Motherhood and Infancies in the Mediterranean in Antiquity

Childhood in the Past Monograph Series

The monograph series was established to allow scholars from all disciplines a forum for presenting new, groundbreaking or challenging research into themed aspects of childhood in the past. The Society is happy to consider proposals for future monographs.

Proposals should be submitted to the General Editor of the Monograph Series. Details for submission may be found on the Society's webpage at www.sscip.org.uk.

Dr Sally Crawford FSA
General Editor, SSCIP Monograph Series
The Institute of Archaeology
36 Beaumont Street
Oxford OX1 2PG
United Kingdom
sally.crawford@arch.ox.ac.uk

Motherhood and Infancies in the Mediterranean in Antiquity

Edited by

Margarita Sánchez Romero
and
Rosa Mª Cid López

OXBOW | books
Oxford & Philadelphia

Published in the United Kingdom in 2018 by
OXBOW BOOKS
The Old Music Hall, 106–108 Cowley Road, Oxford OX4 1JE

and in the United States by
OXBOW BOOKS
1950 Lawrence Road, Havertown, PA 19083

Paperback Edition: ISBN 978-1-78925-038-1
Digital Edition: ISBN 978-1-78925-039-8 (epub)

A CIP record for this book is available from the British Library

Library of Congress Control Number: 2018951271

Typeset in India by Versatile PreMedia Services. www.versatilepremedia.com

For a complete list of Oxbow titles, please contact:

UNITED KINGDOM
Oxbow Books
Telephone (01865) 241249, Fax (01865) 794449
Email: oxbow@oxbowbooks.com
www.oxbowbooks.com

UNITED STATES OF AMERICA
Oxbow Books
Telephone (800) 791-9354, Fax (610) 853-9146
Email: queries@casemateacademic.com
www.casemateacademic.com/oxbow

Oxbow Books is part of the Casemate Group

Front cover: Drawing: Andres Marin Jarque at www.pastwomen.net

Contents

List of contributors

Eva Alarcón García
Departamento de Prehistoria y Arqueología
Universidad de Granada, Spain
eva@ugr.es

Luis Arboledas Martínez
Departamento de Prehistoria y Arqueología
Universidad de Granada, Spain
arboledas@ugr.es

Rosa María Cid López
Grupo Deméter. Maternidad, género y familia
Departamento de Historia
Universidad de Oviedo, Spain
rcid@uniovi.es

Pedro David Conesa Navarro
Departamento de Prehistoria, Arqueología, Historia Antigua, Historia Medieval y Ciencias y Técnicas Historiográficas
Universidad de Murcia, Spain/Università degli Studi di Roma "Tor Vergata," Italy
pedrodavid.conesa@um.es

Ana Delgado Hervás
Grup de Recerca d'Arqueologia Mediterrània (GRACME)
Departament d'Humanitats
Universitat Pompeu Fabra, Barcelona
ana.delgado@upf.edu

Almudena Domínguez-Arranz
Grupo de Investigación. Observatorio Aragonés del Arte en la Esfera Pública del Gobierno de Aragón y Fondo Social Europeo (OAAEP)
Departamento de Ciencias de la Antigüedad
Universidad de Zaragoza, Spain
aldomin@unizar.es

Meritxell Ferrer
Grup de Recerca d'Arqueologia Mediterrània (GRACME)
Departament d'Humanitats
Universitat Pompeu Fabra, Barcelona
meritxell.ferrer@upf.edu

Alejandra García García
Departamento de Prehistoria y Arqueología
Universidad de Granada, Spain
alejandragarciamlg@gmail.com

Antonia García Luque
Departamento de Didáctica de las Ciencias
Universidad de Jaén, Spain
agalu@ujaen.es

Agnès García-Ventura
Institut del Pròxim Orient Antic
Universitat de Barcelona, Barcelona
agnes.ventura@gmail.com

Paloma González-Marcén
Centre d'Estudis del Patrimoni Arqueològic de la Prehistòria – CEPAP
Department de Prehistòria
Universitat Autònoma de Barcelona
Paloma.gonzalez@uab.es

Ana Belén Herranz Sánchez
Instituto Universitario de Investigación en Arqueología Ibérica
Universidad de Jaén, Spain
aherranz@ujaen.es

Mireia López-Bertran
Departamento de Historia del Arte
Facultad de Geografía e Historia
Universitat de València, Spain
mireia.lopez@uv.es

Rosa Mª Marina Saez
Área de Filología Latina.
Departamento de Ciencias de la Antigüedad
Universidad de Zaragoza, Spain
rmarina@unizar.es

Silvia Medina Quintana
Grupo Deméter. Maternidad, género y familia
Departamento de Ciencias Sociales y Experimentales
Universidad de Córdoba
silmequin@gmail.com

Borja Méndez Santiago
Grupo Deméter. Maternidad, género y familia
Departamento de Historia
Universidad de Oviedo, Spain
mendezs@uniovi.es

María Dolores Mirón Pérez
Departamento de Prehistoria y Arqueología / Instituto Universitario de Estudios de las Mujeres y de Género
Universidad de Granada, Spain
dmironp@ugr.es

Maria Dolors Molas Font
Departamento de Historia y Arqueología
Universidad de Barcelona, Spain
dmolas@ub.edu

María Isabel Núñez Paz
Grupo Deméter. Maternidad, género y familia
Area de Derecho Romano
Departamento de Ciencias Jurídicas Básicas
Universidad de Oviedo, Spain
npaz@uniovi.es

Juan Jesús Padilla Fernández
Departamento de Prehistoria
Universidad Complutense de Madrid, Spain
juanje155@hotmail.com

Laura Pepe
Dipartimento di Diritto Privato e Storia del Diritto
Sezione di Diritto Romano
Università degli Studi di Milano
Laura.pepe@unimi.it

Susana Reboreda Morillo
Grupo de Estudios de Arqueología, Antigüedad y Territorio (GEAAT)/Grupo Deméter. Maternidad, Género y Familia.
Facultad de Historia
Universidad de Vigo, Spain
rmorillo@uvigo.es

Carmen Risquez Cuenca
Instituto Universitario de Investigación en Arqueología Ibérica
Universidad de Jaén, Spain
crisquez@ujaen.es

Aurora Rivera-Hernández
Grup de Recerca d'Arqueologia Mediterrània (GRACME)
Departament d'Humanitats
Universitat Pompeu Fabra, Barcelona
aurora.rivera@upf.edu

Carla Rubiera Cancelas
Grupo Deméter. Maternidad, género y familia
Departamento de Historia
Universidad de Oviedo, Spain
rubieracarla@uniovi.es

Carmen Rueda Galán
Instituto Universitario de Investigación en Arqueología Ibérica
Universidad de Jaén, Spain
caruegal@ujaen.es

Margarita Sánchez Romero
Grupo GEA. Cultura material e identidad social en la Prehistoria Reciente en el sur de la Península Ibérica.
Departamento de Prehistoria y Arqueología
Universidad de Granada, Spain
marsanch@ugr.es

Chapter 1

Motherhood and infancies: archaeological and historical approaches

Margarita Sánchez Romero and Rosa Mª Cid López

It is the patriarchy that is undoubtedly responsible for defining the prevailing social model in those communities that emerged in the Mediterranean in 'ancient times.' Due to its success, this model required the establishment and maintenance of certain relationships and gender identities that have become a means through which to define women throughout history. In this construction of feminine identity, a transcultural and transhistorical concept of maternity has been of significance; one in which biological and essentialist elements prevail with respect to what women should do or feel. As such, maternal instinct becomes an obligation and those women who do not possess it are considered abnormal. Furthermore, in order to attain acceptance as a universal issue, stereotypes have been generated with respect to mothers that are easy to both retain and transmit. Behind this natural and biological essentialism or this instinctive attitude lies a simplification of what motherhood means, one that strips it of all its claims to possess skills, or of all experiences beyond the natural; the idea that is possesses any form of knowledge or the ability to use technology is denied. It is as if bodily use were not managed by means of cultural factors. All social transcendence is denied, as if the very existence of communities did not hold the process of reproduction as its most transcendental condition. This social and cultural construction that is motherhood has only become an object of interest for archaeology or history in very recent times: these disciplines have treated the subject in a different way, exploring, as this book demonstrates, various theoretical and methodological approaches.

Recent contributions from history and archaeology question former paradigms, given that now discussion concerns mothers and maternity, children as people with defined roles, as active agents in societies. It is now acknowledged that reproduction involves the work, effort, experience and knowledge of women, not to mention the modification of their bodies and the use of technology, and even their feelings (Sánchez Romero 2006). And, specifically, the important role of women is considered through their relationship with their offspring.

Motherhood took time to appear in academic environments of historical studies, including those related to gender and women. Feminism, however, did address the complex relationship between women and motherhood; from its rejection, which was ambiguously put forward by Simone de Beauvoir (1949), to its defence, by Luisa Muraro (1991). For that Italian philosopher, the close bond between mothers and their offspring had the ability to turn motherhood into a weapon of power, and not of submission, unlike the theory propounded by her French colleague. This is a central debate for contemporary feminism, which has been joined by other 20th century thinkers (Cid 2002; 2015). For example, between the two positions, which have now been mostly discarded, were Yvonne Knibiehler's noteworthy contributions in the 1970s. Knibiehler (2000) was a pioneer in the study of motherhood from a historical perspective and published what is considered to be the first book on the history of women in the West, together with Catherine Fouquet (Knibiehler and Fouquet 1980), and to date her research has been linked to motherhood from highly varied approaches. The pioneering work of the French researcher Françoise Thébaud (1986) has also been noted here, although her work focuses on contemporary society. There is no doubt that French historiography expressed an early interest in mothers and motherhood, one that has been increasing in recent decades. This is manifest in the monographic publications on maternity in the *Clio* magazine dossier (2005) or that specifically dedicated to antiquity in *Métis* (2013), although it only deals with the Greek case. From the work of Françoise Thébaud, we have been able to understand that motherhood was indeed the function traditionally assigned to women. The exercise of this role turned them into 'one-dimensional' beings and generated the socially-accepted idea of feminine identity par excellence, i.e. that the social role of women centred on procreation and the care of offspring. The undertaking of motherhood did not question, but rather reinforced, male social supremacy as women were destined to raise the offspring the husband wanted.

Although it is true that this has been the situation of many women of the past, from a historical standpoint we have observed the complex relationship that women have maintained with motherhood. Past societies, from ancient times to the present, offer us examples of women who rejected motherhood. Such attitudes provoked criticism from their peers, but even so they did involve the refusal to act as something other than an inseminated body, or to assume the role of care-giver to their husbands' children. These attitudes took them as far as Medea, who murdered her own children (McDermott 1989; López and Pociña 2002). In other cases, women are presented as mothers, however this is done while recreating normative discourses and attempting to use motherhood in a different sense. This was true of women who strengthened their social role and enjoyed areas of domestic and extra-domestic power, from the display of a motherhood that was occasionally outside the norm. Agrippina in

Imperial Rome is a paradigmatic example, with her keenness to control the life of Nero, according to the representations of Greco-Roman literature (Ginsburg 2006).

Regarding these issues, scholars of antiquity have also made noteworthy contributions. Suzanne Dixon's *The Roman Mother* or, in the case of Greece, the well-known book by Nicole Loraux, *Les Meres en deuil*, among others (Dixon 1988; Loraux 1990) are obligatory as works of reference. Myth, reality, laws, religion, politics and power, among other issues, were presented in these works, which were later reconsidered and expanded, or nuanced and questioned. This can be seen in the recent contributions on motherhood in the ancient Mediterranean (Hackworth and Salzman-Mitchel 2012; Cid 2009; 2010). Over time, the advances made in terms of knowledge regarding motherhood and mothers have led to the tackling of issues as specific as pregnancy or childbirth, by Veronique Dasen (2004; 2015) and Nancy Demand (2006), or the public role of mothers in the cities, through the contributions of notable women, as described in the works of Emily Hemelrijk (2015) and Cándida Martínez (Martínez and Serrano 2016; Martínez and Ubric 2017). Their works are exemplary in terms of understanding female public roles through 'civic matronhood,' an expression that refers to the work of women benefactors in the cities, who transferred their domestic roles into the public environment. These contributions are limited to the case of ancient societies and are only some of the significant examples. In any event, they prove the influence and dissemination of research on motherhood and maternity from the history of women and gender studies, which has served to revise the views on women of the past that are deeply-rooted in traditional historiography.

It is also significant that in the monumental work of Lynn Budin and Macintosh Turfa (2016) (over 1000 pages), which aims to offer a view of the history of women of antiquity, from East to West, with chapters specific to motherhood in almost all societies, from the Egyptian or Cypriot to the Etruscan, Greek or Roman.

In this respect, archaeology has also contributed to a conceptual change in the construction of motherhood in a particularly significant way. The works of Kathleen M. Bolen (1992), Elisabeth Beausang (2000; 2005), Laurie Wilkie (2003; 2010), Emer O'Donnell (2004) or Katharina Rebay-Salisbury (2017) made their contributions by placing motherhood at the centre of the debate on women, which has moved from a belief in naturalisation and immobility in the development of maternal practices and the non-recognition of children as full components of society, to articulating the appropriate methodologies used to recognise maternity practices in the archaeological record of past populations.

In Spain, this line of work has been especially rewarding in terms of the study of prehistoric societies. Interesting hypotheses have been established regarding human behaviour and the experiences and work of women. Almudena Hernando, in her different studies on the identity of women (Hernando 2001; 2012) shows how motherhood has been used by different authors to justify their identity in biological terms, through established dependency relationships. However, she places the origin of this identity type as a result of the consequences that derive from a loss of mobility due to the constant care required by human offspring. Human youngsters are the weakest in the animal kingdom, due to their extended growth rates; a developmental event that occurred in the genus *Homo* some two and a half million years ago and which led to the prolongation of the foetal period to 21 months (although only nine are intrauterine), which makes these offspring totally dependent. This process evolved basically in order to allow our brains to reach half the size they will have in adulthood. It is this need for child care that reduces women's mobility and which engenders new ways of understanding time and space, while determining initially-established inequalities in a very subtle way (Hernando 2005).

Maria Angeles Querol has outlined the model of 'expansion of maternal behaviour to the rest of the group' (Querol 2005). About two million years ago East African hominids lived on the open plains and were exposed to dangers that could only be overcome through the reorganisation of the group's social relations; this helped individuals to feel cohesion through cooperation among themselves and in distribution of defensive tasks. Maria Angeles Querol believes that this cooperation and these mechanisms of solidarity could have had their origin in the most obvious social relations, i.e. maternal relations, which entail socialisation, the transmission of knowledge, the care of others, etc. The propagation of these behavioural characteristics, by means of various mechanisms, was to be one of the keys to the success and survival of these groups.

However, feminist-Marxist perspectives have analysed biological reproduction in depth, from theories on the production of social life, placing emphasis on the tasks of the production of bodies and the maintenance of subjects and objects, through which not only are sexual bodies essential for the social reproduction of the group created, but also that these individuals are cared for, attended to and socialised (Sanahuja 2002; Escoriza and Sanahuja 2005).

Furthermore, Spanish feminist archaeology has worked on the concept of maintenance activities, which has been essential to conceptualise the social significance of maternal practices and to define the strategies of human groups for their survival (Alarcón and Sánchez 2015). This survival depends not only on biological reproduction, but above all on tasks that take place in daily life, which guarantee the reproduction of the economic and social system of any community (Picazo Gurina 1997; Montón-Subías and Sánchez Romero 2008; Sánchez Romero 2014). These are responsibilities that, until the construction of the concept of maintenance activities, were assigned so little value that we did not even possess an analytical category with which to study them. From this perspective, analysis have been made of questions ranging from why history has not valued maintenance activities (Hernando 2005) to how food production and consumption is managed (Montón-Subías 2005; Sánchez Romero 2014), including an analysis of how the learning and socialisation of children is organised (Sánchez Romero 2008a; 2008b; 2017; Sánchez *et al.* 2015), care practices (Montón-Subías 2010) or the connection to the area of everyday life (Sánchez Romero 2015).

Among the main researchers in this archaeology of childhood are those from feminist and gender archaeology who understood the relationships (more or less constructed) between women and infant individuals and the possibilities that a study of these relationships could provide to the historical discourse. They therefore decided to focus their research on children (Baxter 2005; 2009; Lillehammer 2010; 2015). Thus children and childhood have been described in terms of their bodies (Lewis 2006; Mays *et al.* 2017), the processes of learning and socialisation (Kamp 2001; Högberg 2008; Högberg *et al.* 2015) their spaces (Sánchez Romero *et al.* 2015) or their rituality (Ardren 2011; Murphy and Le Roy 2017).

Research into maternal practices becomes more appealing in the study of care practices and in the socialisation of children. Numerous theoretical and methodological approaches have permitted important moments such as childbirth to be recovered. On the Iberian Peninsula, one of the most interesting prehistoric examples is that of a pregnant woman aged about twenty who died during an obstructed labour, found in the Argaric site of Cerro de Las Viñas (Murcia). The burial reveals the remains of the mother with the newborn child still in the birth canal (Malgosa *et al.* 2004). The anthropological analysis of children is becoming one of the most innovative and informative aspects of this age group (Lewis 2006; Mays *et al.* 2017), including specific perspectives such as the bioarchaeology of the foetus (Halcrow *et al.* 2017).

Evidence of child-care practices is also manifest in many objects, as well as in the use of specially designed processes for food, transportation and clothing, in order to provide children with education, socialisation and entertainment. As these were considered to be natural, immutable and universal, no attention has been paid to the amount of work and knowledge involved or to the different technological and social strategies involved in, for example, breastfeeding and weaning practices in prehistoric societies, i.e. in the processes used to replace breast milk. It is obvious that these processes must have been influenced by various factors that were not only biological, but also environmental, cultural, social and concerning public health. The different communities would have met these needs through mechanisms that combined strategies of solidarity, elements of material culture and a broad range of knowledge (Reboreda forthcoming).

Learning and socialisation practices involve common processes through which children acquire skills and knowledge, they learn to use technology, they take on belief systems and instil values and skills in the world around them. Ideas and skills are acquired through the mechanisms of socialisation and learning. We understand learning as the acquisition of specific knowledge and the use of certain technologies that make children capable of performing productive tasks. Children must however also be able to handle other spheres related to identity and the development of normalised rituals within the adult world, i.e. socialisation. Knowing what strategies societies implemented to perform these processes successfully is important in order to discover how the mechanisms of social reproduction functioned in each community, as in the analysis of Bronze Age sites such as Cerro de la Encina (Monachil, Granada) or Peñalosa (Baños de la Encina, Jaén) (Sánchez Romero and Alarcón 2012). Both strategies have been proven to be a highly important source of information with respect to past societies and which managed to turn children into active agents in societies.

As with archaeology, the history of childhood has also developed significantly. Philippe Ariès (1960) declarations regarding the children of the past, which today are difficult to swallow, are now very distant. Nonetheless, Ariès opened up a new area of research by singling out the infant population and emphasising its role in history. Although he denied young men and women their status as social beings, the laws of ancient societies reveal quite the opposite. This French historian may still have several followers, however most specialists affirm and defend that children (boys and girls) considered themselves social beings, with clearly assigned functions, taking their young age into account. This means that they are also historical agents. They were individuals who were preparing for adulthood, with their own presence and family role and, by extension, also a social role.

Greek and Roman sources however inform us of their presence in religious, domestic and public activities, especially in the streets of the ancient cities, and not only in the Greek *oikos* or the Roman *domus*. Those contributions made regarding childhood and education in the classical world are of enormous interest (Mustakallio *et al.* 2005; Evans Grubbs *et al.* 2013), as are those on this subject in the ancient Mediterranean (Justel Vicente 2012). In terms of childhood in the Greek and Roman world, the name Beryl Rawson is worth mentioning. She opened up prolific lines of research, focusing her study on the family, from where she analyses childhood, as in the book *A Companion to Families in the Greek and Roman Worlds* (2011). Alongside her contributions are those of Suzanne Dixon, also focused on family and childhood in Rome (1992; 2001), and not forgetting Veronique Dasen, whose work centred mainly on the relationship between childbirth, motherhood and the early stages of childhood. With respect to the Greek case, this author emphasises the role of children in family environments, in their religious role both inside and outside the home, and in their work activities (Dasen 2004; 2015).

Today the works of Christian Laes (Laes 2011; Laes and Strubbe 2014; Laes and Vuolanto 2017) with their own views of social history, perspectives that do not dispense with the cultural arena, are highly important. This author's works have allowed us to see the importance and the significant role of children in ancient societies, through the most varied testimonies, from iconography to laws. He introduces us to the variety of the child population and his keen reflections on the representations of childhood are noteworthy.

It was in fact the different debates on maternity practices, reproduction, motherhood and childhood and their dynamism, both from archaeological and historical perspectives, that led us to organise the seminar entitled *Maternities and Childhood. Historical and Archaeological Perspectives*, which was held on 27–28 October 2016 at the University of Granada. This meeting sought to delve into relationships between mothers and their offspring (whether male or female) and to assess whether maternity would have been a woman's exclusive function or whether they combined this work with other tasks. It also sought to investigate the emergence of mother-daughter ties and their development from prehistoric to historical societies in the ancient Mediterranean; to discover in greater detail the true social, economic and technological dimension of maternal practices and to reflect on childhood from a gender perspective.

From the start it was based on a concept of maternity and childhood archetypes that broke with the unilateral images of motherhood and the mother and of childhood with the idea of boy and girl; to be precise, it attempted to value diversity. It was attended by specialists in archeology, law, classical philology and ancient history. It was also a matter of discussing views and diverse approaches, as well as different methodologies, although the gender studies perspective remained as the guiding thread. Several presentations gave rise to some of the chapters that comprise this book, however the need to possess a more complete and complex view of maternal practices in the ancient Mediterranean world led us to request the participation of other renowned experts in these matters, so that they could contribute new texts to this volume.

In this book we seek to understand how the very idea of motherhood was established as a social and cultural practice (García Ventura; Rueda *et al.*); how the identity of women was constructed through their relationship with motherhood from a social standpoint (Molas, Marina), a legal viewpoint (Pepe) or in the power relations, either as powerful women (Mirón; Dominguez; Mendez; Conesa) or from their position as slaves (Rubiera). We also try to understand how essential moments are represented and acknowledged in the lives of women, such as pregnancy or childbirth (Delgado Hervás and Rivera), or how relationships and emotions regarding sons and daughters were visualised either through iconographic (Reboreda) or epigraphic (Cid) representations. We will approach the different ways in which care practices were undertaken (Ferrer; Nuñez), review learning processes (Alarcón *et al.*) and seek to understand how the inclusion of children in funeral rituals could have had an apotropaic (López Bertrán) or a symbolic character (González Marcen), both for the children and for the populations at crucial times in the lives of these societies. We also analyse the ways in which current discourses on motherhood and childhood are transmitted by means of diverse educational strategies (Medina; García Luque).

The seminar arose due to the initiative and cooperation of two research groups from Spanish universities, whose work together in recent years has been highly productive. Specifically, that of the *Grupo GEA. Cultura material e identidad social en la Prehistoria Reciente del sur de la Península Ibérica* of the University of Granada and the *Grupo Deméter. Maternidad, Género y familia* of the University of Oviedo. These groups link two I+D projects, that of the Ministry of Economy and Competitiveness of the Government of Spain, *Innovación, hibridación y resistencia cultural. Las sociedades de III y II milenios cal BC en el sur de la Península Ibérica* [HAR2017-82932-P] and *Maternidades y familias. Permanencias, cambios y rupturas. Entre las sociedades antiguas y la contemporánea* [HAR2013-42371 R]. This publication is linked to these projects.

As editors, we would like to thank those people who participated in the seminar, and those researchers who later joined as the authors of this work. We believe that this publication will be a contribution of interest in furthering knowledge regarding mothers and children, who had been marginalised from historical studies until just a few decades ago. Women, girls and boys have been, without doubt, forgotten subjects (Knapp 2011) in historical research for a long time, however their historical agency ought to be acknowledged.

References

Alarcón, E. and Sánchez Romero, M. (2015) Arqueología feminista, de las mujeres y del género en la Prehistoria de Andalucía. *Menga. Revista de Prehistoria de Andalucía* 6, 32–59.

Ardren, T. (2011) Empowered children in classic Maya sacrificial rites. *Childhood in the Past. An International Journal* 4, 133–145.

Ariès, Ph. (1960) *L'enfant et la vie familiale sous l'Ancien Régime*. Paris, Plon.

Baxter, J. E. (2005) *The Archaeology of Childhood*. Walnut Creek, Altamira Press.

Baxter, J. E. (2009) The archaeology of childhood. *Annual Review of Anthropology* 37, 159–175.

Beausang, E. (2000) Childbirth in prehistory: an introduction. *European Journal of Archaeology* 3(1), 69–87.

Beausang, E. (2005) *Childbirth and Mothering in Archaeology*. Gothenburg, University of Gothenburg.

Beauvoir, S. de. (1949) *Le deuxième sexe*. Paris, Gallimard

Bolen, K. M. (1992) Prehistoric construction of mothering. In C. P. Claassen *Exploring Gender through Archaeology. Selected Papers from the 1991 Boone Conference*. Madison, Prehistory Press, 49–62.

Cid López, R. M. (2002) La maternidad y la figura de la madre en la Roma antigua. In A. I. Blanco, B. Domenech, M. F. López and R. Marcos (coords.) *Nuevas Visiones de la Maternidad*. León, Secretariado de Publicaciones y Medios Audiovisuales de la Universidad de León, 11–49

Cid López, R. M. (2009) *Madres y Maternidades. Construcciones culturales en la civilización clásica*. Oviedo, KRK.

Cid López, R. M. (2010) *Maternidades. Representaciones y realidad social. Edades Antigua y Media*. Madrid, Almudayna.

Cid López, R. M. (2015) *La maternidad en Occidente. Reflexiones desde el feminismo y la historia*. In S. Chemotti and M. C. la Rocca (eds) *Il genere nella ricerca storica. Atti del VI Congresso della Societá Italiana delle Storiche*. Padova, Il Poligrafo, 975–995.

Dasen, V. (2004) *Naissance et petite enfance dans l'Antiquité*. Fribourg/Göttingen, Academic Press/ Vandenhoeck & Ruprecht.

Dasen, V. (2015) *Le sourire d'Omphale. Maternité et petite enfance dans l'Antiquité*. Rennes, Presses Universitaires de Rennes,

Demand, N. (2006) *Birth, Death, and Motherhood in Classical Greece*. Baltimore and London, Johns Hopkins University Press.

Dixon, S. (1988) *The Roman Mother*. London, Routledge.

Dixon, S. (1992) *The Roman Family*. Baltimore and London, Johns Hopkins University Press.

Dixon, S. (2001) *Childhood, Class and Kin in the Roman World*. London, Routledge

Escoriza, T. and Sanahuja, M. E. (2005) *La Prehistoria de la autoridad y la relación. Nuevas perspectivas de análisis para las sociedades del pasado*. In M. Sánchez Romero (ed.) *Arqueología y género*. Granada, Universidad de Granada, 109–140.

Evans Grubbs, J., Parkin, T. and Bell, R. (2013) *The Oxford Handbook of Childhood and Education in the Classical World*. New York, Oxford University Press.

Ginsburg, J. 2006 (reprint of 2004). *Representing Agrippina. Constructions of Female Power in the Early Roman Empire*. Oxford/New York, Oxford University Press.
Hackworth Petersen, L. and Salzman-Mitchel, P. (2012) *Mothering and motherhood in Ancient Greece and Rome*. Texas, University of Texas Press.
Halcrow, S. E., Tayles, Nancy and Gail, E. (2017) The Bioarchaeology of Fetuses. In S. Han, T. K. Betsinger and A. B. Scott (eds.) *The Anthropology of the Fetus: Biology, Culture, and Society*. New York/Londres, Berghahn.
Hemelrijk, E. (2015) *Hidden lives, public persons: Women and civic life in the Roman West*. Oxford/New York, Oxford University Press.
Hernando Gonzalo, A. (2001) *Arqueología de la identidad*. Madrid, Akal.
Hernando Gonzalo, A. (2005). Mujeres y Prehistoria. En torno a la cuestión del origen del patriarcado. In M. Sánchez Romero (ed.) *Arqueología y género*. Granada, Universidad de Granada, 73–108.
Hernando Gonzalo, A. (2012) *La fantasía de la individualidad. Sobre la construcción sociohistórica del sujeto moderno*. Buenos Aires, Katz.
Histoire, femmes et sociétés: Maternités (2005) Dossier Clio, 21.
Högberg, A. (2008) Playing with flint: Tracing a Child's imitation of adult work in a lithic assemblage. *Journal of Archaeological Method and Theory* 15, 112–131.
Hogberg, A, Gärdenfors, P. and Larsson, L. (2015) Knowing, learning and teaching. How Homo became Docens. *Cambridge Archaeological Journal*, 1–22.
Justel Vicente, D. (2012) (ed.) *Niños en la antigüedad. Estudios sobre la infancia en el Mediterráneo antiguo*. Zaragoza, Prensas de la Universidad de Zaragoza,
Kamp, K. A. (2001) Prehistoric children working and playing: A southwestern case study in learning ceramics. *Journal of Anthropological Research* 57, 427–450
Knapp, R. C. (2011) *Los olvidados de Roma. Prostitutas, forajidos, esclavos, gladiadores y gente corriente*. Barcelona, Ariel.
Knibiehler, Y. (2000) *Histoire des mères et de la maternité en Occident*. Paris, Presses Universitaires de France.
Knibiehler, Y. and Fouquet, C. (1980) *L´Histoire des mères depuis le Moyen Age*. Paris, Montalba.
Laes, C. (2011) *Children in the Roman Empire. Outsiders Within*. Cambridge, Cambridge University Press.
Laes, C. and Strubbe, J. (2014) (eds) *Youth in the Roman Empire. The Young and the Restless Years*. Cambridge, Cambridge University Press.
Laes, Ch. and Vuolanto, V. (2017) (eds) *Children and Everyday Life in the Roman and Late Antique World*. London/New York, Routledge.
Lewis, M. E. (2007) *The Bioarchaeology of Children. Perspectives from Biological and Forensic Anthropology*. Cambridge, Cambridge University Press.
Lillehammer, G. (2010) Archaeology of Children. *Complutum* 21(2), 15–46.
Lillehammer, G. (2015) 25 Years with the 'child' and the archaeology of childhood. *Childhood in the Past. An International Journal* 8(2), 78–86.
López, A. and Pociña, A. (2002) (eds) *Medea. Versiones de un mito desde Grecia hasta hoy*. Granada, Universidad de Granada.
Loraux, N. (1990) *Les mères en deuil*. Paris, Éditions du Seuil.
Lynn Budin, S. and Macintosh Turfa, J. (2016) (eds) *Women in Antiquity. Real Women Across the Ancient World*. London/New York, Routledge.
Malgosa, A., Alessan, A., Safont, S., Ballbé, M. and Ayala, M. M. (2004) A dystocic childbirth in the Spanish Bronze Age. *International Journal of Osteoarchaeology* 14, 98–103.
McDermott, E. A. (1989) *Euripide´s Medea: The Incarnation of Disorder*. London, Pennsylvania State University Press.
Martínez, C. and Serrano, F. (2016) (eds) *Matronazgo y arquitectura de la antigüedad a la Edad Moderna*. Granada, Universidad de Granada

Martínez, C. and Ubric, P. (2017) (eds) *Cartografías de género en las ciudades antiguas. Memoria y poder de las mujeres*. Granada: Universidad de Granada
Mays, S., Gowland, R. Halcrow S. E. and Murphy, E. (2017) Child bioarchaeology: Perspectives on the past 10 years. *Childhood in the Past* 10(1), 38–56.
Mères et maternités en Grèce ancienne (2013) Dossier *Metis* 5(11)
Montón Subias, S. (2005) Las prácticas de alimentación: cocina y arqueología. In M. Sánchez Romero (ed.) *Arqueología y género*. Granada, Universidad de Granada, 159–175
Montón Subias, S. (2010) Maintenance activities and the ethics of care. In L. H. Dommasnes, T. Hjorungdal, S. Montón Subias, M. Sánchez Romero and N. L. Wicker (eds) *Situating Gender in European Archaeologies*. Budapest, Archaeolingua, 23–33.
Montón Subias, S. and Sánchez Romero, M. (2008) *Engendering Social Dynamics. The Archaeology of Maintenance Activities*. Oxford, British Archaeological Report S1862.
Muraro, L. (1991) *L´ordine simbolico della madre*. Roma, Editori Riuniti.
Murphy, E. M. and Le Roy, M. (2017) (eds) *Children, Death and Burial. Archaeological Discourses*. Oxford, Oxbow Books.
Mustakallio, H., Hanska, J., Sainio, H.-L. and Vuolante, V. (2005) (eds) 2005. *Hoping for Continuity. Childhood, Education and Death in Antiquity and Middle Ages*. Rome, Institutum Romanum Finlandiae.
O´Donnell, E. (2004) Birthing in prehistory. *Journal of Anthropological Archaeology* 23, 163–171.
Picazo, M. (1997) Hearth and home: the timing of maintenance activities. In J. Moore and E. Scott (eds) *Invisible People and Processes. Writing Gender and Childhood into European Archaeology*. London, Leicester University Press, 59–67.
Querol, M. Á. (2005) 'El origen del hombre' y la identidad femenina: los mitos duraderos. In M. Sánchez Romero (ed.) *Arqueología y género*. Granada, Universidad de Granada, 441–456.
Rawson, B. (2003) *Children and Childhood in Roman Italy*. Oxford, Oxford University Press.
Rawson, B. (2011) (ed.) *A Companion to Families in the Greek and Roman Worlds*. Malden/Oxford/ Chichester, Wiley-Blackwell.
Rebay-Salisbury, K. (2017) Bronze Age beginnings: The conceptualization of motherhood in prehistoric Europe. In D. Cooper and C. Phelan (eds) *Motherhood in Antiquity*. London, Palgrave Macmillan, 169–196.
Reboreda, S. (forthcoming) *Visiones sobre la lactancia en la Antigüedad. Permanencias, cambios y rupturas*, Supplément à Dialogues de Historie Ancienne, 45
Sanahuja, M. E. (2002) *Cuerpos sexuados, objetos y prehistoria*. Barcelona, Cátedra. Feminismos.
Sánchez Romero, M. (2006) Maternidad y prehistoria: prácticas de reproducción, relación y socialización. *Las mujeres en la Prehistoria. Exposición Itinerante. Museo de Prehistoria de Valencia*. Valencia, Diputación de Valencia, 119–137.
Sánchez Romero, M. (2008a) An approach to learning and socialisation in children during the Spanish Bronze Age. In L. H. Dommasnes and M. Wrigglesworth (eds) *Children, Identity and the Past*. Cambridge, Cambridge Scholars Publishing, 113–124.
Sánchez Romero, M. (2008b) Childhood and the construction of gender identities through material culture. *Childhood in the Past. An International Journal* 1, 17–37.
Sánchez Romero, M. (2014) Mujeres, Arqueología y Feminismo: aportaciones desde las sociedades argáricas. *Arqueoweb* 15, 282–290.
Sánchez Romero, M. (2015) Las arquitecturas de lo cotidiano en la prehistoria reciente del sur de la península ibérica. In M. E. Díez Jorge (eds) *Arquitectura y Mujeres en la Historia*. Madrdi, Síntesis, 19–58.
Sánchez Romero, M. (2017) Landscapes of childhood: Bodies, places and material culture. *Childhood in the Past. An International Journal* 10(1), 16–37.
Sánchez Romero, M. and Alarcón, E. (2012) Lo que los niños nos cuentan: individuos infantiles durante la Edad del Bronce en el sur de la Península Ibérica. In D. Justel Vicente (ed.) *Niños en la*

Antigüedad. Estudios sobre la infancia en el Mediterráneo antiguo. Zaragoza, Prensas de la Universidad de Zaragoza, 57–98.

Sánchez Romero, M., Alarcón, E. and Aranda, G. (2015) Children, childhood and space: Multidisciplinary approaches to identity. In M. Sánchez Romero, E. Alarcón and G. Aranda (eds) *Children, Spaces and Identity.* Oxford, Oxbow Books, 2–9

Thébaud, F. (1986) *Quand nos grand mères donnaient la vie. La maternité en France dans l'entre-deux-guerres*, Lyon, Presses Universitaires de Lyon.

Wilkie, L. A. (2003) *The Archaeology of Mothering*. New York, Routledge.

Wilkie, L. A. (2010) Infancia en blanco y negro: La experiencia de la crianza en Estados Unidos a principios del siglo XX. *Complutum* 21(2), 197–214.

Chapter 2

The child is dead: decision-making and emigration in Bronze Age Iberia

Paloma González Marcén

Material culture and migration

Mobility is an intrinsic part of the history of humanity, from the itinerant life of the first groups of Palaeolithic hunter-gatherers to the often dramatic migrations of our contemporary society. From cultural anthropology and sociology, a range of proposals have been created in the broad field of mobility concepts, in terms of socio-economic forms and historical contexts. These studies have differentiated nomadism or itinerancy as a way of life associated with sedentary groups which take the decision to move away from their previous places of settlement. In recent years, the analysis of material culture has been introduced in studies on current migration processes as one of the outstanding aspects in the relationship between the place of origin and the processes of linkage and dissociation with the new and variable contexts of life (Basu and Coleman 2008).

In contrast, in archaeology the concept of migration has tended to be associated with large population movements and research has focused on the material expressions of these dynamics, both in time and space (van Dommelen 2014). However, as Catherine Cameron (2013) has recently argued, not enough attention has been paid to the construction of a more accurate conceptualisation of migration and in particular of the movements of small scale groups as a result of wars, fission or fusion processes or demographic decline. More than 20 years ago, Cameron, and Tomka (1993) already promoted a new archaeological focus on the contexts in which migration trajectories begin, that is, the abandonment of long-term living settlements. The concept of abandonment has become popular in archaeological terminology, leading to a wide range of methodological approaches, all of which are related to the management of material culture as physical traces of the social decision to leave a specific place. One of the most relevant lines of research in this field has been to understand abandonment, not only as an isolated functional action – to leave a house or a familiar landscape – but as a set of cultural procedures involving material expressions and social decisions. For example, Mirjana Stevanovic (1997), in her study of the Neolithic settlements of Southeast Europe, suggested how social decisions and the forms of abandonment of houses were complex and intertwined. The causes of house destruction were not incidental fires or reactions to immediate threatening situations, but rather, were braided together with a diversity of cultural practices aimed at the symbolic reproduction of a community.

Currently, a vast literature on the characteristics and modes of abandonment of living places is available for archaeologists and it is becoming increasingly common to also focus on those material assemblages which can be related to specific farewell rituals (Fogelin and Schiffer 2015). These farewell or termination rituals are framed in what has been called 'planned abandonment' and seem to be part of common practice, particularly in contexts of forced migration with differentiated rhythms and expressions. This is the case of abandonment contexts of domestic buildings in the Contreras valley in Belize, an agricultural settlement located in the outskirts of the Classic Maya centre of Minanha. Apparently, between cal AD 800 and 1200, this community was abandoned as a consequence of the Classic Maya Collapse by a gradual process of depopulation (Lamoureux St-Hilaire *et al.* 2015). In this case, the rituals of abandonment were characterised by the deposition of ceramic containers, some of them fragmented, related to the consumption of food and the burning of incense inside and aligned in front of the doors of the buildings, symbolically blocking their access. Interestingly, these abandonment rituals were not detected in all the houses and when they do occur it seems that they were not carried out at the same time. Abandonments appear to have happened unevenly and gradually showing a wide diversity of responses to depopulation and migration. According to the researchers, the decision to carry or not to carry out rituals of termination can be explained by the distinct cultural and psychosocial attitudes towards the process of emigration. What has been found is that certain residential groups seemed to have a weak association to the cultural norms along with a lack of attachment to the territory and perhaps this related to a temporary abandonment without carrying out a farewell ritual act. This variability indicates that, in small communities with weak ties to ceremonial or power centres, the decision to stress the symbolic end of a place were not part of fixed cultural norms. This decision largely depended on the particular experience and attitudes of each of the groups in relation to the process of abandonment.

In contrast to settlements or living places, there are few cases where it is possible to associate specific burial rituals with processes of abandonment of a territory. Termination rituals usually consist, as we have seen, in the placement of objects in strategic parts of the houses, often in the entrances, symbolising the activities that were carried out inside. In fact, with respect to funerary contexts, the concept of abandonment is not commonly discussed, since the existence of specific rituals marking the end of the use of a cemetery is difficult to detect archaeologically. However, this is not always the case in relation to collective tombs, which occasionally show material evidence indicating the termination of their funerary use. Archaeological examples of the ritual closure of collective funerary enclosures are well known, in particular with megalithic constructions (Gibson 2016). These termination rituals are usually related to the sealing of the entrance with stones or earth and, in certain cases, setting fire to their access or to the entire funerary area (Rojo-Guerra *et al.* 2010; Alonso 2015; Jagu and Masset 2016). In fact, it is difficult to establish if whether these ritual closures were accompanied by settlement abandonment or if they are associated with migration processes (Gibson 2016).

Termination rituals and child burials

One prominent example of the connection between an abandonment ritual in relation to a living space with a particular type of funerary practice is the site of La Juella, in northern Argentina. In Juella a house was found with sets of votive objects and architectural remodelling features to the process of its abandonment. Significantly, this appears to coincide with the expansion of the Inca empire to the south, in the 5th century AD. Among the abundant documented ritual materials, the remains of a foetal skeleton of 6–7 months old, was found. This has been interpreted as a ritual specifically related to the liminal character of abandonment, the end of the social use of that specific building (Leibowicz 2017).

It is not uncommon to find burials of infants or very young children in domestic spaces or singular contexts; their social definition as non-persons and, therefore, not full members of the community resulted in their transformation into valuable protective beings, in close contact with a magical or spiritual dimension. Although the most abundant examples of this type of beliefs and practices can be found in Christianised societies (Finley 2000; Gardela and Duma 2014), similar practices have been documented in ancient and prehistoric contexts (Scott 1999; Moore 2013). Clearly, the presence or absence of children and/or juveniles in funerary rituals as well as their proportion with respect to adults, their ritual treatment or their placement, increased our knowledge of the social position, cultural consideration and personhood definitions of children in different types of agrarian or pre-industrial societies (Halcrow and Tayles 2008).

However, we need to take this argument further and raise the question of the social meaning and values not only of living children, but of child death excluding those stillborn or infants. In general, many of the burials of older children are undistinguishable from those of adults. This funerary norm indicates that the social impact of the death of these children was the same as that of an adult member of the community. From an emotional perspective, funerary rituals can be considered as psycho-cultural performances aimed to assimilate loss and to express grief. We may reasonably ask whether it is possible to detect a specific sense of loss with respect to the death of an older child by focusing on special or abnormal burials (Cannon and Cook 2015; Valk 2016; Baitzel 2018). Such approaches emphasise the interpersonal maternal or parental bond and grief in different historical, social and cultural contexts.

However, there is little discussion of the impact of those deaths in the community itself as well as its manifestation within collective experiences.

In traditional agrarian societies, regardless of their status, children are considered as family capital, both for their future potential to become productive and supportive members of the community, as well as for their social role in economic, ritual and cultural exchanges with other communities. Importantly, this acts to reinforce the successful reproduction of the family or co-residential group (Levine and Levine 1985). Any loss of a weaned child who has survived the most uncertain phases of child growth and is able to actively cooperate in the reproduction of its community, generates a shock in traditional farming societies. This is particular the case with groups undergoing demographic decline or weakened by war, socio-economic or environmental crisis. A recent study on age groups in megalithic burials in the north of the Iberian Peninsula surprisingly demonstrates that in addition to the expected predominance of adults, there was also a substantial representation of children and juveniles, spanning an age range between 5 and 18 years (Fernández-Crespo and de Rua 2015). This evidence demonstrates that persons of this age group (from weaned children to adolescents) were already considered full members of the community. These data suggest that the death of an older child in this type of society implies a feeling of double loss: On the one hand, the loss of a member already active in the community, and on the other, the loss of the unfulfilled social potential of the child.

It is possible that some singular or abnormal child burials could be connected with this double loss as, for example, at the Middle Bronze Age (1800–1450 cal BC) settlement of El Cerro, in central Iberia (Blanco-González 2015). Here an abandoned dwelling was found associated with a pit where three children had been simultaneously buried with atypical funerary offerings. According to Blanco-González (2015) it is 'plausible that the concurrent deaths of three young members of a family might have altered their social and cosmological order,' generating an extraordinary reaction in relation to an event of great emotional and social impact. In the context of the deaths of older children from small farming or herding communities, it is highly probable that maternal grief (Baitzel 2018) was also accompanied by a strong emotional impact on the whole group, altering their economic and cultural prospects and expectations for the future. This type of impact may have provoked or accelerated- as in the case of the El Cerro burial pit- processes of abandonment or eventual migration. In what follows we shall attempt to apply this argument to the case of a child burial that was used as part of a termination ritual for a collective interment in a Bronze Age cave in the northeast of the Iberian Peninsula.

A symbolic end: The child burial of the Forat of Conqueta funerary cave

During a geological survey in August 2004, in the municipality of Les Avellanes-Santa Linya (la Noguera, Catalonia), a small gap in a limestone cliff was discovered with human remains and fragments of ceramic and flint clearly visible on the surface. This gap

Figure 2.1: Entrance of the Forat de Conqueta cave (photo: CEPAP/UAB)

probed to be the entrance to a natural corridor leading to a cavity, visible from a second opening located on the top of the cliff (Figure 2.1). The contents indicated that this was a Chalcolithic-Early Bronze Age collective burial, in a good state of preservation with no apparent signs of later human interference. These initial observations were confirmed by later excavations in 2005 and 2006 (González Marcén *et al.* 2010; 2011a; 2011b)

This cavity, Forat de Conqueta, forms part of the karstic system of calcareous massifs within the contact zone between the Catalan central plain, the Pre-Pyrenees and the middle course of the Segre river (Figure 2.2). It is a collective burial cave with successive burials during a long period of time, which began in the last half of the 3rd millennium cal BC and went out of funerary use at some point around 1300–1200 cal BC as demonstrated by the radiocarbon dates. The ritual closure of the cavity is marked by a last burial of a child between 8 and 9 years old.

The type of funerary ritual recorded at Forat de Conqueta is unique since it is characterised by the partial cremation of most bodies. All the data seem to indicate that the cremation process was carried out inside the cavity and as part of the funerary ritual. This can be deduced because of the degree of thermo-alteration of the remains and the fact that, significantly, the cremation cannot not associated with the action of any natural fire. In fact, the archaeological record of Forat de Conqueta allows us to make an accurate reconstruction of the funerary ritual procedures. The corpses

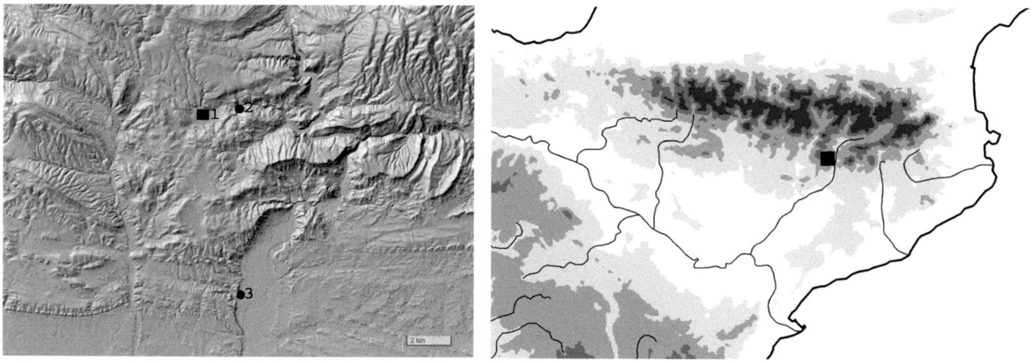

Figure 2.2: Map with the locations of Forat de Conqueta and other archaeological sites mentioned in the text: 1. Forat de Conqueta; 2. Cova Gran; 3. La Colomina (source: Institut Geogràfic de Catalunya)

were wrapped and then place in the cavity, along with some personal belongings or ornaments. In addition, other ritual offerings were put inside the cave-possibly food. Perhaps, giving the presence of ochre in the cave, this may suggest that the bodies of the dead and/or the participants were decorated. These processes seem to have been followed by lighting of a fire at the cave entrance, using as fuel both wood and accumulated organic material. The fact that the cave has two openings – the lateral one of the tunnel entrance and the chimney-like one on the top – would have allowed the circulation of air generating very high temperatures inside the tunnel and the chamber of the cave.

The MNI index calculated from the bioarchaeological study shows 37 individuals, five of whom are children, including all age ranges. While both men and women were buried, the study shows an over-representation of male individuals, either as a result of the limitations of the sex determination methods, or due to differential burial practices in relation with gender. The study of the remains was limited by the poor state of preservation of most of the skeletal material, caused by a variety of factors: the funerary ritual (a combination of inhumation and cremation), the fact that the cavity was reused over a period of more than 1000 years, and the specific taphonomic context of the cave. As a result of the combination of all these factors, the bone remains deposited in the cavity formed a large ossuary where the original patterns of placement of the bodies and funerary offerings were difficult to determine. Among this distorted accumulation of human remains and archaeological materials, it was impossible to trace clear patterns or regularities that could be attributed directly to individuals or ritual gestures, except in four cases in which it was possible to determine the position of the bodies and the original place of their deposition.

It has been impossible to document specific selection or accumulation of bone remains (e.g. skulls, long bones, etc.) in any sector of the ossuary. This is also the case with secondary burials or deliberate displacement of the remains, whether for ritual purposes or to create more space for new interments. It is probable that since most

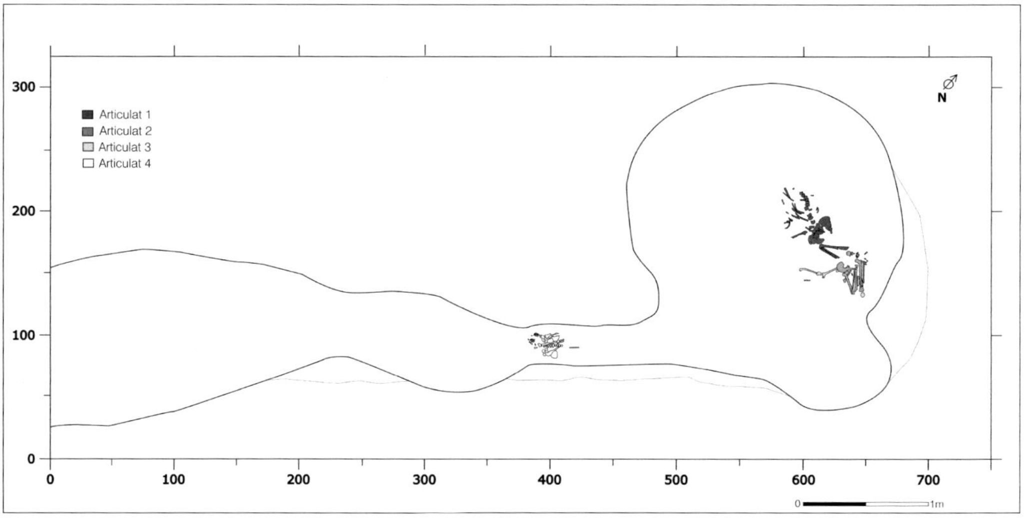

Figure 2.3: Plan of Forat de Conqueta with the four articulated individuals (drawing: Mònica López - CEPAP/UAB)

bodies were burned this contributed to a fragmentation of the material and made it difficult to select specific skulls and long bones and, moreover, this acted to reduce the occupied space by the corpses through combustion.

As already mentioned, only four partially articulated individuals, three adult or juvenile male individuals (Articulat 1, 2 and 3) and one child (Articulat I2), and some other isolated bones maintained some form of anatomical connection. Articulat 1, 2 and 3 were found at the chamber-like bottom of the cave (Figure 2.3). These were buried with distorted positions of the lower extremities, two of them with the legs bent backwards and other with the legs folded over the chest. This position of the bones of the lower extremities and the close anatomical relationships, seem to support the hypothesis that they were brought to the cave and buried already tied and/or wrapped.

In the case of Articulat I2, the skeleton was diagnosed as subadult because the ossification process had not been completed. It was placed in a foetal position, with the legs bent over the chest and the arms around them. The feet appeared at the entrance of the access tunnel and the rest of the body continued into the cavity. At this point, the tunnel has a width of about only 30 cm which conditioned the excavation methodology and the skeleton had to be extracted by parts while advancing towards the interior of the cave (Figure 2.3). These recording difficulties contrast with the very good state of preservation of the child remains, which has allowed us to recover even very small bone fragments such as the epiphysis of the phalanges of hands and feet, with are smaller than 2 mm. The bones of the lower extremities were in perfect articulation. When the bones of the feet, tibias and fibulae were lifted, the two femurs and coxal bones appeared in a somewhat displaced position to the left. Under the femurs and coxals, the sacrum and the vertebrae also appeared, along with the highly fragmented ribs. The vertical position of the metatarsals, as well as other anatomical elements, suggest that either the child was wrapped in some type of plant fibre mat at the time of its burial, or that the decomposition of the corpse took place below layers of sediment.

One noteworthy aspect is that the skeleton was partially burned. Both the colour of the bones and the type of fractures that they presented suggests that the cremation took place at the time of the burial with the soft tissues still present and that it was made in the same place where the remains were deposited without any subsequent transportation. The bones of the feet presented yellowish colouration, as the distal epiphyses of the tibias and proximal femurs. In contrast, the diaphysis of the long bones and most of the ribs and vertebrae showed a blackish colouration, which suggests that the fire did not affect all parts of the body equally. The long bones had longitudinal fractures, which can be explained as a result of the cremation of the bones, and when the soft tissues of the individual were still preserved. The skull was the skeletal element that presented a higher degree of cremation, with a strong black colouration with glassy appearance and very fragmented. It was fractured into an infinity of pieces that were found scattered at the entrance of the cavity.

From the distribution of archaeological materials which may had been related to funerary activities (complete and fragmented vessels, shell and stone beads, small polished axes, flint arrowheads, bone awls and two bronze rings), none of these can be definitively related to any specific individual inside the cave. However, it is possible to identify funerary offerings associated with Articulat I2 found beside the child bones (Figure 2.4): 1 small bowl, 28 beads of *dentalium*, 1 button of fossil resin, 1 perforated suid canine, 1 bone awl, 1 shell pendant and 3 discoidal ceramic tokens.

This buried child of Forat de Conqueta suggests a double reading: first, the ritual closing of a funerary cave used by the same cultural groups for more than 1000 years and second, the added significance of the way in which this closure occurs. The exceptional nature of this termination ritual does not seem arbitrary. The final purpose seems to be linked to an event (the death of the child) that marks the end of a process (the funerary use of the cave). It could be consider simply as a variant of a closure ritual, although it could also be argued that it was related to a more important decision, taken by the community which recognized this place as an ancestral space of reference.

It's time to go: A farewell story in the Pyrenees

The chronological sequence derived from ten C^{14} dates from bones of different individuals deposited in Forat de Conqueta, shows a range of funerary use that would begin in the last half of the 3rd millennium ending between 1300–1200 cal BC (González Marcén 2010). The terminal date of the use of the cave is coeval with the deliberate sealing of the entrance with an older child burial. However, the dynamics of use of Forat de Conqueta as a funerary space raises some questions, since the wide

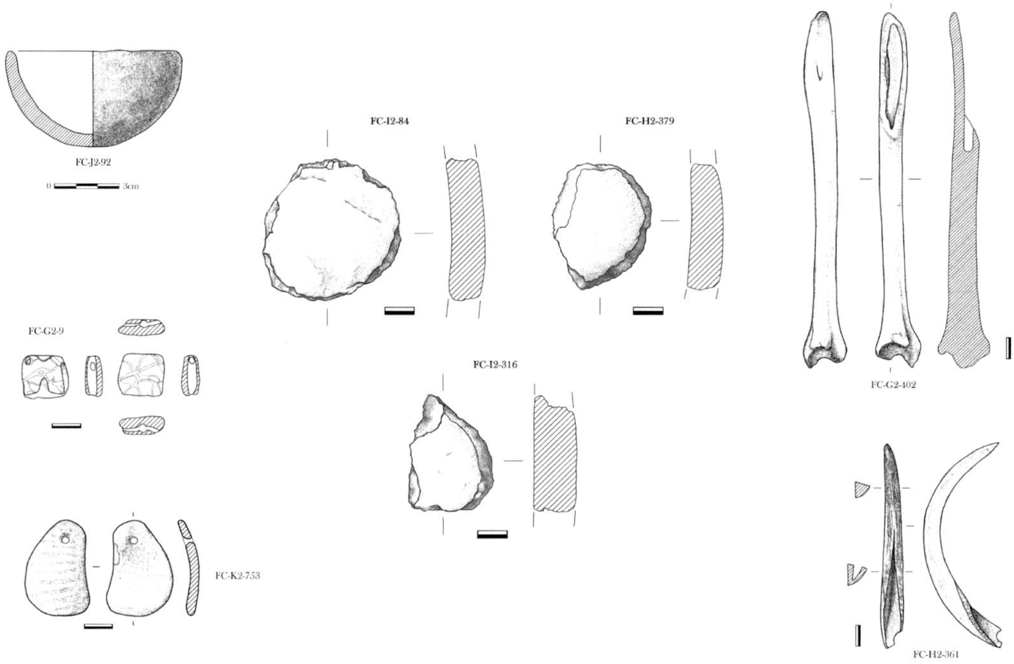

Figure 2.4: Funerary objects associated with the child burial of Forat de Conqueta (Articulat I2). (Drawing: Mònica López – CEPAP/UAB)

temporal range that it covers contrasts sharply with the relatively low number of buried individuals. The contemporaneity of the three first individuals (Articulat 1, 2 and 3) and the apparent coincidence of the radiocarbon dates suggest that there was an intermittent funerary use over the long term with extended periods where no deposition occur. It is possible that during these periods of non-funerary use of Forat de Conqueta, other nearby caves, many of them plundered or little studied (Oms *et al.* 2009), could have assumed the function of ritual places. In any case, the low number of buried individuals, the long duration of Forat de Conqueta as a funerary space, and the recurrence of exactly the same ritual procedure (i.e. cremation inside the cavity), indicate a high degree of rootedness and attachment of these small size communities to this specific landscape. While the material repertoire of the scattered funeral offerings suggested tecnological changes and regional contacts, over all what we see is a image of cultural conservatism.

But what do we really know about the groups which buried their deads in Forat de Conqueta? Systematic and structured research on the first settlers of these pre-Pyrenean valleys is only now beginning to offer an alternative vision to their conventional description as 'cave inhabitants,' as described in the first archaeological studies of this area in the late 19th and early 20th centuries (Oms *et al.* 2009). In the specific case of Forat de Conqueta, the time span of its funerary use corresponds almost exactly to the series of radiocarbon dates obtained in the Holocene occupation floors of the nearby Cova Gran de Santa Linya, located 1 km from the cave (Mora *et al* 2011). In Cova Gran, the intensive practice of herding has been documented since the end of the 3rd millennium and seems to be interrupted around 1300–1200 cal BC, followed by occasional visits until historical times (Polo *et al* 2014). Similar contemporary herding practices to those of the Cova Gran can be also inferred from the layers of animal manure found in other caves from nearby valleys, some of which are located at strategic crossing points (Oms *et al* 2013). These new data support a characterisation of these communities as pastoral groups with seasonal itinerant movements around specific territories marked by caves. It is clear that they had strategic control and extensive knowledge of the north–south routes linking the Pyrenees with the agricultural plains of the Ebro valley and its tributaries.

The ritual closure of Forat de Conqueta, which is currently the only systematically excavated funerary cave in the area, may point to a radical change in funerary rituals and, possibly, in social and economic organisation of the inhabitants of this pre-Pyrenean area. At the end of the 2nd millennium cal BC and particularly throughout the early centuries of the 1st millennium cal BC, a significant number of settlements with rectangular houses associated with cremation tumuli necropolis began to appear on the agricultural plains. At this time also, both agricultural and metal-working activities were expanding, and population seems to have increased (López-Cachero 2007). The nearby settlement and tumuli cemetery of La Colomina, located about 15 km from Forat de Conqueta, shows a clear transition from the herding economy of small groups in the valleys to the growth of farming and metal-working villages in the agricultural plains and near to the main rivers associated with new cultural and also funerary practices (López Melcion 2001). What remains to be explained, is why the way of life associated with the community which buried its dead in Forat de Conqueta and kept its flocks in the Cova Gran de Santa Linya ceased to be culturally and economically viable. It is possible that they lost control of the territory and routes that supplied metal and other tangible and intangible assets to the villagers located on the plain. Clearly this would have affected traditional herding practices or perhaps the new agricultural settlements may have provided more secure and stable living conditions – or alternatively, it may have been a combination of both and other factors.

In any case, it seems clear that only some kind of social crisis related to community survival can explain the abandonment and closure of such a long and conservative funerary practice as we see in Forat de Conqueta. The material expression of this group's ultimate decision can only be understood by the death of the child which became ritualised in a symbolic farewell to a landscape and a way of life. The importance of the closure of the funerary cave lies precisely in the fact that the community chose to mark it with a child burial. Significantly, this burial had a different meaning from others with stillborn, neonates or unweaned babies. The end of the life history of the cave was represented by a child who had already reached the physical and social maturity to be included as a full member of the community. As pointed out previously, it has been established that at least five subadults of all age ranges were interred in the interior of the cave. Why, then, did they not choose to bury this child inside and closure the cave with stones, earth or slabs instead, as is demonstrated by other collective burials? The connection between the child death, the decision to close the funeral space and the abandonment of the area seems a more than plausible explanation.

Conclusions

While there is a great deal of research on the subject of migration processes, however the current bibliography fails to address the specific situations that trigger, at a given moment, decisions to abandon a territorial homeland and journey to a foreign or unknown place. Existing studies on modern or contemporary migrations emphasise the structural and personal conditions that drive emigration experiences, both of the journey itself and of the new contexts of life. But the ultimate decision to leave is hardly treated or analysed – not even in the discussions based on the analysis of life stories (Prat i Carós 2007). From a material culture perspective, contemporary migrations have been approached by scrutinizing what migrants carry in their suitcases and bags and what they transport to their new settle landscapes (Alonso Rey 2012; Svasek 2012; de Leon 2013). Individual and social decisions are not made solely by macro-analysis or by strategic calculations, neither only by cost estimates and earnings, but by the expectations, fears and affections which may be expressed by and through material culture. Significantly, emotional and subjective perceptions play a key role in the how and when of decision making that affects the personal life and the trajectory of a community (Halfacree 2004). It is probable that intense emotional experiences provide a definitive impulse for people to decide to leave at a specific moment and not at another. Frequently, a farewell note, a mark on a closed door or a buried child are the material expressions of the grief of unwanted goodbyes.

In the case of the child burial of Forat de Conqueta, two types of grief are interwoven and merged, into one and the same ritual: the maternal and the community farewells. The first is shown in the meticulous preparation of the dead body, the careful selection and the arrangements of ornaments and toys for the long cosmological journey of a member of the group that is still a child. The second, involves a collective decision by the group to consider this burial as the last interment in the ancestral cave that will be never used again. This decision represented the end point of a place associated with life and cultural identity as well as the beginning of an uncertain journey to a new world.

References

Alonso Fernández, C. (2015) La tumba colectiva de El Hundido (Monasterio de Rodilla, Burgos) y su ritual funerario durante el Neolítico Final y el Calcolítico. *Trabajos de Prehistoria* 72, 84–104.

Alonso Rey, N. (2012) Las cosas de la maleta. Objetos y experiencia migratoria. *Arxiu d'Etnografia de Catalunya* 12, 33–56.

Baitzel, S. (2018) Parental grief and mourning in the Ancient Andes. *Journal of Archaeological Method and Theory* 25, 178–201.

Basu, P. and Coleman, S. (2008) Introduction: Migrant worlds, material cultures. *Mobilities* 3, 313–330.

Blanco-González, A. (2015). Past fragments: From ceramics to social practices in later prehistoric Iberia. *Journal of Social Archaeology* 15, 342–365.

Cameron, C. M. (2013) How people moved among ancient societies: Broadening the view. *American Anthropologist* 115, 218–231.

Cameron, C. M. and Tomka, S. A. (eds) (1993) *The Abandonment of Settlements and Regions: Ethnoarchaeological and archaeological approaches.* Cambridge, Cambridge University Press

Cannon, A. and Cook, K. (2015) Infant death and the archaeology of grief. *Cambridge Archaeological Journal* 25, 399–416.

de León, J. (2013) Undocumented migration, use wear, and the materiality of habitual suffering in the Sonoran Desert. *Journal of Material Culture* 18, 321–345.

Fernández-Crespo, T. and de-La-Rua C. (2015) Demographic evidence of selective burial in megalithic graves of northern Spain. *Journal of Archaeological Science* 53, 604–617.

Finlay, N. (2000) Outside of life: traditions of infant burial in Ireland from *cillin* to cist. *World Archaeology* 31, 407–422.

Fogelin, L. and Schiffer, M. B. (2015) Rites of passage and other rituals in the life histories of objects. *Cambridge Archaeological Journal* 25, 815–827.

Gardeła, L. and Duma, P. (2013) Untimely death: atypical burials of children in early and late medieval Poland. *World Archaeology* 45, 314–332.

Gibson, C. D. (2016) Closed for business or cultural change? Tracing the re-use and final blocking of megalithic tombs during the Beaker period. In J. T. Koch and B. Cunliffe (eds) *Celtic From the West 3: Atlantic Europe in the Metal Ages - Questions of Shared Language*, 83–110. Oxford, Oxbow Books.

González Marcén P. (2010) Les ocupacions prehistòriques del Forat de Conqueta (Santa Linya, Lleida): cronologia i dinàmica d'ús. In P. González Marcén, R. Mora Torcal and X. Roda Gilabert (eds) *El jaciment de Forat de Conqueta: seqüencia arqueológica i cultura material. Treballs d'Arqueologia 16*. Bellaterra, Universitat Autònoma de Barcelona, 115–123.

González Marcén, P., Mora Torcal, R. and Roda Gilabert, X. (eds) (2010) *El jaciment de Forat de Conqueta: seqüencia arqueológica i cultura material. Treballs d'Arqueologia* 16. Bellaterra, Universitat Autònoma de Barcelona.

González Marcén, P., García-Guixé, E. and Pizarro, J. (2011a) El Forat de Conqueta, poblament neolític i usos funeraris del 3r i 2n mil·lenni en el Prepirineu de Lleida. *Tribuna d'Arqueologia* 2009–2010, 99–119.

González Marcén, P., Mora Torcal, R. and Roda Gilabert, X. (eds) (2011b) *El jaciment de Forat de Conqueta: estudis palobiològics. Treballs d'Arqueologia* 17. Bellaterra, Universitat Autònoma de Barcelona.

Halcrow, Siân E. and Nancy Tayles (2008) The bioarchaeological investigation of childhood and social age: problems and prospects. *Journal of Archaeological Method and Theory* 15(2), 190–215.

Halfacree, K. (2004) A utopian imagination in migration's terra incognita? Acknowledging the non-economic worlds of migration decision-making. *Population, Space and Place* 10, 239–253.

Jagu, D. and Masset, C. (2016) Biographies mégalithiques: fermetures partielles, fermetures complètes, condamnations, doubles condamnations. *BSAA Arqueología* 82, 9–33

Lamoureux-St-Hilaire, M., Macrae, S., McCane, C. A., Parker, E. A. and Iannone, G. (2015) The last groups standing: living abandonment at the ancient Maya center of Minanha, Belize. *Latin American Antiquity* 26, 550–569.

Leibowicz, I. (2017) Rituals and abandonment in Juella with the Inca conquest of Humahuaca, Jujuy, Argentina. *Time and Mind* 10, 357–378.

LeVine, S. and LeVine, R. (1985) Age, gender, and the demographic transition: The life course in agrarian societies. In A. L. Rossi (ed.) *Gender and the Life Course*, 29–42. New York, Aldine.

López Melcion, J. B. (2001) L'edat del Bronze. In *La Noguera Antiga. Dels primers pobladors als visigots.* Balaguer, Museu d'Arqueologia de Catalunya -Museu de la Noguera – Ajuntament de Balaguer, 62–95.
López-Cachero, F. J. (2007) Sociedad y economía durante el Bronce Final y la primera Edad del Hierro en el Noreste Peninsular: una aproximación a partir de las evidencias arqueológicas. *Trabajos de Prehistoria* 64, 99–120.
Moore, A. (2013) Hearth and home: The burial of infants within Romano-British domestic contexts. *Childhood in the Past* 2, 33–54
Mora, R., Benito-Calvo, A., Martínez-Moreno, J., González Marcen, P. and de la Torre, I. (2011) Chrono-stratigraphy of the Upper Pleistocene and Holocene archaeological sequence in Cova Gran (south-eastern Pre-Pyrenees, Iberian Peninsula). *Journal of Quaternary Science* 26, 635–644.
Oms, F. X., Bargalló, A., López-García, J. M., Morales, J. I., Pedro, M., and Solé, À. (2009) L'arqueologia prehistòrica a la serralada del Montsec, des del segle XIX fins a l'actual projecte de recerca. *Revista d'Arqueologia de Ponent* 19, 29–50.
Oms, F. X., López-García, J. M., Mangado, X., Martín, P., Mendiela, S., Morales, J. and Yubero, M. (2013) Hàbitat en cova i espai pels ramats ca. 6200–6000 BP: dades preliminars de la Cova Colomera (Prepirineu de Lleida) durant el neolític antic. *SAGVNTVM. Papeles del Laboratorio de Arqueología de Valencia* 45, 25–38.
Polo Díaz, A., Martínez-Moreno, J. Benito-Calvo, A. and Mora, R. (2014) Prehistoric herding facilities: site formation processes and archaeological dynamics in Cova Gran de Santa Linya (Southeastern Prepyrenees, Iberia). *Journal of Archaeological Science* 41, 784–800.
Prat i Carós, J. (2007). En busca del paraíso: historias de vida y migración. *Revista de Dialectologia y Tradiciones Populares* 62(2), 21–61.
Rojo-Guerra, M. A., Garrido-Pena, R. and García-Martínez de Lagrán, I. (2010) Tombs for the dead, monuments to eternity: the deliberate destruction of megalithic graves by fire in the interior highlands of Iberia (Soria Province, Spain). *Oxford Journal of Archaeology* 29, 253–275.
Scott, E. (1999) *The Archaeology of Infancy and Infant Death.* Oxford, British Archaeological Report S819.
Stevanovic, M. (1997) The age of clay: the social dynamics of house destruction. *Journal of Anthropological Archaeology* 16, 334–395
Svasek, M. (ed.) (2012) *Moving Subjects, Moving Objects. Transnationalism, Cultural Production and Emotions.* Oxford, Berghahn
Valk, J. (2016) 'They enjoy syrup and ghee at tables of silver and gold': Infant loss in Ancient Mesopotamia. *Journal of the Economic and Social History of the Orient* 59, 695–749.
van Dommelen. P. (2014) Moving on: Archaeological perspectives on mobility and migration. *World Archaeology* 46, 477–4

Chapter 3

Learning to be ...: learning and socialisation in ceramic productions during Bronze Age in peninsular southeast Spain

Eva Alarcón García, Juan Jesús Padilla Fernández, Alejandra García García and Luis Arboledas Martínez

Learning and socialisation. Key concepts in the study of the societies of the past

The human being is the only animal species that needs to reproduce both biologically and socially for its survival. To achieve this, in both cases, infants and adults need each other from the time of gestation. The care generated in the mother from the moment of gestation has a direct repercussion on the new life. When the infant is born, its fragility, linked to its dependence for nourishment, fosters the specific care on the part of the mother or group of women to which he or she belongs (Hernando 2001; 2005; Sánchez Romero 2006; 2008a; 2008b). Thus, in their first period of life, infants require and need care – from a part of the population at least – and, as they mature physically and mentally, this care is provided by the whole group or the community (Jiménez Arenas 2015). This turns the care of infants into a cooperative task taken on by all members of the group, whose sole objective is to ensure that children reach and enter adult life. The only way of achieving the success of this process is through learning and socialisation.

Learning is a cultural process through which children acquire specific knowledge and begin to use certain technologies that condition and equip them to carry out specific tasks in the adult world (Sánchez Romero 2010). Socialisation, on the other hand, allows them to get to know the world they live in and of which they form part, through rituals, beliefs, the manifestation of distinct modes of identity, etc (Sánchez Romero 2017). Both processes are fundamental for studying the societies of the past, as well as determining factors in the cultural processes. They are a reflection of the changes and continuities that occur in a social group and are direct markers of the processes of reproduction and maternal practices. Both learning and socialisation has been the subject of reflections and analysis from different areas of knowledge, including psychology, education, ethnoarchaeology, etc, and, of course, archaeology and history. In all these cases, the conclusion has been reached that they are formative, social and cultural processes and, as such, are defined (and governed) by the internal rules of each human group. This means any analysis of them must avoid adopting social generalisations in the interpretations of the past.

Given that these are cultural processes, they should be considered as long-term formative and educational processes, whose development is continuous, progressive and cyclical. Observation, imitation, experimentation, instruction and play are called upon as mechanisms based on which knowledge is acquired and the specific skills of each productive technique are developed. The involvement of each of these mechanisms is determined entirely by the social group. For example, among the North American Inuit groups, the learning process is characterised and marked by subtle interactions between children and adults. These interactions may be verbal, through which different social values and roles are taught and transmitted, and/or combined with development, through the imitation of practical skills, techniques and knowledge (Kamp 2010). In other cases, learning is marked by the interaction of different mechanisms, observation, imitation and instruction. This would be the case of the Dii, Duupa and Doayo peoples in the area of Faro (Cameroon), who share cultural, economic and social characteristics. Among the common elements, pottery production plays an important role. In all three cases, this production is in female hands. The women and daughters of each village are charged with carrying out the whole technical process, which begins at a specific age of between seven and nine (when the girls' cognitive ability is already developed). Their period of learning, always under the supervision of the women of the group, lasts from the ages of four to seven and takes place within the framework of daily life. The finalisation of the process is materialised with the celebration of a ritual through which the new potter is blessed by her family nucleus and the community as a whole, assuming her introduction into the adult world, for which purpose she is endowed with the specific implements of her work (Wallaert-Petre 2001).

A similar situation is found in Luxor among a group of potters in Middle Egypt, near the frontier with Libya. In this small village, the production of wheel-thrown common- and cookware signifies, on the one hand, an essential economic means, and on the other, a further characteristic of social identity. Here it has been possible to observe how the learning processes once again play an essential role in their definition as a people. The potteries are domestic production spaces that coexist with the dwelling places to the point that they blend into one (Padilla Fernández *et al.* 2018). This way of understanding the work of the potter turns it into a domestic activity, routine and essential in the learning processes. Children have a direct relationship with this work. Practically from the moment they are born, their lives revolve around the activity, having direct access to both its production and its technical processes. In this environment, observation, experimentation, imitation and instruction become specific learning mechanisms. Very young children (under 5) play with the 'balls of clay,' making anthropomorphic and abstract figures and attempting to imitate the adult work. During this process, the adults (men and women) begin to instruct them in the forms and decorations of the Egyptian Islamic tradition pottery. When they reach the age of eight, the learning process is separated into different parts. The boys are instructed in the whole process of pottery manufacture (except firing) for them to become master potters, while the girls are instructed in painting and decorating the pieces. From then on, both boys and girls are apprentices and helpers at the same time. In both learning processes, experimentation, observation, imitation and instruction is essential. In the case of the boys, it is very important that they learn the positions of the adult hands during the wheel-throwing process. We could call this the interiorisation of the technical gesture; only thus will they be able to reproduce pieces identical to those made by the master potters, albeit in a smaller size. Constant repetition and error correction through instruction determine that in five years the command of the wheel and, therefore, the acquisition of knowledge and the development of skills are almost perfect. Once this stage of learning has been reached (Padilla Fernández 2017), the boys are instructed in the firing, the final step in the technical process of pottery production. Thus they become true master potters and build their own identity within the group, while the girls have become partially effaced in this phase of the process. The exact opposite occurs in the case of the girls of Kusasi in northern Ghana (Calvo *et al.* 2015).

Despite the variability that is a priority in the development of the learning and socialisation processes (location, age of initiation and development, production spaces, social strategies of knowledge transmission, phases, times, learning periods, etc) (Garrido and Herrero 2015; Calvo *et al.* 2015; Sánchez Romero *et al.* 2015), it is true that in the societies of both the past and the present, children imitate behaviours, either in the form of play or in more or less regulated learning. This is the most common method of learning and becoming socialised, reproducing adult attitudes and developing adult thoughts. It is explained by P. Bourdieu (1977) in his *habitus* concept, which is understood as the logical practice and sense of order learned unconsciously through the rules established in daily life.

Pottery production, the framework for learning and socialisation

This study has been carried out in a highly specific temporal and spatial framework: the Bronze Age village of Peñalosa (Baños de la Encina, Jaén) in southeastern Spain (Contreras *et al.* 2000; Contreras and Cámara 2002; Alarcón García 2010) (Fig. 3.1). Peñalosa is included in the Argaric Culture and, as such, is endowed with a certain set of characteristics, among which we find its settlement pattern: the structuring, construction and distribution of its dwellings built on steep hillsides. Its economy was based mainly on farming, intensive stockbreeding and a profuse copper metallurgy activity. It had a very particular funerary ritual, with some family members being buried inside the houses. Lastly, of particular note among its movable material culture, are pottery forms and receptacles that are exceptional due to their technical and morphotypological standardisation and homogeneity (Contreras Cortés *et al.* 1987–88; Aranda 2001).

Figure 3.1: Bronze Age settlement of Peñalosa (Baños de la Encina, Jaén)

Today, after more than 30 years of studies, we are able probe questions related to the sequences of learning practised almost 4000 years ago. A systematic excavation on a microspatial scale led to the find of 21 pottery vessels with their own singularity, as well as differences and similarities that make them the remains of a unique and particular material culture of a specific human group (Fig. 3.2). And it is the material culture, beyond a physical unit, that establishes them as a set of ontological codes belonging to a specific social context; an active agent that creates and, at the same time, reveals the identity of the persons who manufactured and consumed it. In this respect, the technological praxis is conceived as a revealing strategy of great interpretative potential. Apart from that stipulated by the procedural paradigm in consonance with the usefulness of the study of technology in archaeology, this is configured in essence as an authentic social phenomenon. As such, knowledge of the technological aspects is not only useful for analysing the way in which the material objects were made, or for observing the complete sequence of technical actions needed to develop certain types of pottery (García Roselló and Calvo Trías 2013); it goes far beyond that. If we understand the technological action-deed as a Bourdian *habitus*, in other words, as a 'regime of long-lasting and transferable dispositions, structured structures predisposed to function as structuring structures' (Bourdieu 2008, 86), it plays an important role as a part of and participant in the social dynamics. In other words, it is a system of social structures – stipulated forms of thinking, feeling and

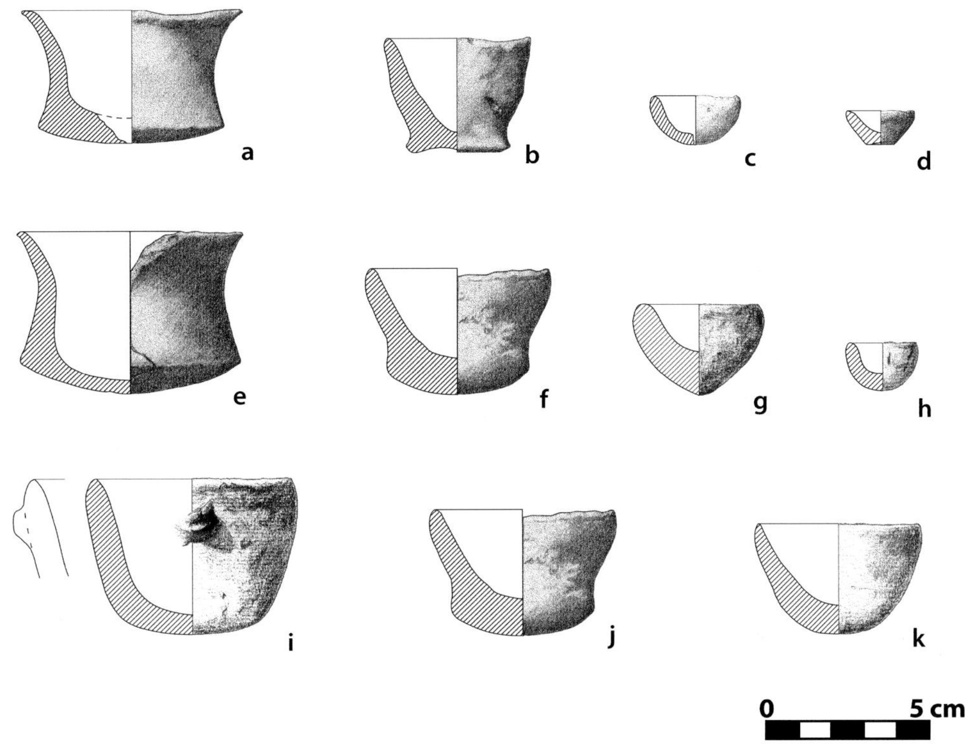

Figure 3.2: Sample pottery vessels with their own singularity from the settlement of Peñalosa

understanding reality – that the person interiorises through primary learning by enculturation (González Ruibal 2006–07, 29).

There can be no doubt that the archaeological record and the finds documented at the Bronze Age archaeological site of Peñalosa are ideal for undertaking social studies and particularly for the definition and identification of the learning and socialisation processes. These processes both form part of and define what we now know as 'childhood.' These are active processes, empirical phenomena and a biological and cultural period through which children acquire skills, develop knowledge, experience the use of technology, take on belief systems and social values and assimilate the specific aptitudes of their behaviour. In summary, these processes are essential not only for understanding the way in which technical knowledge is transmitted (irrespective of the work to be carried out) and in which psychomotor practices are interiorised. The material reality of each of the facets of life impacts directly on the configuration of the *habitus* (Martinelli 1996; Calvo Trías *et al.* 2015). Thus, the materiality, clearly and without the need for the use of language, manifests the set of unwritten rules of behaviour that mark the vicissitudes of a specific sociocultural structure (González Ruibal 2003, 141). The evidence that it is people who create material culture and vice versa – as material culture also creates people (Tilley 2004)

– provides the discipline of archaeology with the opportunity to delve more deeply into the non-verbal information that deciphers different ways of thinking, feeling and acting. In the same way as any other material element, pottery vessels are treasuries of traditions and specific norms of behaviour in the societies of the past (Dobres 2000).

From this perspective, we are faced with an investigation of two fundamental concepts in the study of children: learning and socialisation. For this we will focus on the technological study of the Bronze Age pottery vessels and their educational concepts, which are intimately linked to their specific philosophy and structures. Thus, we propose a technical examination of all the pottery vessels found using the archaeological methodology, all of which are, *a priori*, linked to different moments in the learning process, which in turn is defined on the basis of three elemental technical criteria: first, the ordered and exhaustive description of the pottery cycle; secondly, the detailed definition of each of the gestures and practices used during the manufacturing process; and thirdly, the degree of technical proficiency and skill developed in the technological application. These criteria compile the structuring of the operating chains of the different morphotypological groups, paying individual attention to three major phases or technological periods: 1) the selection, extraction and preparation of the raw materials; 2) the modelling; and 3) the firing (Livingstone 2007; García Roselló and Calvo Trías 2013). To do this, we developed a methodology based above all on the contextual study of each of the pottery vessels analysed. Next, we made a categoric macroscopic profile examination, reinforced by observation with a binocular loupe to check and confirm marks and physical-chemical particularities that are difficult to perceive with the naked eye. Lastly, coupled gas chromatography-mass spectrometry was applied to eleven of the total number of samples (21 pottery vessels from Peñalosa) with the intention of, one the one hand, clarifying the use/functionality hypotheses of these vessels and, on the other, to confirm the technological stages of adult pottery production (Alarcón García 2015).

Materials and production methods and techniques

In contrast to what we see at other Bronze Age settlements on the Iberian Peninsula, such as Cerro de la Encina (Monachil, Granada) or Motilla del Azuer (Daimiel, Ciudad Real) (Sánchez Romero and Alarcón García 2012) at Peñalosa ninety per cent of the pottery vessels linked to the learning processes and knowledge acquisition are documented as part of the movable imaginary of the domestic spaces, enveloped in the occupation floors and adding to the assemblage of small pottery vessels. Above we have already emphasised the high degree of conservation of the archaeological record at Peñalosa. Thanks to this, it has been possible to recover *in situ* each of the elements associated with the two occupation levels identified to date (Phases III0 and IIIA) (Alarcón García 2010; 2015; Contreras *et al.* 2014). In the material assemblage recovered for each period, we have a total of twenty-one pottery vessels. They all share a series of morphotypological and contextual characteristics (Fig. 3.3).

Figure 3.3: Spatial distribution in the domestic context of the pottery vessels analysed

- Small sizes. Miniature scale
- Imitation of larger pottery items
- Asymmetric or slightly symmetric dimensions
- Technological malformations
- Strong temper inclusions
- Little or no surface treatment, either inside or outside
- Very low temperature firings

Tell me who made you and I'll tell you how it was done

A multitude of questions can be asked about the technical pottery-making process. For example: where? (common or segregated areas); when? (was it made); by whom? (a man or a woman, an adult or a child); how? (what were the production processes); for what (to determine their function). In the following pages we will attempt to answer these questions. To do this, we need to look at the archaeometric and chemical aspects.

Select, extract and prepare the clay

The mineralogical composition observed macroscopically in the ceramic matrices of these small pottery vessels suggests that the clay resources used were nearby each other and not far from the Bronze Age village itself, as is also seen in the adult pottery productions (Contreras 2000; Jaramillo 2005). In the general count of minerals observed, we see predominance in the matrices of micaschists, feldspars, quartzes and micas, a composition that is closely linked to the igneous and metamorphic geological horizons predominant in the area around Peñalosa. Moreover, their dominant spherical shape leads us to suppose that the clays would have had a secondary origin with a high degree of erosion, possibly related to the area immediately around the River Rumblar. The small size of the temper and its meagre proportions in most of the pottery vessels analysed indicates a meticulous preparation of the selected clays, probably through decantation by sieving.

With this characterisation in mind, we can say that these pieces would have been made using the same raw material selected and prepared for the manufacture of the adult pottery vessels. This is logical if we take into account that the learning processes were immersed in daily life and therefore impacted directly on the normal undertaking and processes of pottery making. Adults and children would have shared the same spaces, propitiating and generating the strategies necessary for the latter's learning and socialisation (Alarcón García 2015).

In any learning process, memory is an essential factor and even more so in the technology of artisanal activities. In this respect, specific knowledge of the characteristic properties of the different types of clay would have been fundamental for a successful production. The detection of temper with angular edges in some of the analysed fragments, especially in those that imitate forms linked to food preparation (small cooking pots) (Albero Santacreu 2014), could be an obvious sign of the acquisition of this knowledge and the programming of manufacturing sequences in consonance with specific uses. The assimilation of this type of detail would have guaranteed the attainment of products that met the technical and social requirements of the group.

Knead and knead the mass: modelling

The traces and particularities described in the manufacture of the pottery items justifies the initial hypothesis that our study samples are unique and linked *de facto* to learning how to make pottery in the Bronze Age. From a purely technical perspective, all the pieces studied are attempts at smaller imitations of adult forms of Argaric Culture pottery. We see two clearly differentiated execution techniques:

- Simple hollowing out (pinching) (Fig. 3.4). This technique involves discontinuous pinching with the index fingers and thumb to make a central opening in the compact mass of clay prepared for that purpose. In global terms, it is attested as one of the most common and widespread ethnographic technical strategies, due (generally) to

Figure 3.4: Pottery vessel made simple hollowing out pinching

its simplicity and a good guarantee of productive success (Roux 2016). In this case, the clear evidence of irregular surfaces and vertical fractures from the edges to the bases in the smaller specimens documented attests the practice of this learning technique for their manufacture. The presence of these traces reveals the lack of proficiency of the agents charged with making that piece. In view of this, we believe they may have been made by children aged between three and seven, who would have been in the first stages of learning. We must not forget that pottery pieces are three-dimensional objects and, as such, require a series of mental requirements for their manufacture. Anthropological approaches in this respect stress that the ability to appreciate the three-dimensionality of objects is developed at around the age of three, when the human eye acquires its full spectroscopic properties and the brain allows full interaction between electromagnetic radiation and the material (Moore and Moore 1999; Bagwell 2002). Therefore, it makes sense to believe that the age at which those biological mechanisms are acquired would also be when the programmed learning strategies to gain mastery of the pottery technology *habitus* would have begun. At first, it appears that memorisation of the most representative

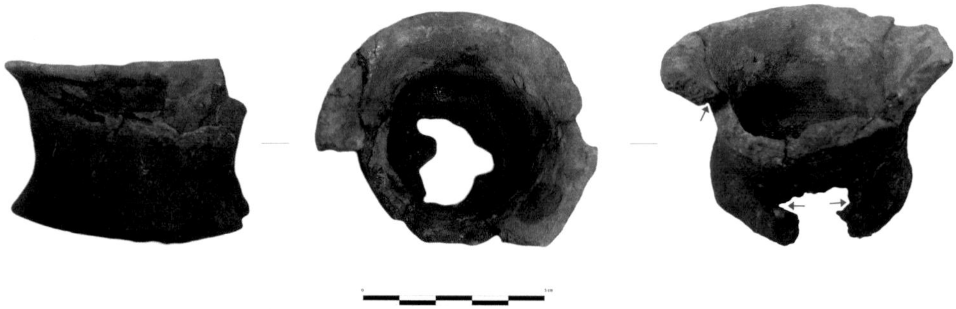

Figure 3.5: Pottery vessel made by coiling. Imitates container related to food preparation

forms of their cultural framework would have been the primordial action to be achieved. To do this such elemental and productive methods as hollowing would have been resorted to. This technique, represented by 52.3% of the samples analysed, indicates the itinerary of the pottery-making learning processes.

- Warping-coiling (Fig. 3.5). This consists of pressing and rolling the clay horizontally on a flat surface or vertically between the hands. This produces rolls of clay or *colombinos* (coil pottery) with sizes that vary according to the technological tradition of each artisan. In this case, they account for 38% of the analysed samples and the size of the rolls used to make the selected pieces is no greater than 5 mm thick and 10 cm long, a measurement adjusted proportionally to their size that in no case coincides with those of the pottery vessels they are imitating. Those are larger, a fact that determines the manufacture with similar-sized clay rolls. Nevertheless, the technical gestures used are identical. The unequivocal identification of traces of flat breakages, profiles full of concave points of intersection and irregular alate veins reveals a continuous superimposition of coils joined by pulling the ends to the edge. Moreover, the existence of horizontal breakages demonstrates the preparation of a small clay base stretched more or less depending on the pottery type reproduced. In these cases, the degree of technical skill is still wanting, but greater than that documented in the case of the sunken method. This means we are looking at a higher stage of learning in which the form and technical gestures are being absorbed and interiorised.

The manufacture of recognisable forms is not exempt from a period of continuous practice that can be glimpsed in the representation of categories of diverse qualities, depending on the degree of skill acquired. In fact, in the analysed sample we can see, albeit sparsely represented with only 9.5% of the total, the coexistence of a hybrid stage (hollowing + coiling) (Fig. 3.6) that perfectly documents the transition from one stage of learning to the next (Table 3.1). Over time, constant observation and repetition of stipulated strategies, together with the correction of errors by the person charged with the teaching, meant that the vessels became more realistic and manufactured with similar techniques to those of the adults. The choice of the technical gestures

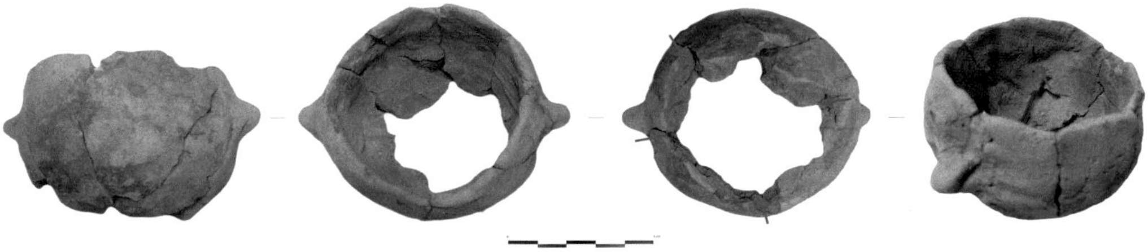

Figure 3.6: Pottery vessel made of a hybrid stage by pinching and coiling

involved in the manufacturing process is fixed in advance by the community to which they belong. Thus, the abandonment of hollowing as a technique would have been determined by that circumstance.

In both cases, although roughly, it is possible glimpse how they also imitated and experimented with certain decorations, such as the typical nail marks on the rim area. Today, it is impossible to know their significance, but we can be sure that they meant something and that this would have been closely linked to their particular concept of the world. Likewise, the vessels that remind us of 'pots' or cooking vessels are found with small mamelons, deformed in many cases and symmetrical in others (Table 3.1).

You in your kiln: the firing

Knowledge of the tasks involved in the firing phase was vital for successfully completing the production process. The work of a potter is eminently constructive and therefore enjoys the privilege of being able to constantly reuse the raw material if an error is made. However, after firing this advantage diminishes to the point that it is practically impossible to reverse the previously taken technological steps. Carrying out a firing without the technical guarantees means that all the technical actions taken up to that point have been wasted. Even so, and in accordance with what we have seen in the vessels analysed, the learning of the gestures linked to this final task was deferred to the effective control of the facets linked to the modelling. In part of them, the post-depositional determining factors completely prevent any conjectures in this respect, as they have undergone powerful oxidising combustion processes due to the burning of the context to which they belonged.[1] The remains, above all those that were attempts to emulate the pottery forms used mainly for food preparation, bear on their surfaces unequivocal evidence of having been heated over open fires. Although it is attested that Argaric household pottery was fired in this type of structure, for example, small holes in the ground, the maximum temperatures reached by the pieces in the studied assemblage did not even reach 500°C. This is a very low temperature for obtaining optimum results in terms of the hardness, durability and, of course, functionality of the vessel. In this way, we have to consider three possibilities. The first concerns the desire for these vessels to reach a certain consistency and durability, having been placed close to sources of fire, such as those that would have been lit in

Table 3.1: Contextual and technological characterisation of the ceramic containers analysed in the Argaric settlement of Peñalosa (Baños de la Encina, Jaén)

Id.	*Context*	*Technical process*	*Surface treatment*	*Dimensions*	*Cooking*	*Represent*	*Weight (g)*	*Technical expertise*
9303	domestic	Coiling	initial polishing	asymmetry	Mixed-oxidise	consumption	67	initial
9427	domestic	simple (pinching)	no	asymmetry	Mixed	consumption	18	initial
9433	domestic	simple (pinching)- coiling	no	asymmetry	Oxidise	food preparation	53	initial
9643	domestic	coiling	inicial	symmetry	Mixed	consumption	63	half/advanced
9706	domestic	simple (pinching)	no	asymmetry	Mixed	consumption	60	initial
9760	domestic	simple (pinching)	smooth out	symmetry	Mixed	consumption	38	media
9761	domestic	coiling	initial polishing	symmetry	Mixed	consumption	67	media
9766	domestic	simple (pinching)	no	asymmetry	Mixed	food preparation	42	initial
91185	domestic	simple (pinching)	no	asymmetry	Mixed	consumption	35	initial
14583	domestic	coiling	initial polishing	symmetry	Mixed	consumption	48	half/advanced
14596	domestic	coiling	initial polishing	symmetry	Mixed	consumption	50	half/advanced
17512-1	funerary	simple (pinching)- coiling	no	asymmetry	Oxidise	consumption	66	initial
25430	domestic	simple (pinching)	smooth out?	symmetry	Mixed	consumption	12	initial/half
25495	domestic	coiling	smooth out	asymmetry	Mixed	food preparation	56	half/advanced
28500	domestic	simple (pinching)	no	asymmetry	Mixed	consumption	16	half
42296	domestic	simple (pinching)	no	asymmetry	Mixed	consumption	12	initial
44385	domestic	simple (pinching)	no	asymmetry	Mixed	consumption	9	half/advanced
50431	domestic	simple (pinching)	no	symmetry	Mixed	consumption		half
50686	domestic	coiling	smooth out	asymmetry	Mixed	food preparation	79	half
50900	funerary	simple (pinching)	no	asymmetry	Mixed	consumption	5	initial
501035	domestic	coiling	polishing (inside and outward)	asymmetry	Mixed	food preparation	58	half

the fireplaces recorded in the domestic spaces. The second and third options would have been directly related to the learning processes. On the one hand, with the firing of these small vessels we would have the whole the technological process of pottery production, and on the other, these learning processes would not have ended with the execution of the object but would have continued to emulate the functions and uses of these vessels; in short, clearly manifesting the socialisation of the children who made them. This last option is supported by the detection of traces of fire identified as oval 'stains' focused on a specific point of the exterior surface. This is exactly the same as that identified on the 'pots' or vessels destined for cooking food.

Tell me about your function

Eleven of the pottery vessels analysed in this study were subjected to gas chromatography coupled with mass spectrometry. The results were very interesting. Firstly, because in all the cases analysed, indications of organic residues were documented, and secondly, because those residues are very homogeneous in their composition and their presence in the vessels. Thus we find that 72% of the samples analysed present linear chain hydrocarbons, clearly suggesting the presence of a waxy material in their interior. In 54.5% of the vessels analysed there were residues of plant origin, due to the presence of unsaturated fatty acids, such as C16:1, C18:1 or C18:2. In only 0.11% of the samples did we find other types of residue, such as citric acid or 9-octadecenamide, considered to be a marker of animal fat.

Conclusions

The analysis of more than 20 pottery vessels in the Bronze Age settlement of Peñalosa leads us to various conclusions regarding the learning and socialisation processes. These are important to describe.

All the pottery vessels studied here are the product of the learning processes that took place more than 4000 years ago in the Bronze Age settlement of Peñalosa. They all repeat the same patterns. Their small size (in no case do they weigh more than 69 g); they reproduce two forms of the adult tableware; they imitate adult decorative motifs (mamelons and small dermatoglyphs); all have been through the firing process, although none at a temperature of higher 500°C, less than that of the adult vessels; and they all demonstrate two specific levels of technical skill: initial and middle-to-advanced.

This materiality clearly marks two stages/moments of the learning processes, unmistakeably determining which technique indicated the beginning of the process and which confirms the assimilation of the ability, having passed through the development of said skill. In other words, in the samples analysed, it is clear that the sunken technique is associated directly with the first stages of learning. A technique that would have been combined and substituted as the child acquired – through practice and instruction – the aptitude and skill needed to develop the coiling or *columbí* technique. In our case, we see how both techniques are combined to make the same vessel, thus marking the passing from one stage of learning to the next. We also possibly have two vessels with great similarities, both in their manufacturing process and their technical gestures, which lead us to believe that they were made by the same individual.

In our case, we have been able to corroborate how the learning and socialisation processes reach their final stage. The linear chain hydrocarbons clearly suggest the presence of a waxy material inside the vessels. This presence can be directly related to the waterproofing of the adult tableware aimed at sealing the pores in the clay. The discovery of these waxy residues is confirmation that the children had fully assimilated the technical process in accordance with that of the adult world.

All the vessels present morphotypological characteristics that allow them to be placed in two concrete groups. On the one hand, we find pieces that reproduce vessels for food preparation, and on the other, those for food consumption. Both activities form part of the tasks linked to food, curiously inserted into the maintenance activities and, evidently, daily life.

The physical determination of exposure to fire and the presence of residues such as fatty acids in the small vessels that imitate the forms related to food preparation highlights two very important questions. On the one hand, that the learning processes included not only acquiring the technical skills of pottery making, but also knowledge of the function and functionality of the vessel produced, in this case cooking and food preparation. On the other hand, it tells us of the culmination of the socialisation process. If that is the case and assuming that generally the tasks related to food practices have been taken as activities carried out by women (Picazo 1997; Alarcón García *et al.* 2008; Alarcón García 2010), we could consider that the persons who made and used these vessels would have been girls in Peñalosa.

In summary, detailed knowledge of the pottery-making learning processes at the archaeological site of Peñalosa provides us with a good account of the application of a perfectly defined *savoir faire* in the Bronze Age that entailed the establishment of a routine and fully specialised manufacture in domestic contexts, immersed in the comings and goings of daily life. Following the logic that pottery and its production methods are necessarily linked to explicit cultural practices or values (Gosselain 2011), we believe that the learning processes in the case of Peñalosa were highly interiorised. Without a doubt, this enhances the social, economic and productive role of the children in this human group. We have to remind ourselves that not only in Peñalosa, but in the Argaric Culture in general, children were considered members of society with full rights. This is confirmed by their presence in the funerary record and their symmetrical treatment with adults in funerary rituals (Sánchez Romero y Alarcón García 2012).

Acknowledgement

This research has been supported by R & D Project HAR2011-30131-CO2-01 funded by the Spanish Ministry of Economy and Competitiveness. A. García acknowledges support from a FPU 13/02389 scholarship from the Spanish Ministry of Education.

Note

1 The settlement of Peñalosa succumbed at least twice to generalised fires that led to the sudden abandonment of the site (Contreras *et al.* 2000).

References

Alarcón García, E. (2015) Social relations between adulthood and childhood in the Early Bronze Age site of Peñalosa (Baños de la Encina, Jaen, Spain). In M. Sánchez Romero, E. Alarcón and G. Aranda (eds) *Children, Spaces and Identity*. Oxford, Oxbow Books, 59–74.

Alarcón García, E. (2010) *Continuidad y cambio social: análisis de las actividades de mantenimiento.* Unpublished thesis, University of Granada.

Alarcón García, E., Sánchez Romero, M., Moreno, M. A., Contreras, F. and Arboledas, L. (2008) Las actividades de mantenimiento en los contextos fortificados de Peñalosa, *Cuadernos de prehistoria y arqueología de la Universidad de Granada* 18, 265–296.

Albero Santacreu, D. (2014) *Materiality, Techniques and Society in the Pottery Production.* London, De Gruyter.

Aranda Jiménez, G. (2001) El análisis de la relación forma-contenido de los conjuntos cerámicos del yacimiento arqueológico del Cerro de la Encina (Granada, España). Oxford, British Archaeological Report S927.

Bagwell, E. (2002) Ceramic form and skill. Attempting to identify child producers at Pecos pueblo, New Mexico. In K. Kamp (ed.) *Children in Prehistoric Puebloan Southwest*. Salt Lake City, University of Utah Press.

Bourdieu, P. (2008) *El sentido práctico*. Salamanca, Siglo XXI.

Calvo Trías, M., García Rosselló, J., Javaloyas, D. and Albero, D. (2015) Playing with mud? An ethnoarchaeological approach to Children´s learning. In M. Sánchez Romero, E. Alarcón and G. Aranda (eds) *Children, Spaces and Identity*, 88–104. Oxford, Oxbow Books.

Contreras Cortés, F. (2000) Análisis histórico de las comunidades de la Edad del Bronce del Piedemonte meridional de Sierra Morena y Depresión Linares-Bailén. Proyecto Peñalosa, *Arqueología. Monografías* 10. Sevilla, Consejería de Cultura.

Contreras Cortés, F. and Cámara Serrano, J. A. (2002) La jerarquización en la Edad del Bronce del Alto Guadalquivir (España). El poblado de Peñalosa (Baños de la Encina, Jaén). Oxford, British Archaeological Report S1025.

Contreras Cortés, F., Capel, J., De la Torre, F., Molina, F. and Esquivel, J. A. (1987–88) Los ajuares cerámicos de la necrópolis argárica de la Cuesta del Negro (Purullena, Granada). Avance al estudio analítico y estadístico, *Cuadernos de prehistoria y arqueología de la Universidad de Granada* 12–13, 135–156.

Contreras Cortés, F., Moreno, M. A., Arboledas, L., Alarcón, E., Mora, A. and Padilla, J. J. (2014) Un poblado de la edad del bronce que tiene mucho que decir, Peñalosa: últimas novedades en la Acrópolis oriental, *Cuadernos de Prehistoria y Arqueología de la Universidad de Granada* 24, 347–390.

Dobres, M. A. (2000) *Technology and Social Agency*. London, Blackwell.

García Roselló, J. and Calvo Trías, M. (2013) *Making Pots. El modelado de la cerámica a mano y su potencial interpretativo.* Oxford, British Archaeological Report S2540.

Garrido-Pena, R. and Herrero Corral, M. (2015) Children as potters: apprenticeship patterns from Bell Beaker pottery of Copper Age Inner Iberia (Spain) (*c.* 2500–2000 cal BC). In M. Sánchez Romero, E. Alarcón and G. Aranda (eds) *Children, Spaces and Identity*. Oxford, Oxbow Books, 40–58.

González Ruibal, A. (2003) *La experiencia del otro. Una introducción a la etnoarqueología.* Madrid, Akal.

González Ruibal, A. (2006–2007) Galaicos: Poder y comunidad en el Noroeste de la Península Ibérica (1200 a.C.–50 d.C.). *Brigantium: Boletín do Museu Arqueolóxico e Histórico da Coruña* 18, 11–272.

Gosselain, O. P. (2011) Fine if I do, fine if I don't. Dynamics of technical knowledge in Sub-Saharan Africa. In B. W. Roberts and M. Vander Linden (eds) *Investigating Archaeological Cultures.* New York, Springer, 211–227.

Hernando, A. (2001) *Arqueología de la Identidad*. Madrid, Akal.
Hernando, A. (2005) Mujeres y Prehistoria. En torno a la cuestión del origen del patriarcado. In M. Sánchez Romero (ed.) *Arqueología y género*. Granada, Universidad de Granada, Granada, 73–108.
Jaramillo, A. (2005) *Una aproximación medioambiental y registro arqueológico en la cuenca del rio Rumblar (norte de Jaén) recursos y materias primas en la Edad del Bronce*. Unpublished thesis, University of Granada.
Jiménez Arenas J. M. (2015) Complexity, cooperation and childhood: an evolutionary perspective. In M. Sánchez Romero, E. Alarcón and G. Aranda (eds) *Children, Spaces and Identity*. Oxford, Oxbow Books, 25–39.
Kamp, K. A. (2010) Entre el trabajo y el juego: perspectivas sobre la infancia en el suroeste norteamericano. *Complutum* 21(2), 103–120.
Livingstone Smith, A. (2007) *Chaîne Operatorie de la Poterie. Référénces ethnografiques, analices et reconstitution*. Tervueren, Musée Royal de l'Afrique Centrale.
Martinelli, B. (1996) Sous le regard de l´aprenti. Paliers de savoir et d´insertions chez les forgerons Moose du Yatenga (Burkina Faso). *Techniques et culture* 28, 9–47.
Moore, K. and Moore, P. (1999) *Embriología clínica*. Ciudad de México, McGraw Hill International.
Padilla Fernández J. J. and Chapon, L. (2015) Gender and childhood in the II Iron Age: The pottery centre of Las Cogotas (Ávila, Spain), In M. Sánchez Romero, E. Alarcón and G. Aranda (eds) *Children, Spaces and Identity*. Oxford, Oxbow Books, 75–87.
Padilla Fernández, J. J., Ruiz Zapatero, G. and Álvarez Sanchís, J. R. (2018) *Algo más que un taller cerámico de la II edad del Hierro: el alfar de las cogotas (Cardeñosa, Ávila)*. In E. Alarcón Garcia, J. J. Padilla Fernández, L. Arboledas and L. Chapon (eds) *Algo más que galbos y cacharros. Etnoarqueología y experimentación cerámica*. Monográfico 3. Menga. Revista de Prehistoria de Andalucía, 217–233.
Padilla Fernández, J. J. (2018) Identidad y tecnología cerámica: el trabajo alfarero en Luxor (Egipto). *Complutum* 28(2), 379–398.
Picazo, M. (1997) Hearth and home: the timing of maintenance activities. In J. Moore and E. Scott (eds) *Invisible People and Processes. Writing Gender and Childhood into European Archaeology*. London, Leicester University Press, 59–67.
Roux, V. (2016) *Des ceramiques et des hommes. Décoder les assemblages archéologiques*. Nanterre, Presses Universitaires de Paris Puest.
Sánchez Romero, M. (2006) Maternidad y prehistoria: prácticas de reproducción, relación y socialización. *Las mujeres en la Prehistoria*. Valencia, Museo de Valencia, 119–138.
Sánchez Romero, M. (2008a). An approach to learning and socialisation in children during the Spanish Bronze Age. In L. H. Dommasnes and M. Wrigglesworth (eds) *Children, Identity and the Past*. Cambridge, Cambridge Scholars Publishing, 113–124.
Sánchez Romero, M. (2008b) Childhood and the construction of gender identities through material culture. *International Journal of Childhood in the Past* 1, 17–37.
Sánchez Romero, M. (2010) Infancia y cultura material en Arqueología. *Complutum* 21(2), 9–13.
Sánchez Romero, M. (2017) Landscapes of Childhood: Bodies, Places and Material Culture. *Childhood in the Past* 10(1), 16–37.
Sánchez Romero, M. and Alarcón García, E. (2012) Lo que los niños nos cuentan: individuos infantiles durante la Edad del Bronce en el sur de la Península Ibérica. In D. Justel (ed.) *Niños en la Antigüedad. Estudios sobre la Infancia en el mediterráneo antiguo*. Zaragoza, Prensas Universitarias de Zaragoza, 57–98.
Sánchez Romero, M., Alarcón, E, and Aranda, G. (2015) Children, and space: multidisciplinary approaches to identity childhood. In M. Sánchez Romero, E. Alarcón and G. Aranda (eds) *Children, Spaces and Identity*. Oxford, Oxbow Books, 2–9.
Tilley, C. (2004) *The Materiality of Stone: Explorations in landscape phenomenology*. Oxford, Berg.
Wallaert-Petre, H. (2001) Learning how to make the right pots: Apprenticeship strategies and material culture, a case study in handmade pottery from Cameroon. *Journal Anthropological Research* 57(4), 471–493.

Chapter 4

Beyond biology: the constructed nature of motherhood(s) in ancient Near Eastern sources and studies

Agnès Garcia-Ventura

The 3000 or so years of cuneiform written sources offer us a rich and varied panorama for reflecting upon the ways in which motherhood was constructed in the ancient Near East.[1] These sources show that the concept of motherhood was neither constant nor unchanging; indeed, different motherhoods are portrayed in different sources and different chronologies. They also prove that these motherhoods were constructed in diverse ways depending on age or status of the potential mothers. Consequently, the primary sources suggest that in ancient Mesopotamia there was no single 'natural' motherhood, but several constructed motherhoods. Despite the wealth of the sources, however, the concept of motherhood has not been discussed in any depth in the secondary literature, and its dimension as a social and cultural construct even less. Fortunately, some recent analyses applying gender studies perspectives have begun to explore new avenues of research in this direction.

In this paper, which comprises three sections plus some brief concluding remarks, I hope to contribute to this emerging line of research. To do so I will consider motherhood as a social institution,[2] built and reinforced through diverse power relationships between the various parties involved.[3] First, I offer some insights into the recent secondary literature on the study of motherhood in ancient Mesopotamia from the point of view of gender studies, and try to establish why the topic has been neglected in spite of the richness of the primary sources. Second, concentrating on these primary sources, I focus on what I consider that is one of the best examples for reflecting on the constructed nature of motherhood: the case of the women consecrated to a divinity, known in Akkadian as *nadītu*, attested in certain legal texts from the beginning of the 2nd millennium BC (the Old Babylonian period). Third, I offer some thoughts on the way the transmission of knowledge, the primary sources and the secondary literature interact. To do so, in this third and last section I examine a text from the 1st millennium BC (the Neo-Babylonian period) allegedly dealing with *nadītu*-women and the way it has been translated and interpreted with regard to the relationship between these women, midwifery and motherhood.

Starting point: some glimpses into the study of motherhood in ancient Mesopotamia

Women's studies and gender studies have grown notably in the last decades (Garcia-Ventura and Zisa 2017, 46–67), and so one might have expected an increase in the studies dealing with motherhood as well. There are indeed some significant examples of research applying gender studies perspectives to the scrutiny of motherhood in ancient Mesopotamia, in order to reassess the interpretations proposed to date and to provide a more complex analysis of ancient women, motherhoods and infancies. The research by Stephanie Lynn Budin (Budin 2011; 2015) and by M. Érica Couto-Ferreira (Couto-Ferreira 2013; 2016a; 2016b) is a good example but these studies are not representative of a more general trend. In my view, in fact, the opposite is true: they stand out as exceptions in a tradition of studies in which motherhood has been largely neglected or, when present, has been described in a very biased way in the secondary literature. Just to take one recent example, in the last comprehensive volume on the family in the ancient Near East, a proceedings volume of the *Rencontre Assyriologique Internationale* held in Paris 2009, none of the 42 papers published dealt exclusively with motherhood (Marti 2014).[4]

In her article *Being mothers or acting (like) mothers? Constructing motherhood in ancient Mesopotamia*, Couto-Ferreira points out several reasons for this under-representation of motherhood as a topic of study (Couto-Ferreira 2016a, 25–26). First, she notes that in the secondary literature dealing with women in ancient Mesopotamia the focus has often been put on marriage but not on motherhood; motherhood is just seen as the 'natural' consequence of marriage. To a certain extent, it could be said that this view corresponds as well to the one reflected in some primary sources, where marriage is presented as the main aim of the life of women.[5] In practical terms it means that, despite the wealth of the primary sources on motherhood, we should not expect them to mention motherhood explicitly, or to prioritize it as a topic.

Second, Couto-Ferreira notes that when attention is paid to motherhood, the concept tends to be portrayed as 'naturalised'; thus, 'mothering labour' and 'birthing labour,' to put it in the terms used by Budin,[6] who also alerted readers to this bias in her volume *Images of Woman and Child from the Bronze Age: Reconsidering Fertility, Maternity, and Gender in the Ancient World*, have traditionally been presented in the secondary literature as a continuum, as unfailingly and biologically linked to women (Budin 2011, 11–20; Couto-Ferreira 2016a, 25–26). In addition, it has been noted that this naturalization is conventionally reflected in a construction of motherhood linked to fertility, and fertility, in its turn, is assimilated to womanhood. However, fertility in ancient Mesopotamia was associated more with men than with women; to quote

Budin, in ancient Near Eastern primary sources 'feminine sexuality focuses on erotic pleasure, with no reference to procreation' (Budin 2011, 17).

So, with regard to these features that make up the naturalisation of motherhood and its link to womanhood, until the critical approach of gender studies began to establish itself in certain academic circles, women were, to quote Orna Donath, 'treated as a natural caregivers' and consequently 'womanhood and motherhood are considered to be synonymous' (Donath 2015, 343). In this scenario, then, the under-representation of motherhood as a topic of study in ancient Near Eastern studies might be interpreted not as a lack of interest in the subject but as the result of the assumption of a 'natural' motherhood which does not need to be studied and analysed, but just 'found' and pointed out in the primary sources. In other words, it responds to the idea of motherhood as a social institution with which we started this article; as Judith Lorber says, it 'creates structure and stability, seeps into the practices of many social roles, has a long history, and is virtually unquestioned' (Lorber 2005, 13).

A third reason, linked not just to the study of motherhood but to the approach to women's history in a broad sense, is that the analysis in ancient Near Eastern studies focuses mainly on goddesses rather than on women of flesh and blood. As a consequence, the motherhoods that come under scrutiny in the secondary literature are not 'real' motherhoods, but 'divine' motherhoods, built literarily and mythologically. This point was stressed by Couto-Ferreira (2016a, 25) in her brief presentation of a state of the art of studies on motherhood in ancient Mesopotamia, in which she noted that the *Reallexikon der Assyriologie*, one of the main reference works in the field, has the entry *Muttergöttin* (mother goddess) but no entry for *Mutterschaft* (motherhood), for instance.

This absence of flesh and blood women is not only blatant with regard to motherhood, but with regard to women in Antiquity in general terms. Indeed, this was the starting point of the monumental volume co-edited by Budin and Jean MacIntosh Turfa, titled *Women in Antiquity: Real Women across the Ancient World*. In her introduction to the volume, Budin spoke of her concern about this absence of 'real women' in the secondary literature, and indeed the main aim of the book is to contribute to filling this gap (Budin 2016, 1). With contributions of this kind, then, the aim is to counteract one of the most frequent androcentric biases in research: the sublimation of women by identifying primarily the images of female bodies with goddesses rather than with mortals, even when there is no evidence for this and the researcher merely applies his or her preconceptions (on this see, among others, Meskell 1995; López-Bertran and Garcia-Ventura 2012, 397–401 with previous literature).

So far, we have seen that the three reasons proposed to explain why motherhood has received little attention in the secondary literature are linked to the presence of certain androcentric biases in research. Consequently, a combination of both an awareness of these biases and the use of new critical approaches using gender studies may be a way to balance the situation. However, there is a fourth reason for the underrepresentation of the topic which, paradoxically, is linked to the *emergence* of feminism in academia rather than to its absence, as in the previous cases. Here I refer to the unease, precisely inside gender studies, provoked by dealing with issues traditionally linked primarily or exclusively to women and even more to women's bodies, such as motherhood (Bolufer Peruga 2012, 59–60). This trend is observable in women's history in all areas and chronologies, and ancient Near Eastern studies are no exception to this rule.[7]

Motherhood beyond biology: the case of the *nadītu*-women of Marduk

At the beginning of the 2nd millennium BC the existence and the activity of women known as *nadītu* is widely attested in cuneiform written sources, mainly in administrative and legal texts. Several translations bringing out different nuances have been proposed for this term, with 'priestess,' 'nun' or 'religious woman' being the most common.[8] The term, however, is multifaceted and none of these translations fully reflects its complexity. A useful working definition may be the one provided by the *Chicago Assyrian Dictionary* (CAD from now on), the reference dictionary for the Akkadian language, which describes *nadītu* as a 'woman dedicated to a god, usually unmarried, not allowed to have children, usually living in a *gagû*.'[9] In this definition it is important to highlight, first, the fact that not all *nadītu* were unmarried, as their marital status depended on the god to whom they were consecrated; and second that whether or not they were married they were not allowed to bear children, that is, they were not allowed to gestate biological children. However, this does not mean that they had no relationship with motherhood at any level, as I will show below.

In this respect, the situation of the *nadītu*-women consecrated to Marduk in the city of Babylon is especially illuminating. These *nadītu*-women were the only ones who were not only allowed to marry, but were expected to do so. Lucile Barberon (2012), whose PhD on these *nadītu* of Marduk is the most comprehensive monograph on these women so far, interprets both the consecration of a daughter as *nadītu* and the marriage of a *nadītu* as a political issue, linked to the creation of the social identity of certain families in the Babylon of the beginning of the 2nd millennium BC (in this respect see especially Barberon 2014, 267–268). It is also in this light that the management of both their marriage and their offspring should be interpreted: as a political and social strategy involving several actors, not only these women in isolation.

Indeed, as a consequence of their marriage and its inseparable link with offspring, these *nadītu* of Marduk were expected to provide their husbands with children. However, as they were not allowed to bear children themselves, this expectation entailed an apparent paradox which had to be resolved in some way. The solution chosen was to create two legal mechanisms to confer on the *nadītu* the legal status of mother of children born to other women. The first was adoption, a common practice, widely attested in ancient Mesopotamia for several purposes and in varied contexts.[10] The second was bigamy, a model in which the *nadītu* was the principal wife and, often, the one responsible for choosing the secondary wife or the slave-woman whose main duty was to give birth to children.[11] This second option is well attested in the Laws of Hammurabi, specifically in five of the laws (137, 144, 145, 146 and 147) which regulate the relationship between the two women as well as the management of the offspring.[12]

In other words, one may say that it is made explicit in the Laws of Hammurabi that the *nadītu*-women were expected to become mothers. Indeed the laws cited above state that the *nadītu* is expected to provide children, but not to bear them, as this duty is to be carried out by another woman. A good example of this is the beginning of law 137, which clearly defines the duty of both women, establishing a clear difference between biological and legal motherhood: 'If a man should decide to divorce a *šugītu* who bore him children, or a *nadītu* who provided him with children ....'[13]

The scenario portrayed in these laws is especially interesting from the point of view of the construction of motherhood because, in practical terms, it granted two mothers to the children born and raised in this way. Indeed, the legal recognition of a dual motherhood for these children would have had consequences in terms of inheritance: for instance, as they were able to inherit from both mothers. This was not the case for those born to slave women, since in this case the biological mother was not legally recognised as mother – a 'charge,' if we may use this word, only reserved to the *nadītu* as the owner of the slave (Barberon 2012, 227–230).

Obviously we cannot know how the motherhood of these *nadītu* women was exercised in practical terms and in everyday life, so we cannot know whether motherhood had any implication outside the legal milieu. What we do know is that they were considered mothers at least in legal and social terms, even though they were not the biological mothers of their offspring.

To sum up, so far we have seen that motherhood is a facet of *nadītu* women that is present in the primary sources, in contrast to their portrayal as 'childless' or as 'fallow women' in some of the secondary literature.[14] The failure to consider them as mothers in the secondary literature, then, may respond to a preconception of a 'naturalised' motherhood which excludes non-biological motherhood(s) from its definition.

Midwifery and the *nadītu*-women: Primary sources, secondary literature and transmission of knowledge

So far I have outlined the definition of the motherhood of the *nadītu*-women consecrated to Marduk, the only ones expected to marry and to provide their husbands with children. But what about the other *nadītu*-women – the ones not allowed to marry, which were the vast majority? First it must be said that they also had the chance to be legal mothers through adoption, but in their case they were the sole mother of the person adopted (often an adult rather than a child), and so the concept of dual motherhood as described above did not apply (Stol 1998, 97–100; Barberon 2012, 225–227; Justel 2014, 77–79). For unmarried *nadītu*, adoption was just one among several mechanisms designed to ensure protection in old age and to secure inheritance rights as well. However, the family of the *nadītu* had other ways to deal with these situations, for instance delegating to their brothers.[15] As a consequence, motherhood was less frequent in unmarried than in married *nadītu*-women. Their relationship with motherhood, then, was different and less frequent partly because even if all *nadītu* shared a certain status as consecrated women, the unmarried ones did not come under the umbrella of marriage (the most common legal framework among adult women, as pointed out above)[16] and outside marriage they were not expected to become mothers, even though, from the legal point of view, they had the chance to do so.

In this scenario, I think it is paradoxical that the secondary literature does not usually emphasise the role of the *nadītu* as mothers, but it does emphasise the alleged and indirect link the *nadītu*, especially those who were not mothers, had with motherhood. Scholars have drawn attention to the possible connection between the *nadītu* and the biological motherhood of other women, attributing them the role of midwives. In this respect the interpretation of two lines of the text KAR 321[17] is especially illuminating.

KAR 321 contains an excerpt of a Babylonian hymn which has come down to us through what appears to have been a school exercise from the 1st millennium BC. So far no full transliteration of the text has been published, but Benjamin Foster (2005, 878) published a complete translation into English and other scholars proposed transliterations and translations (mainly into French and into English) of certain lines. In what follows I reproduce the translations, by four scholars, of the excerpt that interests us here:

1. Wilfred G. Lambert (1992, 143): 'Women who grasp wisdom in their work ... *Nadītus* who preserve the womb by their skill.'
2. Marten Stol (2000, 172): 'Women who have learned insight at their work ... the *nadītu*-women who give the womb life by wisdom.'
3. Benjamin R. Foster (2005, 878): 'Women who have gained understanding in their tasks ... cloistered women who are skilled in keeping the unborn child alive.'
4. Lucile Barberon (2012, 207): 'Les femmes qui sont expertes dans leur travail ... les *nadîtum* qui, par leur science, préservent l'utérus.'

These lines are taken from the excerpt of the text devoted to several religious women who are associated with childbirth (lines 5–9 of the text). In one of the lines (the second sentence of the translations) we find the sumerogram LUKUR.MEŠ and, in the margin, '*na-da-te*' as an explanatory gloss, which has been interpreted as evidence for the reading *nadītu*. However, the univocal equivalence of LUKUR with the Akkadian term *nadītu* is far from clear, for several reasons, so we should be cautious about interpreting the explanatory gloss in KAR 321 in this way. As Alhena Gadotti (2016, 70–71) noted, in lexical lists LUKUR has been equated to several Akkadian terms, *nadītu* being just one of them; and furthermore, the term LUKUR was used at the end of the 3rd millennium BC as an epithet for royal women, and so its use was not necessarily restricted to religious women.

Moreover, it must always be borne in mind that the use and meaning of these terms did not remain unchanged over all the historical period in which they were attested. The way the term *nadītu* was interpreted in the 1st millennium BC – that is, about 1000 years after it was used in the Old Babylonian sources and the consecrated women discussed here were attested to – is likely to have little to do with the reality of the flesh-and-blood *nadītu*-women from the Old Babylonian period. Therefore, taking the explanatory gloss of this text as evidence of what the *nadītu* did at the beginning of the 2nd millennium BC does not seem justified. It also presents us with an interesting example of how the transmission of knowledge may work: here we have an alleged reality of the end of the 2nd millennium BC as recorded in a text from the 1st millennium BC which is, in turn, interpreted by some 20th and 21st century AD scholars in as a reflection of the reality of the 2nd millennium BC.

Thus far I have concentrated on the problems of this transmission of knowledge from the 2nd millennium BC to the 1st. Let me now focus on the next step, the interpretation of the 1st millennium text in current scholarship. In the translations cited above we see certain differences, but the greatest divergences are not in the translations but in the way the use of the word 'womb' has been interpreted in this context. Lambert defended that, as the consecrated women 'were not supposed to bear children, the references can hardly be to their own wombs, since they were allowed to lie fallow, but to the wombs of bearing mothers who received expert obstetrical help from the *nadītus*' (Lambert 1992, 144). Similarly Stol defended that the religious women referred to in this text were all involved in childbirth, and in this regard he added that 'we have no evidence that the Old Babylonian nun *nadītu* in Sippar could function as a midwife, but maybe she could in Babylon' (Stol 2000, 172).

So both Lambert and Stol (who in turn quotes and follows Lambert's proposal as his starting point) take this text as evidence of the relationship of the *nadītu*-women with midwifery. Neither of them produces any further texts to be considered as evidence, and asserting a link between these women with midwifery on the basis of this single text seems unsound, for several reasons. First, it is a really late text: when it was written (as a school exercise, something we should bear in mind) the memory of the activities of the *nadītu*-women of around 1000 years before would have been completely lost. Second, the most important word for us is included in this text just as an explanatory gloss – a weak attestation, especially as it is the only one for the interpretation proposed. Why then do these scholars feel justified in defending this relationship between *nadītu* and midwifery? I suggest that underlying this hypothesis is a preconception about the naturalised bond of women and motherhood, which from certain standpoints does not need to be rigorously tested, but just 'identified' because its identification (however weak) corresponds to this previous assumption.

Maybe for this reason Barberon is much more cautious in her interpretation. Because she does not start from what I see as the preconception underlying the previous proposals, she can present all the evidence and her hypothesis without necessarily assuming the link between these consecrated women and midwifery – a link which she (the only one of the scholars discussing the text cited here who has devoted a monograph to the *nadītu*-women) has not found evidenced in any other text. The lack of any other direct or indirect evidence seems to be an important point in this debate. Specifically regarding the excerpt discussed here, Barberon (2012, 3) presents the following thoughts on the transmission of knowledge and the validity of this source for certain purposes, and stresses the need to find other sources, sources not found to support this argument so far:[18]

> l'apprenti lettré nota en marge, à côté du signe LUKUR, la petite glose *na-da-te* révélatrice du fait qu'il n'était plus familier de ces religieuses et qu'il avait oublié la prononciation akkadienne du titre en question. À son époque, cette pratique religieuse et sociale avait perdu de sa pertinence depuis plusieurs siècles. Il convient donc d'avoir un usage prudent de la littérature d'époque récente, en considérant que si certaines oeuvres furent inspirées de productions anciennes, d'autres reflètent bien plus les mentalités et réalités de leur temps que celles qui avaient cours mille ans plus tôt. Pour éviter un grand nombre d'écueils, il faut autant que possible étudier les femmes détentrices de ces titres au début du IIe millénaire en portant un regard neuf sur les sources de leur époque et en oubliant l'image souvent déformée que les contemporains du 1er millénaire s'en sont faite et ont transmise à la postérité.

Some final thoughts: From childless to childfree?

In this paper I aimed to highlight what I identify as some paradoxes in the secondary literature on motherhood in relation to the *nadītu*-women in ancient Mesopotamia. First there is a certain lack of attention to motherhood as a topic of study. This is partially because motherhood has been 'naturalised,' a process which has led to a portrayal of the *nadītu*-women as 'naturally' bound to motherhood through an alleged link with midwifery, in spite of the scarcity of the primary sources. Second, a first definition of *nadītu* highlights the ban on bearing children and so scholars initially rejected motherhood as a category of analysis. In any case, for the *nadītu*-women of Marduk motherhood is clearly constructed outside the confines of biology, and so the solution of 'naturalisation' is an inappropriate starting point.

To overcome what I identify here as paradoxes and contradictions I prefer not to take the ban on bearing children as a starting point for a characterisation of *nadītu*, because it may hide some important issues. Instead, I propose to consider motherhood, as well as the nuances of the concepts of 'childless' or 'childfree' as tools to approach the primary sources. In my view, considering the *nadītu* of Marduk as non-biological mothers rather than as childless women may help us to interpret the sources – a path explicitly taken, for instance, by Barberon in her monograph on these women.[19] The same, I think, is true of the unmarried *nadītu* who were not adoptive mothers; and at this point we may wonder whether these women were child*less* or child*free*.[20]

The use of the term 'childfree' is of course anachronistic, but I think it may help to better define some nuances of the situation of the *nadītu*-women. It is true that we have no way of knowing whether these women were able to take decisions regarding their future, and indeed it seems more likely that any such decisions would have been a matter for their families. However, thanks to their status as *nadītu* they had the opportunity not to become biological mothers, which was something that was expected of all other women. These women, then, were not barren, and therefore incomplete; by choice (the choice of the families, most probably) they were consecrated women and consequently not biological mothers. In this respect 'childfree,' a term that highlights choice, seems to me more appropriate than 'childless,' a term that highlights incompleteness.

Of course, beyond the issue of choice, not bearing children offered some advantages. One was the potential longevity compared with other women, taking into account the risks of pregnancy and childbirth. This advantage was already pointed out by Rivkah Harris in her pioneering paper about the *nadītu* published as early as 1964 (Harris 1964, 108 and 123). Moreover, these women had the chance, and the duty, to manage business and properties, something that was not expected for other women. Again, it maybe anachronistic to assert that the link of these women to the business world was necessarily positive, but who knows how they, as women of high rank, perceived their duties and their status as women not expected to bear biological children? We will never know the answer, but seen from our perspective, in several ways their situation characterises them more as child*free* rather than child*less*.

Acknowledgement

This paper was written during a Postdoctoral contract Juan de la Cierva-Incorporación, awarded by the Ministry of Economy, Industry and Competitiveness of the Government of Spain.

Notes

1 In this paper I refer to the ancient Near East and to ancient Mesopotamia following the geographical and chronological conventions most commonly accepted in the discipline. For an overview of the sources and of the history of the area see, among others, Kuhrt (1995) and Van de Mieroop (2004), both with previous references. For some criticisms of the most widely accepted conventions see Van de Mieroop (1997).

2 For the use of 'social institution' in gender studies, and even to consider gender itself as such, see Lorber (2005, especially 13–14) for a working definition.

3 In doing so I follow the second of the three main perspectives presented by Mónica Bolufer Peruga (2010, 55) as the main research lines in historical studies on motherhood. For more on these historical approaches and the historiography on the topic, see Bolufer Peruga (2010, 51–58).

4 Although none of the papers deals directly with the construction of motherhood, some of them are devoted to issues which partially discuss, in one way or another, aspects closely related to motherhood: for instance, adoption, the role of queens, or birth and fertility. For a table of selected contents of the volume, see https://www.eisenbrauns.com/assets/NBRF/R/RAI55. PDF [accessed October 2017].

5 See for instance Jana Matuszak's analysis (2016) of some Old Babylonian literary texts which deal with what the author describes as the image of the 'ideal housewife.' On the relevance of marriage for a woman's life and its link with procreation, see especially Matuszak (2016, 249–250). See also (Stol 2016, 60–61).

6 I take 'mothering labour' and 'birthing labour,' as working concepts, from Budin's introduction to her 2011 monograph (see especially Budin (2011, 10), for their definition as such).

7 As far as I know there is no monograph on motherhood, and only a few articles and chapters (such as the ones by the scholars cited above) apply gender studies perspectives in the framework of ancient Near Eastern studies from the 1980s–1990s. For an overview of the main focuses of study during those decades, see Van de Mieroop (1999, 138–160). In the 1980s, Van de Mieroop summarised the main topics such as women as queens or high priestesses in the context of high status women or issues such as marriage, divorce or widowhood for low status women (or at least less privileged ones); again we see that motherhood is not present as a topic (Van de Mieroop 1999, 139–140).

8 For arguments for and against the use of each of these terms, see the following references dealing with *nadītu*, which are among the most recent ones on the topic: Barberon (2012 and 2014); De Graef (2016); Gadotti (2016); Nakata (2016); Stol (2016, 584–607). As a pioneering study on the topic, see Harris (1964) for some of the starting points of the debate.

9 Chicago Assyrian Dictionary N, part I, s.v. *nadītu*, p. 63. On the *gagû*, translated problematically in the secondary literature as 'cloister,' see for instance Richardson (2010), with previous references. Sometimes it is also translated as 'convent' (see for instance Stol (2016, 601–604)). For a different view on the *gagû*, seen as a set of houses, and with criticisms of the translation as 'cloister,' see recent work by Katrien De Graef, for instance (2016, 270–272).

10 For an overview of adoptions in the ancient Near East, see Justel Vicente (2012) and particularly Justel Vicente (2011, 103–104) for a brief state of the art of previous literature. On adoptions in the Laws of Hammurabi see Westbrook (2009). On the role of women in adoption, with a discussion of several case studies, see Justel (2014, 73–102).

11 On bigamy, with previous references and with a text as case study dealing with a *nadītu* in this context, see Justel (2014, 45–47). See also, for polygyny, Justel (2016, 81–82).

12 Here I follow Martha T. Roth in using 'Laws of Hammurabi' rather than 'Code of Hammurabi' (or Hammurapi) which is its other frequent denomination. For a brief presentation of the Laws of Hammurabi and its framework, as well as for the full text of the Laws in Akkadian and in translation into English, see Roth (1995, 71–142). More specifically, on the laws here mentioned concerning the *nadītu*, see also Gadotti (2016, 71–72).

13 Translation from Roth (1995, 107). There is no consensus translation for the term *šugītu*, defined for instance in the CAD just as 'a class of women' (CAD Š, part III, s.v. *šugītu*, 200). These women are often discussed together with religious women due to their context of attestation, and consequently they tend to be presented as religious women too (see for instance Justel (2014, 46); cf. Gadotti (2016, 71)). However, this interpretation has been contested by some scholars, for instance Barberon, who summarises the issue as follows: 'Ce titre n'était pas la marque d'une appartenance à une classe religieuse. Toutefois, l'existence de ces femmes, et donc leur étude, est indissociable de celle des *nadītum* de Marduk, du moins dans les deux Sippar. Leur rôle semble avoir été de faire office d'épouses secondaires auprès de ces dernières de sorte que, lorsque les textes évoquent une *šugîtum* mariée en taisant l'existence d'une première

épouse *nadîtum*, il paraît possible de restituer une telle configuration conjugale' (Barberon 2012, 81). In this direction, see also Stol (2016, 585–585), presenting the *šugītu* as a 'surrogate mother' when attested in this context.

14 On the use of the label 'fallow women,' emphasising a lack for these women, and likening it to the lack of production of a field, see Harris (1964, 108); Lambert (1992, 144). Harris uses the term 'childless' as well.

15 On the care of the elderly in the Old Babylonian period see Stol (1998). For the case of the nadītu women, see Stol (1998, 84–109; 2016, 600–601). See also Justel (2014, 78 and 105–106).

16 On women not under patriarchal authority in ancient Mesopotamia, women whose sexuality was not regulated in the same way as was the sexuality of married women, see Roth (2006, especially 22–23). See also Assante (1998) for a seminal paper deconstructing the way prostitution has been approached in Assyriology, and how certain women have been viewed in this light. It is interesting to note that the case of the *nadītu* was approached from this perspective as early as 1986 by Igor Diakonoff in a paper titled, precisely, *Women in Old Babylonia not under patriarchal authority*.

17 This abbreviation corresponds to the second volume of *Keilschrifttexte aus Assur religiösen Inhalts* (1923), where Erich Ebeling published the *editio princeps* of the text, just as cuneiform copy.

18 Barberon discusses other aspects of the text KAR 321 in several chapters of her monograph. See in this respect Barberon (2012, 182–183 and 207–208).

19 In this respect the title of the last chapter of her monograph, *Vie conjugale et maternité*, is especially illuminating (Barberon 2012, 224–236).

20 For several reflections on the use of the terms 'childless' and 'childfree' and their nuances, see Demetrio and Rigotti (2012).

References

Assante, J. (1998) The kar.kid/*harimtu*, Prostitute or Single Woman? *Ugarit Forschungen* 30, 5–96.

Barberon, L. (2012) *Les religieuses et le culte de Marduk dans le royaume de Babylone* (Archibab 1 = Mémoirs de NABU 14). Paris, Société pour l'Étude du Proche-Orient Ancien.

Barberon, L. (2014) To dedicate or marry a Nadîtu-woman of Marduk in Old Babylonian society. In L. Marti (ed.) *La famille dans le Proche-Orient ancien: réalités, symbolismes, et images. Proceedings of the 55th Rencontre Assyriologique Internationale at Paris 6–9 July 2009*. Winona Lake, Eisenbrauns, 267–274.

Bolufer Peruga, M. (2010) Madres, maternidad: nuevas miradas desde la historiografía. In G. A. Franco Rubio (ed.) *Debates sobre la maternidad desde una perspectiva histórica (siglos XVI-XX)*. Barcelona, Icaria editorial, 51–81.

Budin, S. L. (2011) *Images of Woman and Child from the Bronze Age. Reconsidering Fertility, Maternity, and Gender in the Ancient World*. Cambridge, Cambridge University Press.

Budin, S. L. (2015) Fertility and gender in the Ancient Near East. In M. Masterson, N. S. Rabinowitz and J. Robson (eds) *Sex in Antiquity. Exploring Gender and Sexuality in the Ancient World*. London/New York, Routledge, 30–49.

Budin, S. L. and MacIntosh Turfa, J. (2016) *Women in Antiquity: Real Women Across the Ancient World*. London/New York, Routledge.

Couto-Ferreira, M. É. (2013) The river, the oven, the garden: the female body and fertility in a Late Babylonian ritual text. In C. Ambos and L. Verderame (eds) *Approaching Rituals in Ancient Cultures*. Supplemento Rivista degli Studi Orientali, Nuova Serie LXXXVI. Roma, Fabrizio Serra editore, 97–116.

Couto-Ferreira, M. É. (2016a) Being mothers or acting (like) mothers? Constructing motherhood in ancient Mesopotamia. In S. L. Budin and J. MacIntosh Turfa (eds) *Women in Antiquity: Real Women across the Ancient World*. London/New York, Routledge, 25–34.

Couto-Ferreira, M. É. (2016b) Parteras, nodrizas y cuidadoras en Mesopotamia. In A. Delgado Hervás and M. Picazo Gurina (eds) *Los trabajos de las mujeres en el mundo antiguo. Cuidado y mantenimiento de la vida*. Tarragona, Institut Català d'Arqueologia Clàssica, 105–118.

De Graef, K. (2016) Cherchez la femme! The economic role of women in Old Babylonian Sippar. In B. Lion and C. Michel (eds) *The Role of Women in Work and Society in the Ancient Near East*. Studies in Ancient Near Eastern Records 13. Berlin/New York, de Gruyter, 270–295.

Demetrio, D. and Rigotti, F. (2012) *Senza figli. Una condizione umana*. Milano, Raffaello Cortina Editore.

Diakonoff, I. M. (1986) Women in Old Babylonia not under patriarchal authority. *Journal of the Economic and Social History of the Orient* 29, 225–238.

Donath, O. (2015) Regretting motherhood: a sociopolitical analysis. *Signs: Journal of Women in Culture and Society* 40(2), 343–367.

Foster, B. R. (2005) *Before the Muses. An Anthology of Akkadian Literature*. Bethesda, CDL Press.

Gadotti, A. (2016) Mesopotamian women's cultic roles in late 3rd–early 2nd millennia BCE. In S. L. Budin and J. MacIntosh Turfa, (eds) *Women in Antiquity: Real Women across the Ancient World*. London/New York, Routledge, 64–76.

Garcia-Ventura, A. and Zisa, G. (2017) Gender and women in Ancient Near Eastern studies. Bibliography 2002–2016. *Akkadica* 138(1), 37–67.

Goddeeris, A. (2002) *Economy and Society in Northern Babylonia in the Early Old Babylonian Period (ca. 2000–1800 BC)*. Orientalia Lovaniensia Analecta 109. Leuven: Peeters.

Harris, R. (1964) The *nadītu* woman. In R. D. Biggs and J. A. Brinkman (eds) *Studies Presented to A. Leo Oppenheim June 7, 1964*. Chicago, Oriental Institute of the University of Chicago, 106–135.

Justel, J. J. (2014) *Mujeres y derecho en el Próximo Oriente Antiguo. La presencia de mujeres en los textos jurídicos cuneiformes del segundo y primer milenios a. C.* Zaragoza, Libros Pórtico.

Justel, J. J. (2016) Women, gender and law at the dawn of history. In S. L. Budin and J. MacIntosh Turfa (eds) *Women in Antiquity: Real Women across the Ancient World*. London/New York, Routledge, 77–100.

Justel Vicente, D. (2011) La adopción en Emar en su contexto próximo-oriental antiguo. *Historiae* 8, 103–118.

Justel Vicente, D. (2012) Adopciones infantiles en el Próximo Oriente Antiguo. In D. Justel Vicente (ed.) *Niños en la Antigüedad. Estudios sobre la infancia en el Mediterráneo antiguo*. Zaragoza, Prensas de la Universidad de Zaragoza, 99–148.

Kuhrt, A. (1995) *The Ancient Near East: c.3000–330 B.C.* London, Routledge.

Lambert, W. G. (1992) Prostitution, In V. Haas (ed.) *Aussenseiter und Randgruppen: Beiträge zu einer Sozialgeschichte des Alten Orients*. Xenia 32. Konstanz, Universitätsverlag Konstanz, 127–158.

López-Bertran, M. and Garcia-Ventura, A. (2012) Music, gender and rituals in Ancient Mediterranean: Revisiting the Punic evidence. *World Archaeology* 44(3), 393–408.

Lorber, J. (2005) *Breaking the Bowls. Degendering and Feminist Change*. New York/London, Norton.

Marti, L. (2014) (ed.) *La famille dans le Proche-Orient ancien: réalités, symbolismes, et images. Proceedings of the 55th Rencontre Assyriologique Internationale at Paris 6–9 July 2009*. Winona Lake, Eisenbrauns.

Matuszak, J. (2016) 'She is not fit for womanhood': The ideal housewife according to Sumerian literary texts. In B. Lion and C. Michel (eds) *The Role of Women in Work and Society in the Ancient Near East*. Studies in Ancient Near Eastern Records 13. Berlin/New York, De Gruyter, 228–254.

Meskell, L. (1995) Goddesses, Gimbutas and 'New Age' Archaeology. *Antiquity* 69, 74–86.

Nakata, I. (2016) Economic activities of *nadītum*-women of Šamaš reflected in the field sale contracts (MHET II/1–6). In B. Lion and C. Michel (eds) *The Role of Women in Work and Society in the Ancient Near East*. Studies in Ancient Near Eastern Records 13. Berlin/New York, De Gruyter, 255–269.

Richardson, S. (2010) A light in the *gagûm* window: the Sippar cloister in the late Old Babylonian period. In S. Melville and A. L. Slotsky (eds) *Opening the Tablet Box. Near Eastern Studies in Honor of Benjamin R. Foster*. Leiden/Boston, Brill, 329–346.

Rositani, A. (2012) The role of the nadiātum of Šamaš and of some officials in Old Babylonian Sippar organization of agriculture work. In P. Notizia and F. Pomponio (eds) *Scritti in onore di Pietro Mander* AION (Annali dell'Università degli Studi di Napoli "L'Orientale") 72. Napoli, Annali Dipartimento Asia, Africa e Mediterraneo, sezione Orientale, 113–132.
Roth, M. T. (1995) *Law Collections from Mesopotamia and Asia Minor*. Atlanta, Scholars Press.
Stol, M. (1998) Care of the elderly in Mesopotamia in the Old Babylonian period. In M. Stol and S. P. Vleeming (eds) *The Care of the Elderly in the Ancient Near East*. Leiden/Boston/Köln, Brill, 59–117.
Stol, M. (2016) *Women in the Ancient Near East*. Boston/Berlin, De Gruyter.
Van de Mieroop, M. (1997) On writing a history of the Ancient Near East. *Bibliotheca Orientalis* 54, 285–305.
Van de Mieroop, M. (1999) *Cuneiform Texts and the Writing of History*. London/New York, Routledge.
Van de Mieroop, M. (2004) *A History of the Ancient Near East,* ca. *3000–323 BC*. London, Blackwell.
Westbrook, R. (2009) [1993] The adoption laws of Codex Hammurabi. In B. Wells and F. R. Magdalene (eds) *Law from the Tigris to the Tiber*. Winona Lake, Eisenbrauns, 139–148.

Chapter 5

Death in birth: pregnancy, maternal death and funerary practices in the Phoenician and Punic world

Ana Delgado Hervás and Aurora Rivera Hernández

Introduction

The experiences of pregnancy and childbirth have been relatively neglected themes in the field of Phoenician and Punic studies. The silence surrounding them is not just due to the traditional questions of biology and privacy, which have limited the attention paid to these and other female experiences in analyses of the past, or to the taboos regarding pregnancy and birth today, which have made these facts of female life invisible in our own societies (and, in particular, in academia). It also has its roots in the past itself and in the predominant discourses on reproduction, motherhood and fatherhood.

In fact, Phoenician and Punic contexts contain hardly any textual references or iconographic representations of pregnancy and birth. The very few exceptions are the subject of this chapter. This silence is particularly apparent when seen in contrast to the accounts of procreation and family continuity present in the grand narratives of the Levantine world of the end of the 2nd millennium and throughout the 2nd millennium BC, in which references to the female processes and experiences of pregnancy and birth are conspicuous by their absence. These Levantine narratives and representations are built around what has been called the 'agricultural metaphor,' which underlies the dominant concepts of parenthood and motherhood (Budin 2014; Simkins 2014; Zamora 2016). In this account, the male is the protagonist in the creation and continuity of human life: it is the man who 'makes' new life by planting the seed (the sperm) in the soil (the womb), whose function is to welcome and nurture this new life during pregnancy and after birth. These narratives and iconographies denote and construct a deeply patriarchal ideology of reproduction, which denies the procreative power of women, attributes to them a passive, secondary, subordinate and replaceable role (the seed could be implanted in any other 'soil'), and generates narrow identifications of motherhood as nurturing. Indeed, these same stories and representations exalt images of breastfeeding, to the detriment of experiences of pregnancy and childbirth (Oggiano 2012, 231). The patriarchal discourse underpinning these iconographic representations and literary texts appropriated female voices and silenced the experiences of pregnant women and mothers, voices that today are enormously difficult to revive.

In recent years, however, the archaeology of the funerary spaces of the Phoenician and Punic world has brought forth some interesting surprises. In Phoenician and Punic cemeteries, extending from the Mediterranean Levant to the south of Portugal, tombs of pregnant women have been identified as well as cremations of adult women together with fetal remains – most probably pregnant women or women who died in childbirth. The bodies of these women and the mortuary rituals performed after their death are the subject of this chapter. Through them, the aim is to analyse and explore the incidence of maternal death in these contexts, the different experiences of pregnancy and birth, diverse conceptions of motherhood and corporality, and practices related to mourning and mortuary rituals for women who died during pregnancy or childbirth.

These ill-fated experiences of motherhood offer an opportunity to recreate these women's voices and their stories of maternity in the past. Once silenced by patriarchal discourses and accounts, these stories empower women and their bodies and restore them to their rightful place as indispensable agents in the creation and continuity of human life.

Maternal death among Phoenician and Punic communities

Most academic studies agree that rates of maternal death (defined as deaths caused directly or indirectly by pregnancy, delivery or puerperium) in the human communities of the past must have been very high. The absence of demographic records similar to those kept in most Western industrialised countries since the 19th century means that we have no quantitative data for the ancient world that can be compared with the modern statistical data at our disposal. Nevertheless, a number of studies have explored the incidence of maternal mortality in the ancient world, basing their analysis on literary and epigraphic records, anthropological data, and projections made from data recorded in traditional historical communities (Demand 1994; Oakley 2003; Liston and Papadopoulos 2004). In relation to maternal death in the Mediterranean communities of the 1st millennium BC, most of the information available is from the Greek world. It has been suggested that maternal mortality in this area may have reached rates around 14% (Liston and Papadopoulos 2004, 20). In classical Athens, relatively early marriages for women (around 18 years of age) and a high incidence of maternal death have been postulated as possible causes of the differences in gender longevity, with life expectancy estimated at 45 years for men but only 36.2 years for women (Oakley 2003, 163).

In the case of the ancient Near East we lack specific quantitative studies, but the estimates of the incidence of maternal death are similar to those posited for the Greek world. As in the Greek case, these proposals are based mainly on projections made from data from contemporary non-industrialised communities and on textual references that warn of the dangers of childbirth (Scurlock 1991, 135; Cox and Ackerman 2009; Couto-Ferreira 2014). The anthropological data obtained in funeral areas in the ancient Near East also indicate similar patterns to those of classical Athens. Levantine Iron Age cemeteries reveal a marked difference in the longevity of men and women; in the necropolis of Tyre, for example, the average longevity of men has been estimated at around 36 years of age, while for women the figure falls to 29 years, that is, a drop of seven years (Trellisó 2004, 254). Carol Meyers has drawn attention to the low average life expectancy (20–30 years) of women buried in Iron Age cemeteries of Levantine communities further to the south (Meyers 2016, 420), and associates the marked differences in gender longevity recorded in these cemeteries with high rates of maternal death. She also associates the early death of Levantine women (in comparison with their peers in other contemporary Mediterranean areas such as Athens) with maternity at very early ages; indeed, literary references suggest that in some communities the first pregnancies occurred as early as puberty (Ebeling 2010, 61–64).

Anthropological data indicate that maternal mortality was also high among the Phoenician and Punic communities born in the Levantine diaspora which began at the end of the ninth century and continued throughout the 8th century BC, and led to the settlement and the creation of new communities in the West (Fig. 5.1). Data obtained from Phoenician and Punic cemeteries suggests that life expectancy in these regions was also lower in women than in men (Gómez Bellard 1990, 154; García Teyssandier and Marzoli 2013; Delgado 2016). These western communities also reflect some diversity in the average longevity of women; in some western cemeteries like the Hoya de los Rastros (Ayamonte, Huelva) the average life expectancy of women seems to have been higher than those recorded in the Levant; in the small Huelva cemetery there are no graves of females aged less than 32 years (García Teyssandier and Marzoli 2013). In other Phoenician–Punic settings, however, the average life expectancy of women seems to have been much shorter. Some areas of the cemetery of Puig des Molins in Ibiza contain significant percentages of women who died before the age of 25, and two who died between 15 and 20 years (while no men in this age group are recorded) (Gómez Bellard 1990, 154). This diversity in the anthropological data from cemeteries like Hoya de los Rastros and Puig des Molins may reflect differences in the age of the first pregnancy among the Phoenician and Western Punic communities, and therefore differences in relation to motherhood as well.

Pregnancies at very early ages (under 18) are attested at the western end of the Phoenician world. A tomb in Las Chorreras (Málaga) dated at 840–790 cal BC holds the incinerated remains of a newborn or a full-term fetus and a young girl of about 17–18 years of age (Martín *et al.* 2007). The mortuary ritual performed (incineration of the corpses) means that we cannot state conclusively that the foetus was still inside the womb when the woman died and so we do not know whether she died before or during childbirth. However, certain ritual practices recorded in this burial (for example, the

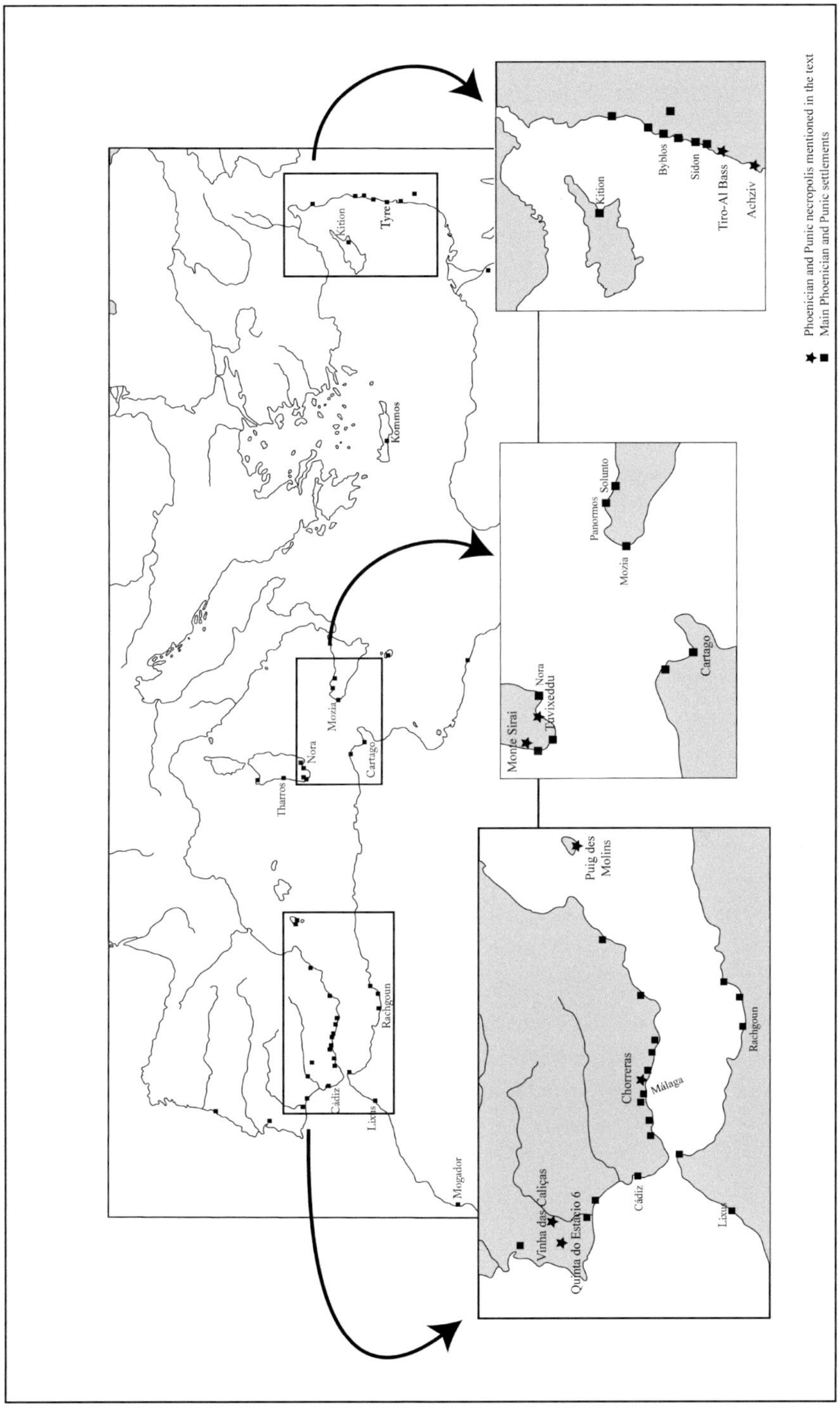

Figure 5.1: Map of the main Phoenician and Punic cemeteries mentioned in the text

fact that the bones of both the woman and the foetus were crushed, or the lack of any difference in the degree of combustion between them; Martín *et al.* 2007, 570, 575 and 579) seem to suggest that she had not yet given birth. Similar interpretations have been made in other Mediterranean tombs holding incinerated remains of a woman and a newborn or full-term foetus – among them the tomb known in the archaeological literature as 'the rich Athenian lady,' probably the most famous tomb of the Greek Geometric period (Liston and Papadopoulos 2004).

The invisibility of maternal death

Even though maternal death must have been relatively frequent in the ancient world, the archaeological evidence in the funerary record of women who died during pregnancy or childbirth is very limited.[1] The archaeological invisibility of maternal mortality is even more marked in the case of deaths of women who managed to give birth. In the Phoenician and Punic domains, the anthropological evidence of women who died during pregnancy or childbirth is extremely scarce. For the period spanning the 9th century and the 2nd century BC, and over the wide geographical area from the Phoenician communities of the central coast of the Mediterranean Levant to the 'hybrid' communities of modern-day Portugal, only nine cases have been identified to date: two in the Levant: Achziv, Tomb L04–102 (Mazar 2009, 125–26), and probably Tyre-Al Bass, Urn 3/5 (Trellisó 2004, 263), three in Sardinia: Monte Sirai, Tomb 316 (Piga *et al.* 2016; Pla Orquín 2011, 16–18; 2014–15) and Tuvixeddu, T. 173 and T. 242 (Salvi *et al.* 2016), one in Ibiza: Puig des Molins, Tomb 33 (Gómez Bellard 1990), one in the Andalusian Mediterranean: Las Chorreras, mentioned above (Martín *et al.* 2007), and finally two in Portugal: Quinta do Estácio 6, Tomb 4 (Pereiro *et al.* 2017) and Vinha das Caliças, Tomb 54 (Arruda *et al.* 2017) (Fig. 5.2).

In contrast to other contemporary areas in the Mediterranean (Terranova 2013; Margarity 2016 among others), in the Phoenician and Punic contexts no textual or iconographic data on women who died in childbirth is available. In the Levant we have only two Biblical references, recorded by Cox and Ackerman (2009): the death of Rachel after the birth of her son Benjamin,[2] and the death of Phineas' wife after giving birth to her son Ichabod.[3] From the archaeological point of view Cox and Ackerman's text is especially interesting, because they analyse the treatment and memorialisation of the bodies of these women who died in childbirth. In the case of the death of Phineas' wife the Biblical account evades this question, but in the case of Rachel it tells how her body was buried in the place where she died, next to a road, and how the site of the grave was marked by a stela or cultic standing stone. Several authors have found it puzzling that Rachel, in spite of her lineage and social status, was buried not in the family tomb but in a separate, far-away grave (Cox and Ackerman 2009; Stavrakopoulou 2010, ns 49 and 73). Indeed, far from being made invisible, the site was transformed into a place of worship and pilgrimage (Hays 2011, 154–155), later becoming a landmark which acquired enormous significance in the definition of political territories (Stavrakopoulou 2010, 13).

Figure 5.2: Tomb of a pregnant woman of the cemetery of Monte Sirai (Tomb 316), showing in detail the grave good and the reconstruction of the fetus position (copyright Michele Guirgis)

Some authors consider that the unique nature of Rachel's tomb is related to the fact that she died as a result of giving birth (Cox and Ackerman 2009, 140). In many human communities, both past and present, the death of women in childbirth is considered unnatural, unhappy or 'bad' and their bodies (like other corpses in this category) are seen as tremendously dangerous or powerful (Liston and Papadopoulos 2004, 28; Cox and Ackerman 2009, 142). Aztec women who died in childbirth, for example, received funerals similar to those of warriors killed in combat; their bodies were kept and protected because they were considered to have magical and supernatural powers (Aguilar Moreno 2007, 169). In the communities of the Ancient Near East (Van der Toorn 1996, 122–123), among them the Iron Age Levant, the bodies of women after childbirth were regarded as unclean and socially dangerous; they and their newborns were separated from the rest of their family and community, and occupied a different part of the house for days or weeks. The duration of this separation could be extended until the end of postpartum period if the newborn was a girl, or a week if the newborn was a boy (Goodfriend 2008; Cox and Ackerman 2009, 143–147).[4] These same literary passages record the rituals performed by the women who had given birth in order to purify their unclean bodies. These rituals were celebrated in the temple and involved bathing, pouring water and the sacrifice of animals (Goodfriend 2008), mainly birds and lambs (Fulton *et al.* 2017). We find the same offerings in the tophets – funeral areas where the bodies of fetuses and infants, promised by their families to the deities, were deposited and commemorated (Xella 2013, 259).

The taboo that surrounds the liminal act of childbirth, along with the profound social and emotional impact of maternal loss on families and communities, is expressed in many human societies in the form of mortuary ceremonies and mourning and burying rites which in time develop significant traits of their own and break away from the standard funeral practices. These traits can affect the ceremonies and rituals, the objects and people that participate in them, and the structure of the tombs and their spatial disposition. In England, for example, the practice of burying women who died in childbirth outside the wall enclosing the consecrated ground of the churchyard, along with people who had died in other 'anomalous' circumstances, is recorded in the late 15th century (Parker Pearson 1999, 15). The presence of isolated tombs or separate cemeteries for women who died in childbirth has also been proposed for the Etruscan world, where no pregnant women or women accompanied by perinatal skeletons have been recorded in the burial areas excavated to date. Indeed, some Etruscan cemeteries, for example those in Tarquinia, also contain a much higher proportion of adult men than of adult women. These two features highlight the probability that these women (and children too) were buried in separate areas or cemeteries (Becker 2007, 289).

As in the Etruscan world, the burial of women who died in childbirth outside the family or communal funerary space may also have been a common practice among Phoenician and Punic communities. Just as in Tarquinia, a high proportion of males is found in a great many Phoenician cemeteries, especially in the Levant (Trellisó 2004, 254). The under-representation of women's tombs is particularly noticeable in some parts of the Tyre-al Bass cemetery, where corpses appear to have been grouped according to family ties; in some parts of this cemetery, women represent only 25% of the total, while men account for 53.6% and those of indeterminate sex 21.4% (Trellisó 2004, 254).

Mourning pregnant women: funerary practices in Phoenician and Punic cemeteries

Among Phoenician and Punic communities, taboos around childbirth and the bodies of women giving birth appear to have had a profound effect on the mortuary rituals associated with maternal deaths, especially those caused by childbirth. The burials of pregnant women in Phoenician and Punic cemeteries diverge from the norm; the few pregnant women found in archaeological excavations of these areas are placed in funerary spaces or present evidence of ritual performances which set them apart from other 'standard' burials.

The practical absence of burials of this kind in the archaeological record suggests that the bodies of women who died during childbirth or shortly afterwards were probably buried in isolated areas, separated from other members of their family or community. In death as in life, the taboo regarding their bodies remained solidly in place.

Along with the literary evidence we have seen in the case of Rachel's tomb, there is also some archaeological evidence of the separation of pregnant women in funeral areas. In the Levant, the Phoenician cemetery of Achziv provides a single case of a burial of a pregnant woman (Tomb L4–102). The woman was buried away from the family graves, in an area of the cemetery populated almost exclusively by children (Mazar 2009, 70). The same arrangement is seen in other Phoenician–Punic necropolises including Monte Sirai, in Sardinia. In this cemetery, tomb T316 houses the remains of a pregnant woman, about 20–25 years of age, with a foetus of 38–40 weeks of gestation in a transversal position between the bones of the pelvis. The age and position of the foetus suggest that the woman probably died as a result of a dystocic birth (Fig. 5.2) (Guirguis 2011; Pla Orquín 2014–15, 145; 2017, 325–326; Piga *et al.* 2016). Along with the body, the mourning community deposited two jugs, a glass, and two plates, which gave material form to the food and drink necessary in the afterlife. The objects in the funeral ritual indicate the same mortuary practices as those witnessed in most of the female tombs in this cemetery (Piga *et al.* 2015, 100). The taboo surrounding this type of maternal death is reflected in the site chosen for this tomb, in an area reserved for children and other women (Pla Orquín 2014–15, 146).

Another possible case of an isolated burial of a woman who may have died in childbirth is the tomb of Las Chorreras, which we mentioned above. Radiocarbon dating places the chronology of this tomb between 840–790 cal BC (Martín *et al.* 2007, 575), and so it is related to the first generations of Phoenicians who migrated and settled on the Mediterranean coast of Andalusia. The tomb is located at a high point of the promontory of Las Chorreras and there are no other graves nearby. However, its location – in an area which has undergone considerable urban development in recent times and in which other 'isolated' tombs of different characteristics are known – (Martín 2014–15) the circumstances of its discovery and the fact that the tomb is partially destroyed mean that we can determine very little about the funerary landscape surrounding it, or any data relating to its structure or closure. What is clearly exceptional in this case are the grave goods, comprising three gold objects (a swivel ring, a pendant and a bead from a necklace) an amphora and a jug. These items bear witness to the importance of this woman and the significance of her death for her community (Martín *et al.* 2007).

Along with these three isolated tombs located in 'special' burial areas which held women who were separated in death from other members of their family or their community, other Phoenician and Punic cemeteries contain tombs of women inside community or family funerary spaces who died during the last weeks of pregnancy, alongside other graves of men or adult women. These findings suggest a certain diversity in the rituals accompanying maternal death in the Phoenician and Punic communities. In the area known as Lotto 7 of the Phoenician–Punic cemetery of Tuvixeddu in Sardinia, the graves of two women who died in an advanced state of pregnancy have recently been uncovered (Salvi *et al.* 2016). One of them, Tomb 173, contained the body of a woman between 25 and 30 years of age, without any palaeopathological alterations, with a foetus of some 36 weeks of gestation in the pelvis (Fig. 5.3). The tomb also held fragments of the skull and humerus of a second child estimated to be between 3 and 5 months of age. Some of the ritual gestures recorded in this tomb seem once again to show that this body received special funerary treatment, albeit using practices different from those we have seen in the three previous cases.

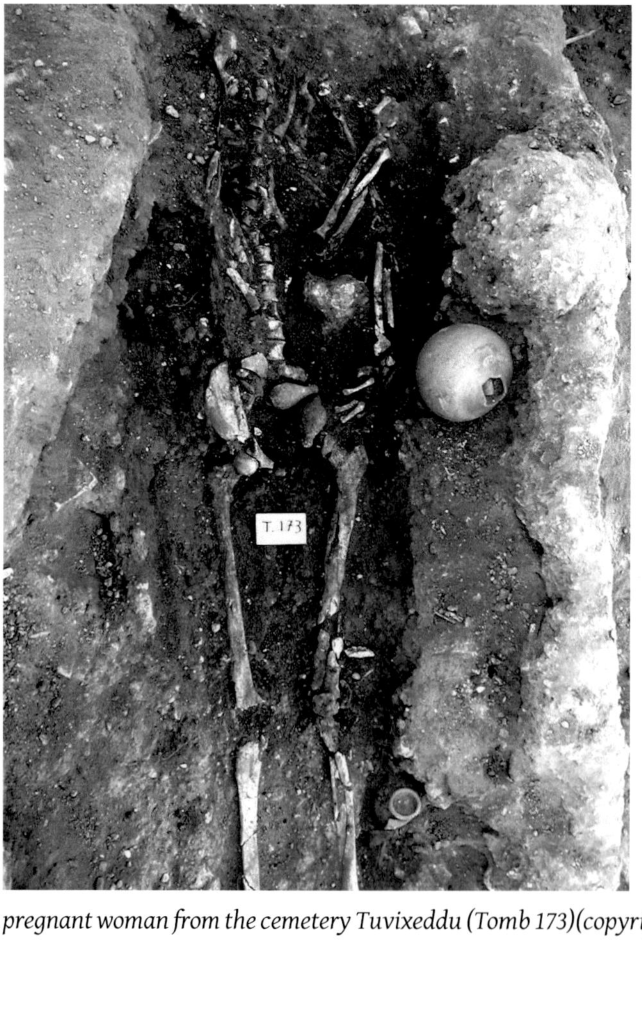

Figure 5.3: Tomb of a pregnant woman from the cemetery Tuvixeddu (Tomb 173)(copyright Donatela Salvi)

The objects deposited next to the woman buried in this tomb include a coin and two glasses, intended to prolong the deceased's life after death. There were also three vessels that would have contained oils used in the cleaning and ritual purification of the bodies. Two of them were placed next to the woman's pelvis, an area where other specific magic or cultic practices would have been performed in the purification of these bodies. On the right, next to the woman's pelvis and femur, a ritual fire was lit on the floor of the pit itself, which left its mark on the floor of the tomb and on the pelvis. Also, before the grave was closed, a large stone was placed on the pelvis. The placement of stones on the dead or on significant parts of their bodies during the closing of the tomb is a ritual gesture that has been recorded in other Punic necropolises such as Monte Sirai. In this area, this practice has been interpreted as an attempt to contain the spirits of the dead inside the graves, so that they should not disturb the living (Bartoloni 2000). This ritual gesture is probably associated with deaths considered unhappy or 'bad' – for example, maternal deaths, whose ghosts were regarded as active and powerful (as suggested by the passages in the Bible regarding the ill-fated Rachel; Cox and Ackerman 2009, 147).

Ritual practices related to the purification of these bodies and the containment of their ghosts inside the tomb also appear to have been performed after maternal deaths in other Phoenician-Punic communities and in other closely associated contexts. With regard to purification, the necropolis of Quinta do Estácio 6 in southern Portugal offers us some interesting evidence. This cemetery contains the grave of a woman bearing a fetus between 38 and 40 weeks of gestation, in the pelvis (Pereiro *et al.* 2017, 312–313). The tomb is part of a small rural necropolis (probably belonging to a family) and contains a set of grave goods similar to the ones found in other female burials. It presents clear evidence of rituals related to the purification of the bodies, very similar to the ones recorded in the necropolis of Tuvixeddu. A small ritual fire was lit on the woman's belly just before the tomb was closed (Pereiro *et al.* 2017, 312–313).

The necropolis of Puig des Molins, in Ibiza, offers us an example of specific mortuary practices designed to keep the powerful ghosts of these women from leaving their graves. Tomb 33 contained the incinerated bone remains of a woman aged between 20 and 25 years and of an infant with an estimated age of less than 3 months. The research team that analysed them considered that the woman was probably in an advanced stage of pregnancy (7–9 months) with a full-term foetus (Gómez Bellard 1990, 116–117 and 154). Her skeletal remains were accompanied by a small bowl, a bone lid – perhaps used to close a container made of organic material which has not survived and which may have held spices or a liquid – and a bronze knife. The deposition of knives in tombs has been linked with the shaving of the corpses, as a part of the ritual purification (Delgado and Ferrer 2012, 140; Acquaro 2017, 12).

This tomb in Puig des Molins also presents several distinct features with respect to other graves excavated in this extensive necropolis, mainly due to the importance given to its closure and the protection of the bones. Most incineration tombs in Puig des Molins were made in small natural pits or hollows of the land, which were then simply covered over with soil. However, tomb 33, despite being located in a natural hollow large enough to contain it, was dug into the rock so that the bodies could be deposited at a greater depth. In addition, the burial was sealed by a compact layer of red clay and protected with a circular stone structure that formed a small mound, built with highly compacted clay and stones of different sizes (Gómez Bellard 1990, 116). This funerary structure seems to have had the same objective as the large stone placed on the belly of the pregnant woman in tomb 173 at Tuvixeddu: to prevent the powerful ghosts of these women from leaving their graves and disturbing the world of the living.

The funerary practices associated with pregnant women buried in Phoenician and Punic cemeteries show some diversity, but all of them present a series of ritual gestures – isolation, purification or containment of the ghosts in the tomb – which suggest that the corpses (and their spirits) were conceived as dangerous or powerful. All these ritual gestures are associated with pregnant women with foetuses of more than 36 weeks of gestation, an indication perhaps that their death occurred around the time of delivery, and probably as a consequence of it – suggesting that in these contexts this kind of death was considered unhappy or bad.

Along with women who probably died in childbirth, some graves of pregnant women with foetal remains of gestational age less than 36 weeks are also found in Phoenician and Punic cemeteries. One such grave is Tomb 242 in the necropolis of Tuvixeddu which contains a woman with a foetus with an estimated gestational age of around 34 weeks in the abdominal cavity (Salvi *et al.* 2016, 354). This tomb is not isolated or separated from its community; on the contrary, it is located in an area with a large number of graves. Nor do we find evidence of any ritual gestures that might be associated with the purification of the body or the containment of its spirit. The tomb has no grave goods and the pit where the body was laid to rest is so small that the corpse had to be forced inside it, as some parts were even left outside the grave itself. All this suggests that the burial was carried out without any great care, reflecting perhaps the scarce social significance of this particular death.

A similar case is tomb 54 in the cemetery of Vinhas das Caliças, in Beja, Portugal, which houses a woman bearing the remains of a foetus in her pelvis with an estimated gestational age of around 26 weeks (Arruda *et al.* 2017, 191). This tomb is located in a funeral space containing other women and adult men, as well as children (Arruda *et al.* 2017, 187–189). Her grave goods comprised necklace beads in bronze and glass paste and perforated shells, but does not present any significant differences with respect to other female tombs; nor is there any evidence of ritual practices related to a more intense purification of this body or the containment of its spirit. These ritual practices are also absent in Urn 3 in the Tyre-al Bass cemetery, which contained the remains of an adult woman and a fetus, and also appears in a probable grouping of family graves. The lack of data about the gestational age of the fetus in Urn 3 means that we should cannot draw any firm conclusions about the absence of ritual gestures (Trellisó 2004, 254).

Nevertheless, the women buried in tomb 242 of the cemetery of Tuvixeddu and in tomb 54 of Vinhas das Caliças introduce a new factor of diversity into the range of ritual practices that we have reported in the burials of pregnant women in Phoenician and Punic contexts. The gestational ages of these fetuses seem to be somewhat lower than those recorded in the other graves, suggesting that perhaps maternal death due to causes other than childbirth did not require such powerful magical-religious or cultic protection. This distinction places the focus of attention on childbirth as the liminal moment *par excellence*.

Childbirth among Phoenician and Punic communities: liminality, magic-religious practices and obstetric care

Mortuary practices and funerary landscapes are suggestive contexts for a material exploration of the predominant conceptions of pregnancy and childbirth among the Phoenician and Punic communities and, more specifically, of maternal deaths that occurred during or close to the moment of birth. The widespread absence of these burials in the funerary record and the unusual extent of the deployment of ritual practices in the few known burial sites suggest that these deaths were surrounded by a powerful taboo. To a large extent, this taboo is due to the fact that these communities conceived birth as a liminal moment and the bodies of pregnant women, especially those women giving birth, as liminal bodies. This perception prepares the way for the magical (or religious) ambiguity of bodies considered at the same time powerful (or blessed) and dangerous (or unclean) that we find both in the funerary record and in some literary texts from the Syrian-Palestinian area.

These communities saw childbirth as a moment of danger, an event that caused great pain to the mother and put her life at risk (Oggiano 2012, 230; Couto-Ferreira 2014, 292). They would have understood this danger as a consequence of the liminal nature of childbirth and also of the bodies of the women giving birth, which they conceived of as an open door through which the acts of demons and other evil forces could pass (Willet 2002). For this reason, inside these communities, the knowledge and practices designed to care for women during pregnancy and to help them during labour simultaneously included therapeutic practices such as the application of potions, medicinal remedies, massages and obstetrics (Couto-Ferreira 2014; 2016), and magical-religious acts such as the recitation of prayers and incantations to accelerate the birth and protect the mother and the child,[5] the use of magical and apotropaic objects,[6] and maybe also the playing of music, as some representations of the god Bes suggest (Velázquez Brieva 2007, lam. IV, figs 3 and 4; Kozma 2006, fig. 7).

The iconographic representations and textual references to childbirth in the Levantine and Phoenician-Punic world indicate that, here as elsewhere, this was a sphere of feminine knowledge and engagement (Wegner 2009, 482–491; Couto-Ferreira 2014, 307; 2016; Töpfer 2014, 320–323). Terracottas with scenes of childbirth, like the one in the Hecht Museum at Haifa University[7] and the well-known group of Cypriot women (Oggiano 2012, 245; Boucher 2016), always include one or two women behind the mother-to-be, holding her back or shoulders, pressing her belly with their hands, or standing in front of her to aid the delivery of the newborn. The women who appear in these representations may well be midwives; indeed, there are numerous references to midwives in texts from the Syrian-Palestinian area (Benjamin 1989; Willett 2002; Marsman 2003, 725)[8] and from Mesopotamia (Couto-Ferreira 2014; 2016). These women were held in high esteem[9] as guardians and transmitters of knowledge, of remedies, obstetric techniques and cultic practices and rituals designed to help women during conception, abortion (either spontaneous or induced) (Xella 2013, 271), pregnancy and childbirth. Textual references also record the participation of women from the family or from the community at times of birth, who used their knowledge and their experience of their own bodies to care for other women.[10]

The representations of scenes of childbirth also indicate the positions adopted by women during labour in the Phoenician and Punic world. A wide variety of positions were used: some women are depicted giving birth in the upright position, helped by

Figure 5.4: Amulet of woman giving birth found in the hypogeum no. 14 of the cemetery of Puig des Molins (MAEF inv no. MAI 3839, copyright Museu Arqueològic d'Eivissa i Formentera)

two other women supporting them;[11] some in the sitting position, with their backs inclined, resting on another woman (this is a common representation in the terracottas of the Cypriot group);[12] and finally, in the squatting position, depicted in an amulet from a funerary hypogeum of Puig des Molins which represents a woman giving birth (Fernández 1981, 22) (Fig. 5.4). The squatting position is also known from Levantine textual references and is the most common in the iconographic representations of the Ancient Near East (Battini 2006) and Ancient Egypt (Wegner 2009; Töpfer 2014).

Conclusions

There are few iconographic representations and literary references existing in the Phoenician-Punic world regarding pregnancy, and specifically labour and birth. Those that we have, however, highlight the centrality of women's bodies and experiences, and also of practices and knowledge related to procreation and the continuity of human life, the family, and the community which were safeguarded and transmitted by women. They show how pregnancy, labour and birth were a sphere of feminine power that challenged the patriarchal discourse on human reproduction that prevailed in these communities. That patriarchal power, which controlled the grand narrative and a large part of the iconographic representation, erased the processes and experiences of pregnancy and birth and rendered them invisible in the stories about creation and the continuity of life.

Thanks to some iconographic and literary fragments, and especially to the archaeological data from Phoenician and Punic funerary areas, we have been able to restore some of these silenced experiences of (uncompleted) maternity and, in a certain way, reclaim them from the taboo that enveloped them.

Acknowledgements

This study is part of the project 'HESTIA: Comidas, cocinas y prácticas de consumo en espacios coloniales mediterráneos (siglos VIII-V a.C.),' funded by MINECO (HAR2015-69842-P). We would like to thank Michele Guirguis (Università degli Studi di Sassari), Donatella Salvi (Soprintendenza Archeologica di Cagliari) and the Museu Arqueològic d'Eivissa i Formentera for their courtesy in allowing us to use their images.

Notes

1 Some examples are compiled in Halcrow *et al.* (2018); Piga *et al.* (2016, table 3); Wells (1975, 1237).
2 *Gen.* 35: 16–20.
3 *Sam.* 4: 19–21. For other textual references from the Near East of the 1st millennium BC, see Couto-Ferreira (2014, 292–293).
4 See also Lev. 12–15.
5 On the recitation of incantations or prayers during birth in the Levant, Mesopotamia and Egypt, see Michel (2004); Wegner (2009); Ebeling (2010, 99–100); Stavrakopoulou (2010); Couto Ferreira (2014; 2016) .

6 On the use of stones in rituals for pregnant women in Ugarit, see Nougayrol (1968), 29; Matoïan (2010, 218).
7 Ref. n. H-3307 Hecht Museum (Haifa University, Israel).
8 *Gen.* 35.17, *Gen.* 38.28 and *Ex.* 1.15–21.
9 *Gen.* 38: 27–29; *Gen.* 35:17.
10 1 *Sam.*: 19–21.
11 Ref. n. H3307 Hecht Museum.
12 On the use of childbirth chairs or birth stools in Mesopotamia and the Levant, see Ebeling (2010, 102); Ulanowski (2014, 14).

References

Acquaro, E. (2017) La quaglia di Eracle/Melqart: un'inusuale escatologia funeraria punica in rasoi di Cartagine? *Gerion* 35(1), 11–17.

Aguilar-Moreno, M. (2007) *Handbook to Life in the Aztec World*. Oxford, Oxford University Press.

Arruda, A. M., Barbosa, R., Gomes, F. and de Sousa, E. (2017) A necrópole da Vinha das Caliças (Beja, Portugal). In J. Jiménez Ávila (ed.) *Sidereum Ana III. El Río Guadiana y Tartessos*. Mérida, Consorcio de la Ciudad Monumental, Histórico-Artística y Arqueológica, 187–225.

Bartoloni, P. (2000) *La necropolis di Monte Sirai-I*. Collezione di Studi Fenici 41. Roma, Consiglio Nazionale delle Ricerche.

Battini, L. (2006) Les images de la naissance en Mésopotamie. In L. Battini and P. Villard (eds) *Médecine et médicines au Proche-Orient ancien*. Oxford, British Archaeological Report S1528, 1–37.

Becker, M. J. (2007) Childhood among the Etruscan: Mortuary programs at Tarquinia as indicators of the transition to adult status. In A. Cohen and J. B. Rutter (eds) *Constructions of Childhood in ancient Greece and Italy*. Princeton, American School of Classical Studies at Athens, 281–412.

Benjamin, D. C. (1989) Israel's God: mother and midwife. *Biblical Theology Bulletin*, 19(4), 115–120.

Boucher, A. (2016) Mettre au monde il y a 2500 ans sur l'île de Chypre. *Archéologia* 543, 22–23.

Budin, S. L. (2014) Fertility and gender in the Ancient Near East. In M. Materson, N. S. Rabinowitz and J. Robson (eds) *Sex in Antiquity: Exploring gender and sexuality in the Ancient World*. London, Routledge, 30–49.

Couto-Ferreira, E. (2014) She will give birth easily: therapeutic approaches to childbirth in 1st millenium BCE cuneiform sources, *Dynamis* 34(2), 289–315.

Couto-Ferreira, M. E. (2016) Parteras, nodrizas y cuidadoras en Mesopotamia. In A. Delgado Hervás and M. Picazo (eds) *Los trabajos de las mujeres en el mundo antiguo. Cuidado y mantenimiento de la vida*. Tarragona, Institut Català d'Arqueologia Clàssica, 105–118.

Cox, B. D. and Ackerman, S. (2009) 'Rachel's Tomb'. *Journal of Biblical Literature* 128(1), 135–148.

Delgado Hervás, A. (2016) Mujeres, grupos domésticos y prácticas cotidianas en las comunidades fenicias y púnicas occidentales, *Treballs del Museu Arqueològic d'Eivissa i Formentera* 74, 47–84.

Delgado Hervás, A. and Ferrer Martín, M. (2012) La muerte visita la casa: mujeres, cuidados y memorias familiares en los rituales funerarios fenicio-púnicos. In L. Prados (ed.) C. López and J. Parra (coords.) *La Arqueología funeraria desde una perspectiva de género*. Madrid, UAM Ediciones, 123–155.

Demand, N. (1994) *Birth, Death, and Motherhood in Classical Greece*. Baltimore, Johns Hopkins University Press.

Ebeling, J. R. (2010) *Women's Lives in Biblical Times*. London, T&T Clark.

Fernández, J. H. (1981) *Un hipogeo intacto en la necrópolis del Puig des Molins. Eivissa*. Trabajos del Museo Arqueológico de Ibiza, 6. Eivissa, Museu Arqueològic d'Eivissa i Formentera.

Fulton, D. N., Hesse, P. and Hesse, B. (2017) Considering carcasses: Sheep and goat sacrifice at Carthage, Tunisia and Al Qisha, Yemen. In J. Lev-Tov, P. Wapnish and A. Gilbert (eds) *The Wide*

Lens in Archaeology. Honoring Brian Hesse's Contributions to Anthropological Archaeology. Atlanta, Lockwood Press, 245–256.

García Teyssandier, E. and Marzoli, D. (2013) Phönizische gräber in Ayamonte (Huelva, Spain). Ein vorberich, *Madrider Mitteilungen* 54, 89–158.

Gómez Bellard, C. (1990) *La colonización fenicia de la isla de Ibiza.* Excavaciones Arqueológicas en España 157. Madrid, Ministerio de Cultura.

Goodfriend, E. A. (2008) Tazria Leviticus 12:1–13:59: Purity, birth, and illness. In T. C. Eskenazi and A. L. Weiss (eds) *The Torah: A women's commentary.* New York, Women of Reform Judaism.

Guirguis, M. (2011) Gli spazi della morte a Monte Sirai (Carbonia-Sardegna). Rituali e ideologie funeraria nella necropoli fenicia e púnica (scavi 2005–2010). *Journal of Fasti* Online. http://www.fastionline.org/docs/FOLDER-it-2011-230.pdf.

Halcrow, S. E., Tayles, N. and Elliott, G. (2018) The bioarchaeology of fetuses. In S. Han, T. K. Betsinger and A. B. Scott (eds) *The Anthropology of the Fetus: Biology, culture and society*. New York, Berghahn Books, 83–110.

Hays, C. B. (2011). *Death in the Iron Age II and in First Isaiah.* Tübingen: Mohr Siebeck.

Kozma, C. (2006) Historical review. Dwarfs in Ancient Egypt. *American Journal of Medical Genetics* 140A, 303–311.

Liston, M. A. and Papadoulos, J. K. (2004) The 'rich Athenian lady' was pregnant: the anthropology of a Geometric tomb reconsidered. *Hesperia* 73, 7–38.

Margarity, K. (2016) A mother's gaze: Death and orphanhood on Classical Attic grave reliefs. *BABESCH* 91, 87–104.

Marsman, H. J. (2003) *Women in Ugarit and Israel: Their social and religious position in the context of the Ancient Near East.* Leiden, Brill.

Martín, E., Recio, A., Ramírez, J. D. and Macías, M. (2007) Enterramiento fenicio en Las Chorreras (Vélez-Málaga, Málaga). *Mainake* 29, 557–581.

Martín, E. (2014–15) Sarcófago fenicio del siglo VIII a.C. en Las Chorreras (Vélez-Málaga, Málaga). *Mainake* 35, 67–88.

Matoïan, V. (2010) Étude d'iconographie levantine. Bès à Ougarit. *Semitica et Classica* 3, 213–22

Mazar, E. (2009) *The Northern Cemetery of Achziv (10th-6th Centuries BCE): The Tophet Site; the Sam Turner Expedition: Final Report of the Excavations 1992-2004.* Cuadernos de Arqueología Mediterránea 19–20. Barcelona, Bellaterra,

Meyers, C. (2016) Women's lives. In S. Niditch (ed.) *The Wiley Blackwell Companion to Ancient Israel.* Chichester, Wiley, 415–432.

Michel, C. 2004. Deux incantations paléo-assyriennes. Une nouvelle incantation pour faciliter la naissance. In J. G. Dercksen (ed.) *Assyria and Beyond: Studies Presented to Mogens Trolle Larsen.* Leiden, Nederlands Instituut voor het Nabije Oosten, 395–420.

Nougayrol, J. (1968) Textes suméro-accadiens des archives et bibliothèques privées d'Ugarit. In C. F. A. Schaeffer (ed.) *Ugaritica V. Nouveaux textes accadiens, hourrites et ugaritiques des archives et bibliothèques privées d'Ugarit. Mission de Ras Shamra* XVI. Paris, Paul Geuthner, 1–447.

Oakley, J. H. (2003) Death and child. In J. Neils and J. H. Oakley (eds) *Coming of Age in Ancient Greece. Images of Childhood from the Classical Past.* New Haven: Yale University Press, 163–193.

Oggiano, I. (2012) Scopi e modalità delle azioni rituali femminili nell'area siro-palestinese del I millennio a. C.: Il contributo dell'archeologia. In V. Nizzo and L. La Rocca (eds) *Antropologia e archeologia a confronto: Atti del 2° Congresso Internazionale di Studi.* Roma, E. S. S. Editorial Service System, 223–249.

Parker Pearson, M. (1999) *The Archaeology of Death and Burial.* Texas, A&M University Press.

Pereiro, T., Mataloto, R. and Borges, N. (2017) Alentejo, a sul de Beja: a necrópole sidérica da Quinta do Estácio 6. In J. Jiménez Ávila (ed.) *Sidereum Ana III. El río Guadiana y Tartessos.* Mérida, Consorcio de la Ciudad Monumental, Historico-Artística y Arqueológica, 305–331.

Piga, G., Guirguis, M. and Allue, E. (2015) Funerary rituals and ideologies in the Phoenician-Punic necrópolis of Monte Sirai (Carbonia, Sardinia, Italy). In T. Thompson (ed.) *The Archaeology of Cremation: Burned human remains in funerary studies*. Oxford, Oxbow Books, 97–121.
Piga, G., Guirguis, M., Thompson, T. J. U., Isidro, A., Enzo, S. and Malgosa, A. (2016) A case of semi-combusted pregnant female in the Phoenician-Punic necropolis of Monte Sirai (Carbonia, Sardinia, Italy) *HOMO - Journal of Comparative Human Biology* 67(1), 50–64.
Pla Orquín, R. (2014–15) *Le donne nella Sardegna fenicia e púnica: tradizioni ed evoluzione della identità. Il caso di Monte Sirai* (Ph. D diss. Università degli Studi di Sassari).
Pla Orquín, R. (2017): Il mondo femmenile e l'infanzia. In M. Guirguis (ed.) *La Sardegna Fenicia e Punica: Storia e materiali*. Nuoro, Ilisso Edizzioni, 317–325.
Salvi, D., Sariggu, M., Puscedu, V. and Zamora J. A. (2016) Sepolture Tardo Puniche dal Lotto 7 di Tuvixeddu: due storie di bambini mai nati e alcune osservazioni epigrafiche. *Quaderni* 27, 347–367.
Scurlock, J. A. (1991) Baby-snatching demons, restless souls, and the dangers of childbirth: Medico-magical means of dealing with some of the perils of motherhood in Ancient Mesopotamia. *Incognita* 2, 137–185.
Simkins, R. A. (2014) The embodied world: Creation metaphors in the Ancient Near East. *Biblical Theology Bulletin* 44(1), 40–53.
Stavrakopoulou, F. (2010) *Land of our Fathers: The roles of ancestor veneration in biblical land claims*. Library of Biblical Studies 473. New York, T&T Clark.
Terranova, C. (2013) Morire di parto nell'a antica Grezia. La storia di Plangon di Platea. *FORMA VRBIS* 10, 4–11.
Töpfer, S. (2014) The physical activity of parturition in ancient Egypt: textual and epigraphical sources. *Dynamis* 34(2), 317–335.
Trellisó, L. (2004) The anthropological study on the human skeletal remains. In M. E. Aubet (ed.) *The Phoenician Cemetery of Tyre-Al Bass. Excavations 1997-1999*. Bulletin d'Archéologie et d'Architecture Libanaises Hors Série I. Beirut, Direction Générale des Antiquité, 247–478.
Ulanowsky, K. (2014) The influence of creation and pursuit of immortality on human status in Mesopotamia. *Miscellanea Anthropologica et Sociologica* 15(3), 13–30.
Van der Toorn, K. (1996) *Family Religion in Babylonia, Ugarit and Israel: Continuity and Changes in the Forms of Religious Life*. Leiden, Brill.
Velázquez Brieva, F. (2007) *El dios Bes: de Egipto a Ibiza*. Treballs del Museu Arqueològic d'Eivissa i Formentera 57. Eivissa, Museu Arqueològic d'Eivissa i Formentera.
Wegner, J. (2009) A decorated birth-brick from south Abydos: New evidence on childbirth and birth magic in the Middle Kingdom. In D. P. Silverman, W. K. Simpson and J. Wegner (eds) *Archaism and Innovation. Studies in the Culture of Middle Kingdom Egypt*. Charlestown, Sawyer, 447–496.
Wells, C. (1975) Ancient obstetric hazards and female mortality. *Bulletin of the New York Academy of Medicine* 51, 1235–1241.
Willet, E. A. R. (2002) Infant mortality and family religion in the Biblical periods. *DavarLogos* 1(1), 27–42.
Xella, P. (2013) Tophet. An overall Interpretation. In P. Xella (ed.) *The Tophet in the Phoenician Mediterranean. Studi Epigrafici e Linguistici sul Vicino Oriente Antico* 29–30, 2012–13. Verona, Essedue, 259–281.
Zamora López, J. A. (2016) Hijos y padres, cazadores y guerreros, reyes y héroes. Masculinidades en las construcciones culturales fenicio-púnicas (a través de la tradición literaria ugarítica). *Treballs del Museu Arqueològic d'Eivissa i Formentera* 74, 9–45.

Chapter 6

Looking after dead infants: the materialisation of care in Sicilian child burials (10th–7th centuries BC)

Meritxell Ferrer

Introduction

In recent years, several studies deriving from feminist and postprocessual perspectives and applying different theories and methodologies have stressed that infancy and maternity are predominantly social and cultural constructions (Lillehammer 1989; 2008; 2010; Demand 1994; Wilkie 2003; Baxter 2005; Sánchez 2006; Sánchez Romero 2006; Budin 2011; Sánchez Romero *et al.* 2015; Beckman 2016; Couto 2016; Freucht 2016). In this conception, these two clearly differentiated categories nonetheless converge in a constant relationship of interdependence. This relationship lies, mainly, in the fact that the successful transformation of children into full members of the adult group is not just due to the biological reproduction of their progenitors, but also to the participation of certain members of the adult group in the process of their socialisation. Whether or not these adults are the children's biological parents, they take on the role of parenting – and, specifically, of mothering – and act as the key agents in the construction of an arena in which children learn to be, to feel, and to develop their potential. Over time, this agency helps children to form their own identity and to be included as full members in the group of adults (Sánchez Romero 2004, 378; 2006, 124).

Recent studies have begun to recognise the importance of infancy and maternity in the creation of a fuller, more complex reading of past societies (Baitzel 2018). In fact, the incorporation of these two categories in the archaeological analysis offers new insights that help us to go beyond the traditional strongly androcentric readings that consider certain adult men as the only active agents in the historical dynamics of a society. Despite this gradual acknowledgement of the importance of infancy and maternity, as Sánchez Romero (2006, 124) points out, their archaeological study still presents several difficulties. On the one hand, we still lack a reliable methodology of analysis that does justice to the agency of children and mothers. On the other, the practices and contexts in which the two categories and their relationship of interdependence can be best observed, such as domestic spaces and activities, have traditionally been neglected. Habitually associated with the female sphere, these contexts are seen as static and unchanging over time and, therefore, as secondary (or even entirely unconnected) to the shaping of the social, political and identity dynamics that prevail in any society.

The main aim of this chapter is to analyse the relationships of interdependence that existed between infancy and the practices of parenting in central and western Sicily during the first half of the 1st millennium BC, through the study of infant burials. Specifically, this paper explores the study of the attitudes and affections of the members of the group that took on the parenting functions – in particular, mothering[1] – addressing the premature death of children at three local sites dated between the 10th and 7th centuries BC.[2] These necropoleis are Mokarta (10th–9th centuries BC), Morgantina (8th century BC) and Polizzello (8th–7th centuries BC) (Fig. 6.1).

The choice of funerary contexts and, particularly, child burials to explore the categories of infancy and maternity and to analyse their relationships of interdependence is due, first, to the scarcity of the archaeological evidence available for central and western Sicily during the first half of the 1st millennium BC. Although the interest in archaeology in Sicily has increased since the 1960s, most of the studies published have focused on areas traditionally associated with power, such as city-walls and collective ritual spaces, or on funerary contexts that may provide intact artefacts suitable for display in museums (Ferrer 2013, 213). This bias in the Sicilian archaeological record, at the expense of other spaces such as the domestic sphere, makes burial sites a key context for approaching the study of native Sicilian peoples during this period.

Secondly, child burial represents one of the main contexts in which a given society's concept of infancy takes on a material form (Kamp 2001; Baxter 2005; De Lucia 2010; Baitzel 2018). Furthermore, these sites are places devoted to the expression of grief (Tarlow 2012, 176; Canon and Cook 2015; Baitzel 2018) in which practices of parenting, and especially mothering, are reified through the physical act of caring and through the affection that these adults professed for their dead children during their last physical interaction with them (Baitzel 2018, 178). As a result, the analysis of child burials is the best archaeological context currently available to us for the study of infancy and maternity and the relationships of interdependence that existed between them in the local Sicilian world of the 1st millennium.

Sicilian funerary landscapes in the 1st millennium BC

From the end of the 2nd millennium BC and throughout the 1st millennium BC, the local Sicilian people settled on hilltops at strategic points along routes of travel and transport and within easy reach of the island's river network. This practice favoured communication with other settlements and, from the mid-eighth century BC onwards, also with the colonies scattered along the coast (Fig. 6.1).

The internal organisation of these sites was governed by the topography: that is to say, the three areas that usually made up these settlements were placed at different

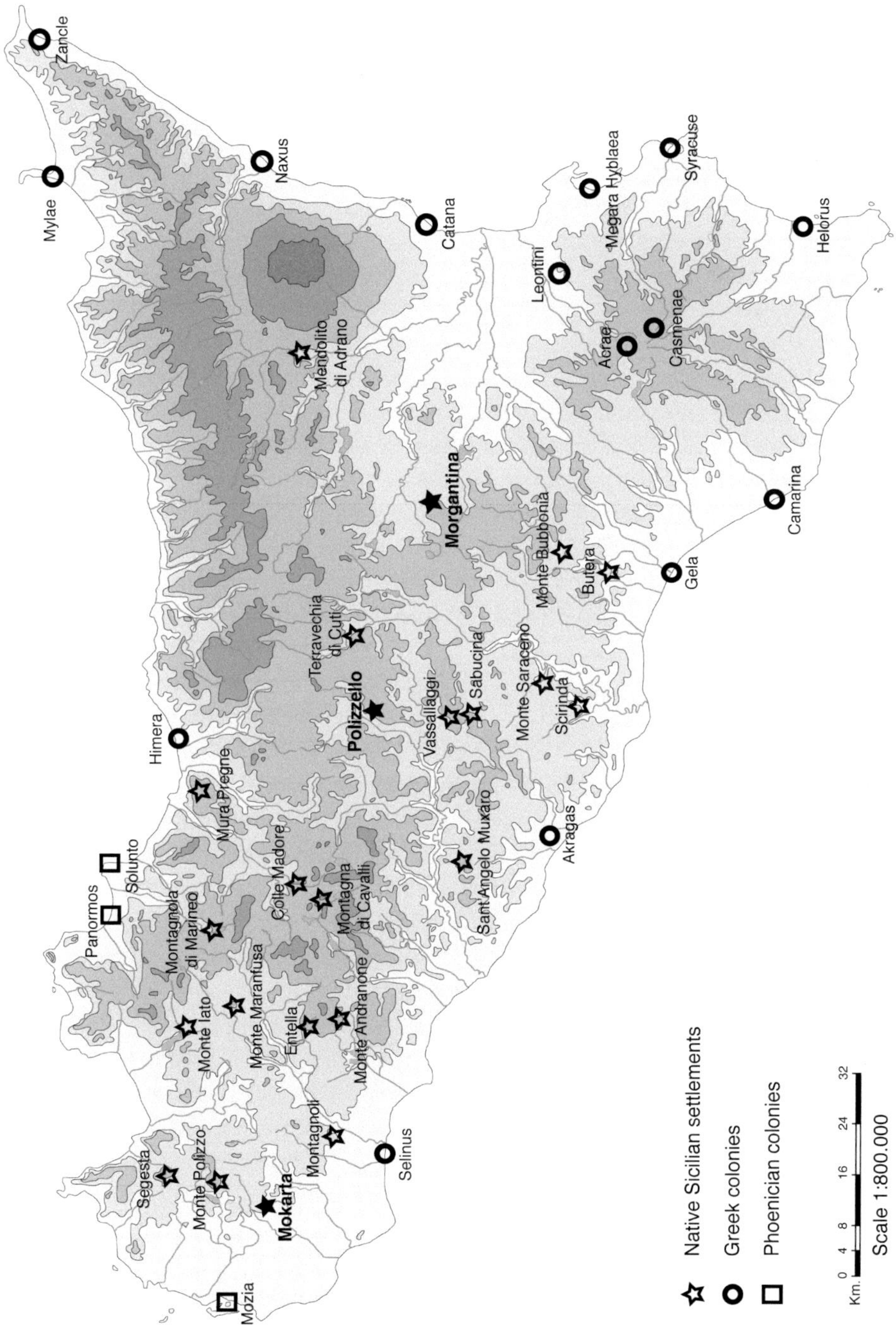

Figure 6.1: Map of Sicily showing the main native settlements of the 1st millennium BC as well as the Greek and Phoenician colonies

heights on the hillside. In the higher or more visually prominent areas we find the acropolis or spaces devoted to the celebration of communal ritual ceremonies. At the second level were the houses, following a system of artificial terraces. Finally, further down the slopes of the hillside, we find the cemeteries (Ferrer 2012; 2013).

The situation of the cemeteries in the lower areas of the slopes made them a constant spatial and visual reference point for all the residents of the settlements or their surroundings. Indeed, they were liminal spaces, crossed daily as one enters or leaves the settlement, and they would have become mnemonic reference points for all the members of the community. The participation of these funerary spaces in the construction of a Sicilian social landscape is stressed by the predominant use of rock-cut chambers, which give an appearance of small beehives attached to the hills. This particular feature increases their visibility at short and medium range and also made the cemeteries ideal territorial markers, central points in the construction of a new Sicilian landscape (Albanese Procelli 2003, 56).

Likewise, the large-scale investment of energy and labour in the construction of these tombs reflects the importance that the world of the dead had for the people – not just in the creation of a funerary landscape, but more importantly in the construction and strengthening of a sense of belonging to a settlement and a community. The monumental nature of these constructions, and their close links to the earth and especially to the hill, offered an image of stability and durability over time that would have played an active part in the creation and legitimation of this sense of belonging. This feeling was strengthened by the re-use of the same tombs over several generations, as evidenced by their periodic reopening and the removal of bodies, and also in some cases by their stratigraphy.

This constant relationship between the settlement (the world of the living) and the cemetery (the world of the dead) is also evidenced through the morphological changes we see in the funerary chambers. During the first centuries of the 1st millennium BC there is a gradual change from circular or elliptical plans to rectangular ones, thus reproducing the transformation recorded in domestic contexts (Albanese Procelli 2003, 57). These trends are also found in the ceiling of the chambers, which, as in the domestic constructions, change from domed to flat.

In sum, the funerary space of the local Sicilian world during the first half of the 1st millennium BC seems to show a society in transformation in which the dead, or at least some of the dead, were a key element in the construction of a new landscape and in the creation of new collective identities that were deeply rooted in the territory and, in particular, on the hillside on which they settled. Furthermore, the reduction of the number of inhumations recorded inside the funerary chambers (Albanese Procelli 2003), their greater simplicity and above all the close relationship between the funerary and domestic spheres all seem to suggest the emergence of a society in which the local collective identity was mainly based on, and conceived as, an amalgam of the different households that made up the settlement. This relationship also suggests that most of the funerary rituals, among them the disposal of the bodies, were actions carried out at the family level, managed by members of the dead person's household.

Despite the importance of funerary spaces and practices for these people as well as for archaeologists, infant burials in the Sicilian context have attracted little attention from researchers. Although some studies on the colonial world have been published, both Greek (Shepherd 2007; Elia and Meirano 2012; Vassallo 2014; Lambrugo 2015) and Phoenician (Spatatafora 2014), to date only one paper has investigated the local context (Cultraro 2015).

Similarly, the scarcity of records of infant burials in local cemeteries may appear surprising in view of the high infant mortality rates estimated for protohistoric societies, which several studies have situated around 30% (Golden 1992; Dasen 2010). This scant documentation seems to be due first of all to the limited availability of funerary records for central and western Sicily during this period. These areas of the island have less tradition of funerary archaeology than the eastern part, where several large cemeteries, both colonial and local, have been excavated since the end of the 19th century. Furthermore, the long-standing practice of clandestine excavations (ever since ancient times) has led to the disappearance of some funerary remains.

Secondly, we should consider the possibility that some children's bodies may not been documented, for taphonomic reasons (Stodder 2008; Gowland *et al.* 2014). Indeed, although the bones of children have the same mineralisation as adult ones, their higher porosity and vascularity may have hastened their disappearance (Gowland *et al.* 2014, 78). Finally, we must also bear in mind that some children were not buried – or, as we will see below, they were buried outside the tombs.

Mokarta: evidence from the Final Bronze Age to the Early Iron Age

Mokarta is located at the western tip of the island, less than 25 km from the sea both to the south and to the west. The site is on a low hill delimited by two small streams, which give it the appearance of a perfect fortified hill fort. The two extremes – Castello de Mokarta (290 m) in the west and Cresta di Gallo (365 m) in the east – are the highest and most important points on this hill (Fig. 6.1).

In Cresta di Gallo, there is evidence of a settlement as early as the Middle Bronze Age, which was then continuously occupied until the Final Bronze (Spatafora and Mannino 1992; Mannino and Spatafora 1995). Following the traditional pattern of Sicilian occupation mentioned above, several funerary areas have been recorded on the slopes of this hill, just below the inhabited area. The eastern and centro-meridional slopes show evidence of some rock-chamber tombs that seem to be dated in the Early Bronze, while the more recent ones, dated to the Final Bronze, are located in the north-eastern area. Although most of these tombs present a poor state of preservation because of the natural erosion of the rock and the clandestine excavations of ancient times, a project led by the Soprintendenza di Trapani in the 1990s was able to identify

61 individual tombs. All were dated to the Final Bronze and 34 of them were excavated (Spatafora and Mannino 1992; Mannino and Spatafora 1995).

These individualised tombs present the traditional Sicilian funerary morphology, the rock-cut chamber, in use from prehistoric times until the first half of the 1st millennium BC (Albanese Procelli 2003). The tombs at Cresta di Gallo comprise a funerary chamber with a circular or elliptical plan,[3] accessed through a small corridor or *dromos*,[4] and with a hemispherical or *tholos*-shaped ceiling. The dominant ritual in this necropolis at that time was inhumation, in which the corpses deposited in the supine position in the middle of the chamber or along its walls, but their feet were always pointing towards the entrance. It is also worth noting that these burials tend to be collective involving between two and seven individuals, although in this cemetery a few individual tombs have also been recorded (Mannino and Spatafora 1995). Alongside the corpses, a few objects have sometimes been recorded, probably deposited as grave goods. Most of them are vessels placed around the head of the dead person. However, a few vessels have also been recorded in the corridor, which are interpreted as the remains of ritual practices connected with the cult of the dead rather than as grave goods (Mannino and Spatafora 1995, 30).

Although no anthropological studies are available, the descriptions offered by archaeologists document a total of 81 individuals. Following their reports, we can infer that most of the individuals deposited in this cemetery were adults (71 individuals), being also recorded four subadults (adolescents and children) and six undetermined due to the scarcity of remains recorded.[5] These data indicate that non-adult individuals were not usually buried in this cemetery, since subadults account for only 4.9% of all the burials recorded – an extremely low rate in view of the infant mortality rates estimated for protohistoric societies which, as we noted above, were around 30%. Furthermore, if we consider that of these four subadults only one is specifically described as a child, the presence of children is even lower (1.2%).

The scarce presence of children in the Cresta di Gallo necropolis suggests that the people of Mokarta did not usually bury children in this funerary space, which seems to have been reserved for adults. This practice suggests several possibilities with regard to the treatment for children who died prematurely. On the one hand, it may be that the funerary rituals carried out after the death of a child or a young member of this community did not involve burial; if we consider the low volume of inhumations documented in this necropolis over a considerable period of time, this practice might also extend to certain adults of the same group. On the other hand, it may also be that children were buried in their houses or in areas nearby, as in some contemporary settlements in eastern Sicily and, especially, in the Italian peninsula. Finally, we might also speculate that children were deposited in a funerary space which was designed specifically for them but has not been archaeologically recorded to date.

Whatever the reason for the absence of child burials in the Cresta di Gallo necropolis, the finding in tomb 39 of a child along with an adult shows that the normative practice of burying only adults in this space might not always be observed. In this particular case it seems that the household to which the child belonged – and specifically the adults that took care of him or her – considered it important not to follow the norms established for this community. In other words, in this phase of the mortuary ritual this child was not treated like the other children who died prematurely in this community but, on the contrary, was deposited in a rock-chamber tomb and treated almost in the same way as some members of the adult group. However, the position of the two bodies inside the tomb – the adult is placed along the wall, while the child is in front of the entrance – indicate that the adult was deposited first. This time sequence in the deposition indicates that the people who managed and carried out this burial had taken the decision not to leave the child unaccompanied inside the rock-chamber, probably because this was not thought of as a place where a child could be alone; and evidencing that child needed the protection and care of an adult, even after death.

Morgantina: evidence from the Iron Age

Morgantina is located in Serra Orlando, at the westernmost end of the Catania plain. It would have been a highly strategic vantage point, from where one could watch over the whole of the plain as well as the Gornalunga and Gela rivers, the natural connection between the interior of the island and the coastlines of Catania and Gela respectively. In the eastern area of Serra Orlando we find Farmhouse Hill; Cittadella (578 m) is its highest point, which was occupied continuously from protohistoric times to the Hellenistic period (Fig. 6.1).

The specific topography of Farmhouse Hill – entirely surrounded by cliffs, with the sole exception of the western side, which is connected with Serra Orlando – is ideally suited for the reproduction of the traditional Sicilian pattern of settlements, in which the funerary areas are located in the lower areas of the slopes. Archaeological studies carried out on this hill[6] have recorded four clearly distinct funerary spaces.[7] In all of them rock-chambers predominate, and most of them in small clusters inside the cemeteries. Although most of these tombs were constructed in the protohistoric and archaic periods, they were in use until Roman times (Lyons 1996, 7).

In spite of the considerable volume of tombs published, for the protohistoric period we have only a few rock-chamber tombs, discovered in Necropolis IV in 1970. Most of these tombs had been violated and only three of them were found perfectly sealed (Allen 1974; Leighton 1993). These three tombs lay out alongside a small terrace, from where the Gornalunga valley can be clearly seen. These tombs are smaller than the ones constructed in the archaic period,[8] and present an elliptical plan with a vaulted ceiling, a shape that once again recalls the contemporary domestic architecture (Fig. 6.2). Their small dimensions may well indicate that the individuals were deposited in their interior perpendicular to the access point, which was sealed with one or two perfectly cut stone slabs (Leighton 1993, 97).

Of these tombs, tomb 4 was used for an individual burial, and tombs 5 and 6 for a group burial. From the individuals buried in these tombs we can infer that this space

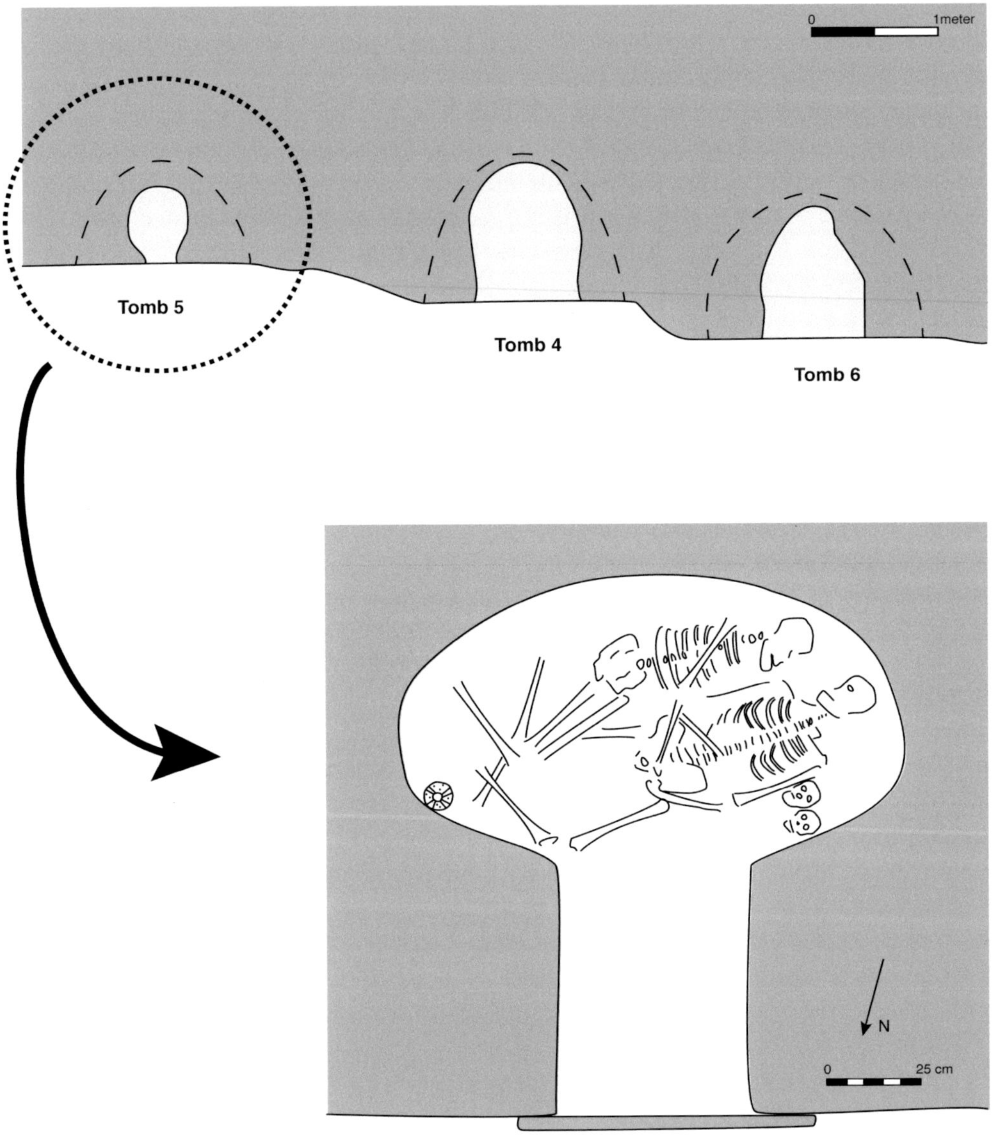

Figure 6.2: Iron Age tombs from Morgantina, Area III Necropolis IV and tomb 5 (after Leighton 1993, figs 27, 29)

was intended to host adults almost exclusively. Indeed, of the 11 individuals recorded, only two (18.2%) are children – once again, a rate far below the estimated infant mortality for this period (Spatatafora 2014). The scarce presence of children in these tombs seems to suggest that in this community the necropolis was not considered an appropriate site for their burial, and that they would have been laid to rest somewhere else – perhaps outside the houses, a place well known to the children and close to the people who had cared for them during their short lives. In Morgantina this seems all the more probable in view of the presence of a child burial inside a *dolia* deposited outside a domestic structure in Area III/trench 31 in Cittadella (Leighton 1993, 43–44).

The location of this child burial just outside a house suggests, first, that certain members of this household (probably those who had carried out parenting and above all mothering functions) did not want to be physically distanced from the child after his/her premature death. Secondly, the location of the burial just outside the house, a busy place where daily activities were carried out, bears witness to the importance given to this child, at least after his/her death when s/he would have become a constant reference for all the members of the household. Finally, the deposition of this child in an external area well protected by the eaves of the roof also indicates that the space was carefully chosen. Probably, this location wanted to prolong after death the protection and care provided by certain members of the family, in particular the ones who had acted as parents and above all as mothers.

Although the necropolis does not seem to have been the most favoured place to bury children, two children were laid to rest alongside two adults in tomb 5 (Fig. 6.2). As in Mokarta, the position of these children inside the funerary rock-chamber – right next to its entrance – indicates that they were the last to be deposited, after the placement of a small jug and the two adults. Once again, this time sequence in the deposition seems to highlight that this space was not considered appropriate for children, who had to be accompanied by adults from the very first moment. But the deposition of these two children in this tomb also evidences that some households challenged the normative funerary practices of the community by burying their youngest and most vulnerable members in this space that was closely connected with the house, and accompanied by other household adult members who would continue to guard, care for and protect them after their death.

Polizzello: the evidence from the Iron Age and the Archaic period

Polizzello is a natural bastion surrounded by the valleys of the Fiumicello and the Belice, two affluents of the Platani river. Polizzello offers an impressive vantage point over the fertile lands of central Sicily and over the main communication roads between the coast and the interior of the island (Fig. 6.1).

The spatial organisation of Polizzello reproduces the traditional tripartition of the Sicilian settlements, in which the funerary areas are located at the lower part of the hill. Although two cemeteries have been documented at this site, the archaeological study has focused exclusively on one of them, the East Necropolis.[9] Most of the tombs excavated in this cemetery date from between the end of the 8th century BC and the beginning of the 6th century BC, and thus cover most of the life of this settlement.[10] Furthermore, it is worth noting that some of these tombs were often re-used over the period, as illustrated by the three overlapping levels of use recorded in Tomb 5, or the five from Tomb 25 (De Miro 1988, 35).

This necropolis is also dominated by the rock-cut chambers arranged in small artificial terraces which, in accordance with the pattern observed previously, mainly hosted multiple adult burials.[11] With regard to their morphology, these tombs are characterised by a small *dromos* providing access to the main funerary chamber. Likewise, the chamber might be either elliptical or rectangular, thus reproducing the architectural changes recorded in contemporary domestic architecture.

Unlike Mokarta and Morgantina, in this cemetery the use of natural cavities to bury certain individuals has also been documented, as well as the existence of small external enclosures associated with certain clusters of tombs. These spaces, closely related to the tombs, seem to have been used for the celebration of ritual ceremonies associated with the funerary sphere, either during the funeral or later on as a part of ritual commemorations. These ritual enclosures seem to have been considered as ideal spaces for the deposition of child remains, as evidenced by the ones located in front of tombs 14/15/16/17 and 24/25 (De Miro 1988, 35, figs 7 and 9). At its southern end, just in front of tomb 24, tomb 25 presents a rectangular structure that seems to protect the access to the chamber, and beside it are two child burials inside *pithoi*, and a ritual pit. To the north of tomb 25 are two small well-documented spaces. The first one, nearer the tomb, is delimited by a small stone platform that might have been used as a sacrificial table. Inside this area some child burials in *pithoi* have been recorded. The second space is clearly marked by a U-shaped wall and seems to have been used as a meeting place where the dead might be honoured (De Miro 1988, 35, fig. 9; Fiorentini 1999, 197) (Fig. 6.3).

The deposition of several children in these spaces bears witness to the great care taken in the choice of places where children could (and should) be buried. Indeed, the considerable presence of child burials in these enclosures seems to indicate that in Polizzello the belief persisted that the children should not be buried in the rock-cut chambers but should be laid to rest in these liminal areas with a strong ritual meaning. Here they would be protected both by the nature of the site and by the vicinity of certain adult individuals buried inside the funerary chambers and, to a lesser extent, in the *dromos* or the enclosures. Furthermore, the burial of children in these external enclosures made them a constant and immediate reference point of the necropolis, with a key presence in the celebration of ceremonies related to the funerary sphere – both funerals and the remembrance rituals. Finally, this position outside the funerary chamber allowed those who had cared for them during their lives to prolong these practices after their death in a very direct and immediate way, without any physical barriers like the slabs that closed the chambers between the living and the dead.

The importance that children who die prematurely seem to gain in this community is underlined by the evidence in tomb 2. This rock-cut tomb is located near the southern extreme of Sector C of this necropolis[12] and it presents an elliptical plan of considerable size.[13] The access to its funerary chamber was via a *dromos* which, once the chamber was sealed, was used as a funerary space. In it were buried ten individuals deposited in three archaeological levels that bear witness to at least three different events.[14] The earliest level revealed a woman 20–25 years old deposited along with two children: one a newborn and the other aged 6–9 months. The second comprised a man and a child 3–4 months old, and the latest comprised a woman of 15–20 years together with a 5–6-year-old child, and

Figure 6.3: Enclosure related to tombs 24 and 25 from Necropolis east of Polizzello, sector B (after De Miro 1988, fig. 9)

a man, a newborn and a child of 3–4 years (Di Salvo *et al.* 2012; Sole 2012, 94). The three events recorded in this *dromos* reassert once again the idea that the spaces excavated in the rock (either chambers or *dromos*) were not considered the most appropriate for child burial because here, in contrast to the external sites, the children are never alone; they are always accompanied by adults to care for them and watch over them. In other words, whatever relationship they may have had with the children during their lives, after their death these adults took on the main functions of parenting.

This constant need to protect the children buried in the rock-cut chambers is also documented inside the funerary chamber in tomb 2, where two levels of deposition are recorded. The earlier one comprises exclusively adults – at least 12, some of them elders.[15] The later level, in contrast, presents children deposited in a single event. The osteological analysis has identified 120 children, among them ten preterm (born between their 7th or 8th month of gestation), 40 newborns, 24 between 1–6 months, three between 6–12 months, 14 between 1–2 years, 12 between 2–3 years, four between 3–4 years, nine between 4–5 years, two between 5–6 years and one between 6–8 years (Messina 2011; Sole 2012, 96–7; Di Salvo *et al.* 2012, 991). The deposition of all these children in a single event has been interpreted as the result of a specific episode in the life of Polizzello dated to the beginning of the 6th century BC, a moment near the time of the abandonment of this site (Palermo 2009, 310) which may perhaps have corresponded to a sudden outbreak of disease (Sole 2012, 111).

In spite of the exceptional nature of this tomb, it presents the same patterns of behaviour as the ones we observed above. Children might be buried in internal areas as long as they were accompanied by adults, because they would need the care and protection of the elders during their stay in this specific funerary space. Furthermore, the data offered by this tomb with regard to the grave goods that accompanied the child burials suggests that they were very similar to the ones found near the adults: mainly vessels related to consumption such as *oinochoai*, bowls and cups, and items of personal adornment and dress such as fibulas or beads (Sole 2012). Interestingly, some of these vessels are undersized, indicating perhaps a desire to adapt the grave good to the individual – in this case, one of the youngest members of the household. This differentiation may also apply to the fauna remains recorded within this tomb. While in most of the tombs the deposition of adult bovines predominates (they represent 70% of all the faunal remains) at this level, which includes exclusively child burials, the fauna is completely dominated by ovicaprines, in particular by animals aged less than 3 years and, in some cases, less than 6 months (Messina 2011, 146; Di Salvo *et al.* 2012, 995). In this regard, we might infer that both the objects and the fauna deposited in child burials are meant to reproduce the same actions and materialities recorded in the adult burials. However, the differences (that is, the undersized objects and the distinct fauna) highlight the fact that child burials present a materiality that is fully adapted to the world of children. This feature probably aimed to materialise a specific socio-cultural category – childhood – but also to reproduce, and preserve after death, the distinct forms of care that would have been given to the children of the household and of the community during their lifetime.

Conclusions

In spite of the limitations of the data available, the analysis of child burials at these three sites during the first centuries of the 1st millennium BC clearly bears witness to the importance attached to children in these communities, and also to the relationships of interdependence established between them and the people who took on the function of parents and, especially, of mothers.

Indeed, the detailed study of these burials presents a serious challenge to the traditional ideas regarding children in Antiquity. On the one hand, there has been a tendency to consider children as individuals excluded from the community, because they do not yet possess the status of 'social person' within the group. However, the funerary treatment given to children who died prematurely shows that, although the rock-cut tombs were not considered suitable places for their burial, other spaces were available for them; indeed, these spaces were visible and accessible on a daily basis, far more so than the chambers cut into the rock. This circumstance gave these children a real significance after their death, a significance that would endure in the memory both in the household and the community to which they belonged.

On the other hand, the theory put forward by Ariès (1973) suggested that neither the families nor the community would have made a great material or affective investment in their children, due to the high rates of infant mortality: 'People could not allow themselves to become too attached to something that was regarded as a probable loss' (Ariès 1973, 37). However, these three sites show that, when children died, those who had taken care of them in life sought, in various ways – by burying them next to an adult, in the most appropriate spaces, and by apportioning them the most suitable grave goods – to extend the provision of this care into the afterlife.

Acknowledgement

This study is part of the project 'HESTIA: Comida, cocina y prácticas de consumo en espacios coloniales mediterráneos (siglos VIII-V a.C.),' funded by MINECO (HAR2015-69842-P).

Notes

1 Although we have no archaeological, iconographic or textual information about those members of the household who took care of children in this Sicilian world, it's pretty probable that these practices – performed both during the lives of children and after their deaths – were carried out by some of the women of the household.

2 It is worth noting that this period comprises the foundation of the first Phoenician and Greek colonies in Sicily.

3 The diameter of these chambers ranges between 1.25 m (T. 44) and 1.70 m (T. 31), while the elliptical ones, which are considerably bigger, present a longitudinal axis between 1.05 m (T. 41) and 2 m (T. 26) and a transversal axis between 1.20 m (T. 30) and 2.42 m (T. 26). Likewise, the height of these chambers range between 0.80 m (T. 42) and 1.15 m (T. 40) (Mannino and Spatafora 1995).
4 The size of the *dromos* varies between 0.27 m and 1.95 m in length, between 0.35 m and 0.85 m in width (Mannino and Spatafora 1995).
5 In relation to the six who were undetermined, we should bear in mind that Mannino and Spatafora only mention 'human remains', and does not specify whether they are from adults, subadults or children.
6 The first systematic excavations were directed by Paolo Orsi at the beginning of the 20th century. Since 1957 Princeton University has run an archaeological project that covers all the periods documented in Morgantina.
7 Most of the published tombs are located in four funerary areas: Necropolis II, on the eastern slope; Necropolis IV, on the western slope; Necropolis V, on the northern slope; and Necropolis VI, at the bottom of the southern slope (Lyons 1996).
8 The smallest tomb is Tomb 5, with a main axis of 1.41 m and a height of 0.85 m; the largest Tomb 6 has a main axis of 1.70 m and a height of 1.18 m.
9 For a preliminary account of the excavations carried out by the Soprintendenza di Agrigenti during the 1980s (De Miro 1988; 1988–89; Fiorentini 1999). For the preliminary results of the excavations directed by Soprintendenza di Caltanissetta between 2004 and 2006 (Messina 2011; Sole 2012; Di Salvo *et al.* 2012).
10 According to the findings recorded at the Polizzello acropolis, this site was continuously occupied between the end of the 9th and the beginning of 6th century BC. (Palermo 2009; Ferrer 2012).
11 The preliminary publications of the excavations in the 1980s do not establish the number of individuals (either adults or subadults) located inside the funerary chambers. However, the preliminary publications of the 2004–2006 excavations report the existence of child burials inside the funerary chambers. With the sole exception of Tomb 2, it seems that they were less frequent than adult burials (Messina 2011; Sole 2012).
12 Sector C is an area occupied by tombs 14/15/16/17 (De Miro 1988, 36, Fig. 7).
13 The rock-cut chamber is 2.20 m long and 1.60 m high (Sole 2012, 61).
14 The grave goods recorded in each of these depositions indicate that these burials were performed over a period of time. The first one dates from the 7th century, and the later one from the end of 7th century or beginning of the 6th century BC. (Sole 2012, 94).
15 Because of the plundering of the tomb at the end of the archaeological campaign this level has not been determined in its entirety (Sole 2012, 110).

References

Albanese Procelli, R. M. (2003) *Sicani, Siculi, Elimi: Forme di identità, modi di contatto e processi di transformazione*. Roma, Longanesi.

Allen, H. L. (1974) Excavations at Morgantina (Serra Orlando), 1970–72. Preliminary report XI. *American Journal of Archaeology* 78, 361–383.

Ariès, P. (1973) *Centuries of Childhood*. London, Jonathan Cape.

Baxter, J. (2005) *The Archaeology of Childhood: Children, gender and material culture*. Oxford, AltaMira Press.

Baitzel, S. (2018) Parental grief and mourning in the Ancient Andes. *Journal of Archaeological Method and Theory* 25, 178–201.

Beausang, E. (2000) Childbirth in prehistory: An introduction. *European Journal of Archaeology* 3, 69–87.
Beckman, G. (2016) Birth and motherhood among the Hitites. In S. L. Budin and J. Mackintosh Turfa (eds) *Women in Antiquity: Real women across the ancient world*. London, Routledge, 319–328.
Budin, S. L. (2011) *Images of Woman and Child from the Bronze Age: Reconsidering fertility, maternity, and gender in the Ancient world*. Cambridge/New York, Cambridge University Press.
Cannon, A. and Cook, K. (2015) Infant death and the archaeology of grief. *Cambridge Archaeological Journal* 25, 399–416.
Couto, E. (2016) Being mothers or acting (like) mothers? Constructing motherhood in ancient Mesopotamia. In S. L. Budin and J. Mackintosh Turfa (eds) *Women in Antiquity: Real women across the ancient world*. London, Routledge, 25–34.
Cultraro, M. (2015) L'infanzia e l'archeologia della norte nella Sicilia protostorica: alguni percorsi di ricerca. In I. E. Buttita and S. Mannia (eds) *La morte e i morti nelle società euromediterranee*. Palermo, Fondazione Ignazio Butitta, 21–43.
Demand, N. (1994) *Birth, Death and Motherhood in Classical Greece*. Baltimore/London, John Hopkins University Press.
Dasen, V. (2010) Archéologie funéraire et historie de l'enfance dans l'Antiquité: Nouveaux enjeux, nouvelles perspectives. In A. M. Guimier-Sorbets and Y. Morizot (eds) *L'enfant et la mort dans l'Antiquité I*. Paris, De Boccard, 19–38.
De Miro, E. (1988) Polizzello, centro della Sicania. *Quaderni di Archaeologia* 3, 25–42.
De Miro, E. (1988–89) Gli 'indigeni' della Sicilia centro-meridional. *Kokalos* 34(5), 18–43.
De Lucia, K. (2010) A child's house: social memory, identity and the construction of childhood in early postclassic Mexican households. *American Anthropologist* 112, 607–624.
Di Salvo, R., Messina, A., Schimenti, V., Sineo, L. and Mannino, M. A. (2012) Studio antropológico sul gruppo umano di Polizzello. In S. Tusa (ed.) *Dai Ciclopi agli Ecisti. Società e Territorio nella Sicilia preistorica e protostorica*. Firenze, Edizioni I.I.P.P. , 989–999.
Elia, D. and Meirano, V. (2012) Children and funerary space. Ritual behaviours in the Greek colonies of Magna Graecia and Sicily. In M. Sánchez Romero, E. Alarcón and G. Aranda (eds) *Children, Spaces and Identity*. Oxford, Oxbow Books, 310–326.
Ferrer, M. (2012) *Acrópolis sicilianas: rituales, comunidades y poderes*. Unpublished thesis. Universidad Pompeu Fabra Barcelona.
Ferrer, M. (2013) Feasting the community: Ritual and power on the Sicilian acropoleis (10th–6th centuries BC) *Journal of Mediterranean Archaeology* 26, 211–234.
Fiorentini, G. (1999) Necropoli dei centri indigeni della valle del Platani: organizzazione, tipologie, aspetti rituali. In M. Barra Bagnasco, E. De Miro and A. Pinzone (eds) *Magna Grecia e Sicilia. Stato degli studi e prospettive di ricerca*. Roma, CNR, 195–201.
Freucht, E. (2016) Motherhood in Pharaonic Egypt. In S. L. Budin and J. Mackintosh Turfa (eds) *Women in Antiquity: Real women across the ancient world*. London, Routledge, 319–328.
Golden, M. (1992) Continuity and change and the study of ancient childhood. *EchoCi* 36, 7–18.
Gowland, R. L., Chamberlain, A. and Redfern, R. C. (2014) On the brinck of being: re-evaluating infanticide and infant burial in Roman Britain. *Journal of Roman Archaeology* 96, 69–88.
Kamp, K. A. (2001) Where have all the children gone? The archaeology of childhood. *Journal of Archaeological Method and Theory* 8, 1–34.
Lambrugo, C. (2015) Dying young in Archaic Gela (Sicily): From the analysis of the cementeries to the reconstruction of early colonial identity. In M. Sánchez Romero, E. Alarcón and G. Aranda (eds) *Children, Spaces and Identity*. Oxford, Oxbow Books, 282–293.
Leighton, R. (1993) *Morgantina Studies IV: The protohistoric settlement on the Cittadella*. Princeton, Princeton University Press.
Lillehammer, G. (1989) A child is born. The child's world in an archaeological perspective. *Norwegian Archaeological Review* 22, 89–105.

Lillehammer, G. (2008) Something about children. In L. H. Dommasnes and M. Wrigglesworth (eds) *Children, Identity and the Past*. Cambridge, Cambridge Scholars Publishing, 96–112.
Lillehammer, G. (2010) Archaeology of children. *Complutum* 21, 15–45.
Lyons, C. (1996) *Morgantina Studies V: the Archaic cemeteries*. Princeton, Princeton University Press.
Mannino, G. and Spatafora, F. (1995) *Mokarta: la necropoli di Cresta di Gallo*. Palermo, Quaderni Regionale 'Antonio Salinas'.
Messina, A. (2011) Le sepoltore dei bambini nell'età del Ferro a Polizzello (Caltanissetta, Sicilia). In C. Corti, D. Neri and P. Pancaldi, P (eds) *Pagani e cristiani. Forme e attestazioni di religiosità del mondo antico in Emilia*. Firenze, Edizioni All'Insegna del Giglio, 145–147.
Palermo, D. (2009) L'Acropoli di Polizzello fra l'Età del Bronzo e il VI sec.: problema e proespettive. In R. Panvini, C. Guzzone and D. Palermo (eds) *Polizzello. Scavi del 2004 nell'area del santuario arcaico dell'acropolis*, 297–312. Palermo, Regione Siciliana.
Sánchez Romero, M. (2004) Children in the southeast of the Iberian Peninsula during the Bronze Age. *Ethnographisch-archaologische Zeitschrift* 2–3, 377–387.
Sánchez Romero, M. (2006) Maternidad y prehistoria: prácticas de reproducción, relación y socialización. In *Las mujeres en la prehistoria*. Valencia, Museo de Prehistoria de Valencia, 119–138.
Sánchez Romero, M., Alarcón García, E. and Aranda Jiménez, G. (2015) (eds) *Children, Spaces and Identity*. Oxford, Oxbow Books.
Shepherd, G. (2007) Poor little rich kids? Status and selection in Archaic western Greece. In G. Shepherd and S. Crawford (eds) *Children, Childhood and Society*. Oxford, Archaeopress, 93–106.
Sole, L. (2012) Una tomba di bambibi dalla necropoli orientale di Polizzello. In G. Di Stefano, R. Panvini and L. Sole (eds) *Il Mondo di Ade. Ideologie, spazi rituali funerari per l'eterno banchetto* (VIII–IV secolo a.C.). Caltanissetta, Salvatore Sciascia Editore, 91–119.
Spatafora, F. (2014) Seppellimenti infantili nella necropoli punica di Palermo. In C. Terranova (ed.) *La presenza dei bambini nelle religioni del Mediterraneo Antico*. Rome, Aracne, 291–310.
Spatafora, F. and Mannino, G. (1992) Materiale preistorici dal territorio di Salemi: la Mokarta. In G. Nenci (ed.) *Giornate Internazionale di Studi sull'area elima*. Pisa-Gibellina, Scuola Superiore di Pisa, 567–575.
Stodder, A. L. W. (2008) Taphonomy and the nature of archaeological assemblages. In M. A. Katzenberg and S. R. Saunders (eds) *Biological Anthropology of the Human Skeleton*. Hoboken, Wiley, 71–114.
Tarlow, S. (2012) The archaeology of emotion and affect. *Annual Review of Anthropology* 41, 169–185.
Vassallo, S. (2014) Le sepolture dei bambibi nelle necropoli di Himera: dati preliminari. In C. Terranova (ed) *La presenza dei bambini nelle religioni del Mediterraneo Antico*. Rome, Aracne, 257–290.
Wilkie, L. (2003) *The Archaeology of Mothering: An African-American midwife's tale*. New York, Routledge.

Chapter 7

Creating beings: relations between children and animals in the Iron Age Western Mediterranean

Mireia López-Bertran

Introduction

Children are connected to their mothers in many different ways, as this present volume attests. My contribution intends to explore how this connection could be expressed too through the link to other creatures and things. The material record of the Western Mediterranean throughout the Iron Age shows an association between stillborn and newborn children and animals – above all ovicaprids of the same age. In this paper I focus on two case-studies: child cremations in Phoenician and Punic tophets (8th–2nd centuries BCE) and burials of children beneath domestic structures in eastern Iberia (5th–3rd centuries BCE) (Fig. 7.1).

In these two contexts, children's remains are accompanied by animals in a relation that can be understood in ontological terms. This paper explores the presence of this association between newborn humans and animals in these two societies. After a review of how childhood, motherhood and infancies have been studied in these two settings, I describe the archaeological contexts in which children and animals are clearly associated. Next, I develop some of the theoretical tenets that will underpin my approach. In the last section I scrutinise the relation between animals and children from the standpoints of the archaeology of the body and social zooarchaeology. Both approaches challenge the concept of bodies as closed and single identities and reinforce the social role of animals with high symbolic meanings.

The material culture of children and motherhood

Motherhood and infancy in the Iron Age Western Mediterranean have been approached from various perspectives. Assessments of Phoenician and Punic childhood have been based mainly on data from funerary and ritual contexts (Marín Ceballos 2003; 2016).

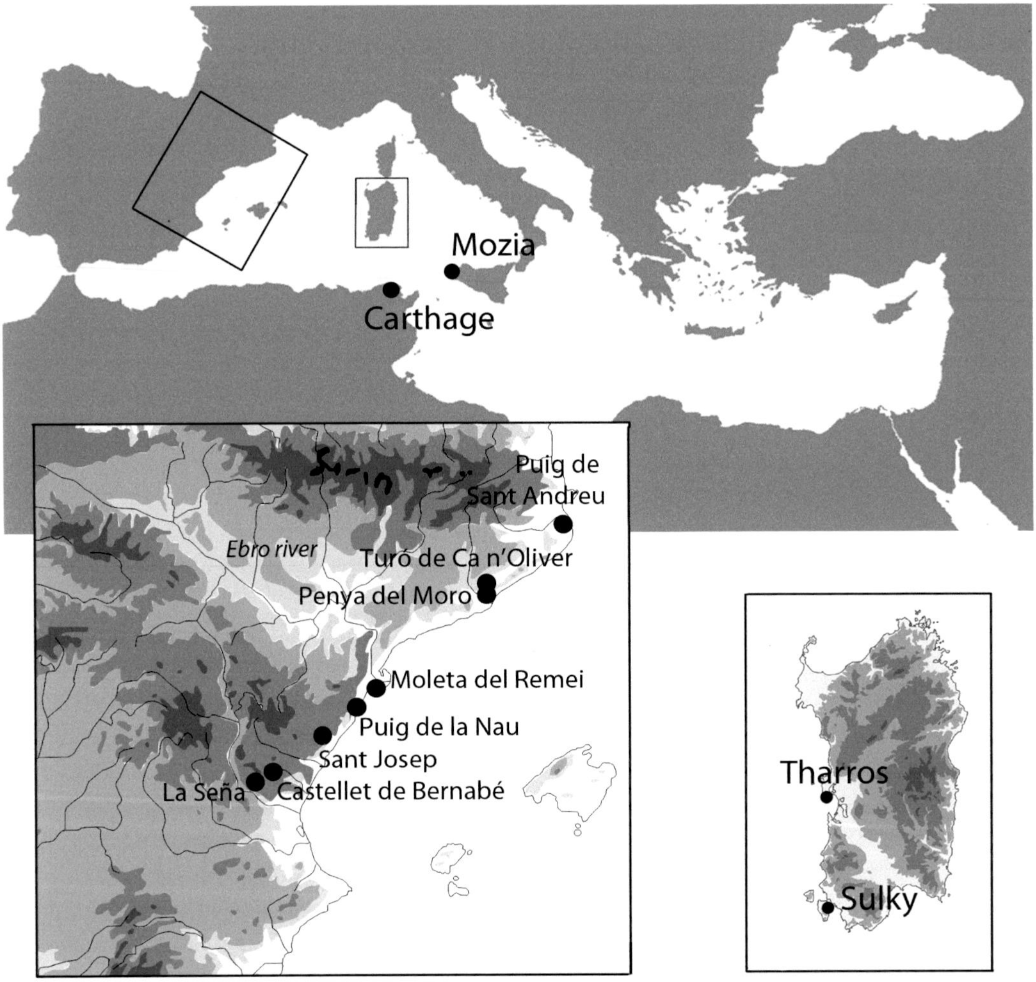

Figure 7.1: Map of the Mediterranean showing the sites mentioned in the text

Inscriptions in tombs stress the importance to the dead of having descendants to remember and honour them in the afterlife. Children's tombs were not isolated nor separated in particular areas of the necropolis, but were placed together with the tombs of their relatives, as shown, for example, in Palermo (Sicily), Monte Sirai (Sardinia) and Hoya de los Rastros (Spain) (García Theyssandier and Marzoli 2013; Spatafora 2014, 303; Guirguis and Pla Orquín 2015, 55). Also striking are the *enkytrismoi* from the Punic period – burials in which children were placed inside amphorae. Children's tombs were heavily protected with the introduction of amulets, miniatures of vessels, feeding bottles or small bells as grave goods (Bénichou Safar 2012; Fariselli 2012–13).

Other materials reflect the concern with fecundity, pregnancy, labour and breastfeeding. Terracotta female figurines with large bellies and holding their breasts, representations of the Egyptian god Bes (the protector of children, pregnant women and the sick) and *kurotrophoi* statuettes are all widespread in the Levant and in the Phoenician and Punic western centres, especially in tombs and sanctuaries (Marín Ceballos 2003; 2016; Oggiano 2012).

There are few representations of children; although some are carved on the stelae of the tophets (see below). The 'temple boys' or 'crouching boys,' votive statuettes of babies made of stone and clay found in Cypriot and Levantine sanctuaries, are also interesting. Their body position is standardised, as they always appear with the right leg bent, indicating that they are still babies who have not yet learnt to walk (Benichou Safar 2013; Marín Ceballos 2016, 93). They also carry an animal or a small round object, interpreted as a loaf of bread (Benichou Safar 2013, 180). They wear long necklaces or diagonal chains bearing small pieces, interpreted as amulets (Caneva and delli Pizzi 2014). Thus, these specimens bear witness to the community's concern with protecting children from disease, the evil eye, or demons.

Finally, recent work has stressed the presence of children in daily contexts and routines. Activities such as the preparation of food would have been female tasks which children would have observed, and in which they would have assisted, both in houses and in public areas. Similarly, the focus on family units in the diasporic communities sheds light on the presence of both women and children as active participants in the Phoenician expansion and domestic economies (Delgado Hervás 2016).

Moving on to the Iberian case, once again data from the funerary realm represent our most significant source of information (Chapa 2003; 2008). Single child burials are not common in Iberian cemeteries. When they occur, grave goods associated with protection, like rings, bells or necklaces of varying materials were included and would have played an apotropaic role (Chapa 2008, 636). Other children are buried close to a cremated adult, presumably the mother – a reminder that cremation was the standard funerary rite for adults among Iberian communities (Chapa 2008, 628).

Issues related to fertility, pregnancy, labour and breastfeeding would have been considered essential but risky activities for mothers and children alike. The material culture reflects their importance in the form of *kurotrophoi* iconographies. A terracotta figurine from La Serreta (Alcoi) and sculptures such as the *Dama de Galera* (Granada) have been interpreted as goddesses associated with breastfeeding and maternity both in the realm of the living and in the afterlife (Olmos 2000–2001).

Researchers of Iberian culture have also explored the development of the depictions of children during the lifecycle. In bronze statuettes from sanctuaries in Jaén babies appear totally wrapped (Prados 1997; Rueda 2011), a representation believed to reflect the practice of showing or offering newborns to divinities in ritual settings. These depictions show how age and gender were constructed since infancy through an array of body modifications. For example, girls appear without veils and with a particular hairstyle – two braids, falling on each side of the chest (Izquierdo 2000) and gathered up with round pieces. Boys also have a special hairstyle covered by a short hood; they hold knives, rather than weapons (a prerogative of adult males) (Chapa 2003; Rueda

2011). Other representations such as the relief called the Bastetan dance from Jaén, or terracotta figurines from La Serreta, make it clear that children played an active part in family and civic rites by performing dances and playing music.

Domestic contexts have also provided information on children. Miniatures have been studied as materials that allow the enculturation of social values; miniature versions of pottery for commensality rituals, weapons or agricultural tools would have been used by children (albeit not exclusively) in order to engage in their group's social and cultural values. It is no coincidence that miniaturised objects emerged at the same time as a social structure based on hereditary power (López-Bertran and Vives-Ferrándiz 2015). Other clay objects have been interpreted as toys, such as the one found in room 49 of Tossal de Sant Miquel (Llíria, Spain) (Bonet 1995, 484). Also in a domestic context in Molinico de Moratalla (Murcia) a small bronze bell, an object usually associated with children in funerary contexts, and small hand-made vases that bear fingerprints have been interpreted as the material remains of children (Lillo-Carpio 1993, 210–211; Chapa 2008, 624).

A surprising relationship? The association of children and animals

The archaeological record offers significant examples of an association between children and animals which has been for the most part unexplored. In this paper I consider two case-studies: Phoenician and Punic tophets, and the burials of newborns and animals in Iberian domestic contexts.

Tophets

The tophet is the prime setting for the study of children in Phoenician and Punic societies. This biblical Hebrew term is conventionally used to denote Phoenician and Carthaginian open air cremation child sanctuaries in the Central Mediterranean from the 8th century BCE to the 2nd century AD (D'Andrea and Giardino 2011; 2013; Xella 2013, 260; Melchiorri 2016). However, the word covers a complex and varied reality and the question of whether tophets were child cemeteries or places of infant sacrifices remains unresolved. Recent work (Bonnet 2011; Quinn 2011; Xella *et al.* 2013) has clearly defined them as sacred places where cremated babies were offered to the good Baal Hammon and the goddess Tinnit. Thus, tophets are 'sacred places where one goes to fulfil a vow, either to ask a god(s) for a favour or because it has been granted' (Xella 2013, 267). The donations to divinities appear to have been specially selected because, generally speaking, the human bones are from newborns and the animal remains are from newborn lambs and kids. In addition, the urns were surmounted by stelae, either blank or incised with votive inscriptions, or by anthropomorphic, vegetable or geometric forms; some tophets also contained small chapels as in Monte Sirai or Mozia. Interestingly, the representation of humans and animals on stone markers is not abundant (d'Andrea and Giardino 2010, 10; Quinn 2012–13, 35) (Fig. 7.2).

Figure 7.2: Tophet of Mozia, Sicily, photograph by By Mboesch (own work) [CC BY-SA 3.0 (https://creativecommons.org/licenses/by-sa/3.0)], via Wikimedia Commons

Tophets have been studied[1] ever since the discovery of the Salammbó Tophet at Carthage (Tunisia) at the beginning of the 20th century.[2] Unfortunately, no comprehensive and reliable catalogues are available because they have not been analysed in a systematic way; depending on their own interests, scholars have focused on specific elements: for instance, stelae, pottery, written and epigraphic sources or osteological analysis (Melchiorri 2016, 6).

There are approximately 40 tophets in all. For reasons of chronological consistency in the Iberian context I will leave aside the later chronology and focus on the ones that were in use before the 3rd century BCE. The 'classic' sites include the oldest ones already mentioned (Carthage, Sulky, Mozia) and five others located in Sardinia (Tharros, Monte Sirai, Nora, Bithia and Cagliari). However, I will focus specifically on the ones where osteological analyses have been carried out: Tharros, Mozia, Sulky and Carthage (Melchiorri 2013; d'Andrea 2014) (Table 7.1).

At Tharros, 95% of the burials are newborns (0–6 months). The animals buried are ewes or newborn lambs (Fedele and Foster, 1988). In Mozia, newborn human remains are mixed with ovicaprids, either newborn or young. Other species are *Bos Taurus*, birds, *Turtur*, unspecified types of fish and *Sus scrofa* (Ciasca et al. 1996; Di Salvo and Di Patti 2005; Melchiorri 2013, 231–233). Sulky has 79 urns with reliable contents. The ones in which only animals are found contain neonates lambs and to a

Table 7.1: Information from the tophets mentioned in the text (based on tables 1.1–1.3 from d'Andrea 2014 and Melchiorri 2013)

Tophet	*Chronology*	*Location*	*Urns*	*Urns with content analysis*	*Humans*	*Animal/humans*	*Animals*	*Undetermined*
Carthage (Tunisia)	First half of the 8th century BCE	South of the settlement on a low plain	26,000/ 30,000	484	346	84	54	
Sulky (Sardinia)	First half of the 8th century BCE	North of the settlement on a rocky hill. Close to the cemetery	*c.* 2000	79	11	37	31	
Tharros (Sardinia)	Beginning of the 7th century/3rd-2nd centuries BCE	North of the settlement, on small height. Probably close to the harbour	*c.* 3000	372	217-18	74–75	80–81	
Mozia (Sicily)	End of the 8th century BCE	North of the settlement on small height. Close to the cemetery	*c.* 800	792	150	338	53	251

lesser extent *Columba palumbus*. The humans are 'individuals of infantile age between the peri-natal phase and the first year of life' (Wilkens 2012; Melchiorri 2013, 238). Carthage offers a complex panorama due to the fragmentation of the data; the sample analysed from the Dutch collections shows an association between newborn humans and lambs, while other samples offer a combination of human newborns with lambs and, in lesser numbers, young goats and other undetermined species (Schwartz *et al.* 2010) (Table 7.1).

Although the data from these four tophets vary in terms of their quality and quantity, all contain urns with humans and animals. The most usual combination comprises young humans (0–6 months old) and young lambs and kids. So we can say that the humans and animals buried share the same age-rank. Unfortunately, the sex cannot be determined.

The urns may contain exclusively babies, babies and animals, or exclusively animals. It has been posited that the animals in the tophets are 'accompanying victims' of the children, either because animals were substitutes for children or because they accompanied the deceased child in virtue of being the same age (Xella 2013, 272). It is striking that most humans are newborns, although there are some children of older ages and some stillborn, and the animals are also newborn or young, mostly lambs and goats. But I do not find this explanation entirely satisfactory. P. Xella (2013, 266) has rightly asked 'Why are both animal and human bones sometimes mixed in the same urn?' and

'Can we evaluate these animals as "accompanying victims" of the children, or should we presume some other analogies between them (e.g., both were very young, newborns in most cases)?' I will come back to these questions later, applying an ontological perspective that breaks down the margins between humans, animals and objects.

Iberian houses

Houses and households have been key analytical units in the archaeology of Iberian communities. Political entities of diverse scale and traits of social hierarchy and inequality have been identified in eastern Iberia (Berrocal-Rangel and Gardes 2001). The settlement patterns show complex organisational systems that can be identified in a diversity of sites, from hillforts and *oppida* with massive defensive systems to farms or hamlets, some of them with fortifications. Inside the settlements there is also a variety of domestic spaces. Houses vary in terms of size and layout, and there is no simple relation between the size of sites and the type and the wealth of the houses.

Apart from the massive defensive structures, few public buildings with a political or religious role have been identified to date. This suggests that domestic, private spaces were probably important places in daily routines. In fact, houses were the locus for an array of economic activities and crafts, from metalworking to weaving; households would have controlled material resources such as land and metals and would have exchanged knowledge and labour as well as symbolic capital. Household practices and strategies were devoted to the maintenance and accumulation of property and, in the process, larger social units were established (Vives-Ferrándiz 2013).

The presence of child and animal burials beneath the floors of houses is a fruitful avenue of study for grasping the symbolic significance of these places, although not all the houses, and not even all sites, have provided deposits of this kind. Children buried in domestic contexts have been identified in eastern Iberia since the 1960s (Tarradell 1965; Gusi 1970; Belarte and Sanmartí 1997). This practice, which can be traced back to the Late Bronze Age, consisted in simple deposits of stillborns and newborns without grave goods. More recently, burials of animals have also been recognised as a feature of these dwellings (Belarte and Sanmartí 1997; Belarte and Valenzuela 2013). Two models can be distinguished: animals that present evidence of processing and consumption before their deposition and animals that were not consumed.

Because these occurrences are scarce and the largest concentrations of deposits have been documented in wealthy and complex residences, it has been suggested that this rite may have been reserved to high-status households (Chapa 2008, 637; Belarte and Valenzuela-Lamas 2013, 181). An interesting example comes from the Iberian *oppidum* of the Puig d'Alcoi (Alacant) where a ritualised deposit has been documented in a house which, given its architectural features, appears to have belonged to high-status families (Grau *et al.* 2015, 82).

Two explanations have been proposed with regard to child burial. Some scholars interpret it as a funerary rite; they assume that these babies were not considered full members of the society and so were not entitled to burial in accordance with the normative funerary rite – that is, cremation and deposition in cemeteries outside the settlements. Other researchers propose that child burials might have been the result of ritual sacrifices when houses were constructed or renovated (Grau *et al.* 2015), possibly in the belief that the spirit of the infant would protect the household. According to this interpretation the sacrifice of a child would sometimes have been substituted by the offering of an animal; this may explain why animal deposits outnumber human ones in dwellings (Gusi and Muriel 2008, 295). Therefore, the relation between children and animals is explained in terms of the substitution of the baby by an animal.

Less attention has been paid to the ontological relations between infants and animals sharing the same burial context, whether a pit or a room in a house. I will focus on the contexts where animals have been buried without any marks of consumption, because they bear more similarities to infant deposits (Table 7.2). I will try to broaden this debate by arguing that, from an ontological point of view, children and animals might have been perceived as sharing certain features. Before going into detail, let us briefly consider the theory-informed perspectives on personhood and the ontology of beings.

Ontologies of humans and animals

Ontology is defined as 'a fundamental set of understandings about how the world is: what kinds of beings, processes and qualities could potentially exist and how these relate to each other' (Harris and Robb 2012, 668). The interest in studying ontologies and theories of being from an archaeological point of view may be expressed in many forms (Alberti 2016). One fundamental point, and essential to my approach, is that ontologies provide a theory of being in the world that encompasses bodies and objects. Bodies are the arenas in which people create and construct their views of the world, while objects are fundamental actors in constructing these views.

Human bodies are not static in time and place; they change as they engage with other bodies (human, animal or other) and objects and spaces. Corporality is key in this situation, and an essential trait of corporality is its relationality. Bodies and material culture, both understood in a wider sense, interact in a relational way, creating webs of complex meanings that can be fluid and multimodal. This idea blurs our contemporary Western conception of bodies as entities with clearly limited boundaries: it shows that they can be extended beyond our flesh and connect with other bodies and other materials and entities (e.g., inert beings) in so far as they possess animated qualities. Thus, among some societies personhood is always relational (Harris and Robb 2012; Robb and Harris 2013; Fowler 2016; Alberti 2016). Relational ontologies, or modes of being, are not exclusively a human issue. For this reason, we need to identify the strategies and the ways in which human and non-human bodies, objects and spaces interact with each other.[3]

Table 7.2: Houses with children and animal deposits in the same space. I have excluded those cases where animals present marks of consumption

Site	*Space*	*Children*	*Animal*	*Chronology (BCE)*	*References*
Puig de Sant Andreu, Ullastret, Girona	Aristocratic dwelling with multiple rooms	2 newborn	73 ovicaprid deposits	4th century	Belarte and Sanmartrí 1997 Grau *et al.* 2015
Turó de Can'Olivé, Cerdanyola del Vallès, Barcelona	Room 2	1 newborn in middle of room. Together with preparation pavement of room	1 whole sheep below stairs entrance and an egg	4th–3rd centuries	Belarte and Sanmartí 1997; Belarte and Valenzuela-Lamas 2013
	Room 8	<1 year. Northeast angle of room	5 deposits of ovicaprids		
Penya del Moro, Sant Just Desvern, Barcelona	Spaces B-E,	1 newborn	2 ovicaprids	4th century	Belarte and Sanmartí 1997
	Space Y	1 newborn	4 ovicaprids		
	Space X	1 newborn	1 ovicaprid		
Moleta del Remei, Alcanar, Montsià	Open air. Access to square. Inside a natural cavity	1 stillborn 9.5 months gestation	Legs of a horse and remains of bronze		Belarte and Sanmartí 1997
Puig de la Nau, Benicarló, Castelló	Space 3800	2 inhumated babies	Pigs, piglets	5th century	Oliver 2006
Sant Josep, La Vall d'Uixò, Castelló		1 inhumation	1 young ovicaprid		Almagro-Gorbea and Lorrio 2011
Castellet de Bernabé, LLíria, Valencia	Department 6	1 inhumation in urn 6 month old	Urn with remains of ovicaprids	4th century	Guérin 2003, 330–331
La Seña, Villar del Arzobispo, Valencia	Department 3	Inhumated baby inside an urn	Rooster inside the urn. Adult, male	5th–4th centuries	Iborra 2004, 205

One of the topics that have been studied from this perspective is the interaction between human and animals under the 'animal turn' or 'social zooarchaeology.' This approach considers the animal–human interaction as mutually constructed and strongly relational. In these theories, animals are seen as non-human persons that participated actively in the social and cultural dynamics. Animals possess capacities which, in Western thinking, tend to be restricted to humans; but a relational approach reconsiders not just human–animal interactions, but also social engagements with people, animals, landscapes or artefacts and focuses on the permeable, fluid or even non-existent boundaries between humans and animals (Russell 2012; Hill 2013).

In an attempt to go beyond the study of animals merely as objects for consumption by humans (whether as a form of subsistence or as a symbolic resource) and to recognise their more active role in social dynamics, archaeologists have tried to conceptualise the relationship between humans and animals in three ways: association, transformation and substitution (Miracle and Borić 2008, 104). 'Association' means that animals and humans appear together in a variety of forms: for instance, they might share the same deposit, or humans might wear body decorations made from animal parts like bones or skin. 'Substitution' happens when humans and animals are interchangeable, while 'transformation' is related to hybrid beings, for instance, burials with human bodies and animal heads, or sculptures representing mixed figures. These material ways of intermingling animals and humans are considered as participating in body worlds where the borders between human and animal may have been blurred and understood as permeable rather than rigid (Borić and Robb 2008, 8; Borić *et al.* 2013, 40).

Shared ontologies?

The contexts mentioned above make clear the close association between animals and children. Moving one step further, we can find a more specific association: the connection between stillborns, newborns up to 6 months and animals, which were slaughtered in their first 12 months. Another connection between these beings is their treatment: in the case of Phoenician and Punic tophets, both animals and newborns were cremated, whereas in the Iberian case children and animals were deposited mostly intact and the animals do not present signs of having been cut or chopped.

These features suggest that we may be dealing with a specific way of understanding and defining one kind of human corporality. Newborn humans and some species of young animals might have been perceived as sharing certain qualities, and for this reason they could be deposited in the same spaces, be it a room in a house in the Iberian case or in a cinerary urn in a tophet.

Newborns and stillborn foetuses might have been regarded as not yet fully human. From this standpoint, they might have shared qualities with certain types of animals rather than with other members of their families. This understanding of personhood is based on the idea that a person and its body is not an individual entity; it is connected and created with other bodies (human or not) objects and places through an array of material practices (Fowler 2004; 2016). These ideas stress that personhood and bodies are multimodal, which means that people do not have a single, exclusive way of understanding their bodies. So bodies, personhood and ontologies are contextual and related to issues of class, gender, kinship, age and the lifecycle. In our case study, stillborn and newborn human personhood has more in common with young animals than with other humans.

Children and animals as animated food

Burials of infants and animals in the tophet were sacrificial offerings (Xella *et al.* 2013, 1202). This idea is strongly supported by the epigraphic evidence, which is clearly votive rather than funerary. The kind of offering is not explicitly inscribed, and indeterminate expressions like 'gift' (*mtnt*) or 'offering' (*ndr*) are attested. Yet some inscriptions explicitly refer to human victims and their age, with expressions like 'a person who has not yet reached maturity' (*»zrm »ˇs (t))* or the 'offering of a lamb' (*mlk mr)* or a person (*b'l)* or an individual or human being (*'dm*) (Amadasi Guzzo 2007–08, 350; Amadasi Guzzo and Zamora 2013, 170–71). Thus, it has been argued that the offering (baby, animal, or the two together) was in response to a prayer. The arguments in favour of this three-model deposition are quite practical: 'the dedicant asked the god for a favour and vowed in return his/her next child. If the deal could not be fulfilled in a reasonable amount of time, sheep and goats perhaps made *acceptable alternatives*' (my emphasis added) (Xella *et al.* 2013, 1204). I argue that, as in the Iberian case, newborn children were interchangeable with animals in certain rituals because they were conceived in similar ontological terms.

If babies and animals were gifts to the gods, namely Baal Hammon and Tinnit, it is conceivable that they were also offered to feed divinities in a symbolic or physical way. As shown in the Late Bronze Age Ugaritic myths, gods and goddesses had certain human features, including the need to consume food and beverages; thus, humans are responsible for feeding them, especially when they are formulating vows. Ugaritic texts and Punic inscriptions make it clear that the most precious gifts are animals (calves, kids and lambs) (Zamora 2015, 62). So both children and animals became food for the gods. Significantly, from a relational and ontological point of view, this food was animated; the living qualities of young humans and animals make the offering special and are transferred to the divinities. Children and animals are not separate beings but become a new one in the act of sacrifice to the gods. I contend that this new entity arises as animated food, made up of human and animal corporalities.

This idea of humans and animals as food is also attested in the Old Testament, where we find the expression 'sacrifice as food' (Ez 16, 20–21) in relation to human sacrifices in Israel (Xella 2013, 264). These written sources make it clear that sacrifices were not restricted to firstborns and those sisters or daughters may have been sacrificed too. The seasonality of the rite has also been addressed from the perspective of the lambing cycle, which happens only once or twice a year at fixed periods. Thus, it is possible that people went to tophets only at specific times, probably during sacred feasts or celebrations (Fedele and Foster 1988; Docter *et al.* 2003, 424; Xella 2013, 268).

The creation of this powerful and animated food is quite exceptional and does not seem to occur in other ritual contexts like cemeteries or temples, or in houses. The total number of deposits in each tophet suggests that it occurred only very rarely: for example, one or two depositions per year in the tophets of Mozia, Tharros and Sulky (Xella 2013, 270). Probably, then, people would have attended this ritual only in exceptional circumstances, at a critical point in their lifecycle.

Children and animals as protective beings

In the Iberian case, the vast majority of child burials do not contain grave goods and animals are buried in simple deposits, without traces of any attempt to mark it (for instance, in stone or clay). Interestingly, babies buried (either cremated or not) in cemeteries present grave goods such as body decorative objects (Chapa 2008). At Castellet de Bernabé (Llíria), a fortified farm, two baby burials found in rooms 1 and 3 were deposited inside urns, one of which contained grave goods such as a miniature pickaxe, a small bronze ring, a small bronze bell and a marine shell. The infants buried were around six months old (Guérin 2003, 332).

Perhaps stillborn and newborns lacked a sufficient biography to be linked to other humans in their families, in terms of the accumulation of objects embedded with family stories and traditions. This argument has been used to suggest that these babies did not yet qualify as members of the group and consequently did not deserve public rites in cemeteries. From this perspective, these children were seen as inferior – less important than other members of the community – and that is why they appeared close to animal deposits, if we understand animals as being subordinate to humans. However, I argue that newborns and young animals, mostly ovicaprids, were significant persons and this is why they were buried beneath floors of houses.

From the data available we cannot say whether the depositions of children and animals correspond to single or repeated events. Nevertheless, the depositions of beings in dwellings suggest that spaces could also possess personhood and should be seen as animated beings because the burial of other creatures has been interpreted as animating buildings (Sanmartí Belarte 1997, 23; Belarte and Valenzuela-Lamas 2013, 179; Carter *et al.* 2015, 106). In addition, dwelling and working structures became highly charged spaces, not just because they were central loci for social strategies (Vives-Ferrandiz 2013), but also because they contained other beings in addition to living humans.

As already noted, the animals appear to have been selected deliberately; they mostly comprise sheep, goats, and to a lesser extent domestic fowl. Regarding the anthropic marks, there are no traces of chopping but there are cut marks indicating evisceration and disarticulation, thus suggesting that some animals were deposited partially intact, with the skin and hair still attached (Belarte and Valenzuela-Lamas

2013, 175–178). Domestic animals were preferred, especially animals that were the most commonly eaten. This selection is significant considering the domestic locus of the deposits, conforming to the logic of protecting or feeding the household and forging bonds between all the inhabitants.

Acknowledging the creation of a new ontological category comprising animals, stillborns and newborns means that domestic spaces are accompanied during their life cycle by these creatures which had special features and played specific roles in relation to buildings and their inhabitants. The infants and animals deposited must have maintained the links between living people, dead babies and animals and houses over long periods; in fact, some houses present several deposits.

Conclusions

The Iberian and the Phoenician cases present both differences and similarities. The ontological understanding of babies and animals is similar in the two instances, but in the Iberian case, the new being is created for apotropaic reasons. In contrast, in the Phoenician and Punic tophets babies and animals share the same space in different ways because they have the same role: they become a powerful food as their living qualities serve to feed divinities, and so they become animated food or animated objects.

In spite of their differences, the Iberian and the Phoenician cases have in common the importance of family rites that affect the wellbeing of households and all their members (people, objects, spaces, ancestors, the unborn, animals and divinities). This is clearly seen in the Iberian case, but it is also present in the tophet if we consider these sanctuaries and the rituals performed there as extensions of households in institutional contexts (Ferrer Martín and Lafrenz Samuels 2016, 544).

In this paper, I have tried to demonstrate that stillborn and newborn humans were considered unique bodies for their families which conceived them in the same terms as certain animals such as young ovicaprids. For the living human adults, both present the same features and share the same personhood, blurring the ontological borders between humans and animals and creating new categories of creatures. Another point to highlight in this relational web between diverse beings is the emotional dimension. It has been claimed that affection was not a strong emotion in ancient history due to the high infant mortality rates, and that this attitude would have underpinned people's behaviour with regard to premature babies, neonates and stillborns (Ariès 1962). However, this argument has been refuted in several cultures (Greek, Phoenician, medieval British *inter alia*) (Gilchrist 2005; Chaniotis 2012; Delgado and Ferrer 2012; Marín Ceballos 2016). I contend that the death of a baby, regardless of the reason (sacrifice, infanticide, natural death) is an emotionally intense moment and the family members negotiate their loss by transforming them into powerful other beings which feed divinities and protect the household. These creatures are formed and created through their association with animals, and in this transformation children and animals are understood not as separate entities but as unified beings with the same ontologies.

Acknowledgement

This study was written as part of the MINECO research project 'METIPO: Metales, tierra y poder durante la Edad del Hierro en el sureste de la Península Ibérica' (HAR2014-54414-P). A first draft of this article was written thanks to a DAAD (Deutsches Akademischer Austausch Dienst – German Academic Exchange Service) scholarship at the Eberhard-Karls Universität Tübingen (Tübingen, Germany) in summer 2017. I would like to thank the DAAD for the funding received and especially Prof. Jens Kamlah for supporting my proposal and accepting me as a research partner.

Notes

1 For a comprehensive recent approach to the topic with detailed references, see the edited volume by Xella (2013).
2 In fact, some of the north African tophets were excavated before the Salammbo one, but they were labelled as sanctuaries rather than tophets (d'Andrea 2104, 24).
3 See Fowler (2004) and Robb and Harris (2013) for multiple case-studies.

References

Alberti, B. (2016) Archaeologies of ontology. *Annual Review of Anthropology* 45, 163–179.

Almagro-Gorbea, M. and Lorrio, A. (2011) *Teutates. El Héroe fundador.* Bibliotheca Archaeologica Hispana 36. Madrid, Real Academia de la Historia.

Amadasi Guzzo, M. G. (2007–08) Il *tofet*. Osservazioni di un'epigrafista. In Bartoloni, G. and Benedettini, M. G. (eds) *Sepolti tra i vivi/Buried among the Living. Evidenza ed interpretazione di contesti funerari in abitato.* Scienze dell'Antichità XIV. Roma, Edizioni Quasar, 347–62.

Amadasi Guzzo, M. G. and Zamora, J. Á. (2013) The epigraphy of the Tophet. In Xella. P. (ed.) *The Tophet in the Phoenician Mediterranean.* Studi Epigrafici e Linguistici sul Vicino Oriente Antico 29–30. Verona, Essedue Edizioni, 159–92.

Ariès, P. (1962) *Centuries of Childhood: a social history of family life.* New York, Knopf.

Belarte, M. C. and Sanmartí, J. (1997) Espais de culte i pràctiques rituals a la Catalunya protohistòrica. *Quaderns de Prehistòria i Arqueologia de Castelló* 18, 7–32.

Belarte, M. C and Valenzuela-Lamas, S. (2013) Zooarchaeological evidence for domestic rituals in the Iron Age communities of north-eastern Iberia (present-day Catalonia) (sixth–second century BC). *Oxford Journal of Archaeology* 32(2), 163–186.

Bénichou Safar, H. (2012) Le statut de l'enfant punique et les objets funéraires. In A. Hermary and C. Dubois (eds) *L'enfant et la mort dans l'antiquité. III. Le matériel associé aux tombes d'enfants, Actes de la table ronde international organisée à la Maison des Sciences de l'Homme et de la Méditerranée d'Aix-enProvence, 20-22 janvier 2011.* Bibliothèque d'archéologie méditerranéenne et africaine 12. Aix-en Provence, Errance, 263–272.

Bénichou Safar, H. (2013) Les temple-boys: des desservants en puissance pour le sanctuaire. In F. Briquel-Chatonnet, C. Fauveaud and I. Gajda (eds) *Entre Carthage et l'Arabie heureuse.* Paris, De Boccard, 117–191.

Berrocal-Rangel, L. and Gardes, P. (2001) *Entre celtas e iberos. Las poblaciones protohistóricas de las Galias e Hispania.* Bibliotheca Archaeologica Hispana 8. Madrid, Real Academia de la Historia.

Bonet, H. (1995) *El Tossal de Sant Miquel de Llíria. La antigua Edeta y su territorio.* Valencia, Diputación Provincial de Valencia.

Bonnet, C. (2011) On gods and earth. The tophet and the construction of a new identity in Punic Carthage. In E. Gruen (ed.) *Cultural Identity in the Ancient Mediterranean.* Los Angeles, Getty Research Institute, 373–387.

Borić, D. and Robb, J. (2008) Body theory in archaeology. In D. Borić and J. Robb (eds) *Past Bodies. Body-centered research in archaeology*. Oxford, Oxbow Books, 1–8.

Borić, D., Harris, O. J. T, Miracle P. and Robb, J. (2013) The limits of the body. In J. Robb and O. J. T. Harris (eds) *The Body in History. Europe from the Palaeolithic to the Future*. Cambridge, Cambridge University Press, 32–63.

Caneva, S. G. and Delli Pizzi, R. (2014) Classical and Hellenistic statuettes of the so- called 'Temple Boys': A religious and social reappraisal. In C. Terranova (ed.) *La presenza dei bambini nelle religioni del mediterraneo antico. La vita e la morte, i rituali e i culti tra archeologia, antropologia e storia delle religioni.* Ariccia: Aracne, 495–521.

Carter, T., Haddow, S., Russell, N. Bogaard, A. and Tsoraki, C. (2015) Laying the foundations. Creating households at Neolithic Çatalhöyük. In I. Hodder and A. Marciniak (eds) *Assembling Çatalhöyük.* Themes in Contemporary Archaeology. Leeds, Maney Publishing, 97–110.

Chaniotis, A. (2012) Moving stones: Stones: The study of emotions in Greek inscriptions. In A. Chaniotis (ed.) *Unveiling Emotions: Sources and methods for the study of emotions in the Greek world.* Stuttgart, Franz Steiner, 91–129.

Chapa, T. (2003) La percepción de la infancia en el mundo ibérico. *Trabajos de Prehistoria* 60(1), 15–38.

Chapa, T. (2008) Presencia infantil y ritual funerario en el mundo ibérico. In F. Gusi, S. Muriel and C. Olària (eds) *Nasciturus, infans, puerulus vobis mater terra. La muerte en la infancia.* Sèrie de Prehistòria i Arqueologia. Castelló, Servei d'investigacions prehistòriques i arqueològiques-SIAP, 619–642.

Ciasca, A., Di Salvo, R., Castellino, M. and Di Patti, C. (1996) Saggio preliminare sugli incinerati del 'tofet' di Mozia. *Vicino Oriente* 10, 317–346.

D'Andrea, B. (2014) *I tofet del nord d'Africa dall'età arcaica all'età romana (VIII sec. A.C.–II sec. D.C. Studi Archeologici.* Collezione di Studi Fenici 45. Roma-Pisa, Fabrizio Serra Editore.

D'Andrea, B. and Giardino, S. (2011) 'Il Tofet: dove e perchè.' Alle origini dell'identità fenicia. *Vicino e Medio Oriente* XV, 133–157.

D'Andrea, B. and Giardino, S. (2013) Il Tofet: dove e perchè. L'identità fenicia, il Circolo de Cartagine e la fase tardo punica. *Bolletino di Archeologia Online* 4(1), 1–29.

Delgado Hervás. A. (2016) Mujeres, grupos domésticos y prácticas cotidianas en las comunidades fenicias y púnicas occidentales. In *Aspectos de la vida y la muerte en las sociedades fenicio-púnicas. XXIX Jornadas de arqueología fenicio-púnica.* Treballs del Museu Arqueològic d'Eivissa i Formenetera 74. Eivissa, Museu Arqueològic d'Eivissa i Formentera, 47–84.

Delgado, A. and Ferrer, M. (2012) La muerte visita las casas: mujeres, cuidados memorias familiares en los rituales funerarios fenicio-púnicos. In L. Prados (ed.) *La arqueología funeraria desde una perspectiva de género. II Jornadas internacionales de Arqueología y Género en la UAM.* Colección de Estudios 145. Madrid, Universidad Autónoma de Madrid, 123–156.

Di Salvo, R and and Di Patti, C. (2005) Gli esemplari incinerati del tofet di Mozia. Indagine osteológica. In A. Spanò Giammellaro (ed.) *Atti del V Congresso Internazionale di Studi Fenici e Punici* (Marsala-Palermo, 2–8 ottobre 2000). Palermo, Università de Palermo, II, 645–652.

Docter, R., Smits, E., Hakbijl, T., Stuijts, I. and van der Plicht, H. (2003) Interdisciplinary research on urns from the Carthaginian tophet and their contents. *Palaeohistoria* 43–44, 417–433.

Fariselli, A. C. (2012–13) Bambini e campanelli: note preliminari su alcuni 'effetti sonori' nei rituali funerari e votivi punici. *Byrsa. Arte, cultura e archeologia del Mediterraneo púnico* 21–22 and 23–24, 29–44.

Fedele, F. and Foster, G. V. (1988) Tharros: ovicaprini sacrificali e rituale del tofet. *Rivista di Studi Fenici* 14(1), 29–46.

Ferrer, M. and Lafrenz Samuels, K. (2016) Women's ritual practice in the western Phoenician and Punic world. In S. L. Budin and J. Mackintosh Turfa (eds) *Women in Antiquity. Real women across the Ancient world.* London/New York, Routledge, 533–551.

Fowler, C. (2004) *The Archaeology of Personhood. An Anthropological Approach.* Cambridge, Cambridge University Press.

Fowler, C. (2016) Relational personhood revisited. *Cambridge Archaeological Journal* 26(3), 397–412.

García Teyssandier, E. and Marzoli, D. (2013) Phönizische Gräber in Ayamonte (Huelva, Spanien): ein Vorbericht. *Madrider Mitteilungen* 54, 89–158.

Gilchrist, R. (2005) Cuidando a los muertos: las mujeres medievales en las pompas fúnebres familiares. In P. González Marcén, S. Montón Subías and M. Picazo Gurina (eds) *Dones i activitats de manteniment en temps de canvi.* Treballs d'Arqueologia 11. Bellaterra: Universitat Autónoma de Barcelona, 51–72.

Girguis, M., and Pla Orquín, R. (2015) Morti innocenti e fragili resti. Le sepolture infantili della necropoli fenicia e punica di Monte Sirai (VIII-IV sec. a.C.). *Sardinia, Corsica et Baleares Antiquae. An International Journal of Archaeology* XII, 37–66.

Grau Mira, I., Amorós López, I., de Miguel Ibánez, M. P., Iborra, P. and Segura Martí, J. M. (2015). Fundar la casa: prácticas rituales y espacio doméstico en el *oppidum* ibérico de El Puig d'Alcoi (Alacant). *Archivo Español de Arqueología* 88, 67–84.

Guérin, P. (2003) *El Castellet de Bernabé y el horizonte pleno edetano.* Serie de Trabajos Varios 101. Valencia, Servicio de Investigación Prehistórica.

Gusi, F. (1970) Enteramientos infantiles ibéricos en vivienda. *Pyrenae* 1, 65–70.

Harris, O. J. T and Robb, J. (2012) Multiple ontologies and the problem of the body in history. *American Anthropologist* 114(4), 668–679.

Hill, E. (2013) Archaeology and animal persons toward a prehistory of human-animal relations. *Environment and Society: Advances in Research* 4, 117–136.

Iborra, M. P. (2004) *La ganadería y la caza desde el Bronce Final hasta el Ibérico Final en el territorio valenciano.* Trabajos Varios 103. Valencia, Diputación Provincial de Valencia.

Izquierdo, I. (2000) *Monumentos funerarios ibéricos: los pilares-estela.* Serie de Trabajos Varios 98. Valencia, Diputación Provincial de Valencia.

Lillo-Carpio, P. (1993) *El poblado ibérico fortificado de los Molinicos de Moratalla (Murcia).* Serie arqueología 3. Murcia, Servicio de Patrimonio Histórico.

López-Bertran, M. and Vives-Ferrándiz, J. (2015) Miniatures from domestic contexts in Iron Age Iberia. *World Archaeology* 47(1), 80–93.

Marín Ceballos, M. C. (2003) El niño. In J. Á. Zamora (ed.) *El hombre fenicio. Estudios y materiales.* Roma, Escuela Española de Historia y Arqueología en Roma/CSIC, 199–215.

Marín Ceballos, M. C. (2016) La infancia en el mundo fenicio-púnico. In *Aspectos de la vida y la muerte en las sociedades fenicio-púnicas. XXIX Jornadas de arqueología fenicio-púnica.* Treballs del Museu Arqueològic d'Eivissa i Formenetera 74. Eivissa, Museu Arqueològic d'Eivissa i Formentera, 85–105.

Melchiorri, V. (2013) Osteological analysis in the study of the Phoenician and Punic tophet: A history of research. In P. Xella (ed.) *The Tophet in the Phoenician Mediterranean.* Studi Epigrafici e Linguistici sul Vicino Oriente Antico 29–30. Verona, Essedue Edizioni, 223–258.

Melchiorri, V. (2016) Child cremation sanctuaries ('tophets') and Early Phoenician colonisation: Markers of identity? In G. J. Burgers, L. Donnelan and V. Nizzo (eds) *Contextualising Early Colonisation, Proceedings of the International Congress.* Forum Romanum Belgicum 13(10). Roma, Belgisch Historisch Instituut Rome, 13–10.

Miracle, P. and Borić, D. (2008) Bodily beliefs and agricultural beginnings in Western Asia: animal-human hybridity re-examined. In D. Borić and J. Robb (eds) *Past Bodies. Body-Centered Research in Archaeology.* Oxford: Oxbow Books, 101–113.

Oggiano, I. (2012) Scope e modalità delle azioni rituale femminile nell'area sirio-palestinese del I millennio a. C. Il contributo dell'archeologia. In V. Nizzo and L. La Rocca (eds) *Antropologia e archeologia confronto: rappresentazioni e pratiche del sacro.* Roma, Editorial Service System, 223–249.

Oliver, A. (2006) *El Puig de la Nau, Benicarló.* Castelló, Proyecto Cultural de Castellón.

Olmos, R. (2000–01) Diosas y animales que amamantan: la transmisión de la vida en la iconografía ibérica. *Zephyrus* 53–54, 353–378.

Prados, L. 1997. Los ritos de paso y su reflejo en la toréutica ibérica. In R. Olmos and J. A. Santos Velasco (eds) *Iconografía ibérica, iconografía itálica: propuestas de interpretación y lectura.* Serie varia 3. Madrid, Universidad Autónoma de Madrid, 273–282.

Quinn, J. C. (2011) The cultures of tophet. Identification and identity in the Phoenician diaspora. In E. Gruen (ed.) *Cultural Identity in the Ancient Mediterranean.* Los Angeles, Getty Research Institute, 388–413.

Robb, J. and Harris, O. J. T. (2013) Body worlds and their history: some working concepts. In J. Rob and O. J. T. Harris (eds) *The Body in History. Europe from the Paleolithic to the Future.* Cambridge: Cambridge University Press, 7–31.

Rueda, C. (2011) *Territorio, culto e iconografía en los santuarios iberos del Alto Guadalquivir (ss. IV a.n.e. - I d.n.e.)* Textos CAAI, 3. Jaén, Universidad de Jaén.

Russell, N. (2012) *Social Zooarchaeology. Humans and animals in Prehistory.* Cambridge, Cambridge University Press.

Schwartz, J. H. Houghton, F., Macchiarelli, R. and Bondioli, L. (2010) Skeletal remains from Punic Carthage do not support systematic sacrifice of infants (http://www.plosone.org/article/info:doi/10.1371/journal.pone.0009177)

Spatafora, F. (2014) Seppellimenti infantili nella necropoli punica di Palermo. In C. Terranova (ed.) *La presenza dei bambini nelle religioni del mediterraneo antico. La vita e la morte, i rituali e i culti tra archeologia, antropologia e storia delle religioni.* Ariccia: Aracne, 291–308.

Tarradell, M. (1965) Enterramientos infantiles en el interior de habitaciones ibéricas. *Pyrenae* 1, 174–175.

Vives-Ferrándiz, J. (2013) Del espacio doméstico a la estructura social en un *oppidum* ibérico. Reflexiones a partir de la Bastida de les Alcusses. In S. Gutiérrez Lloret and I. Grau Mira (eds) *De la estructura doméstica al espacio social. Lecturas arqueológicas del uso social del espacio.* Alicante, Publicaciones de la Universidad de Alicante, 95–110.

Wilkens, B. (20129 Le offerte animali da alcune urne del *tofet* di Sulky. *Sardinia, Corsica et Baleares Antiquae. An International Journal of Archaeology* X, 45–59.

Xella, P. (2013) 'Tophet.' An overall interpretation. In P. Xella (ed.) *The Tophet in the Phoenician Mediterranean.* Studi Epigrafici e Linguistici sul Vicino Oriente Antico 29–30, 259–281. Verona, Essedue Edizioni.

Xella, P., Quinn, J. C., Melchiorri V. and van Dommelen, P. (2013) Phoenician bones of contention. *Antiquity* 87, 1199–1207.

Zamora, J. Á. (2015) 'Que coman y beban los dioses.' Religión y alimentación en el mundo fenicio (desde sus precedentes orientales al occidente púnico). In F. J. García Fernández, F. Lozano Gómez and A. Pereira Delgado (eds) *El alimento de los dioses. Sacrificio y consumo de alimentos en las religiones antiguas.* Spal Monografías XX. Sevilla, Universidad de Sevilla, 57–88.

Chapter 8

Maternities in Iberian societies. From day-to-day life to sacredness

Carmen Rueda Galán, Carmen Rísquez Cuenca and Ana B. Herránz Sánchez

The maternal function and its symbolic dimension. Proposals from (Iberian) archaeology

In this study we approach the analysis of maternity or, more correctly stated, maternities, as the plural of the term combines a diversity of situations and realities. Our intention in this study is to approach maternities as social experiences, as well as cultural constructions involving diverse defining aspects such as, for example, how to deal with procreation and maternity strategies and how their symbols are used. For this reason, we believe it is better to speak of the maternal function or maternal practices, as they bring us closer to multidirectional readings of the societies of the past, in our case, the Iberian societies (4th–3rd centuries BC).

The maternal function or practices bring us face to face with the importance of reproduction in the construction of the identity of the women of the past that, in the most traditional and conservationist 'theses', are justified fundamentally by dependency relations (Hernando 2005). However, the term maternity encompasses more than that; it goes beyond the exclusively biological and physical to take us into the social reality, as it denotes a status and confers a social and political role on women, incorporated into a fiercely private dimension. However, as we will see in the case of the Iberian societies, it is also public, at least in some aspects (Rísquez and Hornos 2005; Rísquez 2015; Prados 2016).

As other authors, such as Margarita Sánchez, have also accurately pointed out, maternity as a trans-historic concept has led to it traditionally being left out of the historiographic debate in archaeological practise (Sánchez 2008, 123–124). As a natural event, a necessary part of life, it has been taken for granted and not in need of archaeological analysis as a cultural process. Al this has resulted in it being conceived as a static activity that can be dealt with ahistorically. Only very recently has it been incorporated into the archaeological debate linked to feminist archaeology and the re-evaluation of the activities related to the female sphere. Far from these perceptions, we see maternal practise as a dynamic activity that obliges us to analyse it in a way that contextualises it in a historic space and time. The explanations must come from the social processes, not exclusively from the biological readings, which are unavoidably linked to reproduction.

Taking these approaches into account, the maternal functions in Iberian societies, as historical and cultural dynamics, are of course perceived as a process involving physiological aspects, together with others of a social, formative and learning nature.

Here we will focus mainly on the Iberian ritual context, in which the religious dimension of maternity provides us with fundamental clues for understanding the different moments or phases of maternity, taking into account their cyclical rather than linear nature. We have recently studied how in the rites of a cyclical nature the symbolic dimension of the important biotic cycles is also expressed (Rueda *et al.* 2016). Thus, at some sanctuaries, which we will look at later, we find the 'life changes' demarcated. These changes become essential moments that are heavily ritualised as symbols of individual and social learning. In this way, the introduction to maternity, basically the transition from virginity to the reproductive phase, becomes a primordial stage that is reflected in the votive record.

This is the perspective we have selected: from the day-to-day to the sacred, to be able to explain how a strong symbolic and religious dimension emanates from the maternal function. In this way, the biological experience of pregnancy and giving birth, as well as the psychological experience of maternity, is very rich in religious consequences. Knowledge of the pain or anguish brings a woman very close to a position of religious creativity (Marian-Balasa 2013) and symbolic devices are generated that situate the maternal function as a cultural activity sustained by the mechanisms of ritual learning and sanction (transformation, protection, propitiation, aggregation, etc.). These norms are taken on and learned through reiteration and also contribute to the transmission of certain values and tools that are included in the mechanisms of teaching functions, in which those of maternity are incorporated (López-Beltrán and Vives-Ferrándiz 2015, 10–11). The succession of these stages (we insist on evaluating maternity as a dynamic experience) contributes to the survival of the established social models and the conservation of the social roles (Montepaone 1999, 14) defined and organised by rules established by the society, in this case that of the Iberians, and more specifically in our study, the peoples of the Alto Guadalquivir.

The maternal practices, therefore, are reflected in the archaeological record, as well as in the religious or ritual dimension, understanding that the rite is a fundamental part of the symbolic language that projects the values of a specific society (Bell 1992). From a methodological perspective, the religious manifestations have a materiality, sometimes intentional and inherent to the cult that originated them, subject to acts of fossilisation of a petition through survival resources. From that materiality, albeit with lacunas and inaccuracies, we can approach some of the nuances of the ritual practices, as well as aspects of behaviour, feelings and fears, as the 'immaterial' is conceptualised and expressed in material forms. Under these perspectives we go beyond the passive concept of the objects and look in depth at aspects that surpass mere visual representations, investigating the channels of sensorial and emotive empathy necessary, for example, in the mythological constructions and ritual (Hamilakis 2015), in which we frame the religious dimension of maternity.

On the other hand, from this methodological point of view, it is necessary to evaluate the importance of the ritual actions inserted into their cultural landscapes, their political and social territories, approaching the whole from a coherent interdisciplinary practise, distanced from the traditional historical-cultural perspectives. This forces us to look at the archaeological record and include all the variables of analysis, without underestimating the information contributed by aspects or finds, that are traditionally perceived as secondary. Under these approaches, the archaeological analysis of the image is an outstanding point in our analysis. The figurative image offers us key data, albeit taking into account a contextualised reading, understanding it as another part of the liturgical framework. The body, as a social construction and space of memory, becomes a valid tool for interpreting aspects related to the religious identities of the communities involved in that cult. Likewise, we focus on the forms in which the experiences created through the bodies generate an ideal framework for understanding the cultural system from an internal reading, in other words, of a religious structure organised for a territory, a shrine, a town, etc. (Hamilakis *et al.* 2002; Fisher and DiPaolo 2003, 228–229; Joyce 2005; Boric and Robb 2008; Boric 2013). In this context we integrate the analysis of the female iconography and the construction of the body of the woman associated with the maternal functions in their preparative phase; as a gestating body and, finally, linked to the achievement of maternity.

Maternal practices as a dynamic and the rite as a process

Our analysis begins with the 4th century BC, because that is the phase in which the aristocratic system became fully consolidated in the Iberian societies as the key structure in the development of social and political relations (Ruiz and Molinos 1999; 2007; Aranegui 2012 for an in-depth view of the Iberian societies). From the religious point of view, this stage coincides with the moment in which votive contexts begin to be perceptible as true treasuries that accumulate offerings of various kinds (García Cardiel 2013). Thus, for example, the supraterritorial sanctuaries of Cástulo, Collado de los Jardines (Santa, Elena, Jaén) and La Cueva de la Lobera (Castellar, Jaén) (Nicolini *et al.* 2004; Rueda 2011; Risquez *et al.* 2015), on which we focus a large part of our analysis, become key centres for analysing the forms of religiosity specific to the 4th and 3rd centuries BC. As places of cohesion, to which pilgrimages were held on certain dates, they took on a fundamental role in the political organisation of a vast territory (Nicolini 1969; Prados 1992; Rueda 2011). In sanctuaries vital rituals were performed for a very wide religious community and can be seen through their votive deposits, with many thousands of offerings that include huge numbers of personalised offerings and figurative representations. The bronze ex-votos are a clear example of this process (Nicolini 1969; Prados 1992; Rueda 2011). As an offering that projects the image of the bestower, their attitude and their ritual motivations, they form part of and participate in a system of socio-ideological codes that includes aspects related to the social, political, religious, gender or age spheres. Beyond a merely formal reading, the systematic incorporation of this iconography speaks to us of the expansion of social participation in the cult, as the preceding models that exclusively represented the aristocracy become fractured and transformed and the image of the clientele is incorporated as a formula of cohesion (Rueda 2008). In the same way, the offering of the ex-voto involves a public display that contributes to strengthening community ties and has an immediate consequence: the transmission of religious identity, as well as cultural identity.

The ritual organisation is show in these places of worship as a sequence of the biotic cycle in which the change stages indicate central moments in social learning. In this context, the ritual practices related to maternity are not associated with an independent religiosity and are categorised as secondary or minor. Far from this idea, they are integrated into this religious structure and illustrate the complex relations between the masculine and the feminine, which are incorporated as attributable aspects in the official religious system.[1]

From these perspectives, the rites related to maternity are perceived, on the liturgical plain and in those sanctuaries, as a process or cycle in which it is possible to demarcate different phases or moments. This temporality (the times in the ritual) marks a progressive chain of learning in which habits of religious behaviour are acquired. These share a common feature, as they are linked to transformation, in other words, 'to the event of coming-to-be or becoming.' The key is in the transforming force that intervenes as a constant concept in these rituals and is linked to ceremonies related to propitiation (procreation); protection (gestation and delivery), healing (post-partum) and aggregation (maternity). Following this dynamic and this process we approach the different moments of ritual behaviour related to maternity in the sanctuaries of the Alto Guadalquivir (Fig. 8.1).

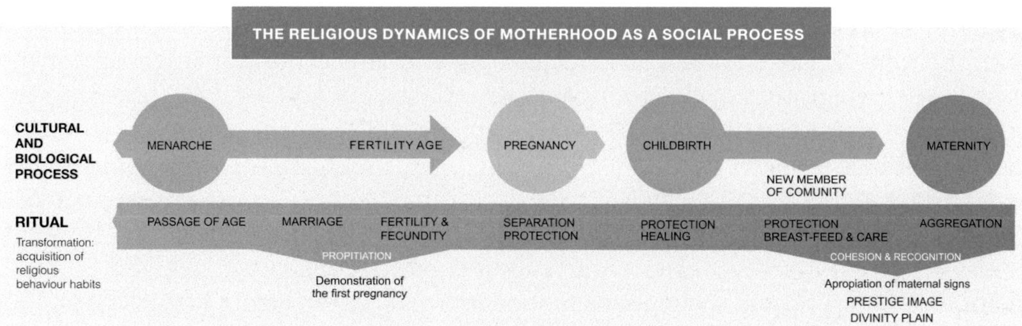

Figure 8.1: The religious dynamics of motherhood as a process. Interpretive scheme

The transition from virginity to the reproductive stage

In the Iberian societies and in the female sphere, the passage from virginity to fertility would have been sanctioned as a key moment, heavily ritualised and standardised through practices aimed at visualising the changes and markers of the transition to a mature age. Coming of age rites mark the beginning of the ritual chain of this religious structure in the analysed places of worship.[2] They delimit a fundamental moment in the individual life that is related to the introduction into the active social life that supports social maintenance and reproduction and that we sense would have been subject to complex and highly structured rituals. As a symbolic and functional reference of the introduction to the community, the rites of age are promotional within the religious structure (Bernardini 1986, 81–82) and become necessary for the survival of the established social models, as well as for maintaining the religious legacy in which they are included (Montepaone 1999, 14). The functions acquired following the initiation rite are demarcated by gender, in such a way that the female universe tends to be linked to the biological and reproductive cycle and female education is linked to the initiation process itself. In this respect, the initiation rite should be understood as a transition to the sexed world (*puberalii* rites) and in the female sphere it is linked to the menarche.

The rites of passage cycle is formalised with the participation of the spouse and is thus visualised in these shrines through a very precise iconography,[3] which involves special formulas uniquely linked to this ritual. In this way, we see two moments in the rite: the preparation-presentation of the ceremony, in which the traits of youth are present and identifiable through formal and attributive aspects, such as the hairstyle; and the moment the coming of age rite is reached, which involves transformation and the adoption of a new identity that marks access to the community. On a formal level, this change involves, among other things, the cutting of the hair and the adoption of the signs specific to the mature age, a ritual act that is of considerable consequence in specific cults in the Greek world, such as the worship of Artemis or Persephone,[4] or that of Latia, with the shrine of Lavinium[5] as a reference.

The cutting and offering of hair in public ceremonies can be understood as a prenuptial rite alluding to prosperity linked to the future social role (Garwood 2011, 262), which is of extreme importance for the whole of the aristocracy in the case of the Iberians.[6] As a promotional action charged with learning resources it is consummated with the re-aggregation of the transformed person. This is the starting point for the progressive integration of the young people into society and, in particular, into the structure of rites specific to adulthood (Fig. 8.2).

The periodic dynamic of the worship, that begins with these coming of age rites, is also adapted to a ritual calendar set according to the natural and agricultural cycle. Thanks to recent research, including archaeoastronomic analyses (Esteban *et al.* 2014), we have been able to partially reconstruct the ritual calendar of these shrines. In both of them the equinoxes appear to play a regulating role in the annual or seasonal customs, along with astrological phenomena linked to the sanctury, in the case of Collado de los Jardines, and to the sunset, at Cueva de la Lobera. In the latter

Figure 8.2: Images in bronze that represent the rite of step of age. Offerings proceeding from the sanctuary of Collado de los Jardines (archive G. Nicolini)

sanctuary it was possible to define a visual phenomenon interpreted as the hierophany of a female deity that alludes to a possible divine mythical narration. This would have contributed to objectivising the rite as experiences undergone collectively and understood and codified within this religious community (Rísquez *et al.* 2015). The importance that marks and defines the turn of the seasons must be related directly to the agricultural calendar and the festivities that derive from farming activities, which are set within these temporal frameworks. In this regulation of time, once again we see constant reference to the concept of transformation.

Procreation strategies

Procreation strategies are channelled through specific practices related to fertility and fecundity. Marriage may have been the explicit condition for celebrating these propitiatory rites aimed at evaluating the ability to conceive. These rituals occupy a very important place in the structure of the Cástulo sanctuaries. On a quantitative level, they predominate as one of the best-represented practices, in which female participation is perfectly regulated by diverse formulas. This empowers a language of complementarity, in which the spouse is the protagonist and the nude the formula used in this type of petition. It is a resource charged with symbolic intentionality

Figure 8.3: Strategies of procreation: the approximation of the bodies (Álvarez-Ossorio 1941: pls lxviii; Nicolini 1969: pls. xxxii)

and a correct form of presenting oneself before the divinity, which is sometimes accompanied by resources of exaggeration and hypertrophy that allude to the sphere of sexual maturity and procreation (Rueda and Olmos 2012, 78–80).

The spouse appears in gestural syntony, showing himself in an equivalent situation and sharing the offering. In some cases, the construction of the naked male and female bodies is so similar that only the indication of the sex helps us differentiate their genders (Álvarez-Ossorio 1941, pls xxv, xxvi, xxxii, lxviii and xcviii; Nicolini 1969, pl. xxxii, 3). This is an intentional process: the body is conceived in exactly the same way in terms of proportions and resources, even sharing such traits as the breast and the navel that, in some male representations appear as common attributes. In this sacred context, the petition is transferred from the female to the male sphere; it is shared, indicating the social importance of procreation and reproduction, which transcend strict biological limits (Fig. 8.3).

This does not exclude an exclusively female corporal and gestural language, which is related to and shares a similar ritual context in which the women redirect themselves, exclusively (and individually) towards a 'body language of exhibition'. In this respect, in the territory of Cástulo we have an abundant and quite homogeneous type of iconography that depicts women as completely veiled; on presenting themselves to the divinity, they open their robes and show their breasts or pubis, sometimes indicated by an incision in the metal (Rueda 2012, n° 44). This is a direct language that focuses on a precise moment in the ritual, involving a body language, robes and attributes specific to women (Fig. 8.4).

Protection rituals during pregnancy and before labour

Reproduction and pregnancy become a fundamental expression of collective worship, as they go beyond the individual dimension and are contextualised socially. As we have already indicated, for women the experiences linked to gestation are, in large part, culturally determined. In this way, their fears and the channels through which they are remedied cannot be separated from the social structure and established modes of religiosity.

Figure 8.4: Strategies of procreation: the bodies and the gestures in feminine. Offerings in bronzes of the Archaeological Museum of Seville, Museum of Jaen and Museum of Castellar (Rueda et al. *2016)*

Pregnancy (conceptually) can be included in an extensive range of rites of passage, in the manner in which it is a temporal, liminal period in the life of a woman that summarises and binds together a present condition and a future circumstance (Lee 2012, 23). In societies such as the Iberian, the first pregnancy takes on a vital importance as a testimony to the ability to gestate and, consequently, to assume an important family and social role (Giuman 1999, 47). In ritual terms they must have had their own channels of development, that may have been different to the ceremonies held within the framework of the protection rites, whose culmination is the re-aggregation of the woman.

Taking into account these presuppositions, the image of gestating women is practically imperceptible in the territorial sanctuaries of Cástulo. We have only one example from Collado de los Jardines that alludes to gestation, in which the gestural (hands and belly) and attributive (fruit such as quince or grenadine) symbology is quite explicit (Izquierdo 2004) (Fig. 8.5). This panorama can be applied to the rest of

Figure 8.5: The protection of the childbirth and the maternity: ritual offerings and funeral symbols. Images in terracotta of the tomb 127A of the Albufereta and votive offering in bronze of the sanctuary of Collado de los Jardines (Museum Conde Valencia de Don Juan) (images: Léxico de Iconografía Ibérica, CSIC; Moreno Conde 2016)

the Iberian territories, in which images of gestating women are almost completely absent. There are some exceptions to this rule, such as the acephalous image from the shrine of Torreparedones (Baena, Córdoba) (Cunliffe and Fernández Castro 1999, fig. 6.39) or the terracotta piece deposited in the Tomb 127A of La Albufereta (Alicante) necropolis (Olmos 2007). This latter example is particularly interesting because of its context. It is an interment dated to the 2nd century BC (as the most recent limit) that is defined as a symbolic accumulation of materials from different periods, in which the female image, on diverse media and from different chronologies, has an obvious protagonism. In this closed context, of particular note is a set of terracotta pieces through which the woman is depicted as nurturing (*kourotrophos)* and gestating. These could be related, together with the Attic iconography, to discourses focusing on initiation rites and youth. And all this without being able to completely separate the image of the gestating woman and mother from a mediating function that endows the context with the afterlife.

Returning to the sanctuaries of Cástulo, the scarcity (or rather almost complete absence) of iconography alluding to this rituality perhaps shows us that the rites related to gestation would have been included in the practices of separation, prior to the re-aggregation into the community marked by the post-partum period. It is

Figure 8.6: Illustration of a childbirth in the Iberian period (Iron Age) (Rumor for GENDAR Project)

possible that the private sphere took precedence and that the rituality would have been carried out in the bosom of the family (Fig. 8.6). As an individual experience, framed within a collective (not public) dimension, pregnancy and the ways of managing the rituals would have been linked mainly to the home.[7] The footprint in the archaeological record is, therefore, more difficult to identify. On the other hand, we should not lose sight of the fact that, as a separation rite, the gestation period would have involved important religious and symbolic aspects, such as the concept of contamination associated with the vulnerability during a period of major physical and psychological changes. These determining factors for this condition are incompatible with the processes of ritual mobility, such as long-distance pilgrimages to visit the place of worship. Whether they are explicit prohibitions of the presence of gestating women in sacred places or due to taboos or reasons of protection, the ritual dynamics in the analysed sanctuaries mark a parenthesis in the ritualised biotic cycle itself. The chain is broken to exclude these ritualities, which remain framed in other development contexts. In the future we will need to study them in greater depth.

We have many more limitations when it comes to approaching the practices related to protection before birth, although they were probably part of the mechanisms designed to bring about the success of the whole gestational process. In other Mediterranean areas, the prescriptions related to the protection of childbirth are perfectly integrated (Dillon 2003). In the Iberian religious space these protection mechanisms must have existed, possibly also assigned to a family or private area and linked to precautions taken against dangers, maledictions or contamination. At the analysed sanctuaries there are no representations that allude to childbirth or to related surgical instruments (or their miniaturisation). Therefore, an indirect reading could complete this partial and complex-to-approach panorama from the archaeological record. Thus, the analysis of the female divinity present in these shrines contributes to delineating the modes of religiosity and channels of empathy, emotional preparation and relationship with the divine sphere, also in relation to the adoption of symbolic models linked to maternity. An exceptional image associated with Collado de los Jardines shrine alludes to construction of a divine iconography through the image of maternity. Far from defending the platitudes that have linked maternity with the image of the divinity and distancing ourselves from the generic models extrapolated from different contexts and images (Couto-Ferreira 2016), we analyse this iconography as part of its religious system and its own ritual-visual expression. It is an exceptional image (Olmos 2000–2001; Rueda 2012) from different points of view. Firstly, although it is made of bronze, it is not an ex-voto. The configuration of the piece, which is larger than normal, leads us to believe that it is a figure of worship, conceived to be displayed in some part of the shrine. The circular pedestal contains an orifice for fitting a rod, which has not been preserved, but would have allowed it to be exhibited in a prominent position. This is a truly remarkable technical feature. The other exceptional aspect is its specific iconography. It depicts a female figure holding a child in her arms, who is suckling at her left breast. Another feature, equally as important, completes the image: the presence of the duck on the pedestal, which would have framed symmetrically (although only one is preserved) the setting of the scene. In Iberian iconography, the bird is a sign linked to the female divinity that has among its connotations a link to the sphere of fecundity and female initiation (Olmos and Tortosa 2010). It is also associated with the corpus of bronze ex-votos from these shrines, accompanying images of girls going through the coming of age rites.[8] Under these presuppositions, this image can be interpreted as a deity, in its significance as a *kourotrophos*. This appears to confirm that these places of worship were under the tutelage of a female divinity of a territorial nature, depicted as a nurturer, but also as an icon of the transformative force of Nature, as can be seen in the hierophany of Castellar. Therefore, it seems that the cult was largely sustained by the myth of the female divinity that, as an aggregator of diverse functions, explains this complex religious system that includes practices related to maternity.

Puerperium rituals

At this point we introduce a type of ex-voto that alludes symbolically to the ritual space and directly to the area of female reproductivity: the anatomic ex-votos

Figure 8.7: Votive offerings in bronze that represent uteruses and female breasts. They come from the sanctuaries of Collado de los Jardines and La Cueva de la Lobera (Museum of Jaén, Rueda et al. *2016)*

that depict uteruses and breasts. This iconography, which is habitual in cultural contexts such as the Etruscan or the Italic – in which they are documented in very many complexes – (Comella 1981), is less represented at Iberian religious sites. Nevertheless, they appear as a very numerous votive category in the votive deposits of the Cástulo shrines, always made in bronze (Prados 1991; 2013). Within the uterus category we see typological differences (Álvarez-Ossorio 1941, pl. cxlvii; Moreno Conde 2006, 539; Rueda 2011, fig. 58; Vives-Ferrándiz 2013, 36). On the one hand, there is a more numerous type that depicts a general scheme of the female reproductive apparatus, combined with others that depict the vagina or perhaps the placenta.[9] With respect to the depiction of female breasts, diverse resources are used that vary from the more schematic to the more realistic examples, although those made on plaques appear to predominate (Fig. 8.7).

Traditionally framed in the sphere of maternity propitiation rites, they must undoubtedly be conceived as symbols of the feminine, that may summarise diverse aspects or meanings. Therefore, we cannot understand them from a static point of view, but rather the opposite; they are images that can be integrated into different moments of the ritual linked to female fertility and maternity. In other words, they evoke maternity, but we cannot rule out a link to the rituals of protection or even of healing related to gestation and giving birth. The affections deriving from labour could be accompanied by the offering of this type of image, within the sphere of the healing cults, as documented in other areas (Oberhelman 2014, 57–58).

The success of pregnancy and childbirth

The positive outcome of pregnancy and labour, especially when it is the first pregnancy, would involve the re-aggregation of the woman and her incorporation into the ritual structure. This new relational context involves specific symbolic and ritual expressions related to the sphere of infancy, which is intimately linked to the female space.

In it we have to understand the very few representations of newborns documented solely at Collado de los Jardines (Fig. 8.8). They are an outstanding iconographic medium for analysing diverse aspects related to the projection of the image of the child, an intentionally ambiguous image, devoid of social or religious attributes, in which it is not possible to determine the gender in iconographic terms (*bambini in face*). Their presence leads us to propose certain questions regarding infancy, as well as its significance, if in their deposition we only have to see the ex-votos of women seeking a petition linked to fertility and a healthy maternity (propitiation rituals), or if we

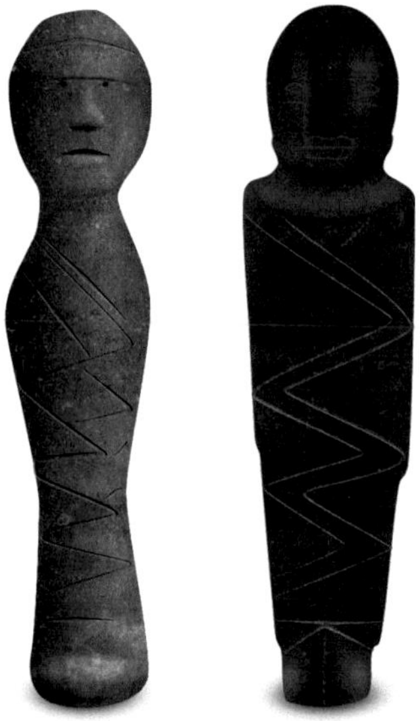

Figure 8.8: Representations of newborns documented at sanctuary of Collado de los Jardines (Rueda et al. *2016)*

should perceive an idea more subordinate to other aspects of the community, such as a petition for the survival of the little ones and linking them also to the sphere of death (protection rituals) (Prados 2013, 333–335). But this type of representation is highly exclusive and minimal, and we do not believe they should be read as part of the collective dynamic and identified as a symbolic representation of the community. Other interpretations link these offerings to rituals of presentation, tutelage and divine protection. Should they be associated with the aristocracy as class images? We can expand on this idea.

The mother–child relationship is more evident in a singular image. We are referring to a piece from Collado de los Jardines that depicts a woman holding a small child in her arms.[10] Made of terracotta, it depicts this scheme of the maternal relationship that, far from interpreting it as a deity, we believe alludes to the sphere in which maternity takes place, in a line of representation very close to those found in others sacred contexts, such as La Albufereta necropolis (Olmos 2007). In the terracotta piece from Despeñaperros we see accentuated the communicative language with the deity of both protagonists (mother and child), who are presented in true corporal and gestural syntony (Fig. 8.9).

This iconographic formulation alludes to the maternal practise in the explicit relationship between the female sphere and early infancy, in which the role of the woman in relation to nurturing and education is especially important (Sánchez 2008, 123). This relational space is transferred to the shrine, framed in practices of presentation-protection, being one of the few examples (together with the aforementioned image of the newborns) in which earliest childhood is included in the community space of religious identity. In fact, this type of representation is exclusive; it is not serialised, nor reiterated. Once again, we are faced with a *unicum* that, understood in the context, could be related to the adoption of 'free and unique formulas of representation' specific to the aristocracy.[11] We suggest that in this context of strongly hierarchised relations, access to these presentation rites (and the ways in which they are visualised) could be linked directly to the aristocratic class. Thus, use of the universal language alluding to the link between mother and child is restricted, as a sign of prestige, to those men or women who make it possible to perpetuate the lineage. In this way, the presentation rites (exhibition of the legitimate children) and protection of infancy (continuity of the

Figure 8.9: A maternal image: terracotta from the sanctuary of Collado de los Jardines. Museum of Jaén (Rueda et al. *2016)*

lineage) become fundamental practices for the aristocracy, as well as those connected to overseeing the education of 'the best' by the divinity.

Some reflections by way of conclusion

The study of maternal functions in the Iberian religious space reveals that it is an analysis with a high degree of complexity. As soon as we distance ourselves from the perspectives that view maternity as an ahistorical factor and delve more deeply into it from the social readings, we observe the richness of the nuances, which can only be understood in the specific social context. In the case of the Iberian society, through an analysis from a religious perspective and from the ritual structure that identifies southern Oretania for the 4th–3rd centuries BC, we observe how maternity is conceived liturgically as a process and is linked to the importance of female rituality, which occupies an essential space especially linked to the rites of aggregation (Cenerini 2002, 126).

The analysis of a specific ritual system, understood and contextualised in its social structure and political territory, allows us to perceive nuances in the use and function of maternal practices and their symbols of representation. Thus, from the reading of processes, we document how the resources are heterogeneous and serve to give value to different aspects:

1. The cohesion of the community. The stages of the maternal cycle related to the propitiation of fertility and the protection of pregnancy and labour are integrated into the social identification practices, which incorporate different strata of the community. They are evaluated from a ritual point of view, being the most representative liturgical practices in these sanctuaries, as well as from a symbolic point of view, as they represent the channels for achieving the success of procreation strategies that are reinvested on a community social and religious level. At this point we particularly observe the importance of female rituality in the aggregation practices that accentuate the complementarity with the masculine sphere, as well as occupying its own unique area of development and visualisation.
2. Maternity as an image of prestige, that is incorporated based on unique and restricted models, such as the maternal-child image or the representation of infancy. These highlight the practices linked to the perpetuation of the lineage and the recognition of the legitimate children who take on an important role in the community from an early age: daughters and sons who increase the power and prestige of a lineage. The symbols of maternity, associated with infancy, are used as an image of class and a channel for claiming parental ties.
3. Maternity linked to the divine plain. The image of the nurturing divinity is incorporated as a symbol that contributes to the regulation of the cycles and complements the divine language of the transformation linked to Nature, a concept, we emphasise, that is constant in the cycle related to maternal practices.

The approach we take in this article opens the way to an investigation of the archaeological analysis of the record related to the sphere of maternity. In the future we will need to incorporate other areas that will undoubtedly enrich the proposals made in these pages, such as the funerary sphere and the domestic environment, where the imprint of women and their spaces of development will allow us to expand the map of relations linked to the maternal functions.

Acknowledgement

This paper has been prepared as part of the Resources for the investigation of the archaeology of women and gender in Spain Excellence Project, GENDAR (HUM-1904). Junta de Andalucía.

Notes

1 For other areas of contrast, cf. Cid (2014, 10).

2 Although not restricted to them, the rituals related to coming of age are documented in diverse territories and shrines, framed in equally heterogeneous religious structures. Cf. Rueda (2013); Grau and Amorós (2013); Machause *et al.* (2014); Ruiz *et al.* (2015).

3 For the male variations, cf. Álvarez-Ossorio (1941, pl. xli); Nicolini (1969, pl. xiv, 5–6); Prados (1992, 331–333, nos 359, 361, 371 and 376). For the female examples, cf. Álvarez-Ossorio (1941, i and ii); Nicolini (1969, pl. xx, 1–4); Prados (1992, 343, no. 556); Moreno Conde (2006, no. 14); Rueda (2012, no. 2).

4 Of particular note are depictions alluding to the cutting and offering of hair, as in the reliefs from the sanctuary of Lokri, in which we can see this type of representation, cf. Dillon (2003, 225).

5 Associated with the cult of *Athena Ilias*, in which the age for holding these rituals is set at around 15, cf. Torelli (1984).

6 Aspects that are also transferred to and visualised in other religious areas, such as burial sites and grave goods. In this case, we also have to highlight the presence of objects that allude to the female rites of passage in a strongly prestigious language. Thus, the Attic crater of the Bath of Helena, documented in the princely chamber of Piquía that, forming part of an assemblage of grave goods and a more complex narrative programme, alludes to the preparation of the bride in an imported, but perfectly understandable language in the heart of the Iberian religious traditions. Cf. Rueda and Olmos (2015).

7 In some cases, such as in the Hittite societies, it is formalised in what has been defined as 'family abduction', cf. Beckman (2016).

8 There is an exceptional example from Collado de los Jardines. The young woman is wearing ritual attire linked to the rites of passage and she is holding a bird, representing the offering of the moment prior to the consummation of the rite. Cf. Álvarez-Ossorio (1941, pl. i); Prados (1992, 349).

9 For the difference in types, cf. Rueda *et al.* (2016, 66–67).

10 It is an example that has its closest parallel in the terracotta piece from the La Algaida sanctuary, attributed to the 4th–2nd centuries BC, identified as a nurturing divinity in one of the formulations of the Mediterranean mother goddess. It is a model of expression specific to the central and western Mediterranean present in the Iberian world from the 4th century BC and whose first prototypes may have been reproduced from imported moulds. Cf. Rueda (2011, fig. 66); Rueda *et al.* (2016, 68–69).

11 In an overall reading of the thousands of offerings we have at our disposal, we can see how individuality is a way of differentiating class that contrasts with seriation, a resource related to clientele representation that adapts to a series of standardised codes. Cf. Rueda (2008).

References

Álvarez-Ossorio, F. (1941) *Catálogo de los exvotos ibéricos del Museo Arqueológico Nacional.* Madrid, Museo Arqueológico Nacional.

Aranegui, C. (2012) *Los iberos ayer y hoy. Arqueologías y culturas.* Colección Historia. Madrid, Ed. Marcial Pons.

Beckman, G. (2016) Birth and motherhood among the Hittites. In S. Budin and J. Macintosh Turfa (eds) *Women in Antiquity: Real women across the ancient world rewriting antiquity*. London/New York, Routledge, 319–328.

Bell, C. (1992) *Ritual Theory, Ritual Practice*. Oxford, Oxford University Press.

Bernardi, B. (1986) Initation rites and post-puberal transition. In U. Bianchi (ed.) *Transition Rites. Cosmic, Social and Individual Order.* Storia delle Religione 2. Roma, L'Erma di Bretschneider, 81–90.

Boric, D. (2013) Mortuary practices, bodies and persons in the Neolithic and Early-Middle Copper Age of southeast Europe. In C. Fowler, J. Harding and D. Hofmann (eds) *The Oxford Handbook of Neolithic Europe*. Oxford, Oxford University Press, 1–23.

Boric, D. and Robb, J. (2008) *Past Bodies: Body-centered research in archaeology*. Oxford, Oxbow Books.

Cenerini, F. (2002) *La donna romana. Modelli e raltà*. Bologna, Ed. Il Mulino.

Cid, R. Mª (2014) Los santuarios suburbanos y la religión de las matronas. El Templo de Fortuna Muliebris en la Roma republicana. In J. Mangas and M. A. Novillo (eds) *Santuarios suburbanos y del territorio en las ciudades romanas*. Madrid, Universidad Autónoma de Madrid, 9–29.

Comella, A. (1981–82) Tipologia e diffusione dei complessi votivi in italia in epoca medio e tardo republicana. Contributo alla storia dell'artigianato antico. *Antiquité* 93. Melanges de l'ecole Française de Rome, 717–803.

Couto-Ferreira, M. E. (2016) Beging mothers or acting (like) mothers? Constructing motherhood in ancient Mesopotamia. In S. Budin and J. Macintosh Turfa (eds) *Women in Antiquity: Real women across the ancient world rewriting antiquity*, 25–34. London/New York, Routledge.

Cunliffe, B. and Fernández Castro, Mª C. (1999) *The Guadajoz Project. Andalucía in the first millennium BC. Volume 1: Torreparedones and its hinterland*. Monograph 47. Oxford, Oxford University Committee for Archaeology.

Dillon, M. (2003) *Girls and Women in Classical Greek Religion*. London/New York, Routledge

Esteban, C., Rísquez, C. and Rueda, C. (2014) An evanescent vision of the divinity. The equinoctial sun at the iberian sanctuary of Castellar. *International Journal of Mediterranean Archaeology and Archaeometry* 14(3), 99–106.

Fisher, G. and Dipaolo, D. (2003) Embodying identity in archaeology: introduction. *Cambridge Archaeological Journal* 13(2), 225–230.

Garwood, P. (2011) Rites of passage. In T. Insoll (ed.) *The Oxford Handbook of the Archaeology of Ritual and Religion*. Oxford, Oxford University Press, 261–283.

García Cardiel, J. (2013) De la hierogamia a la ofrenda. El contacto con la divinidad en el mundo ibérico. *Mediterráneo Antico* 16(1), 277, 308.

Giuman, M. (1999) *La dea, la vergine, il sangue. Archeologia di un culto femminile*. Milano, Longanesi & C. Biblioteca di Archeologia.

Grau, I. and Amorós, I. (2013) La delimitación simbólica de los espacios territoriales ibéricos: el culto en el confín y las cuevas-santuario. In C. Rísquez and C. Rueda (eds) *Santuarios Iberos: territorio, ritualidad y memoria. Actas del Congreso El santuario de La Cueva de la Lobera de Castellar. 1912–2012*. Jaen, ASODECO, 183–212.

Hamilakis, Y. (2015) *Arqueología y los sentidos. Experiencia, memoria y afecto*. Madrid, JAS Arqueología Editorial.

Hamilakis, Y., Pluciennik, M. and Tarlow, S. (2002) *Thinking Through the Body: Archaeologies of corporeality*. New York, Kluwer Academic/Plenum.

Hernando, A. (2005) Mujeres y Prehistoria. En torno a la cuestión del origen del patriarcado. In M. Sánchez (ed.) *Arqueología y género*. Granada, Universidad de Granada, 73–108.

Izquierdo, I. (2004) Exvotos ibéricos como símbolos de fecundidad: un ejemplo femenino en bronce del Instituto y Museo Valencia de Don Juan (Madrid). *Saguntum (P.L.A.V.)* 36, 111–124.

Joyce, R. (2005) Archaeology of the body. *Annual Reviews in Anthropology* 34, 139–158.

Lee, M. M. (2012) Maternity and Miasma. Dress and the transition from Parthenos to Gune. In L. Hackworth and P. Salzman-Mitchell (eds) *Mothering and Motherhood in Ancient Greece and Rome*. Austin, University of Texas Press, 23–42.

López-Beltrán, M. and Vives-Ferrándiz, J. (2015) Miniatures from domestic contexts in Iron Age Iberia, *World Archaeology* 47, 80–93.

Machause, S., Pérez, A., Vidal, P. and Sanchís, A. (2014) Prácticas rituales ibéricas en la Cueva del Sapo (Chiva, Valencia): más allá del caliciforme. *Zephyrus* LXXIV, 157–179.

Marian-Balasa, M. (2013) Maternity as a souce of religion. *Journal of Ethnography and Folklore* 1–2, 101–108.

Montepaone, C. (1999) *Lo spazio del margine. Prospettive sul femminile nella comunitá antica.* Roma, Donzelli Ed.

Moreno-Conde, M. (2006) *Exvotos Ibéricos.* Vol. I: *El Instituto Valencia de Don Juan.* Jaén, Instituto de Estudios Gienneses.

Nicolini, G. (1969) *Les Bronzes Figurés des Sanctuaires Ibériques.* Paris, Presses Universitaires de France.

Nicolini, G., Rísquez, C., Ruiz, A. and Zafra, N. (2004) *El santuario ibérico de Castellar, Jaén. Intervenciones arqueológicas 1966–1991.* Arqueología Monografías. Sevilla, Junta de Andalucía.

Oberhelman, S. M. (2014) Anatomical votive reliefs as evidence for specialization at healing sanctuaries in the ancient Mediterranean world. *Athens Journal of Health* 1(1), 47–62.

Olmos, R. (2000–2001) Diosas y animales que amamantan: la transmisión de la vida en la iconografía ibérica. *Zephyrus* 53–54, 353–378.

Olmos, R. (2007) El lenguaje de la diosa de los pebeteros. Signo icónico y función narrativa en dos tumbas de La Albufereta (Alicante). In Mª C. Marín Ceballos and F. Horn (eds) *Imagen y culto en la Iberia prerromana: los pebeteros en forma de cabeza humana.* Sevilla, Universidad de Sevilla, 367–390.

Olmos, R. and Tortosa, T. (2010) Aves, diosas, mujeres. In T. Chapa, T. and I. Izquierdo (eds) *La dama de Baza. Un viaje femenino al más allá.* Actas del encuentro Internacional Museo Arqueológico Nacional. Madrid, Ministerio de Cultura, 243–258.

Prados, L. (1991) Los exvotos anatómicos del santuario de Collado de los Jardines (Santa Elena, Jaén). *Trabajos de Prehistoria* 48, 313–332.

Prados, L. (1992) *Exvotos ibéricos de bronce del Museo Arqueológico Nacional.* Madrid, Museo Arqueológico Nacional.

Prados, L. (2013) ¿Por qué se ofrecían los exvotos de recién nacidos? Una aproximación a la presencia de 'bebés enfajados' en el santuario ibérico de Collado de los Jardines (Santa Elena, Jaén, España). In C. Rísquez and C. Rueda (eds) *Santuarios Iberos: territorio, ritualidad y memoria. Actas del Congreso El santuario de La Cueva de la Lobera de Castellar. 1912–2012.* Jaén, ASODECO, 325–339.

Prados, L. (2016) Women in Iberian culture. 6th–1st centuries B.C. In S. Boudin and J. Mackintosh Turfa (eds.). *Women in Antiquity. Real women across the ancient world. London/New York,* Routledge, 986–1007.

Rísquez, C. (2015) La arqueología ibérica y los estudios de género en Andalucía, *Menga* 6, 61–91.

Rísquez, C. and Hornos, F. (2005) Mujeres Iberas. Un estado de la cuestión. In M. Sánchez (ed.) *Arqueología y género.* Granada, Universidad de Granada, 283–334.

Rísquez, C., Rueda, C., Nicolini, G., Ruiz, A., Zafra, N. and Esteban, C. (2015) El santuario de la Cueva de la Lobera de Castellar. In A. Ruiz and M. Molinos (eds) *Jaén Tierra Ibera. 40 años de investigación y transferencia.* Jaén, Universidad de Jaén, 203–218.

Rueda, C. (2008) Las imágenes de los santuarios de Cástulo: los exvotos ibéricos en bronce de Collado de los Jardines (Santa Elena) y Los Altos del Sotillo (Castellar). *Palaeohispánica* 8, 55–87.

Rueda, C. (2011) *Territorio, culto e iconografía en los santuarios iberos del Alto Guadalquivir (ss. IV a.n.e.-I d.n.e.).* Textos CAAI 3. Jaén, Universidad de Jaén.

Rueda, C. (2012) *Exvotos Ibéricos. Vol, II: El Instituto Gómez-Moreno. Fundación Rodríguez-Acosta (Granada).* Jaén, Instituto de Estudios Gienneses.

Rueda, C. (2013) Ritos de paso de edad y ritos nupciales en la religiosidad ibera: algunos casos de estudio. In C. Rísquez and C. Rueda (eds) *Santuarios Iberos: territorio, ritualidad y memoria. Actas del Congreso El santuario de La Cueva de la Lobera de Castellar. 1912–2012.* Jaén, ASODECO, 341–383.

Rueda, C. and Olmos, R. (2015) Las cráteras áticas de la cámara principesca de Piquía (Arjona): los vasos de la memoria de uno de los últimos linajes iberos. In A. Ruiz and M. Molinos (eds) *Jaén Tierra Ibera. 40 años de investigación y transferencia.* Jaén, Universidad de Jaén, 375–391.

Rueda, C.; Rísquez, C., Herranz, A.; Hornos, F. and García, A. (2016) *Catálogo de la Exposición "Las Edades de las mujeres iberas. La ritualidad femenina a través de las colecciones del Museo de Jaén."* Jaén, Universidad de Jaén.

Ruiz, A. and Molinos, M. (1999) *The Archaeology of the Iberians*. New Studies in Archaeology. Cambridge, Cambridge University Press.

Ruiz A. and Molinos, M. (2007) *Iberos en Jaén*. Textos CAAI Ibérica, 2. Jaén, Universidad de Jaén.

Ruiz, A., Rueda, C., Bellón, J. P. and Gómez, F. (2013) El factor ibero en la Batalla de Baecula: los efectos colaterales de la guerra. *Cuadernos de Prehistoria y Arqueología de la Universidad de Granada* 23, 199–225.

Ruiz, A., Molinos, M., Fernández, R., Pérez, M. and Rueda, C. 2015. El santuario de la Puerta del Sol. In A. Ruiz and M. Molinos (eds) *Jaén Tierra Ibera. 40 años de investigación y transferencia*. Jaén, Universidad de Jaén, 93–106.

Sánchez, M. (2008). Maternidad y Prehistoria: prácticas de reproducción, relación y socialización. In *Las mujeres en la Prehistoria*. Valencia, Museo de Prehistoria de Valencia, 119–138.

Torelli, M. (1984) *Lavinio e Roma. Riti iniziatici e matrimonio tra archeologia e storia*. Roma, Ed. Quasar.

Vives-Ferrándiz, J. (2013) *Imágenes para las divinidades*. Valencia, Museo de Prehistoria de Valencia.

Chapter 9

Motherhood, gender and identity in the Athenian *polis*

M. Dolors Molas Font

'Certainly, human history consists, at least to certain extent, in putting names to things in order to absorb them into the human world of dialogue, consciousness and reflection, into the life of words and writing, without which these things do not belong to us' (Cortina 2017, 17).

Introduction

Pericles' citizenship law, passed in the year 451 BC,[1] reinforced the political weight of motherhood for Athenian women. *Politeia* (passed down in the blood line) became the exclusive prerogative of those born to a monogamous, legitimate marriage between an Athenian (male) citizen and the legitimate daughter of another (male) citizen, i.e. between a *polites* and an *aste*. Thus, the motherhood of the *astai* was henceforth situated at the very heart of the system founded on the rights and duties of the *politai*. As such, the existence of the citizen-based state required control over the lives and reproductive bodies of women, control that was performed by women´s relatives. This system responded to the belief that transgression of the norms of feminine conduct, laid down by the masculine-organised system, would disturb the correct functioning of the *polis*. It was for this reason that the *politai* held the right to take part in public punishments of unfaithful wives,[2] sanctions whose purpose was to show an example to other women.

The dominant discourses on the values of the *polis* instilled the idea that only reproduction within marriage could give meaning to the life of the Athenian women, who internalized their fate through socialization and ritual.[3] Festivals promoting Athenian women's fertility and fecundity were central to the religious calendar of the *polis*, clearly demonstrating the political importance of both maternity and symbolic representations of Athenian women's value as mothers. For example, the *Thesmophoria*, devoted to Demeter Thesmophoros (Bruit Zaidman 1991, 388–391; Blundell 1995, 163–165), was a festival in which only Athenian married women could take part, and which thereby also proved that their marriages were legitimate.[4]

This political view of motherhood projected a powerful image of the woman as wife and mother which transcended the ideological and sociopolitical spheres in which it had its original function and meaning to become a universal, essentialist idea of womanhood, bound by definition to maternity. Clearly, this is an unbalanced view of Athenian social reality, which has obscured the richness and diversity of femininities represented by the other women who lived in the city: Athenian women of uncertain status, foreign women and female slaves.[5] Demosthenes' well-known aphorism from the speech *Against Neaera*, addressed to Athenian men, shows that many of these women had both temporary and permanent relationships with citizens, some also having children by them:

> Mistresses we keep for the sake of pleasure, concubines for the daily care of our persons, but wives to bear us legitimate children and to be faithful guardians of our households (122)

Demosthenes was referring to women of diverse legal status and social class, women whose identity was given shape by their sexual relationship with a (male) citizen, which may not necessarily have been intended to give him children. The orator is explicit about what male citizens wanted – and needed – from women, and how legitimate motherhood was reserved for an exclusive group and, therefore, could not be a determining factor in the identity of many women residents of Athens. Whatever the case, we should remember that the male citizens involved in the lawsuits that we know through public speeches belonged to the wealthy classes, and it is these whom Demosthenes is addressing. For this reason we should add to his list of women the prostitutes, free or enslaved, normally seen in literature and research studies as sellers of sexual pleasure to men of the lower classes (Glazebrook 2011, 34–59).

In this paper, through the lens of Attic legal oratory, specifically Demosthenes LIX and Isaeus III and VI, I explore the meaning of motherhood in the construction of the identity of those women whose marriage with an Athenian citizen was prohibited by law. To this end we should remember that the orators' rhetoric distorted the image of women, especially the *hetaera* and prostitutes, to cast a negative light on their behaviour and thereby discredit the opposing party of the lawsuit (Glazebrook 2005, 126). We should also bear in mind the context of these juridical texts in Athens in the 4th century BC, when the meanings of the word 'woman' came from the dominant discourses of a masculine-hegemonic, phallocentric society which conceptualized women as bodies of various categories: bodies for reproduction, bodies for (predominantly male) pleasure and bodies for both work and pleasure.

Some of the life stories emerging from the legal oratory show that many women who had relationships with (male) Athenian citizens out of wedlock were in a situation of legal uncertainty. This arose when they were mothers and the male partner's relatives questioned the legal capacity of their children to inherit from the father and, in the case of girls, to be offered in marriage to a *polites*. This shows that many of the women living in Athens, like many of the men also, frequently lacked a clear juridical status.

The construction of otherness: *heteara*, prostitutes and concubines

The speech *Against Neaera* attributed to Demosthenes is an exceptional text of Athenian oratory.[6] Firstly because a woman is both the accused and the main figure in the story, and secondly because Neaera, while not an *aste,* was living in an apparently legitimate marriage with a citizen named Stephanos. From previous relationships Neaerea had brought two sons and a daughter named Phano, and Stephanos claimed to have adopted these, thus conferring legitimacy on them.

For these reasons, the various circumstances coming together in the figure of Neaera make the text a privileged source that illustrates the construction of feminine-gender identities in classical Athens. These circumstances show how the concept of the woman varied according to the interaction between different identity categories, in this case age, status and class. In other words, the text reveals the existence in Athens of distinct femininities diverging from the hegemonic model.

Against Neaera makes explicit the mechanisms with which this Otherness was constructed, in this case in opposition to the figure of the legitimate wife. Aiming to prove the illegality of Neaera and Stephanos' marriage and thereby the illegitimacy of the sons and daughter, Demosthenes dwells on the dissolute conduct of Neaera as not being that proper to a wife of a citizen, but rather to a *hetaera*, whom he sometimes calls a prostitute (*porne*), thus stressing Neaera's otherness and with it her inferior status:[7]

> When he came back here, bringing her with him, he treated her without decency or restraint, taking her everywhere with him to dinner where there was drinking and making her a partner in his revels; and he had intercourse with her openly whenever and wherever he wished, making his privilege a display to the onlookers. He took her to many houses to gay parties ... and in that place many had intercourse with her when she was drunk, while Phrynion was asleep, among them even the serving-men of Chabrias (33)
>
> She remained at Megara two years, that of the archonship of Asteius and that of Alcisthenes; but the trade of prostitution did not bring in enough money to maintain her establishment – she was lavish in her tastes ... (36)
>
> ... a creature who in many and obscene ways has bestowed her favours many times a day on all comers, as each one happened to desire (114)
>
> Has she not been everywhere in the Peloponnesus, in Thessaly and in Magnesia in the company of Simus of Larisa and Eurydanus son of Medeius, in Chios and most of Ionia, following in the train of Sotadas the Cretan, and was she not let out for hire by Nicarete so long as she belonged to her? What do you suppose a woman does who is subject to men who are not her kinsfolk, and who follows in the train of him who pays her? Does she not serve all the lusts of those who deal with her?

> Will you, then, declare by your vote that a woman of this stamp, who is known by everybody beyond all question to have plied her trade the whole world over, is an Athenian citizen? (108)

By insisting on the licentious conduct of the accused, Demosthenes reveals the masculine Athenian's imaginary of the hegemonic, normative femininity represented by the *gune gamete*. The ideal wife was the *sophron gune* (Glazebrook 2006, 128), the woman whose identity embraced the necessary requisites such as chastity, passivity, lack of mobility, abstention from drinking wine, belonging to only one man and living far from the gaze of men not of her family. Thus, the orator constructs the identity of the courtesan as the opposite of the hegemonic, normative feminine Self; the condition of the *hetaera* is that of the Other; and therefore, sexual promiscuity, luxury, drinking wine, visibility and spatial mobility are the most distinctive features of Neaera's Otherness: she is a woman completely lacking in *sophrosyne*. The identity of the *hetaera*, then, leaves no room for maternity, since her body is conceptualized as devoted to selling pleasure to men, as opposed to providing legitimate offspring to them. Demosthenes needed to persuade the citizen tribunal that the indecent life of the accused was radically opposite to that of the Athenian woman socialised for the production of sons for the *oikos* and the *polis* and daughters for the reproduction of the state system.

Demosthenes' main argument in persuading the jury of Neaera's guilt (and that of Stephanos) and of the illegitimacy of her sons and daughter is based solely on making her condition of the Other visible, i.e. in revealing Neaera's identity as a courtesan. This is the connecting thread which binds his speech together.

The events of Neaera's life, seen through the masculine gaze, biassed and intentionally distorted, show the dynamic, dialectical and discursive nature of identity. In her childhood Neaera was a child prostitute; in her youth she was freed from slavery and gained foreign resident status in Athens; with the profession of *hetaera* she was able to control the earnings of her own work; and she became the mother of three children and, at some point, the apparently legitimate wife of a citizen. We do not know how Neaera saw herself throughout the changing course of her life; however, her public identity did not only depend on her own view of herself or how she wanted others to see her, but to a large extent on how others really saw her.

The construction of a woman's identity in Otherness in order to present her as of inferior status and thereby locate her offspring outside the law is also documented in Isaeus, III, *On the State of Pyrrhus*. This speech illustrates a concubine's[8] motherhood and foregrounds the legal ambiguity of her sons and daughters. Born as illegitimate or *nothoi*, the offspring of a *pallake* lacked inheritance rights, with the possible exception of the 'legitimate portion' Blundell (1995, 125). The practice of concubinage among wealthy (male) Athenians was a means of satisfying the sexual desires of the husband without increasing the size of the family. Through the practice of concubinage, if the legitimate sons and daughters died, the rich (male) Athenian could then have recourse to a stock of potential children for adoption who could take on the role of the dead offspring.

In the lawsuit over the inheritance of the citizen Pyrrhus, there were two contending parties: one of the nephews of the deceased, son of his daughter; and Xenocles, representing his own wife Phile, who claimed that her mother had legally married Pyrrhus and therefore she was her legitimate daughter. We also find the recurring anonymity of women in Greek oratory in this example: neither Pyrrhus' sister nor Phile's mother are named in the speech. On this occasion, and in contrast to Neaera, the anonymous mother of Phile was an Athenian, according to the parentage cited in the text. Phile's ambiguous position, and that of her mother, revolved round whether her mother was legitimately married to Pyrrhus or was his concubine, his *pallake*; as a result, doubt is shed on whether Phile, the daughter, was the legitimate daughter or in fact illegitimate. The issue which interests us here is that the party suing for the inheritance, represented here by Isaeus, uses the same argument to discredit Phile as Demosthenes in *Against Neaera*. The oratory argues that the dishonest behaviour of Phile's mother is the antithesis of the hegemonic, normative femininity, that of the *sophron gune*; and to sow confusion and hammer home his rhetoric aimed at discrediting Phile, Isaeus uses the terms concubine and courtesan indifferently and perversely, also adding that of 'lover.'

> That the woman, whom the defendant has deposed that he gave in legal marriage to our uncle, was a courtesan who gave herself to anyone and not his wife, has been testified to you by the other acquaintances and by the neighbours of Pyrrhus, who have given evidence of quarrels, serenades, and frequent scenes of disorder which the defendant's sister occasioned whenever she was at Pyrrhus's house. Yet no one, I presume, would dare to serenade a married woman, nor do married women accompany their husbands to banquets or think of feasting in the company of strangers, especially mere chance comers (III, 13–14)
>
> Did you not know that by the demand that the estate should be adjudicated an attempt was being made to bastardize your niece? (III, 41)

Furthermore, to heighten the image of her licentiousness he adds that she aroused passion in men, i.e. that she was an active seductress, which was an improper role for an honest woman:

> ... on the other hand, if our uncle, under the influence of his passion, contracted a marriage with a woman of this character, clearly he who gave her in marriage would have been all the more careful to procure an agreement from the other party stating that he received money with her, so that it might not be in the latter's power easily to get rid of the woman whenever he wished (III, 28)

Another example of the construction of feminine identity through Otherness in which the status and indecent behaviour of the woman are used to legally incapacitate her offspring is in Isaeus VI, *On the Estate of Philoctemon*. In this case the story concerns a supposed freedwoman named Alpe, who according to the speech had duped the rich, elderly Philoctemon so that she could live on his wealth and achieve legitimate paternity for her children, born to a freedman. Two brothers were the petitioners for the inheritance in the case that came to court. The pejorative view of women's lifestyles gains more weight in this speech, with the accusation that Alpe had used seduction and drugs to beguile Philectemon, the alleged father of the petitioners. However, the most devastating argument in discrediting her as a wife and legitimate mother is that she had been a slave. Thus, both conduct and status intertwine decisively in the construction of Alpe's identity, moulded by the orator into that of a promiscuous and perverse slave, an identity within which motherhood could have absolutely no place. In other words, the legal status of former slavery was seen as an impenetrable barrier to any possible legitimacy for the sons and daughters:

> Yet the mother of these young men, being admittedly a slave, and having always lived a scandalous life, who ought never to have entered the temple and seen any of the rites performed there, had the effrontery to join in the procession when a sacrifice was being made in honour of these goddesses and to enter the temple and see what she has no right to see (VI, 49–50)

Allegations of a woman's disorderly behaviour in order to sow doubt on her condition as *gune gamete* and in consequence deny her children the right to the paternal estate, or even the mother's dowry, are also made against Plangon, the daughter of Panphilus, who appears in Demosthenes' speeches XXXIX: *Mantitheus against Boeotus in Regard to the Name* and XL: *Mantitheus against Boeotus Regarding his Mother's Marriage-Portion.* For example, in order to undermine Plangon's legal status, Mantitheus, the plaintiff in both lawsuits, states that she was beautiful, that Matias, the father, was in love with her, and that passion existed in that relationship, insinuating that neither passion nor love had anything in common with marriage. To stress the doubt, Mantitheus hints that her lifestyle was that of a *hetaera*, since she had a host of female slaves and lived lavishly, and for this reason she had made his father to underwrite many of her expenses.[9]

Motherhoods: core, eccentric/peripheral and trangressive

The condition of motherhood, rather than a biological fate determining women's being, is an ideological-cultural construct charged with political meanings. On the basis of an understanding of identity as dialectical, dynamic and discursive, i.e. fluid, we can view motherhood from a gender and identity perspective, allowing its different dimensions (in the same sociocultural context) to appear: distinct realities which require new, specific words to name them and thereby lift them out of invisibility.

Thus, we may use the term 'core motherhood' to indicate that being a mother was the core of the *gune gamete* identity, situated at the very heart of the institution of citizenship. In contrast, 'eccentric motherhood' – which could also be named as peripheral- signifies that maternity was not a distinctive feature of a woman's identity, due to her status, origins, ethnic group or social class. With these two terms we can encompass the types of motherhood of most of the women living in ancient Athens:

concubines, foreign women, *hetaerae* and slaves. However, we also need to account for free Athenian mothers who were neither married nor concubines, whom I have termed mothers of 'ambiguous identity.' Despite the self-serving silence of the primary sources, there is no doubt that they existed, especially among the poorer classes, many of them taking up prostitution in order to feed their children:

> ... then the trade of the harlot will absolutely make its way to the daughters of citizens, who through poverty are unable to marry .... Demosthenes, LIX, 113

These are eccentric or peripheral motherhoods, all with their own specific features, evidencing the frequent fluidity of identity. For example, in the case of the concubine, eccentric or peripheral motherhood could become core motherhoods if the partner adopted her 'illegitimate' sons and daughters, thereby conferring legitimacy on them, as this passage from Demosthenes demonstrates:

> If one should involuntarily kill another [...] catching him on top of his wife or mother or sister or daughter or a concubine that he has taken to father freeborn children, then for these charges he should not be exiled. Demosthenes, *Political Speeches, Against Aristocrates*, 53.

A legal orator could use the ambiguous status of the freeborn foreign woman to call into question the legality of her children when these were potentially in receipt of a paternal estate. It is for this reason that the issue of freeborn foreign women's motherhood arises constantly in Attic oratory (Hong 2016, 679–680). We should note that freeborn women whose lives were seen as honourable were praised in funeral epitaphs in the same terms as those defining normative Athenian femininity, thereby proving that the Athenian ideal of motherhood was linked to honest behaviour (Hong 2016, 680).

Reduced to the status of animate objects, slaves could be exploited without restriction by anyone, male or female, who legally owned them, often for example as prostitutes by a brothel owner.[10] Employed in the production of goods for both use and exchange, slaves' bodies were also exploited for pleasure by male owners, possibly also female owners, although in this case the primary sources have nothing to say, as is normally the case for sexual relationships between women (Boehringer 2007; Ormand 2009, 67). In other words, female slaves were bodies used for pleasure, as were both young slaves of both sexes and children. But women slaves also took part in another type of production, that of bodies: the reproduction of the unfree labour force (Hong 2016, 680).

Although referring to Roman society under the Empire, Strong (2012, 130) cites Seneca's opinion that the prostitute's licentious way of life was incompatible with that of the virtuous wife and mother, thus stressing that maternity was not fitting for a prostitute, who should avoid it through contraceptives and abortion. Seneca, then, sees the prostitute mother as a violation of the norm, and thus further underlines her Otherness.

Trangressive motherhood

Critical reading of Attic oratorial texts allows us a glimpse into a much richer and more diverse society than that portrayed in the dominant discourses on normative femininity. Affective (or otherwise) relationships between people of differing wealth and status could compel them to break the law, knowing that this involved a sanction, and thereby giving rise to ambiguous legal situations. Added to this, the ruling classes' economic interests and often partial legal interpretations sometimes increased this juridical uncertainty.

Neaera's transgressive motherhood was situated within this context. She is the main character in a speech in which, while citizenship is the fundamental issue, the key topic is maternity, since in the Athenian *polis* there could be no citizenship without motherhood. By attempting to give her daughter Phano legal status, Neaera had violated the political order.

Leaving aside Demosthenes' accusations aimed at discrediting her on the basis of her alleged promiscuity and lifestyle, Neaera is portrayed as a woman of uncertain origins, lacking a family line. These were the conditions which, under Pericles' citizenship law, still in force in 343 and 339 BC, blocked her access to *gune gamete* status and with it legitimate motherhood. Despite this Neaera, aided and abetted by the Athenian Stephanos, broke the law of citizenship, seeking for herself and especially for her daughter Phano (whom they twice attempted to marry to another Athenian citizen) the legal, social and economic status which had been denied them. Neaera, then, was a resilient and agentic woman: she shows a great capacity for taking action, overcoming obstacles and using her ingenuity to bend the rules discriminating against herself and her daughter, fruit of her marginal motherhood (Molas 2006; 2007). The relationship between mother and daughter is constant throughout their hectic adult lives (Strong 2012, 133): a relationship of unflagging mutual aid in the face of a masculine society which was hostile towards them due to their Otherness. The actions of Neaera and Phano, however, neither call into question nor subvert the values of the *polis*, but instead uphold them, since both wished to belong to a system which discriminated against them, and struggled to legitimise their offspring.

Body, power and motherhood

The body is the *locus* where power invests the individual from birth, the material basis for the construction of identity and the site where relations of power are played out (Reverter 2004, 134). Therefore the reproductive female body is a site of the political struggle to appropriate and control the produce of motherhood.

References to the sexual positions of men and women are explicit in the laws on adultery in Attic juridical oratory. These show how, through control of women's bodies and sexuality, men appropriated the products of motherhood; in other words, the positions of the bodies in the sexual act were a paradigm of masculine dominance and hegemony, which made heterosexuality a decisive category for feminine identity and being a woman synonymous with heterosexuality (Wittig 2006).

> If one should involuntarily kill another ... catching him on top of his wife or mother or sister or daughter or a concubine that he has taken to father freeborn children, then for these charges he should not be exiled. Demosthenes, *Political Speeches, Against Aristocrates*, 53.
>
> For a woman who has been taken in adultery is not permitted to attend any of the public sacrifices ... and if they do attend them and defy the law, any person whatsoever may at will inflict upon them any sort of punishment, save only death, and that with impunity; and the law has given the right of punishing these women to any person who happens to meet with them. Demosthenes, LIX, *Against Neaera*, 85–86.

It was not by chance that this law on the sexual positions also appears in the story of Lilith, Adam's first wife:

> When God created the first man Adam alone, God said, 'It is not good for man to be alone.' [So] God created a woman for him, from the earth like him, and called her Lilith. They [Adam and Lilith] promptly began to argue with each other: She said, 'I will not lie below,' and he said, 'I will not lie below, but above, since you are fit for being below and I for being above.' She said to him, "The two of us are equal, since we are both from the earth.' The Alphabet of Ben Sira, 10th century.[11]

The male-superior physical position[12] signifies phallocentrism and normative heterosexuality for women, defining their sexuality as exclusively reproductive. This position is both the expression of power and an exponent of the conceptualisation of the Other (i.e. the woman) as a passive being reduced to an object to be penetrated and dominated by the referential masculine Self the active component in the sexual act. Thus the positioning of the male body over the female aims to establish that the male is the main agent of procreation, since he is the active part of the relationship and therefore the sons and daughters born from the union are his property. Symbolically the woman's body is conceptualised as a body with holes to be penetrated, and thereby fertilisation, but which can never penetrate in its turn, in contrast to the male; and for this reason, the woman can never be dominant. As a consequence, the law on the two bodies' sexual positions was an expression of the relations of force and power between women and men, and this domination of the female body was one of the key strategies of masculine power.

Thus, the symbol of Lilith is a powerful precedent, as she was the first woman in the Jewish tradition, apparently invented by the Bible interpreters, and therefore her disobedience would have taken place during the period of the construction of the masculine hegemonic order. Her act of resistance is focused on the fact that she saw herself as equal to the male and an active partner in the sexual act. This equality would entail her having the same rights over her offspring, since the sexual position determined the property of the children. In consequence, Lilith's disobedience and defiant attitude subvert the order in construction and make her a model for the woman who is agent of her own life. We not should be surprised, then, that after she had left Adam and disobeyed God, the Jewish tradition recasts Lilith as a promiscuous being, a winged demon preying on children. This was not a chance characterisation, and turned Lilith into a figure representing anti-motherhood, the opposite side of the mirror, where women should never see themselves reflected. In short, the masquerade of the mirrors makes Lilith a model of women's agency and insubordination against phallocentrism and the institutional constraints of motherhood, always disguised by the representation of maternal feelings as organic needs (Butler 1990, 310).

Acknowledgement

This essay was written as part of the research project 'Motherhood and families: permanence, change and rupture in history. Between classical societies and the contemporary world' (HAR2013–42371-R), and under the aegis of the research group GRC Creació i Pensament de les Dones, 2014 SGR 44.

Notes

1 Aristotle, *Athenian Constitution,* 24. 4; Plutarch, *Life of Pericles,* 37.
2 Demosthenes, LIX, *Against Neaera,* 85–86; Aeschines, *Against Timarchus,* 183.
3 On the importance of motherhood for Athenian women in the 5th and 4th centuries BC see Hong (2016, 673–675).
4 Isaeus, III, *On the Estate of Pyrrhus,* 3. 80.
5 In her essay Hong (2016) shows that Athenian women were not a homogeneous group and examines the motherhood of citizens, freedwomen and slaves.
6 On Neaera see for example Herter (1985); Mossé (1993); Hamel (2003); Molas Font (2006; 2007); Glazebrook (2005; 2011; 2016).
7 Futo Kennedy (2015) analyses the use of the term *hetaira* in archaic and classical Athens to denote a type of both status and of conduct, and points out the error in associating the terms *hetaira, simposio* and prostitute, urging a re-examination of the conflation of the three terms. This false identification gained ground in the democratic period, when, in a deliberate and perverse way, orators used it to discredit their opponents. Kennedy shows that these intentional confusions are repeatedly found in later authors such as Athenaeus.
8 On concubines see for example Blundell (1995, 124–125). There are two differing interpretations of the Athenian concubine. The majority view is that it was a legal institution, while another sees it as proof of the existence of polygamy in ancient Greek society. In the legal institution, a father would hand over his daughter to a citizen without a contract (*enque*) or dowry (*proix*). The resulting offspring would then be accepted as natural and obtain citizenship if the father adopted them. In fact, having one or more concubines ensured that the rich Athenian would have heirs in case there were no children from a legal marriage. Also, concubinage allowed the male to have sexual relationships without risk of increasing the number of legitimate heirs with claims on his property.
9 Demosthenes, XL, *Mantitheus Against Boeotus Regarding his Mother's Marriage-Portion*, 51.
10 For example, Lysias IV, *On a Wound by Premeditation,* 1, 8–10.
11 https://en.wikipedia.org/wiki/Alphabet_of_Sirach#Lilith.www.comayala.es/catequesis/unasolacarne.htm

12 The male-superior position in sex is also documented in Egypt, where on only two occasions do we find a representation of a woman having sex over a man, in both cases a goddess (Orriols Llonch 2012, 27 and note 42). The relationship between sexual position and control over offspring also appears among the Yamana, a hunter-gatherer people who lived in Tierra del Fuego (Argentina). Their myths, collected by ethnographers, show discrimination against and exploitation of women by men, and how men symbolically appropriated reproduction through the control of female sexuality. They tell that when at the beginning of time woman dominated men, they positioned themselves on top of the man in the sexual act; and when women were defeated the physical roles were reversed, and at this moment men finally understood who was the father (Vila Mitjà and Ruíz del Olmo 2001, 287; Vargas 2004, 220).

References

Blundell, S. (1995) *Women in Ancient Greece*. London, British Museum Press.

Boehringer, S. (2007) *Homosexualité féminine dans l'Antiquité grecque et romaine*. Paris, Les Belles Lettres.

Bruit Zaidman, L. (1992) Las hijas de Pandora. Mujeres y rituales en las ciudades. In G. Duby and M. Perrot (dirs) *Historia de las Mujeres. La Antigüedad*. Madrid, Taurus, 373–419.

Butler, J. (1990) Variaciones sobre sexo y género: Beauvoir, Wittig y Foucault. In S. Benhabib and D. Cornell (eds) *Teoría feminista y teoría crítica. Ensayos sobre la política de géneros en las sociedades de capitalismo tardío*. Valencia, Ediciones Alfons el Magnànim, 303–326.

Cortina, A. (2017) *Aporofobia, el rechazo al pobre. Un desafío para la democracia*. Barcelona, Paidós.

Futo Kennedy, R. (2015) Elite Citizen Women and the Origins of the *Hetaira* in Classicla Athens. *Helios* 42(1), 61–79.

Glazebrook, A. (2005) The making of a prostitute: Apollodoros's Portrait of Neaira. *Arethusa* 38(2), 161–187.

Glazebrook A. (2006) The bad girls of Athens. The image and funcion of Hetairai in judicial oratory. In Ch. A. Faraone and L. K. Maclure (eds) *Prostitutes and Courtesans in the Ancient World*. Madison, University of Wisconsin Press, 125–138.

Glazebrook, A. (2011) Porneion: Prostitution in Athenian civic space. In A. Glazebrook and M. Henry (eds) *Greek Prostitutes in the Ancient Mediterranean 800 BCE-200 CE*. Madison, University of Wisconsin, 34–59.

Glazebrook, A. (2016) Prostitutes, women, and gender in Ancient Athens. In S. L. Budin and J. Macintosh Turfa (eds) *Women in Antiquity. Real women across the ancient world*. London/New York, Routledge, 703–713.

Hamel, D. (2003) *Trying Neaira: The true story of a courtesan's scandalous life in ancient Greece*. New Haven, Yale University Press.

Herter, H. (1985) Il mondo delle cortigiane e delle prostitute. In G. Arrigoni (ed.) *Le donne in Grecia*. Roma/Bari, Laterza, 363–398.

Hong, Y. (2016) Mothering in Ancient Athens: class, identity, and experience. In S. L. Budin and J. Macintosh Turfa (eds) *Women in Antiquity. Real women across the ancient world*. London/New York, Routledge, 673–682.

Molas Font, M. D. (2006) Prostitutas y adúlteras. Cuerpos usados y espíritus seducidos. In M. D. Molas Font, S. Guerra López, E. Huntingford Antigas and J. Zaragoza Gras (eds) *La violencia de género en la antigüedad*. Madrid, Instituto de la Mujer, 109–134.

Molas Font, M. D. (2007) Cuerpos usados y espíritus seducidos en la oratoria ática. In M. D. Molas Font (ed.) *Violencia deliberada. Las raíces de la violencia patriarcal*. Barcelona, Icaria, 89–105.

Mossé, Cl. (1993) Neera, la cortigiana. In N. Loraux (ed.) *Grecia al femminile*. Roma/Bari, Laterza, 197–227.

Ormand, K. (2009) *Controlling desires: sexuality in ancient Greece and Rome*. Westport, Praeger.

Orriols Llonch, M. (2012) Mujer ideal, mujer infractora. La transgresión femenina en el antiguo Egipto. *Lectora* 18, 17–40.
Reverter, S. (2004) La (in)vestidura de los cuerpos. *Lectora* 10, 133–140.
Strong, A. K. (2012) Mother-daughter bonds among ancient prostitutes. In L. Hackworth Petersen and P. Salzman-Mitchell (eds) *Mothering & Motherhood in Ancient Greece and Rome*. Austin, University of Texas, 121–139.
Vilà Mitjà, A. and Ruíz del Olmo, G. (2001) Información etnológica y análisis de la reproducción social. El caso Yamana. *Revista Española de Antropología Americana* 31, 275–291.
Vargas, I. (2004) Ideología y dominación masculina en las sociedades cazadoras recolectoras. El caso de la sociedad yamana. *Boletín Antropológico* 22(61), 209–237.
Wittig, M. (2006) *El pensamiento heterosexual y otros ensayos.* Barcelona, EGALES.

Classical authors

Aeschines, *Speeches.* English translation by C. D. Adam, London, Loeb Classical Library, 1919.
Aristotle, *Athenian Constitution. Eudemian Ethics. Virtues and Vices.* English trans. H. Rackham, London, Loeb Classical Library, 1935.
Demosthenes, III, English trans. J. H. Vince, London, Loeb Classical Library, 1964.
Demosthenes, IV, English trans. A. T. Murray, London, Loeb Classical Library, 1965.
Demosthenes, VI, English trans. A. T. Murray, London, Loeb Classical Library, 1964.
Isaeus, *Isaeus.* English trans. E. S. Foster, London, Loeb Classical Library, 1962.
Lysias, *Lysias.* English trans. W. R. M. Lamb, London, Loeb Classical Library 1930.
Plutarch, *The Parallel Lives,* III. English trans. B. Perrin, London, Loeb Classical Library, 1914.

Chapter 10

Childhood and motherhood in Ancient Greece: an iconographic look

Susana Reboreda Morillo

The purpose of this study is to analyse what the society of the Ancient Greek civilisation, especially during the Classic period, thought and transmitted about childhood, from birth to death, with special emphasis on the relationship between child and mother. The context of reference is the citizenship, the group about which we have the most information. Methodologically, we will mainly analyse iconographic sources, without forgetting literary and archaeological references. There will be two main settings: the domestic and the ritual, both coinciding with the main activities of women. From giving birth, mothers acquired the difficult responsibility of ensuring their descendants survived, at the same time as carrying out the tasks of raising and educating their offspring, which went beyond teaching basic skills (walking, talking, eating, and so on), since they were also responsible for instilling into their children the need to respect the rules of patriarchal society based on the *poliade* community.

Introduction and difficulties

We are aware that the subject under study entails certain problems that it is important to raise before beginning the exposition and analysis of the facts. In first place, the scarcity of testimonies in which children were the main figures, an indicative aspect of the scarce interest that they stirred, although we will see differences between genders and periods in time; this factor influences the challenge meaning that defining their trajectories reaches greater dimensions. We know that, in the first stages of childhood, the environment of children was the *oikos*, therefore, a feminine environment (Gherchanoc 2012); where girls remained until reaching the age of marriage, whereas boys continued their learning outside of their home. In both cases, the objective was to prepare them for their respective roles allocated by a society which followed the example of the *polis*. Of all the sources that refer to this stage in life, the most prolific is iconography, whose analysis is not exempt of difficulties. Thus, we enter the second issue: we cannot overlook the fact that the scenes depicted do not always reflect reality and, might, in certain cases, show what 'it should be' (Molas Font 2016, 71). However, it is obvious that, from this archetype depicted in images, it is always possible to extract interesting information which serves as a bridge to bring us closer to this reality. We will see how these portrayals evolve and that can only be related to the changes taking place in society, an aspect that shows their usefulness as a source of information. We will also make use of some written testimonies and archaeological findings. This will allow us to outline an introduction to the childhood activities in relation to motherhood, in close connection with the future roles that society assigned to both genders.

The third problem we face is ambiguity, such as stated by Sourvinou-Inwood (1990, 45), we have to bear in mind that we are analysing a period with cultural differences to our own, due to which we should avoid associating it with our immediate environment, even if the relationship is sometimes evident. We must always be aware that the concept of childhood itself is eminently cultural, varying between societies, periods, and even the particular circumstances surrounding each individual. Therefore, we will avoid making generalisations which include, for example, all members of society or even the different *poleis*. We will focus on Attica because it has more portrayals in its ceramic paintings as well as reliefs and sculptures.

The structure of the present work follows chronological issues. Thus, we will begin our exposition with birth and will end with marriage which, at the time, was considered the end of childhood for girls.

Explanatory questions about childhood in Ancient Greece and its portrayal

In Ancient Greece, the word for childhood, *país/paides*, was cloaked in certain ambiguity because it had other associated meanings. Thus, it was also used to contrast a small boy with an adult or a small boy with an adolescent (Cohen 2007, 3–4). The complexity increases on verifying its use to refer to other groups, such as *eromenoi*, which can refer to the youth in a homoerotic relationship or to a slave. It is possible to infer that the connotation of the word implies an inferior status, in a state of dependency (Golden 2003, 14). This lack of precision extends to iconography, especially in the Archaic period, in which slaves and children were portrayed in the same way: with the scaled-down body of an adult. Only very clear contexts allow the identification of the difference between children and slaves that could be adults. As of the 6th century BC, and progressively so, artists make an effort to capture children in a more natural body; for example, emphasis is given to the head, the extremities become more appropriate to the age, and the body is drawn to make them more plump. Furthermore, their presence in the scenes becomes more recurrent and they frequently appear beside their mothers. These artistic changes are reflecting the transformation, if not of the strict reality, then that of the archetype, which shows a greater interest, which, in the words of Beaumont (2004, 59), is 'a well-deserved respect.' The reason is associated with the abandonment of aristocratic ideals and conceding prominence to the citizenry, whose most essential elements are the citizens and, consequently, the necessary hope for the survival of the children (Beaumont 2004, 75).

It is not until the end of the 5th century BC and the beginning of the 4th century BC that different iconographic groups, which seek to show the different stages which Greek society established throughout childhood and puberty, from birth to maturity, are established. It is not easy to determine its limits, as made clear by the lack of unanimity when determining the ages included in the different groups. On the assumption that these limits were lax and flexible (Beaumont 2012, 19; 2015, 40–42), we assume the following schematic: the first would comprise birth to three years of age, the second from 3 to 7 years of age, and the third from 7 to 14/15, the age of marriage for girls. Other authors (Lawton 2007, 43–55; Grossman 2007, 310) opt for more generic schematics: babies, preadolescents, early adolescents and maidens.

Each age group is determined in iconography through social conventions which are shown in external aspects such as dress (or nudity), hairstyles, clothing and behaviour. As pointed out by Molas Font (2016, 68), it is about cultural constructs that reflect the different roles that society assigned to each phase. Logically, details are more profuse in reliefs and sculptures than in ceramic paintings, whose ages are better determined by gestures and attitudes (McNiven 2007, 85–93). Cohen (2007, 261) warns of the possible manipulation of some artists, who could, consciously, change some social realities, such as, to give an example, the large difference in age between young women, much younger than their husbands. This fact is very clear in mythical kidnappings, with the intention of hiding the transgressive sexuality of the adults.

First stage. Infants/babies: from birth until the age of three

The main role of women in Ancient Greece was, without a doubt, motherhood, not in just any circumstance, but in the bosom of marriage; the only possibility for acknowledged procreation and, therefore, heir to the paternal status. With the setup of the *poleis*, the interest was focussed on the continuity of the citizenry. In Athens, Pericles' citizenship law of 451 BC would, among other consequences, bring the imperative of marriage between citizens. Women lacked this status in a practical sense, but they would be indispensable for the transmission of the highest social distinction: only people whose parents both had the status of citizens would be citizens themselves. Thereon, the different roles are determined, men participate in politics and war, and women are wives and mothers, and keep watch over the maintenance of the *oikos*. We should not lose sight of the fact that this is a common denominator of all *poleis*, independently of the ruling political system; citizenship came to be the most essential element of the political-territorial structure, whose prized independence relied mainly on the decisions of this collective.

With this premise, it is obvious that, after the marriage celebration, young women should get pregnant, and in order to succeed, they would seek divine, as well as human, help. This help would continue being essential during the pregnancy and especially at the critical moment of the birth, which involved a real risk to the life of the mothers, as well as the newborns. To the women's youth, we add their limited knowledge of gynaecology and obstetrics, among other aspects (Reboreda Morillo forthcoming). The often-repeated words of Medea in Euripides' eponymous work show that women were very aware of this risk: 'Then people also say that while we live quietly and without danger at home, the men go off to war. Wrong! One birth alone is worse than three times in battlefield behind a shield.'[1] No doubt the reason for this statement goes beyond the intense pain that was systematically associated with giving birth, but was due to the high mortality of mothers as well as newborns. As pointed out by Nicole Loraux, the mothers' death was recognised with respect by the *polis* (Loraux 2004, 43–97; Demand 2004, 122–129), and, for this reason, it was brought to life in portrayals on steles and *lekythos*, showing the unsettled figure of a woman, with messy hair and clothes, partially sitting on a *kline*, with a leg resting on a stool and surrounded by the women who helped during birth. On occasions, a baby, who did not take away any of the mother's importance, was included in this scene (Oakley 2003, 185–186); in fact, no particular data is provided, about its gender nor its destiny, playing a secondary, inactive role (Hirsch-Dyczek 1983, 39–40). Actually, the baby's presence seems to have the task of highlighting the heartbreaking impossibility of them continuing their lives together (Grossman 2007, 312). The gender not being determined may be due to lack of either interest or social identity (Molas Font 2016, 72).

In general, the contexts in which they appear tend to be of a ritual nature, as part of a grave, in the case of steles or *lekythos*, or in tribute to a divinity or a hero. In any case, the purpose is to show the loss more painfully, thanks to the presence of dependent beings that are left unprotected without a father or a mother. Babies are usually portrayed swaddled or sometimes, as in Paestum, with a pointed hat (McNiven 2007, 142), or naked, and, almost always, in the arms of a woman, who is assumed to be the mother or wet nurse.

In spite of the fact that there is evidence that mothers took on the duty of breastfeeding (Reboreda Morillo 2017), in Athens, unlike in Etruria, in the south of Italy, and Sicily, no images of mothers breastfeeding their babies are found on either ceramics or in reliefs, leading to the conclusion that the subject was taboo. Beaumont (2015, 52–53) states that the sight of women's breasts had a very strong sexual connotation for men, which clashed with the concept of the ideal of the maternal figure.

The second scene where this age group is depicted is incorporated in the celebration of a rite, which can be associated with different circumstances. If, unlike previous examples, childbirth was successful, then after the paternal acknowledgement, which took place in the privacy of the home (*amphidromia*) and has never been depicted (Neils 2003, 144), came the public ceremonies (*dekate*). The most important part was probably thanking the deities involved in the successful birth, at the same time as requesting that the baby be kept alive. In Thessaly, a marble relief dating from around 300 BC,[2] which is very illustrative for learning the rituals included in this exclusively feminine ceremony, has been documented (Morizot 2004, 159–170). A woman identified as the wet nurse is carrying the baby in her arms and is presenting it to Artemis. A male slave is leading an ox to the altar, in order for it to be sacrificed; a female slave, also identified by her lesser stature, is carrying offerings of food. The mother, who is at the back of the procession, and who is identified by the veil she is wearing, holds another offering in her hand, a *pyxis*.

We have seen how this ceremony referred to the success of the birth and to the continuation of life, the following concern shared by all mothers. Although it is difficult to estimate the percentage of child mortality, it is thought that only half would reach adulthood (Oakley 2003, 163). Therefore, during this first stage, several votive offerings were made: swaddled terracotta babies with amulets around the neck, which were used against bad luck, disease or the evil eye, such as those found in Paestum (Ammerman 2007, 142–148). These amulets around the neck are customary in the portrayal of small children. Figurines of women carrying a child in their arms, known as *kourotrophos*, were also offered; this offering was already in use in Archaic times (Beaumont 2003, 61).

Another public ceremony with a more civic nature is the *Apotouria*, celebrated annually and in which the father presented the boy to the bosom of the *phatry*, and very likely the girl as well, when they turned one (Neils 2003, 144–145). On this occasion, the children were also presented before the guardian deity of the *polis*. A fragmented relief found in the Acropolis of Athens, which shows a father with his son before Athena,[3] has been associated with this ceremony (Lawton 2007, 46).

Another quite common depiction, which portrays an inactive baby in the arms of an adult woman, is a relief that was used as an offering, reproducing the practice of a family tribute (Fig. 10.1). In general, the group goes in procession towards the deity, who is almost always enthroned, carrying offerings and/or animals to be sacrificed (Lawton 2007, 43–45). These scenes reflect real worship acts, although it is not confirmed on the ceramics (Hirsch-Dyczek 1983, 41). The baby's role is also secondary in this case; the family unity showing respect to the deity is highlighted, as well as their participation in the worship since the earliest ages (Dillon 2002, 31–36). The same situation is repeated in portrayals that recreate family visits to the tombs of a loved one, as can be noted in several *lekythos* attributed to the painter from Berlin (Oakley 2003, 163).

There are certain aspects in which this age group coincides with the following one, due to the common denominator of the bond with the *oikos*, such as the fact that few differences are noted, as we will see, between the activities of boys and girls, although the girls are always dressed and the boys naked, no doubt a symbolic nakedness (Molas Font 2016, 73). The scenes showing children in such a domestic environment are very scarce, the exception being a few glasses with red figures from the end of the 5th century BC (Beaumont 2015, 106–114), where the disjunctive of

Figure 10.1: Attica. Votive relief found in the sanctuary of Artemis of Brauron. Archaeological Museum of Brauron (340 BC) (photo: author. © Hellenic Ministry of Culture and Sports/Ephorate of Antiquities of East Attica. Inv. 1151, reproduced by permission

naked boys and dressed girls is maintained. On occasions, the accompanying women are carrying out activities related to weaving.

Second stage. Pre-puberty: from 3–7 years of age

Other than in very specific contexts, we will see that it is very complicated to determine the age of those depicted in the iconography. They belong to this group, not so much because of their physical appearance, which is generally imprecise, but more in relation to their gestures, attributes and objects. Beaumont (2015, 24–36) highlights the following features: size, height and body shape, hair length, facial and body hair, clothes, gestures, attributes and compositional connection with other figures. These peculiarities, although not always concurrent, can be compared with reliefs with epigraphic information, such as the stele of the Ikaria Acropolis,[4] in which a woman is portrayed with five children, according to the inscription, three children and two siblings, understood to be between 1 and 16 years old. The smallest is being carried (first group), the middle one crawls in search of the mother and the third youngster, naked, is standing before her (both in the second group). The two siblings, the oldest in the group, are wearing tunics. The difference between them is shown in their manifestation of pain, more intense in the youngest, who holds his hand to his head (third group) and, more rigid in the oldest (fourth group), who extends his right hand towards her as if saying goodbye (Oakley 2003, 180). We will analyse these gestures in more detail, in relation to the funeral rite.

Figure 10.2: London. Attic Choes: boy and girl crawling (425–420 BC)(image: British Museum. Attica red-figure chous boy. Inv. 1842, 0728, 1123 and Inv. 1933, 0613, 5, reproduced by permission)

Three years of age is taken as the beginning of a new stage which is considered less vulnerable, because the possibilities of reaching adulthood increased notably. The Athenian society celebrated this transition with a rite of passage in one of the most significant festivities of the *polis*: the *Anthesteria* in honour of Dionysus. Specifically, the second day was known as *Choes*, 'the feast of wine jugs', so called because there was a drinking competition among adults (Neils 2003, 145 and Beaumont 2004, 75), and 3-year-old children tasted wine for the first time, a ritual that celebrated their survival. The objects that symbolised this event were the *choes* themselves, small glasses decorated with different activities related to childhood, which serve to show us an approximation of what their lives were like. Thus, they show games of skill or imitation, comic scenes and daily events accompanied by pets (Moreno Conde 2015, 37) that allow us to learn some of the children's entertainments. The most common pets are dogs and, among the games they played, the most recurrent are the wheeled stick and the carts. Occasionally, older youngsters are also depicted (Beaumont 2015, 69–84). Although portrayals of boys are more frequent than of girls, there are not too many differences between the genders, except for the nakedness of the boys, in contrast with the clothed bodies of the girls (Fig. 10.2), of whom only one case of nakedness has been confirmed (Beaumont 2015, fig. 2.3 a). In other words, games, pets, and gestures seem interchangeable between both. These coincidences are also documented in funeral objects (Oakley 2003, 178) and in funerary steles. The most common objects in burials were terracotta figures of animals, miniature glasses, toy furniture, balls, dolls, and knucklebones; all could be used as offerings at the time in which they began a new stage, marriage for girls, and a new educational phase for boys, which would introduce them to the male universe (Beaumont 2015, 128–34).

Most *choes* have been located among children's funeral objects, sometimes as property of the deceased, but other times as an object that they would have owned if they had lived, but death prevented them from taking part in this festivity. It is a situation comparable to that of young women who died before getting married and were buried with *loutrophoroi*, containers characteristic of the wedding ritual. In both cases, it nostalgically confirms the impossibility being able to proceed towards new social situations. The death of a young woman was cloaked in special sadness due to not having achieved the main role that society assigned to women (Foley 2003, 132).

Even though the age of the *choes* can be determined because we know the associated ritual, in general, it is practically impossible to specify the age of the individuals, beyond that of belonging to a particular group. It is important to keep in mind that in ancient times it was not important to determine the exact age of an individual (Beaumont 2015, 17). The funerary steles, much influenced by the socioeconomic circumstances of the *polis* (Hirsch-Dyczek 1983, 8), constitute an excellent subject of study. Small children usually appear together with a woman, very probably their mother. Unlike the previous stage, they show a greater autonomy of movement, crawling, standing, or sitting on her knees, the latter being the oldest motif (Hirsch-Dyczek 1983, 39). The most common gesture is with their arms raised, showing their dependence, such as corresponds to this stage of coexistence, for both boys and girls, in the *oikos*, dominated by the feminine universe. In this phase, the mother carries out an important educational task, which goes beyond physical abilities such as eating, walking and speaking, in order to go into the necessary respect for the rules of the patriarchal society and, especially, for the values of the citizenry, fundamental to maintaining the continuity of the *poleis* (Reboreda Morillo 2012). When the steles include two children with the mother and one of them is a baby, it usually corresponds to death during the last birth (Oakley 2003, 185). Another group of funerary reliefs, not very common, but meaningful, are those that depict a boy or a girl alone, the former being more frequent. We can cite the famous stele that depicts two brothers[5] as being exceptional. They are often accompanied by pets and toys: birds, dogs, knucklebones, balls, and spinning tops are common to both sexes. Dolls or mirrors (objects that are maintained in the following stage) are exclusive to girls and wheeled sticks, hoops and, less often, lyres, hares and cats are for boys. With the exception of the repeated nakedness of the boys and the girls being dressed, we can see that most objects and pets are interchangeable. The scenes conjure up moments of happiness, probably with the purpose of perpetuating this image of eternal play (Oakley 2003, 191). Fondness and pain caused by the separation is also expressed, the same feelings reflected by painters of funerary urns, where the child is about to leave in Charon's boat, a common theme; however, the images never describe time spent in Hades (Oakley 2003, 173).

As in the first age group, boys and girls took part in religious rituals, no longer in the arms of an adult, but more actively. Thus, they take part in processions which were going to make an offering or a sacrifice to a deity, or accompanying women to get water for the bride's ritual bath, or taking part in the wedding party that accompanies the newlyweds to their new home.

Another recurrent religious context is the funeral rites. We start from the principal that death was a normal experience in Ancient Greece, and from this daily nature, the

Figure 10.3: Paris. Pinax (Votive plaque) from Athens. Prothesis attributed to painter of Sappho (about 500 BC). Paris, Museum of Louvre. Inv. MNB 905

scenes show the functions that society attributed to both genders in relation to the age group in which they were integrated. To illustrate this statement it is customary to refer to a terracotta funeral plaque attributed to the painter Sappho at the beginning of the 5th century BC[6] (Fig. 10.3). It depicts an *ekphora*, the moment in which the corpse, after being washed and anointed by the women, is exhibited before the loved ones so that they could say their last goodbyes. The women, near the deceased's head, openly express their pain with eloquent gestures of sorrow: they pull their hair and beat their chest and cheeks; it is an open and spontaneous display of their feelings. The group of men, placed at the feet, in a contained gesture, send an austere salute by raising their right arm in a contained gesture. The girls, placed among the women, imitate the female mourning, foreseeing their future role in the learning process. The boys' attitude usually follows the external display of pain of the women, as a consequence of their dependency laid down by the *oikos* environment. However, we believe that there is another possible interpretation, at least on occasions such as this, midway between both defined groups, both physically in the scene and also because of their particular gesture, which is customary and which varies between male austerity and the female explosion of feelings. Thus, the boys are not holding back their feelings and do express their grief, but in a more restrained way than the women, the common denominator in different funeral portrayals is the wish to reach out to whoever has passed away, generally by extending their arms towards the deceased (Oakley 2003, 166; 170–173). This same expression is the one shown on the painted glasses that describe Charon: the boy, about to leave, turns towards his parents and stretches is arms out towards them, as a kind of a painful farewell. They sometimes carry toys with them, such as a bag of knucklebones or a toy cart, remembering those happy childhood moments.

Third stage. Puberty: from 7–14 years of age

As of 7 years of age, portrayals show that boys and girls took different paths, a circumstance that corresponds with the beginning of their preparation for carrying out their respective roles that society assigned to them. For the young girls, the end of this stage, which coincided with their biological ability to be mothers, took them directly to marriage. The young boys would still have to wait until 30 years of age, after completing a training process which was considered more complex than that of the girls, in accordance with the future performance of their political and military obligations demanded by their *polis* as citizens.

Let us analyse what the iconography says about those girls, whose breasts are, unlike the previous stage, already perceived under their clothing. During this period they stayed in the *oikos* in a feminised environment, adding to the role plays, real learning practices. Both prepared them to be good wives and mothers, i.e. organising the home and the tasks of the servants, cooking, taking care of the sick, bringing children into the world, making sure they survived and educating them in the values of the *polis* (Reboreda Morillo 2016).

For this reason, the most meaningful scenes, which are very rare, are set in a domestic context. Perhaps the most illustrative is the well-known terracotta Boeotia from the beginning of the 5th century BC, which depicts an adult woman cooking with a young girl and that has been unanimously interpreted as a mother teaching her daughter to cook[7] (Foley 2003, 112; 120). No doubt the most recurrent image is the one that shows women in relation to the activity of weaving, symbol of their virtue par excellence. Although different ages are represented, it is not easy to identify the relationship between them, but it seems evident that mother and daughter weaved together, the mother being responsible for teaching, as confirmed by written records. Thus, Xenophon, in his work *Oeconomicus* (VII, 6), states that learning about wool was the most meaningful task, together with controlling appetites. In the epigraphy we have evidence that the final product went beyond the limits of the self-sufficiency of the *oikos* to become a regular joint offering, from mother and daughter, to the gods, particularly the female ones (Beaumont 2003, 117–118).

Another feminine domestic scene which combines different age groups is the one that describes the wedding preparations of a young woman in which the mother plays an important role, since she is considered responsible for fulfilling all the required rituals. This theme, in various dimensions of the event, is profusely shown on ceramics and the main figure is always the maiden (Lissarrague 1991; 1996). Just as in the previous case, it is also complicated to identify both the other women and their relationships, but written sources describe this motherly prominence as an act that will signal the end of their cohabitation, since the girl would depart to the home of her husband's family after the celebrations.

Once again, we broach the religious context. In addition to domestic training, the girls had to know and pass a series of rites dedicated to certain goddesses, whom they had to worship, many times in relation to their roles in society. In these rituals, dancing and music occupy a prominent place, as shown in the iconography (Beaumont 2015, 149–152). Although there is no information on this subject, it is very likely that learning these skills took place at home, taught by female adult relatives. In the setting of the temples, in Athens we have evidence of three rituals, reflected in the iconography as well as written sources, although the information is limited (Dillon 2002, 57–63). Everything points to a minority position, probably led by the daughters of the wealthier families, and it is quite probable that this privilege was passed from mothers to daughters.

In *Lysistrata*, Aristophanes states that, at the age of 7, two or perhaps four girls, acted as *arrephoros*, carriers of secret objects in the night festival known as *Arrhephoria* and in the another festival; *Chalkeia* (Beaumont 2015, 170–175). Furthermore, they lived in the acropolis for a while, they were considered servants of the goddess and for a year they took part in weaving *peplos,* which were given as an offering to Athena. At the age of 10, they assumed the role of *aletris*, grain grinders, the only activity of which no portrayals are known, and *kanephoros*, carriers of baskets which contained objects related to sacrifices and led the sacrificial processions (Neils 2003, 149–151; 158). Along with this tribute to Athena, the most extended ritual of the *polis* in Attica took place in Brauron, at the sanctuary of Artemis (Reboreda Morillo forthcoming), where an abundance of iconography related to childhood, particularly of girls, but also of boys (Fig. 10.4) has been found (Beaumont 2015, 174–186).

As an example, a great many sculptures are documented, of small children accompanied by birds, balls, and rabbits, the boys naked and the girls dressed; the reason for these offerings varied. In general, they called for protection, they gave thanks for having overcome a disease or for having held a prominent position in a ritual at the service of the deity (Beaumont 2015, 154–156). Other depictions are directly associated with the confinement period of Athenian girls between the ages of 10 and 14 classed as *arktoi* (bear cubs). The end of their stay closed the childhood stage, associated with a wild nature, and they were now considered to be ready for sexual maturity and its consequences (Marinatos 2002, 36–39), i.e., being good wives and effective mothers. We do not know the length of the stay; it is even possible that it varied depending on the era, although some specialists believe that it would be about one year. The tasks that they performed in this sacred place have not emerged either. In his play, *Lysistrata,* (645), Aristophanes states that acolytes, dressed in saffron-coloured suits (a substitute for bear skin), known as krokoton, and 'shed' the 'bear skin.' This activity was associated with that portrayed in the *krateriskoi* (Nielsen 2009, 81–83), small kraters specific to the tribute of that goddess and also documented, for example, in the sanctuary of Artemis Mounichia in Piraeus. They were decorated with girls of different ages in procession, dancing and running, generally dressed in a tunic and, less frequently, naked. This 'bear dance' prepared them for pregnancy and giving birth, probably due to the association of this animal with great maternal traits. The saffron colour described by Aristophanes was associated with the erotic properties that the Greeks attributed to the crocus flower. Another ritual shown is that of the

Figure 10.4: Attica. Votive sculptures: girls and boy found in the sanctuary of Artemis of Brauron. Archaeological Museum of Brauron.

hunt of a female bear, a role that was taken on by one of the girls, portrayed with a bear mask (Nielsen 2009, 88).

Before concluding the feminine references of this stage, we must mention the famous *kore* from the Archaic period which, although previous to our chronological framework, cover the dangerous liminal period of a young girl who was considered neither child nor adult, but rather a figure in transit, a transit of short duration, who has to be protected from the external masculine threats as well as her own instability (Beaumont 2000, 45). They are sculptures of young aristocrats, which served as an offering to the goddesses, at the same time as making their availability for marriage public, as well as the possible dowry that their family was willing to hand over. The end of the *parthenos* period was determined not so much by marriage, but more by their ability to bear children, which raised them to the status of *gyne*.

In this entire group, the age most portrayed is that close to marriage, proving the importance given to her fertility, which made her an essential element for the continuation of the *polis* (Molas Font 2016, 80).

We will add little with respect to the males who, upon entering the masculine universe, are usually no longer linked to their mothers' actions, moving away from the aim of this study. A new, very different learning process starts for them, away from home, with the purpose of them learning the specific and essential skills to develop their role as citizens (Beaumont 2015, 134–146). Thus, they are shown in private schools, learning reading, writing, and music; modestly dressed in *himation* or capes or naked in the gymnasium, doing physical exercise or in scenes of conquest with adult males with whom they maintained homoerotic relationships as a part of their education and training. Once they have proved their ability to perform their role as citizens, they join the army. The most common scenes in which mothers and sons are reunited are known as 'the farewell of the warrior,' where the mother is shown in distress because of the very possible, terrible fate of her son (Beaumont 2005, 110–111). Prior to this time, in the 6th century BC, the luxurious sculptures of the *kouros*, athletic youths, naked, who represented the idealized aristocracy are of interest. Their fate, just as we saw with the *kore*, was to become an offering in a shrine. The difference is that these statues were used in the cemeteries to mark graves. In these latter contexts, as warriors or athletes they are usually portrayed on funerary steles that now no longer recall happiness through games, but through competition and war.

By way of conclusion

The initial approach of this paper was to deal with the perception of childhood in Athens during the Classical period through images and texts, but as I worked on the subject, I became aware that the richness transmitted by the iconography, as pointed out by specialists, surpassed that of the texts themselves. While aware that in many examples an ideal is depicted, this, necessarily, informs us of a reality, a factor which we can verify through both the scenes selected by the artists and the influence that social changes exert on the portrayal itself. It is true that the children were not usually naked, but no doubt their worth to society was highlighted in this nakedness, whereas the girls, except for a few exceptions, always appeared dressed, a symbol of their respectable future role as mothers and wives. The political-territorial structure of the *polis* brings with it the imperious need for citizens, even female citizens after Pericles' law, and society becomes more aware of the relevance of its children, an aspect which is shown through a portrayal which is more in line with their real forms, no longer being adults on a smaller scale. Furthermore, their presence becomes more frequent, also besides their mothers. The images through gestures, complements and contexts, show the different stages into which the Hellenes divided childhood. The smallest children, inactive, only showed their existence. From the age of 3, their participation becomes more active. Until the age of 7, when boys and girls lived together in the *oikos*, they hardly showed any differences, the same happens with their funeral objects on the graves and in the portrayal of funerary steles. From this age onwards, just as in their lives, their images are separated.

The most common context portrayed is the religious context, showing the interaction of this world with the daily nature of individuals. Thus, they are included in votive and funeral reliefs, in offerings and as a part of the rituals, both as main figures and taking part in the worship of deities or funerary ceremonies. The second, much less usual, scene is the domestic setting, from which boys disappear as soon as they begin their training in order to be able to carry out the roles that society has assigned them, more valued than the feminine roles, and so requiring more time. Girls married as soon as they were able to bring citizens into the world. The wedding preparations are the last scenes that link them to their mothers, who are profusely depicted in paintings on ceramics, where the maidens, just as in the reality of the event, held the most meaningful place.

Acknowledgements

This publication belongs to the I+D+I Research Project, funded by the Ministry of Economy and Competitiveness and directed by Rosa Cid López from Oviedo University, entitled 'Motherhood and families: continuity, changes, and breakdowns in history. Between ancient and contemporary societies.' (HAR 2013–42371-R).

Notes

1 Euripides: *Medea*, trans. George Theodovids, 2005. www.poetryintranslation.com
2 Archaeological Museum of Lamia, AE 1041.
3 Acropolis Museum, Athens, 3030.
4 Kataphygion, Ikaria, Schoolhouse.
5 New York, The Metropolitan Museum of Art 11.185.
6 Paris, Louvre Museum, MNB 905.
7 Boston, Museum of Fine Arts, H.10.7

References

Ammerman, R. M. (2007) Votive terracottas end the welfare of infants. In A. Cohen and J. R. Rutter (eds) *Constructions of Childhood in Ancient Greece and Italy*. Princeton/New Jersey, American School of Classical at Athens, 131–151.

Beaumont, L. A. (2000) The social status and artistic presentation of ′adolescence' in fifth century Athens. In J. S. Derevenski (ed.) *Children and Material Culture*. London/New York, Routledge, 39–50.

Beaumont, L. A. (2003) The changing face of childhood. In J. Neils and J. H. Oakley (eds) *Coming of Age in Ancient Greece. Images of Childhood from the Classical Past*. New Haven/London, Yale University Press, 58–83.

Cohen, A. (2007) Introduction: Childhood between past and present. in A. Cohen and J. R. Rutter (eds) *Constructions of Childhood in Ancient Greece and Italy*, 1–24. Princeton/New Jersey, American School of Classical at Athens.

Demand, N. (2004) *Birth, Death and Motherhood in Classical Greece*. Baltimor/London, Johns Hopkins University Press.

Dillon, M. (2002) *Girls and Women in Classical Greek Religion*. London/New York, Routledge.

Foley, H. (2003) Mothers and daughters. In J. Neils and J. H. Oakley (eds) *Coming of Age in Ancient Greece. Images of Childhood from the Classical Past*. New Haven/London, Yale University Press, 113–137.

Foley, H. (2007) Gendering the age gap: boys, girls, and abduction in Ancient Greek Art. In A. Cohen and J. R. Rutter (eds) *Constructions of Childhood in Ancient Greece and Italy*. Princeton/New Jersey, American School of Classical at Athens, 257–278.

Gherchanoc, F. (2012) *L'oikos en fête. Célébrations familiales et sociabilité en Grèce ancienne*. Paris, Publications de la Sorbonne.

Golden, M. (2003) Childhood in Ancient Greece. In J. Neils and J. H. Oakley (eds) *Coming of Age in Ancient Greece. Images of Childhood from the Classical Past*. New Haven/London, Yale University Press, 12–29.

Grossman, J. B. (2007) Forever young: An investigation of the depictions of children on Classical Attic funerary monuments. In A. Cohen and J. R. Rutter (eds) *Constructions of Childhood in Ancient Greece and Italy*. Princeton/New Jersey, American School of Classical at Athens, 309–322.

Hirsch-Dyczek, O. (1983) *Les representations des enfants sur les steles funeraires attiques*. Varsovia, PWN-Editions Scientifiques de Pologne.

Langdom, S. (2007) The awkward age: art and maturation in Early Greece. In A. Cohen and J. R. Rutter (eds) *Constructions of Childhood in Ancient Greece and Italy*. Princeton/New Jersey, American School of Classical at Athens, 173–191.

Lawton, C. L. (2007) Children in Classical Attic votive reliefs. In A. Cohen and J. R. Rutter (eds) *Constructions of Childhood in Ancient Greece and Italy*. Princeton/New Jersey, American School of Classical at Athens, 41–60.

Lissarrague, F. (1996) Regards sur le mariage grec. In O. Cavalier (dir.) *Silence et fureur. La femme et le mariage en Grèce. Les antiquités grecques du Musée Clavet*. Avignon: Mussée Clavet, 415–433.

Lissarrague, F. (1991) Una mirada ateniense. In G. Duby and M. Perrot (eds) *Historia de las mujeres en Occidente*, 1. Barcelona, Taurus, 183–250.

Loraux, N. (2004) *Las experiencias de Tiresias. Lo masculino y lo femenino en el mundo griego*. Barcelona, El Acantilado.

Marinatos, N. (2002) The *Arkteia* and the gradual transformation of Maiden into a Woman In B. Gentilo and F. Perusino (eds) *Le orse di Brauron. Un rituale di iniziazione femminile nel santuario di Artemide*. Pisa, Edizione ETS, 28–42.

McNiven, T. J. (2007) Behaving like a child: Immature gestures in Athenian Vase painting. In A. Cohen and J. R. Rutter (eds) *Constructions of Childhood in Ancient Greece and Italy*. Princeton/New Jersey, The American School of Classical at Athens, 85–99.

Molas Font, M. D. (2016) Las niñas en la *polis* ateniense. Cuerpos vestidos y vulnerables. In M. D. Molas Font and A. Santiago Bautista (eds) *La infancia en femenino: las niñas. Imágenes y figuras de la filiación*. Barcelona, Icaria, 67–85.

Moreno Conde, M. (2015) Las edades de la vida. Infancia y vejez a través de la iconografía griega. In A. Iriarte and L. Ferreira (eds) *Idades e género na literatura e na arte da Grécia antiga*. Universidade de Coimbra, Coimbra, 31–60.

Morizot, Y. (2004) Offrandes à Artémis pour une naissance. Autour du relief d'Achinos. In V. Dasen (ed.) *Naissance et petite enfance dans l'Antiquité. Actes du colloque de Fribourg, 28 novembre–1 décembre 2001*. Fribourg, Academic Press Fribourg, 159–170.

Neils, J. (2003) Children and Greek religion. In J. Neils and J. H. Oakley (eds) *Coming of Age in Ancient Greece. Images of Childhood from the Classical Past*. New Haven/London, Yale University Press, 138–161.

Nielsen, I. (2009) The Sanctuary of Artemis Brauronia. Can architecture and iconography help to locate the settings of the rituals? In T. Fischer-Hansen and B. Poulsen (eds) *From Artemis to Diana. The Goddess of Man and Beast*. Copenhagen, Museum Tusculanum-Press University of Copenhagen, 83–116.

Reboreda Morillo, S. (2012) Madres dependientes en la Antigüedad Griega. Su importancia en la preservación de la *polis*. In F. Reduzzi (ed.) *Dipendenza ed emarginazione nel mondo antico e moderno. Atti del XXXIII Convegno Internazionale G.I.R.E.A. dedicati alla memoria di Franco Salerno.* Rome, Aracne, 331–341.

Reboreda Morillo, S. (2016) La maternidad: desde la infancia a la adolescencia en la antigua Grecia. In A. Hervás Delgado and M. Picazo Gurina (eds) *Los trabajos de las mujeres en el mundo antiguo: cuidado y mantenimiento de la vida*, 119–128. Tarragona, Huc et Nunc.

Reboreda Morillo, S. (2017) La lactancia en la antigua Grecia entre el mito y la historia. *Dilemata* 25, 23–35.

Reboreda Morillo, S. (forthcoming) De Comadronas a diosas: panorama del parto en la Antigua Grecia. In R. M. Cid López (ed.) *Las madres y el parto en las sociedades del Mediterráneo antiguo. Entre el mito y la historia.* Oviedo, Trabe.

Sourvinou-Inwood, C. (1990) Lire l'*arkteia* -lire les images, les textes, l'animalité. *Dialogues d'Histoire Ancienne* 16(3), 45–60.

Chapter 11

The (ir)relevance of being a mother. A legal perspective on the relationship between mothers and children in ancient Greece

Laura Pepe

Sometimes, while considering some specific historical periods, we realise that it is possible to establish a bi-univocal relationship between law and art. This is conceivable, for example, for late antiquity of Roman empire. Mosaic is the most typical form of decorative art of this era; and mosaic is made of many little pieces that are put together in order to create (or rather to give the illusion of creating) a unity. It is tempting to compare the structure and the shape of the mosaic with that of the main legal work of this period, the *Digest* of Justinian; also the *Digest* is made up of (mainly) short fragments of earlier jurists, put in sequence in order to give the impression of some unity. In both cases, however, in the final result the idea of a real, actual, and full unity is lacking.

The same comparison between law and art can be made also as far as classical Greece is concerned. The most powerful artistic expression of classical Greece is sculpture; and if we take a look at Greek statues, we see many *kouroi* – young boys with athletic bodies, symbol of balance and perfection – and several *korai* – chaste, virginal young girls, not yet married, not yet mothers. It is hard, in classical art, to find scenes which show, for instance, a moment of intimacy between a mother and her baby. In truth, many vase-paintings actually portray women; but mostly these women belong to a particular category. They are *hetairai*, courtesans, high-profile prostitutes that normally attended the *symposia* (inaccessible to 'honest' women, like mothers, daughters, sisters, and wives of citizens), with the task of cheering young and less young men. But these women are not a symbol of any virtue: they are just bodies, objects of lust. Hence, apparently art is interested in women only when their body is young, desirable, attractive – in a word, not yet damaged by a pregnancy.

If we now shift our focus from art to literature, we see that in this field too it is hard to find any information concerning mothers, or the relationship between mothers and their children; moreover, the scant information we have is far from being positive, or favorable to women. Apart from archaic times – in the *Iliad,* Andromache is portrayed in moments of deep tenderness with her son Astyanax (*Il.* 6.399–410; 22.484–507), and Thetis is depicted as a very affectionate mother, desperate for the sad fate of her son Achilles (*Il.* 1.414–8; 18.37–64, 429–461) –, the myths of the classical period often talk about terrible, unstable mothers who do not hesitate to kill their children. The most notorious example is of course that of Euripides' Medea,[1] but there are many other stories about other destructive women: Althea, mad at her son Meleager, causes his death by throwing in the fire the piece of wood to which his life was tied ([Apollod.] *Bibl.* 1.8.2–3); Ino, daughter of Cadmus and Armonia, in an outburst of madness kills Melicertes, one of her children ([Apollod.] *Bibl.* 1.9.2; 3.4.3); and, in Euripides' *Bacchae*, Agave, struck with Dionysian madness, tears apart his son Pentheus.

What about law? Like art and literature, also the legal rules show almost no interest in mothers and childhood and, accordingly, in the relationship between mothers and sons. There are however some exceptions that are worth considering. In so doing, I will divide the analysis that follows in two distinct sections. In the first one I deal with Athens, the Attic *polis* that in our popular imagination represents Greek democracy in its best, and whose laws are well-known thanks to many literary and epigraphic sources. In the second section I consider Gortyn, a Cretan *polis* of Doric origins – like Sparta – known especially for its 'code' on family law. Between these two models it is possible to find some differences, sometimes noticeable. This is quite normal; in fact, it is important to remind that ancient Greece was not a unitary country, but a complex of many *poleis*, which were independent from a political perspective and, at least sometimes, had different legal rules.[2]

Athenian laws dealt almost exclusively with men, and in particular with citizens, the only individuals who represented the *polis*, and the only ones who benefitted from the rights recognised and assured by the *polis*. Athenian laws were very detailed in specifying the duties and the rights of citizens, in fixing the penalties for citizens who did not abide by the rules, in regulating the economic relationships among citizens. In a sentence, Athenian laws were male-oriented – and, if we consider them from our perspective, sometimes they can even appear sexist (a concept that was of course unknown to ancient Greeks and ancient people in general). Women were taken into account by the laws of the city only seldom, and in most cases only indirectly, when their activity interfered, by chance or by necessity, with that of men. And one of the most typical circumstances in which female and male activities came into contact with each others was of course the reproduction of children. In considering the rules that regulated this topic, it is first important to recall very briefly the historical frame in which these laws were enacted.

Athens was a 'closed city'; since it was a direct democracy, where citizens were asked to participate actively in, and to take vital decisions for, the health, the safety, and in general the life of the *polis*, citizenship was granted on a very narrow basis. Whereas until the middle of the 5th century it was enough to be born from just one

Athenian parent (usually the father) in order to be Athenian, in 450/1 BC, when Athens was at the height of its glory, Pericles – one of the most renowned Athenian statesmen – established with a non-retroactive statute that 'only those whose parents on both sides were Athenians should be reckoned Athenians.'[3]

Athenian women were thus given a prominent role by the law. Before that moment, it was not necessary to have an Athenian mother in order to be an Athenian citizen, and aristocratic families usually arranged for their sons a marriage with illustrious foreign women;[4] from that moment on (albeit with some discontinuity)[5] only Athenian women were titled to be mothers of children who would become Athenian citizens, when they came of age. Their maternity – in the sense of the generation process that they ensured – was extraordinarily important.

The link between law and women, however, ends here. As for the law, the role of a woman was relevant only as far as she was meant to 'produce' new citizens; there was no interest at all in her 'being mother', after the baby came to life. In fact, many sources underscore that she was just a vessel, a womb for her child:[6] once it was born and became independent from her body, it belonged to the father, who had to power to decide whether it had the right to become a legitimate member of the family or, on the contrary, it should be exposed and left to destiny.[7]

The fact that, from the very first moment of the life of the newborn, there is no more connection between a mother and her child explains the silence of Athenian law about their relationship and mutual duties; as a matter of fact, there was no reason for the law to take into account something that, at least from a legal point of view, did not even exist. Since the children was related only to the father, the law regulated only the duty of the father to rear the children, especially the sons, and to teach them a job – providing a sort of sanction for the fathers who failed to do so[8] (of course mothers had to teach their daughters how to weave, how to cook, how to take care of the house, so that they could be good wives in the future; but this is something that had only a social, not a legal relevance). Since there was no kinship tie between mothers and children, the latter could not inherit from the family of their mothers, but only from that of their fathers; as for the woman, in the rare cases when she was allowed to inherit something – since, according to the Athenian law, women could not be owners of the family estate –, she could only inherit from the collateral relatives of her original family.[9]

It seems, however, that there could be an exception to the rule that Athenian law was not interested in women; in fact, we know of a statute concerning *oikoi eremoi*, 'lonely households' that lacked a father, a head of the family. The most relevant source for this law is a passage in the speech *Against Macartatus*, attributed to Demosthenes:

> Ὁ ἄρχων ἐπιμελείσθω τῶν ὀρφανῶν καὶ τῶν ἐπικλήρων καὶ τῶν οἴκων τῶν ἐξερημουμένων καὶ τῶν γυναικῶν, ὅσαι μένουσιν ἐν τοῖς οἴκοις τῶν ἀνδρῶν τῶν τεθνηκότων φάσκουσαι κυεῖν. Τούτων ἐπιμελείσθω καὶ μὴ ἐάτω ὑβρίζειν μηδένα περὶ τούτους. Ἐὰν δέ τις ὑβρίζῃ ἢ ποιῇ τι παράνομον, κύριος ἔστω ἐπιβάλλειν κτλ. ([Dem.] 43.75)

> Let the archon take care of orphans, heiresses, and families that are about to become extinct [*oikoi exeremoumenoi*], and of women who remain in the houses of their deceased husbands declaring that they are pregnant. Let him take care of these, and not permit anyone to mistreat them. And if anyone mistreats them or does anything contrary to law or custom, he shall have power to penalize him.

This information is confirmed also in the *Athenaion Politeia* attributed to Aristoteles (*Ath. Pol.* 56.7), as well as in a speech by Isaeus (Isae. 7.30). The rule, apparently enacted by Solon[10] – one of the most ancient Athenian lawgivers – accorded a special protection to specific categories of people belonging to a household where there was no *paterfamilias* left; among these people there were pregnant widows and orphans (no need to say that of course, for the Greeks, an orphan was a minor who did not have a father, but could still have a mother). In particular, the law said that it was one of the magistrates, the archon, who had to take care of their well-being; hence, if somebody mistreated them (the Greek word is *hybrizei*, which indicates an intentional and particularly serious violence), or did something contrary to law or custom, the archon had the power and the duty to summon him and take him in front of the popular court, so that he could be judged and, if found guilty, appropriately punished.

At first glance, it looks like this statute aims at safeguarding the relationship between mothers and children in the absence of a father. But is it really so? Unfortunately I doubt it. In fact, if we take a closer look at the law, contextualising it in the historical frame of ancient Athens, we realise that it had only a patrimonial goal. Its purpose was to guarantee that the house, *oikos*, did not fail short of a legitimate heir, and it is indeed undeniable that it had to do with the preservation of inheritance lines in households that were vulnerable under this point of view: first of all, those households where there was a child without a father (an 'orphan'), who had to stay only with his mother; and moreover those where there was a pregnant widow, whose womb had to be protected in order to make sure that the family could have a heir.

The conclusion that can be drawn from the analysis of both laws – the Periclean and the Solonian one – is that, at least from a legal point of view, Athens is not at all interested in women as mothers, and in the relation they could have with their children. The *polis* that surpassed all the other ancient cities as far as freedom and democracy were concerned, the *polis* that, for this very reason, we usually take as a paradigm of inspiration, this *polis* was – exactly like most of ancient cites – definitely lacking in the protection of women and of their being mothers.

Of course, ancient Greece was not just Athens, even though it is hard to deny that the concept we have of ancient Greece is mostly focused on Athens – it is 'Athenocentric.' However, if we want to find an attitude towards mothers which is closer to our sensitivity, it is to other *poleis* that we should direct our glance. It is well-known that Sparta, and Doric cities in general, had a consideration of women very different from that of the Athenians. As a matter of fact, in the Doric area women had an independence, a freedom, and – most of all – a financial position which are hardly comparable to that of Athenian women. I will not re-examine here the general status of Spartan and more generally Doric women; I would only like to stress that their autonomy was relevant especially under a legal point of view, and, as far as our topic is concerned, in the relationship between mothers and children.

The *polis* I will consider is Gortyn, a small Doric city in the middle of Crete. Here, several years ago, the Italian archaeologists unearthed a monumental series of legal inscriptions on stone – usually known as 'the Code of Gortyn' – which is still displayed in the site of the ancient town. The Gortynian code deals with family law, and reveals that women here were clearly 'emancipated,' at least if we compare their position to that of Athenian women.[11]

As we just said, in Athens the destiny of the babies born from *iustae nuptiae* was placed exclusively in the hands of the fathers. If he decided not to recognize them as legitimate children, they were excluded from the family, and there was no chance that anybody else could stop him from doing so, or could object to his decision. But what happened when a pregnant wife was repudiated by her husband? And what happened to the newborn baby? Athenian laws, as far as we know, do not say a word on this point, probably because their fate did not interest the city and its institutions. Gortynian laws, instead, evaluate this possibility in a quite detailed way. In fact, we read in the lawcode that:

> Αἰ τέκοι γυνὰ κ-
> ε[ρ]ε[ύο]νσα, ἐπελεῦσαι τῶι ἀ-
> νδρὶ ἐπὶ στέγαν ἀντὶ μαιτ-
> ύρον τριῶν. Αἰ δὲ μὲ δέκσαι-
> το, ἐπὶ τᾶι ματρὶ ἔμεν τὸ τέκ-
> νον ἒ τράπεν ἒ ἀποθέμεν (*IC* IV 72 col. III 44–49)

> If a divorced woman gives birth, she shall go to the ex-husband place together with three witnesses. If (the ex husband) does not acknowledge (the baby as his own), she shall decide whether to rear or to expose the baby.

This rule is incredibly important, since it admits the possibility that a lonely mother, divorced from the previous husband, could actually rear the baby; moreover, it implies that in this case the baby does not get the name of the father – who decided not to recognise him as his legitimate son – but instead becomes part of the family of the mother – who decided to bring it up –. At the same time, exactly as it allows the protection of the tie between a mother and her child, the law acknowledges that a lonely woman could decide not to rear the baby born after the end of the marriage. Her only duty is to inform the ex husband about the birth of the newborn, so that he can be the first one to decide what to do. Of course, there are penalties in case the mother does not abide by this rule:

> Υ-
> υνὰ κερεύονσ'αἰ ἀποβάλοι
> παιδίον πρὶν ἐπελεῦσαι κατ-
> ὰ τὰ ἐγραμμένα, ἐλευθέρο μ-

ἐν καταστασεῖ πεντέκοντα
στατερανς, δόλο πέντε καὶ ϝ-
ίκατι, αἴ κα νικαθεῖ (*IC* IV 72 col. IV 8–14)

If a divorced woman has exposed the baby before going to the ex-husband, as stated, she shall pay fifty staters, if free, twenty-five staters, if slave. But if there is no house where to go, or the husband cannot be seen, she shall not pay anything in case she decides to expose the baby.

The Gortynian woman has of course some duties towards the previous husband; but, at the same time, she also have some rights on the newborn, even though these rights come after those of the father. What is worth stressing, however, is that the baby is not an exclusive property of the man. Gortynian laws, as far as the relationship mother-child is concerned, are far more advanced than the Athenian ones. They granted the woman a freedom that the Athenians – our ideal 'ancestors' – could not even imagine to concede.

Acknowledgement

This publication belongs to the I+D+I Research Project, funded by the Ministry of Economy and Competitiveness of Spain, entitled 'Motherhood and families: continuity, changes, and breakdowns in history. Between ancient and contemporary societies.' (HAR 2013–42371-R).

Notes

1 Euripides' tragedy, where Medea kills her sons, of course reproduces one of the available versions of the myth. It is however important to note that the poet does not depict Medea as a bad and vicious mother; she clearly loves her children (Eur. *Med.* 1019–1080), even though she realises that only by killing them she will fully accomplish her plan of revenge against their father Jason.

2 Scholars have debated at length, and are still debating, whether it is possible to conceive Greek law as a homogeneous system, or it is better to emphasise the differences among the law of the different *poleis*, or at least the law of each of the three groups that lived in ancient Greece (the Doric, the Ionic and the Eolic one). One of the main supporters of the latter idea is Finley (1966), whose theories were shared by Talamanca (1981). New contributions to the topic have been recently brought by Gagarin (2005), who thinks that it is possible to speak of unity of Greek law only as far as procedural (not substantial) law is concerned; by Barta (2010), 159 ff., according to which the general homogeneity of Greek culture included also the legal field; and by Phillips (2014), who shows that there are concepts, like that of *hybris*, where it is possible to speak of unity also from a substantial point of view.

3 Plut. *Per.* 37.3: Περικλῆς ... νόμον ἔγραψε μόνους Ἀθηναίους εἶναι τοὺς ἐκ δυεῖν Ἀθηναίων γεγονότας; cf. also *Ath. Pol.* 26.4: Περικλέους εἰπόντος ἔγνωσαν μὴ μετέχειν τῆς πόλεως, ὃς ἂν μὴ ἐξ ἀμφοῖν ἀστοῖν ᾖ γεγονώς, 'an enactment was passed on the proposal of Pericles confining citizenship to persons of citizen birth on both sides.' For a detailed analysis of the law see generally Patterson (1981). It is debated whether the law – clearly quoted both by the *Ath. Pol.* and by Plutarch in an abridged form – required also the *iustae nuptiae* of the parents

of the prospective citizen or not; for the former hypothesis see Humphreys (1974); Rhodes (1978); Patterson (1990); Ogden (1996); for the latter see Harrison (1968, 63 ss.); MacDowell (1976; 1978, 68); Cantarella (1997).

4 To quote just a few examples, two of the most important Athenian statesmen of the 6th and 5th centuries BC were born from foreign mothers. Cleisthenes, traditionally known as the father of democracy in 508/7, was the son of Agariste, daughter of the tyrant of Sycion who had given her to the Athenian Megacles (Hdt. 6.126–131); Cimon, a leading general in 470/60 BC, was the son of the Athenian Miltiades and of a Thracian woman named Hegesipyle (Plut. *Cim.* 4.1).

5 Since it was re-enacted in 403/2 BC (see Aesch. 1.39), it is easy to infer that during the Peloponnesian war the law, albeit probably not officially annulled, was not really enforced.

6 See *e.g.* Aesch. *Eum.* 658–661; Arist. *Gen. anim.* 728a; 729a-b.

7 On this point see esp. Pepe (2012; 2014 with further bibliography).

8 Normally the sons had the duty of *gerotrophia*, meaning that they had to support their parents once they were too old to work; in case that the father did not teach them a job, however, the sons were exempted from this duty (see Plut. *Sol.* 22). On the topic see lately Cantarella (2016).

9 Isae. 7.19; 11.1–3, cf. [Dem.] 43.51. For the restricted financial capacity of Athenian women, who could not own anything and were moreover forbidden to contract for the disposal of more than a bushel of barley, see Isae. 10.10.

10 See Scafuro (2006, especially 179 f).

11 Main editions of the code are Guarducci (1950) and Willetts (1967). The most important works on the code, some of which dedicated in particular to the Gortynian woman, are those of Maffi (1997; 2012a; 2012b), Gagarin (2008; 2012a; 2012b), Kristensen (2004; 2007); Gagarin and Perlman (2016).

References

Barta, H. (2010) *'Graeca non leguntur?.' Zu der Ursprüngen des europäischen Rechts im antiken Griechenland.* Wiesbaden, Harrassowitz

Cantarella, E. (1997) Filiazione legittima e cittadinanza. In G. Thür and J. Vélissaropoulos Karakostas (eds) *Symposion 1995. Vorträge zur griechischen und hellenistischen Rechtsgeschichte.* Köln-Weimar-Wien, Böhlau, 97–111.

Cantarella, E. (2016) Gerotrophia. A controversial law. In D. Leão and G. Thür (eds) *Symposion 2015. Vorträge zur griechischen und hellenistischen Rechtsgeschichte.* Wien, Austrian Academy of Sciences Press, 55–66.

Finley, M. I. (1966) The problem of the unity of Greek law, In AA.VV. *La storia del diritto nel quadro delle scienze storiche. Atti del primo congresso internazionale della Società Italiana di Storia del Diritto.* Firenze, Società italiana di storia del diritto, 129–142.

Gagarin, M. (2005) The unity of Greek law. In M. Gagarin and D. Cohen (eds) *The Cambridge Companion to Ancient Greek Law.* Cambridge, Cambridge University Press, 29–40.

Gagarin, M. (2008) Women and property at Gortyn. *Dike* 11, 5–25.

Gagarin, M. (2012a) Women and the Law in Gortyn. *Index* 40, 57–67.

Gagarin, M. (2012b) Women's property at Gortyn. *Dike* 15, 73–92.

Gagarin, M. and Perlman, P. (2016) *The Laws of Ancient Crete, c. 650–400 BCE.* Oxford, Oxford University Press.

Guarducci, M. (1950) *Inscriptiones Creticae. IV. Tituli Gortynii.* Roma, La Libreria dello stato

Harrison, A. R. W. (1968) *The Law of Athens. The family and property.* Oxford, Clarendon Press

Humphreys, S. (1974) The nothoi of Kynosarges. *Journal of Hellenic Studies* 94, 88–95.

Kristensen, K. R. (2004) Codification, tradition and innovation in the Law Code of Gortyn. *Dike* 7, 135–168.

Kristensen, K. R. (2007) Inheritance, property, and management: Gortynian family law revisited. In E. Cantarella (ed.) *Symposion 2005. Vorträge zur griechischen und hellenistischen Rechtsgeschichte.* Wien, Austrian Academy of Sciences Press, 89–100.

MacDowell, D. M. (1976) Bastards as Athenian citizens. *Classical Quarterly* 26, 88–91.

MacDowell, D. M. (1978) *The Law in Classical Athens.* London, Thames and Hudson.

Maffi, A. (1997) *Il diritto di famiglia nel codice di Gortina.* Milano, CUEM.

Maffi, A. (2012a) Lo statuto dei 'beni materni' nella Grecia classica. *Index* 40, 91–111.

Maffi, A. (2012b) Ancora sulla condizione giuridica della donna nel codice di Gortina. *Dike* 15, 93–123.

Ogden, D. (1996) *Greek Bastardy in the Classical and Hellenistic Periods.* Oxford, Clarendon Press.

Patterson, C. (1981) *Pericles' Citizenship Law of 451/0 a. C.*, New York, Arno Press.

Patterson, C. (1990) Those Athenian bastards. *Classical Antiquity* 9, 39–73.

Pepe, L. (2012) Pregnancy and childbirth, or the right of the father. some reflections about motherhood and fatherhood in ancient Greece. *Rivista di diritto ellenico* 2, 255–274.

Pepe, L. (2014) Abortion in Ancient Greece. In M. Gagarin, A. Lanni (eds) *Symposion 2013. Vorträge zur griechischen und hellenistischen Rechtsgeschichte.* Wien, Austrian Academy of Sciences Press, 39–63.

Phillips, D. D. (2014) Hubris and the unity of Greek law. In M. Gagarin, A. Lanni (eds) *Symposion 2013. Vorträge zur griechischen und hellenistischen Rechtsgeschichte.* Wien, Austrian Academy of Sciences Press, 75–97.

Rhodes, P. J. (1978) Bastards as Athenian citizens. *Classical Quarterly* 28, 89–92.

Scafuro, A. C. (2006) Identifying Solonian laws. In J. H. Blok and A. P. M. H. Lardinois (eds) *Solon of Athens. New Historical and Philological Approaches.* Leiden, Brill, 175–196.

Talamanca, M. (1981) Il diritto in Grecia. In M. Bretone and M. Talamanca (eds) *Il diritto in Grecia e a Roma.* Bari, Laterza, 3–89.

Willetts, R. F. (1967) *The Law Code of Gortyn.* Berlin, de Gruyter.

Chapter 12

The Queen and her children: Royal motherhood in Hellenistic Greece

María Dolores Mirón Pérez

Royal families are political institutions, in the sense that political power is biologically and socially reproduced within them. Although monarchical power is held by a specific person, the king or queen (usually also the head of the family), all the members of royal families share royal power to some extent. Everything that happens within royal families (marriages, births, deaths and conflicts) has political significance.

Although formal political power has historically been a male-dominated sphere, royal women have also shared it to some degree, and they have even exercised it occasionally. Regardless of the manner and the extent to which their proximity to power materialises in practice, women fulfill a key political role: to transmit royal power and produce heirs to the throne. Providing and raising future political leaders is a political act in itself. Royal women usually also take part in the self-representation constructed by monarchies to justify and maintain power, by exalting the virtues and attitudes that qualify for government. In the case of royal women, their 'domestic' virtues and attitudes, linked to their gender, are commonly emphasised. Thus royal motherhood is an affair of state.

These features are observed in the monarchies that, resulting from the dismemberment of the empire of Alexander the Great, dominated the Greek world during the Hellenistic period (323–30 BC). Royal women within those monarchies often played a prominent public role, but political power never ceased to be masculine in essence. The king (*basileus*) had an obvious function as a political military leader, but the figure of the queen never had a clear definition. In fact, the world *basilissa* does not quite correspond to what has been understood as a queen in the subsequent history of Europe. The title was not always formally given to all the wives and mothers of kings, whereas sometimes it was granted to royal women who were not the wives or mothers of kings.[1] The different Hellenistic kingdoms had varied practices for queenship, as well as varied individual circumstances. Thus, although the cultural framework was fairly similar, the ways of being queen could be very different,[2] as could the ways of being a mother.

Although motherhood was central to Hellenistic queens, modern historians have not paid very much attention to this aspect of queenship. As a matter of fact, the ancient sources offer little information. Ancient authors particularly tend to be sparing when dealing with the relationship between queens and their children, except to report political family conflicts. In this respect, it should be noted that much of the surviving literary information on Hellenistic monarchies comes from Roman or pro-Roman authors, i.e., from the point of view of an enemy who finally prevailed. It was common to attack rivals by censuring their domestic conduct, and politically powerful queens were usual targets of this practice. But also the documentation produced by these monarchies themselves, including propaganda, does not particularly emphasize the maternal role of queens, as seen from epigraphy and iconography.

To find the most extensive information on the relationship between royal mothers and children, we must look back to the late classical Macedonian monarchy, more specifically to Olympias and her famous son, Alexander the Great (Mirón 2002; Carney 2006). This information ranges from Alexander's birth to Olympias' death, and results from different and sometimes contradictory traditions, nourished and transformed over the centuries, encompassing more or less verifiable historical facts and more or less apocryphal anecdotes. Therein, Olympias is shown as being directly interested in her son's education, and interacting with him in the context of royal Macedonian polygamy and rivalry between the different children and wives of Philip II. Later, during the reign of Alexander, she collaborated with him – not without conflicts and discrepancies – trying to influence his government with varying degrees of success and, finally, avenging her son's death and engaging in a struggle for the throne on the side of her grandson. Notwithstanding the occasional conflicts, a strong loving relationship between mother and son is inferred, and indeed, their relationship was, in antiquity, an example of mother–son love, even according to the most unfavourable sources. The current widespread image of Olympias as a domineering mother and Alexander's Oedipus complex is as recent as Freudian theory.

Information about the maternal aspects of Hellenistic queens is scarce both in quantity and quality, and focuses mainly on the numerous political and family conflicts that arose. A main source of conflict in Hellenistic monarchies, especially in their early stage, derives from the continuance of royal Macedonian polygamy, with mothers struggling for power in favour of their children against other royal mothers and children. This is the case of Arsinoe II, who plotted to ensure her children prevailed over their stepbrothers in the court of her first husband, Lysimachus of Thrace, causing the death of his firstborn son, Agathocles. Subsequently, she had to helplessly watch the murder of two of her children at the hands of her second husband, her stepbrother Ptolemy Ceraunus, who in turn had been removed from the succession to the Egyptian throne by his father in favour of Arsinoe's full-brother,

Ptolemy II (Carney 2013, 31–48). A daughter of the latter, Berenice, married the Seleucid king Antiochus II of Syria, bore a son by him, and conflicted with his first wife, Laodice I, who had both mother and son murdered. On this episode there is a story, perhaps apocryphal, with the grief-stricken Berenice taking arms and chariot to chase and kill her son's executor.[3] Of another Syrian queen, Laodice II, it is said that she aided her youngest son, Antiochus III, in his struggle for the throne against her eldest son, Seleucus III.[4] As matter of fact, some Hellenistic queens favoured one of their children against the others, acting in intrigues aimed at obtaining and maintaining power.

In this sense, the most conflictive context for mother–son relations were regencies and power-sharing arrangements, circumstances where the status of mother and political leader were mixed and could conflict with each other, as occurred in various examples from the Seleucids of Syria and, mostly, the Ptolemies of Egypt (Bielman 2012). A paradigmatic case is Cleopatra Thea, Ptolemaic princess and queen of Syria.[5] Married to three Seleucid kings (the usurper Alexander Balas, Demetrius II Nicator and his brother Antiochus VI Sidetes), relations with her husbands and sons were unequal, and her story was quite dramatic. Her firstborn, Antiochus VI Dionysus, son of Alexander Balas, was killed by a usurper shortly after he was proclaimed king when Demetrius II was captured by the Parthians. When the latter returned, Cleopatra had to send Antiochus IX, her son by her third husband, to Cyzicus to protect him from his uncle. Particularly stormy were the relations with the two sons she had with Demetrius, whose murder was attributed to her. Regarding the elder, Seleucus V Philometor, Cleopatra seems to have assumed the regency, and it is said that, when the youth wanted to exercise power, she had him murdered. Cleopatra Thea was formally associated in royal power with the younger son, Antiochus VIII Grypus, although *de facto* she exerted it alone. History repeated itself, although with a different ending, as the son forced his mother to drink the poison she had prepared for him. In sum, Cleopatra Thea appears as an anti-mother, at least to her second husband's children, but actually she did not act very differently from her male relatives. We should also take into account that much of her black legend could be a construct of Grypus, as well as Roman prejudices towards Hellenistic monarchies and women's power. Thus, most of the acts attributed to her should be, at the very least, nuanced, as occurs with many of the Hellenistic queens.

The image the dynasties created of royal motherhood and the relationship between queens and their children was quite different. For example, it was frequent to use epithets referring to love within the family, like Philometor ('who loves his/her mother'), used particularly by children associated in power with their mothers, and regardless of the actual relationship between them, as is illustrated in the case of the above-mentioned Seleucus V. This title was also given to Ptolemy XV Caesarion, associated with his mother, Cleopatra VII, in dynastic propaganda. Iconographic representations reproduce the model of Isis-Horus, the divine couple of mother and son, highlighting the role of Cleopatra as a giver of prosperity and guarantor of the succession to the throne (Puyadas 2016, 84–99). Even so, although Cleopatra's image as a mother was important, especially concerning the legitimacy of Julius Caesar's son, it was not pivotal in her self-representation.

Queens were usually presented as givers of fecundity and protectors of marriage, which implied motherhood (Mirón 2012). Royal fecundity was essential for the peaceful continuity of dynastic power, and, thus, for the peace and welfare of the kingdom, at least theoretically, and symbolised general prosperity, embodied by queens. Furthermore, royal motherhood, particularly of an heir to the throne, had effects on the position of the mother within the court, and, as we have already seen, could give her more opportunities to influence power and even to exercise it directly. Royal births, especially of a male, were publicly celebrated, and, at least in Egypt, the queen and the king together received congratulations and gifts.[6] Also, the members of a royal family were depicted as collaborating in political or diplomatic affairs, as did Apama of Syria with her husband, Seleucus I, and her son, Antiochus I (Nourse 2002, 238–247).

Sometimes royal families presented themselves as a harmonious cooperative unit composed of a royal couple and their children, where the queen and her motherhood played a fundamental role. This is the case of Laodice III, wife of Antiochus III of Syria and the mother of seven children (Widmer 2008; Ramsey 2011). Of these, two sons (Seleucus IV and Antiochus IV) became kings, and a daughter (Cleopatra I) was the first woman in Hellenistic Egypt to exercise power alone. Motherhood played a substantive role in her image and agency in the relationship of royal power with Greek cities, where Laodice undertook intense activity, always in concert with her husband but with her own agenda. In Iasos, she promoted marriage and fertility by creating a foundation to ensure dowries for impoverished girls, and the grateful city instituted a festival in her honour where she was assimilated to Aphrodite as a patroness of weddings, among other honours bestowed on her, her husband and children. Teos dedicated a fountain in the agora to her, the water of which was to be used for civic sacrifices, funeral rituals, and bathwater for brides. Sardes dedicated a festival to her that included a sacrifice to Zeus Genethlios ('of the birth') on behalf of her, her husband and children.[7] Thus, her role as benefactress of marriage and motherhood was stressed. However, she was not distinctively praised for her motherly virtues. Instead, her husband publicly praised her for her love (*philostorgia*) and solicitude (*kedemonia*) towards him (Ma 2000, no. 37). Only the representation of Attalid royal women pivoted around motherhood and the relationship with their children, with Apollonis as the most conspicuous figure. I will focus on her henceforth in this work.

Unlike the other main Hellenistic royal dynasties, the Attalids did not have aristocratic Macedonian descent. The founder, Philetaerus (283–283 BC), was a commander of modest origins who assumed independent power in Pergamon, a strategic city in the region of Mysia (West Anatolia). This power became royal in character during the rule of his great-nephew Attalus I (241–197 BC). His reign and those of his sons Eumenes II (197–159 BC) and Attalus II (159–138 BC) constituted the golden age of the kingdom of Pergamon. Although other royal dynasties vaunted their families' virtues (authentic or not) as part of their virtues for government (Roy 1998), they did not do so to the same degree as the Attalids, who put these qualities at the very core of royal ideology, with features more related to the world of the *polis* than to that of monarchy.[8] Thus, the rulers of Pergamon presented themselves and their power based on a cooperative harmonious family, within which a key role was played by Queen Apollonis, wife of Attalus I, and mother of Eumenes II and Attalus II.[9]

Unlike most Hellenistic queens, Apollonis had no royal blood, but was a plebeian (*demotes*), though from an elite family of Cyzicus, a powerful and wealthy city in the Propontis.[10] When Attalus I married (*c.* 223 BC), he had recently adopted the title of *basileus* and was involved in territorial expansion through Asia Minor, conflicting with Macedonia and the Seleucids, while facing invasions of the Gauls. Modern historians have tended to consider it a marriage without diplomatic implications and even a 'love-match',[11] but this union really had highly political connotations, inasmuch as it reinforced friendship between Pergamon and Cyzicus, which was interesting for commercial, political and military purposes. Furthermore, the union between a king and a citizen woman had the potential to positively affect Attalus' relations with Greek cities, lending greater credibility to Attalid self-presentation as champions of the traditional values of the Greek *polis*.

Apollonis was the mother of four sons (Eumenes, Attalus, Philetaerus and Athenaeus), an exception in a dynasty with many unmarried and/or childless leaders, where, until then, succession had never passed from father to son (Allen 1983, 181–189). The prolific maternity of Apollonis not only guaranteed dynastic continuity,[12] but surely also gave her prestige as a woman, as she fulfilled beyond expectations the main goal of every Greek woman: to produce children, especially male. Moreover, Apollonis was publicly presented and perceived as an integral part of royal power. Her name was frequently included in the public honours bestowed on the royal family by various instances, within or outside the kingdom.[13] Sometimes, a son even identified himself or was identified publicly as 'the son of king Attalus and queen Apollonis'.[14] This mention of maternal filiation was rare for kings, except in Egypt, where queens were usually associated with the king in power.

Ancient sources highlight the harmony that existed between her and her husband and sons. Particularly, Roman or pro-Roman authors present her as a model of honesty and chastity, besides her motherly virtues. Polybius speaks of 'perfect affect and love' in her relationship with her four children till the last day of her life.[15] Plutarch states that she 'always congratulated herself and gave thanks to the gods, not because of wealth or empire', but because of the harmony and trust amongst her four children.[16] The prevailing positive image of the dynasty in these texts is undoubtedly directly related to the fact that the Attalids were Roman allies in war and in general had good relations with Rome (Hansen 1971, 120–128). This image also coincided largely with Roman values, as well as reflecting Attalid self-representation.

An inscription from Hierapolis that perhaps reproduces the royal decree of divinisation of Apollonis after her death,[17] speaks of her in terms such as 'reverence towards her parents', 'her life with her husband was distinguished', 'she consorted with her children in complete harmony', 'having earned conspicuous gratitude from her children', 'having consorted nobly with king Eumenes Soter, Attalus Philadelphus, Philetaerus and Athenaeus', 'she left a most beautiful and praiseworthy sign of her own excellence in her harmonious relations with her children'.

These values were also symbolically present in Attalid architectural and iconographic programmes. In Pergamon, Attalus I remodeled the terrace of the temple of Athena, and erected a memorial of his victories over the Gauls, to which other elements of dynastic celebration were subsequently added (Schalles 1985, 68–104; Thonemann 2013, 40–41), including a statue of Apollonis dedicated by the still prince Attalus, praising her *philostorgia* towards him.[18] In the lower terrace and directly associated with the temple of Athena, Eumenes undertook the construction of the most representative monument of Pergamon: the Great Altar. Its iconographic programme celebrates the dynasty and the queen mother (Fehr 1997; Stewart 2000; Queyrel 2005). In the outer façade, the famous frieze of the Gigantomachy has significantly more female than male figures, and repeatedly depicts children fighting cooperatively alongside their mothers (Fehr 1997; Queyrel 2005, 126–128). Thus, family unity, especially that of mother and children, is exalted.

Inside, a sculpted frieze commemorates the story of Telephus, an ancestor of the Pergamenes. According to the version of this ancient myth reproduced in the frieze (Queyrel 2005, 79–100), Auge, daughter of the king of Tegea (Arcadia) and priestess of Athena, bore a son, Telephus, fathered by Heracles. Auge's father expelled mother and son, who went separate ways. Auge arrived at Mysia, where the king Teuthras adopted her as a daughter. After various adventures, Telephus came to Mysia, saved the country from serious danger, and, as a reward, Teuthras gave him Auge's hand in marriage. On the wedding night, inspired by a divinity, mother and son recognized each other. As Teuthras had no male children, he decided to appoint Telephus as his heir and married him to his biological daughter Argiope. The recognition of the king's mother culminates in one of the main panels of the frieze, where Auge's apotheosis is represented, a divinization after death, as occurred with Apollonis, whereby royal ideology identifies the mythical heroine with the real queen mother.

After Apollonis' death and deification, her sons built her a temple in her home city, Cyzicus. Although it has not been found, we know from literary descriptions that it was decorated with mythological scenes on the theme of love between mother and son, and brotherly love.[19] Some of these scenes are directly related to the iconography of the Great Altar, as the apotheosis of Semele and Alcmene through their sons, evoking that of Auge-Apollonis, or the recognition of Telephus by Auge. There was also a representation of the story of the mythical brothers Cleobis and Biton helping their mother, with a great effort, to reach the temple of Hera.[20] This was a direct evocation of Apollonis' visit to Cyzicus in 183/2 BC,[21] when she toured the temples and the city, accompanied by her sons, who placed her between them and took both her hands, displaying gratitude to and respect for their mother. This display of affection was applauded by the spectators, who recalled the story of the brothers Cleobis and Biton. This clear evocation of the royal visit in the temple served to fix in the collective memory of the Cyzicenes their links with Pergamon through the queen mother. Beyond this, the orderly and complex iconographic programme of the temple, which included myths from all around the Greek (and even Roman) world, symbolically connected the Greek cities with the monarchy of Pergamon, embodied by the mother (Massa-Pairault 1981–1982, 189). In this sense, Apollonis not only linked the Attalids with Cyzicus, but also with all the Greek cities, especially Ionian ones, since Cyzicus was a colony of Miletus.[22]

Modern historians have remarked that Eumenes and Attalus used the figure of their mother to vaunt their own family virtues as mother-loving sons and loyal brothers (Vatin 1970, 104–107; Virgilio 1993, 44–52; Ogden 1999, 201–202; Thonemann 2013, 30–44; among others). Certainly, the Attalids' emphasis on family values, an emphasis that necessarily included both male and female members, must have contributed to Apollonis' central position in dynastic self-representation (Thonemann 2013, 30–44). Although it was true that her sons depicted her figure in this way, there is also ample evidence of her actual authority within the family, her political cooperation with her sons, and her agency in the construction of both her own image and that of the dynasty.

We must consider, firstly, her influence within the family. We have already noted the prestige that motherhood of male children conferred upon Greek women. Also, mothers' authority over children in infancy can evolve into other, more or less strong forms of influence in adulthood. Some family circumstances could favour the continuation and even the reinforcement of Apollonis' maternal authority during her lifetime, such as the fact that, although her children were already adults when their father died in 197 BC, they were still young. The eldest, Eumenes, was around 25 years old, and the youngest, Athenaeus, around 18 (Van Looy 1975, 155–156). Also, Apollonis' life was long and included at least 30 years of widowhood.[23] Her sons' bachelorhood was also long: the first documented marriage (Eumenes and Stratonice) occurred in the last decade of her life.[24] Thus, Apollonis was, for a long time, the only female figure in the royal family, so that the bonds of mother–child affection and her maternal/domestic authority remained unchallenged for decades. All these circumstances could contribute to increase her influence within the family. Being a royal family, where the limits between the public and private realms were unclear, her domestic influence had public significance.

Apollonis' role as educator was one of the aspects that had public resonance and recognition.[25] Education was one of the elements that prepared princes for accession to the throne, and, thus, was important for all the Hellenistic royal dynasties. But, in the case of the Attalids, education, and especially moral education, was also central in their self-representation.[26] They were also the only dynasty where the educational role of the queen enjoyed international recognition. A decree from Athens in 175/4 BC states that Attalus I and Apollonis had 'bequeathed to their sons excellence (*arete*) and good qualities (*kalokagathia*) by looking after their education in a good (*kalos*) and wise (*sophronos*) way'.[27] The annual festival celebrated by the city of Teos in honour of goddess Apollonis involved the performance of choruses of both boys and maidens, who were selected by the *paidonomos*, the official responsible for supervising the education of youths.[28] The Greek choruses of adolescents had a ritual educational function. In the case of boys, it was to assume their future roles as citizens, whereas for girls, it consisted of assuming their role as wives and mothers of citizens (Calame 1977). Thus, Teos indirectly acknowledged the educational work of Apollonis, which resulted in the success of her male offspring and probably served as an example for future mothers. She became a divine patroness of motherhood and education. The association of both concepts was also materially expressed in the urban layout of Pergamon, through the proximity to each other of two major architectural complexes of the Attalid city: the Gymnasium, the institution for comprehensive education of the youths, built by Eumenes II, and the sanctuary of Demeter, a place for the ritual celebration of motherhood, remodeled by Apollonis and possibly devoted to the education of girls (Mirón 2016, 52–53).

The evidence of Apollonis' intervention in conflicts between her sons is not so clear. As has been mentioned above, Plutarch says that she was proud of the harmony and loyalty reigning between her sons, as she saw 'her three sons members of the bodyguard of the eldest, who passed his days without fear surrounded by brothers with swords and spears in their hands'.[29] In the same text (*De fraterno amore*), Plutarch relates an episode where such loyalty and harmony were challenged: in 172 BC, Eumenes II suffered an attack in Delphi, and, believing him dead, his brother Attalus assumed royal power and seemingly married the widowed queen, Stratonice. When Eumenes reappeared, Attalus loyally returned what he had assumed to his brother.[30] Later on, in 168/7 BC, Attalus was tempted by Rome (finally in vain) to seize independent power.[31] Apollonis was probably alive when the episode of the false death of her firstborn occurred, and perhaps also when the second incident took place. In this respect, Massa-Pairault has made an interesting interpretation of one of the decorations of her temple at Cyzicus, namely the scene of the encounter of Ulysses with his mother, Anticlea, during his visit to Hades, where he questions her concerning affairs at home, Ithaca.[32] The author thinks it is an allusion to the death of Apollonis when Eumenes was absent and perhaps related to the news of his false death. In this sense, the mother would ensure from Hades that Stratonice-Penelope remained faithful and Attalus was not just a common suitor. Nevertheless, this image does not necessarily mean that Apollonis died while these events occurred, but it is probably a symbolic representation of the queen mother protecting harmony within the family, from the underworld, though there is also perhaps an underlying allusion to this specific episode.

Moreover, the first document in which Attalus is referred to as Philadelphus ('who loves his brother') is the abovementioned decree of Hierapolis, dated shortly after Apollonis' death. The use of this epithet is typically related to situations requiring special emphasis on the harmony between brothers, particularly if this harmony has been challenged, as in the abovementioned incidents.[33] Ancient sources do not mention any involvement of Apollonis in these events, but the Cyzicene representation and the insistence of the Hierapolitan decree on the harmony between the brothers, and between them and their mother, could be indirect indications of her possible intervention.

There is also evidence of Apollonis' collaboration with her sons in political and diplomatic matters. In the first instance, we must consider her visits to cities, such as the abovementioned visit to Cyzicus and another paid to Teos (Mirón 2015, 86). Royal visits are themselves diplomatic acts, regardless of the specific activities undertaken in their course, but it would be too simplistic to think that Apollonis was there just to be exhibited. In any case, her inclusion in royal visits reasserted the idea that monarchy was equivalent to the power of the family. She also made benefactions to the community, a common practice in Hellenistic monarchies and citizen elites, and a way to justify power and make it more attractive, as well as to secure grateful and loyal communities.[34] In Pergamon, Apollonis undertook the enlargement and renovation of the sanctuary of Demeter and Kore, in thanksgiving to the goddesses,[35] surely referring to her success as a mother and queen, and also publicly expressing her maternal pride, so she seems to have been be the first concerned with her self-representation as mother. Possibly her intervention in the sanctuary should be dated in the late 3rd century BC (Kohl 2009, 148–150; Piok Zanon 2009, 136–144), hence predating the great building projects of her sons, perhaps still little boys. Therefore, Apollonis actively participated from an early stage in the creation of both the dynastic and her own image.

The sanctuaries of Demeter were closely associated with women and especially motherhood. Therefore, they were places where women were frequently honoured by institutions or individuals. In Pergamon, other Attalid mothers were honoured there. Philetaerus and his brother Eumenes built the temple and the altar of Demeter on behalf of their mother, Boas.[36] Also, the people (*demos*) of Pergamon dedicated a statue of queen Stratonice there.[37] Thus, the sanctuary was a place for celebrating women in general and dynastic mothers (real or potential) in particular, associating the reproduction of the city with royal power. The urban topography of Pergamon also has other interesting features relating to royal mothers. The straight line drawn between the sanctuary of Demeter and the temple of Athena crossed over the Great Altar, creating an axis that united the past and the present of the city through the figure of the queen mother. Thus, in this north-south axis, the figure of Auge-Apollonis should be the backbone of the dynastic celebration, appropriately gendered: the military victories of kings and the maternal success of women.

Furthermore, the tribute to her daughter-in-law, Stratonice, represented looking to the future, that is, the continuity of both the monarchy and the dynastic image. When Stratonice married Eumenes, she joined the family's harmonious image centred around Apollonis. The decree of Hierapolis states that Apollonis 'always behaved with goodwill in all circumstances towards Queen Stratonice, believing that the woman who shared her son also shared her own affection'. Stratonice was included in the honours to the royal family,[38] particularly in association with Apollonis,[39] so that the figure of the new queen was shaped by the model of the queen mother, in solidarity and continuance with her. Despite the lesser emphasis on her 'domestic' virtues and the fact that she was a more controversial figure than her mother-in-law,[40] the official documents refer to the affection between Stratonice and her son, Attalus III. He was named Philometor, and emphasised the love of his mother for him.[41]

The image of Apollonis as a loving mother could also influence the public celebration of women outside the Attalid dynasty. In the second half of the 2nd century BC, again in the sanctuary of Demeter at Pergamon, the *demos* and her children dedicated statues to Philotera, praised for her *philostorgia* towards her children.[42] Certainly, the attitudes and values of the cities' elites, among them motherly love (Thonemann 2013, 40–44), could have affected the construction of Apollonis' image, but also her public image as mother could influence the public image of other women, as is exemplified by Stratonice and Philotera. Furthermore, in the late Hellenistic period and especially during the Roman Empire, elite women, some of them very influential in the public realm, were frequently publicly praised for their domestic virtues, although motherly love was not the most widely mentioned (Mantas 1999, 217–228).

The unanimous positive image of Apollonis in ancient literary sources has been noted, and the fact that it could have been favourably affected by the similarity of Attalid and Roman values. Indeed, the queen mother of Pergamon is portrayed under the paradigm of the Roman matron. But it is also likely that, in some respects, she influenced the construction of the public image of the Roman matron. The first woman honoured with a public statue in Rome was presumably Cornelia, mother of the Gracchi.[43] Her father's family, the Cornelii Scipiones, was one of the main agents of the Hellenization of Rome, and it should be recalled that her father and her uncle had had close relations with the Attalids. Although Cornelia was highly educated and influential, her public celebration focused on her motherly virtues, constructing a matron image of her that sustained and was also sustained by the image of the women in Augustus' family, especially Octavia. Ultimately, Apollonis could have been a forerunner of the public image of imperial mothers.

Acknowledgement

This paper is part of the background studies of the project 'Género y arquitectura en la sociedad romana Antigua: matronazgo cívico en las provincias occidentales' (I+D FEM2014–53423-P), financed by the Spanish Ministry of Economy and Competitiveness.

Notes

1 On the origin, meaning, roles and image of the Hellenistic *basilissa*, see Savalli-Lestrade (1994; 2003); Nourse 2002; Bielman (2003); Carney (2010; 2015, 1–26).

2 This variety can be observed in the comprehensive studies of Macurdy (1932), Ogden (1999) or Carney (2000).

3 Valerius Maximus, 9, 10. See Martinez-Seve (2003).
4 Plutarch, *Moralia*, 489A.
5 On Cleopatra Thea, see Muccioli (2003); Bielman (2012, 57–59); Penrose (2018, 54–55).
6 Flavius Josephus, *Jewish Antiquities* 12, 196–221.
7 Iasos: Ma (2000: nos 26 and 28). Teos: Ma (2000: no. 18). Sardis: Ma (2000: no. 2). See Ramsey (2011, 520–523).
8 On the image of the Attalids, see Virgilio (1993); Gruen (2000); Kosmetatou (2003); Thonemann (2013, 30–44). On the Attalid kingdom in general, see Hansen (1971); Allen (1983).
9 On Apollonis and her image, see Van Looy (1976); Virgilio (1993, 44–52); Bielman (2003); Mirón (2015).
10 Polybius, 22, 20,1–2.
11 For example, Ogden (1999, 201); Thonemann (2013, 38). These ideas have been convincingly refuted by Sève (2014, 154–157).
12 Polybius, 18, 41,10.
13 Telmessos (Allen 1983, no. 7); Aetolia (*IG* IX,1^2 1:179); Athens (*OGIS* 248); Colophon Nova (*BCH* 30, 1906, 349–358); Lydia (*TAM* V, 1 690); Pergamon (*OGIS* 292); hinterland of Pergamon (Müller and Wörrle 2002).
14 *Inschriften Iasos* 6; *IG* II^2 3171; *Hesperia* 23 (1954), 252–253.
15 Polybius, 22, 20,3.
16 Plutarch, *Moralia*, 480CD.
17 *OGIS* 308. See Hansen (1971, 456).
18 *Inschriften Pergamon* 169.
19 *Palatine Anthology*, 3. See, among others, Massa-Pairault (1981–82); Queyrel (2003, 24–27); Sève (2014, 157–162).
20 Herodotus, 1, 31.
21 Polybius, 22, 20,4–8; *Suda*, "Apollonias."
22 Strabo, 14, 1,6. See *OGIS* 763.
23 Polybius (22, 20,3) says that she survived her husband for a considerable time. She was certainly alive in 175/4 (*OGIS* 248, l. 56–7), and for sure dead in 164 BC (Müller and Wörrle 2002). Probably, she was still alive in 166 BC (*IG* XII *Suppl.* 250; *cf.* Queyrel 2003, 35).
24 The marriage of Eumenes and Stratonice, daughter of King Ariarathes IV of Cappadocia, was held after 174 BC, as she does not appear in the documents dated before. Cf. Müller (1991, 396–405) contra Allen (1983, 200–206).
25 On the educational role of Greek mothers, see Reboreda (2010).
26 On the education of Attalid princes, see Alonso (2005).
27 *OGIS* 248 l. 41–46.
28 *OGIS* 309. Cf. Mirón (2015, 82–84).
29 Plutarch, *Moralia*, 489C.
30 Livius, 42, 16; Plutarch, *Moralia*, 184AB; 489EF.
31 Livius, 45, 19–20; Polybius, 30, 1–3.
32 *Palatine Anthology*, 3, 8; Massa-Pairault (1981–1982, 182–186).
33 Cf. Muccioli (1994), who, in this specific case, relates the epithet to the political role of prince Attalus in the last years of Eumenes' rule (ibid., 404–407).
34 Ver Bringmann (1993). On the queens as benefactresses, see Mirón (2011).
35 *Anatolische Mitteilungen* 35 (1910), no. 24. On the sanctuary in the Hellenistic period and the intervention of Apollonis, see Thomas (1998); Piok Zanon (2009); Kohl (2009); Mirón (2015).
36 *Anatolische Mitteilungen* 35 (1910), nos 22–23.
37 *Bulletin Épigraphique*, 1971, no. 538.
38 For example, sanctuary of Athena at Pergamon (*OGIS* 291–296); Panion, Thrace (*OGIS* 302–304; *SEG* 49, 876–877).

39 In addition to Hierapolis (*OGIS* 308), mention of the queens (*basilissai*) in Andros (*IG* XII *Suppl.* 250), shared priesthoods in Teos (*OGIS* 309) and Pergamon (*Anatolische Mitteilungen* 33 (1908), 375–379).
40 See the episode of Eumenes' false death. When he actually died, his brother Attalus II married Stratonice and assumed the throne in the name of his nephew, Attalus III, who succeeded him after death. The real identity of Attalus III's father, and even his mother, has been questioned. On this controversy, see, among others, Vatin (1970, 110–112); Allen (1983, 189–194); Ogden (1999, 202–207).
41 *OGIS* 331, 4; 332.
42 *Anatolische MItteilungen* 35 (1910), nos 47–48
43 Pliny, *Natural History*, 34, 14. On Cornelia and the construction of her image, see Dixon (2007).

References

Allen, R. E. (1983) *The Attalid Kingdom. A constitutional history*. Oxford, Clarendon.

Alonso, V. (2005) La *paideia* del príncipe y la ideología helenística de la realeza. *Gerión Anejos* 9, 185–204.

Bielman, A. (2003) Régner au féminin. Réflexions sur le reines attalides et séleucides. In F. Prost (ed.) *L'Orient Méditerranéen de la mort d'Alexandre aux campagnes de Pompée. Cités et royaumes à l'époque héllenistique*. Toulouse, Presses Universitaires du Mireil, 45–61.

Bielman, A. (2012) Quand des reines transgressent les normes, créent-elles l´ordre ou le désordre? *Lectora* 18, 51–70.

Bringmann, K. (1993) The king as benefactor: Some remarks on ideal kingship in the age of Hellenism. In A. Bulloch, E. S. Gruen, A. A. Long and A. Stewart (eds) *Images and Ideologies: Self-definition in the Hellenistic World*. Berkeley, University of California Press, 8–25.

Calame, C. (1977) *Les choeurs de jeunes filles en Grèce archaïque*. Rome, Ateneo.

Carney, E. (2000) *Women and Monarchy in Macedonia*. Norman, University of Oklahoma Press.

Carney, E. (2006) *Olympias, Mother of Alexander the Great*. New York, Routledge.

Carney, E. (2010) Being royal and female in the early Hellenistic period. In A. Erskine and L. Llewellyn Jones (eds) *Creating a Hellenistic World*. Swansea, Classical Press of Wales, 195–222.

Carney, E. (2013) *Arsinoë of Egypt and Macedon. A Royal Life*. Oxford, Oxford University Press.

Carney, E. (2015) *King and Court in Ancient Macedonia*. Swansea, Classical Press of Wales.

Dixon, S. (2007) *Cornelia. Mother of the Gracchi*. New York, Routledge.

Fehr, B. (1997) Society, consanguinity and the fertility of women. The community of deities on the Great Frieze of the Pergamum Altar as a paradigm of cross-cultural ideas. In P. Bilde, T. Engbert-Pedersen, L. Hannestad, and J. P. Zahle (eds) *Conventional Values of the Hellenistic Greeks*. Aarhus: Aarhus University Press, 48–66.

Gruen, E. (2000) Culture as policy. The Attalids of Pergamon. In N. T. Grummond and B. S. Ridgway (eds) *From Pergamon to Sperlonga. Sculpture and Context*. Berkeley, University of California Press, 17–31.

Hansen, E. W. (1971) *The Attalids of Pergamon*. Ithaca, Cornell University Press.

Kohl, M. (2009) Le sanctuaire de Déméter à Pergame et son culte. *Numismatica e antichità classiche* 38, 139–167.

Kosmetatou, E. (2003). The Attalids of Pergamon. In A. Erskine (ed.) *A Companion to the Hellenistic World*. Oxford: Blackwell, 159–174.

Ma, J. (2000) *Antiochos III and the Cities of Western Asia Minor*. Oxford, Oxford University Press.

Macurdy, G. H. (1932) *Hellenistic Queens*. Baltimore, Johns Hopkins University Press.

Mantas, K. (1999) Public and Private. *Polis* 12, 181–228.

Martinez-Seve, L. (2003) Laodice, femme d'Antiochos II: du roman à la reconstruction historique. *Revue des Études Grecques* 116, 690–706.

Massa-Pairault, F.-H. (1981–82) Il problema degli stilopinakia del templo di Apollonis a Cizico. Alcune considerazioni. *Annali della Facoltà di Lettere e Filosofia. Perugia* 19, 147–219.

Mirón, M. D. (2002) *Olimpia*. Madrid, Ediciones del Orto.
Mirón, M. D. (2011) Las 'buenas obras' de las reinas helenísticas: benefactoras y poder político. *Arenal* 18, 243–275.
Mirón, M. D. (2012) Afrodita y las reinas: una mirada al poder femenino en la Grecia helenística. *Feminismo/s* 20, 165–186.
Mirón, M. D. (2015) La reina Apolonis y Afrodita: divinidad, poder y virtud en la Grecia helenística. In E. Ferrer and A. Pereira (coords) *Hijas de Eva. Mujeres y religión en la Antigüedad*. Sevilla, Universidad de Sevilla, 69–95.
Mirón, M. D. (2016) Maternidad, poder y arquitectura: la impronta de la reina Apolonis en el urbanismo de Pérgamo. In C. Martínez and F. Serrano (eds) *Matronazgo y Arquitectura. De la Antigüedad a la Edad Moderna*. Granada, Universidad de Granada, 27–64.
Muccioli, F. (1994) Considerazioni generali sull'epiteto *philadelphos* nelle dinastie ellenistiche e sulla sua applicazione nella titolatura degli ultimi Seleucidi. *Historia* 43, 402–422.
Muccioli, F. (2003) Cleopatra Thea, una regina tolemaica nella dinastia dei Seleucidi. In N. Bonacasa, A. M. Donadoni Roveri, S. Aiosa and P. Minà (eds.) *Faraoni come dei. Tolemei come faraoni*, 105–116. Torino, Ministero Beni e Attività Culturali.
Müller, H. (1991) Königin Stratonike, Tochter des Königs Ariarathes. *Chiron* 21, 393–424.
Müller, H. and Wörrle, M. (2002) Ein Verein im Hinterland Pergamons zur Zeit Eumenes= II. *Chiron* 32, 191–235.
Nourse, K. L. (2002) *Women and the Early Development of Royal Power in the Hellenistic East*. Ph. D. thesis, University of Pennsylvania.
Ogden, D. (1999) *Polygamy, Prostitutes and Death. The Hellenistic Dynasties*. London, Duckworth.
Penrose, W. D. (2018) Queens and their children: Dynastic dis/loyalty in the Hellenistic period. In C. Dunn and E. Carney (eds.) *Royal Women and Dynastic Loyalty*, 49–65. Palgrave, Macmillan.
Piok Zanon, C. (2009) *The Sanctuary of Demeter at Pergamon: Architecture and Dynasty in the Early Attalid Capital*. Ph. D. thesis, University of Pittsburg.
Puyadas, V. (2016) *Cleopatra VII: La creación de una imagen*. Zaragoza, Universidad de Zaragoza.
Queyrel, F. (2003) *Les portraits des Attalides*. Paris, De Boccard.
Queyrel, F. (2005) *L'Autel de Pergame. Images et pouvoir en Grèce d=Asie*. Paris, A. et J. Picard.
Ramsey, G. (2011) The queen and the city: Royal female intervention and patronage in Hellenistic civic communities. *Gender and History* 23, 510–527.
Reboreda, S. (2010) El papel educativo de la mujer en la antigua Grecia y su importancia en el mantenimiento de la *polis*. *Salduie* 10, 159–175.
Roy, J. (1998) The masculinity of the Hellenistic king. In L. Foxhall and J. Salmon (eds.) *When Men Were Men. Masculinity, Power and Identities in Classical Antiquity*, 111–135. London, Routledge.
Savalli-Lestrade, I. (1994) Il ruolo pubblico delle regine ellenistiche. In S. Alessandri (ed.) *Historie. Studi offerti dagli allievi a Giuseppe Nenci*, 415–432. Puglia, Congedo.
Savalli-Lestrade, I. (2003) La place des reines à la cour et dans le royaume à l'époque Hellénistique. In R. Frei-Stolba, A. Bielman and O. Bianchi (eds.) *Les femmes antiques entre sphère privée et sphère publique*, 59–76. Bern: Peter Lang.
Schalles, H.-J. (1985) *Untersuchungen zur Kulturpolitik der pergamenischen Herrscher im dritten Jahrhundert vor Christus*. Tübingen, Verlag Ernst Wasmuth.
Sève, M. (2014) Cyzique et les Attalids. In M. Sève and P. Schlosser (eds.) *Cyzique, cité majeure et méconnue de la Propontide antique*, 151–165. Metz, Université de Lorraine.
Stewart, A. (2000) Pergamo ara marmorea magna. On the date, reconstruction, and functions of the Great Altar at Pergamon. In N. T. Grummond and B. S. Ridgway (eds.) *From Pergamon to Sperlonga. Sculpture and Context*, 32–57. Berkeley, University of California Press.
Thomas, C. M. (1998) The sanctuary of Demeter at Pergamon: Cultic space for women and its eclipse. In H. Koester (ed.) *Pergamon Citadel of the Gods*, 277–298. Harrisburg, Trinity Press International.
Thonemann, P. (2013) The Attalid State, 188–133 BC. In P. Thonemann (ed.) *Attalid Asia Minor*, 1–47. Oxford, Oxford University Press.

Van Looy, H. (1976) Apollonis reine de Pergame. *Ancient Society* 7, 151–65.

Vatin, C. (1970) *Recherches sur le mariage et la condition de la femme mariée à l'époque hellénistique.* Paris, De Boccard.

Virgilio, B. (1993) *Gli Attalidi di Pergamo. Fama, eredità, memoria.* Pisa, Giardini.

Widmer, M. (2008) Pourquoi reprende le dossier des reines hellénistiques? Le cas de Laodice V. In F. Bertholet, A. Bielman and R. Frei-Stolba (eds.) *Egypte - Grèce - Rome. Les différentes visages des femmes antiques*, 63–92. Bern, Peter Lang.

Chapter 13

Mors immatura, childhood and maternal–filial relationships in the *carmina epigraphica*. Case studies from the Iberian Peninsula

Rosa María Cid López

A funerary inscription discovered in *Carthago Noua* tells us about a mother who is unable to bear her daughter's death. Finally, the mother dies as well:

> For your interest, traveller, here lies a daughter and her mother, whom died violently. Cruel almighty fortune first took the daughter away from the mother. Her premature death evidences how much the mother mourned the loss of her child. After the grieving mother honored her daughter with this monument, she surrendered her soul in the midst of all her pain.[1]

In addition to being very moving, this beautiful epigraphic poem speaks volumes about the relationship between mothers and their infants. It specifically deals with the mother's deep affection and grief for her daughter, who died at a very early age. These types of texts are very common among the so-called *carmina epigraphica*, which are found widely across the Roman Empire. Hispania is not an exception. In Ancient Rome, epigraphic poems dealing with children and young people are relatively common and very beautifully written.[2] They are also among those which better convey the experience of pain, particularly parents' grief for a *mors immatura*, that is to say, a premature death.

Because of their characteristics, these poems have been traditionally studied by philologists, but they are also of tremendous value to historical scholarship. These funerary poems offer alternative views on childhood and maternal/paternal–filial relationships, and also show how femininity and masculinity are constructed from an early age. In this sense, they evidence the way in which boys and girls are given specific roles. Childhood is without any doubt a stage that leaves an imprint not only on individual lives, but also on social and family life, as is apparent in the *carmina epigraphica* dedicated to children.

Funerary poems refute the idea that parents did not love their children, a belief grounded on the high rate of infant mortality that existed back then. Parents' tributes to their prematurely deceased children overtly express sorrow and pain. Thus, they contest the ethic of the *severitas* and the alleged coldness of maternal/paternal-filial relationships in Roman society. Among these poems, those dedicated by mothers to their sons and daughters particularly stand out. These compositions showcase the strong relationship that existed between mothers and their children in a society where the father played a prominent role.[3]

Sepulchral *carmina epigraphica*. Children testimonials

The number of texts from the Iberian Peninsula that have been selected to explore maternal-filial relationships is very limited. They make up a list of approximately 20 pieces showing mothers' tributes to their children.[4] Additionally, they reflect what life was like in the rest of the Roman Empire.

In order to understand to what extent this limited number is significant, it is helpful to take some figures into account. Nowadays it is estimated that there are about 280,000 Latin inscriptions in the Roman Empire, including the 4135 *carmina epigraphica* or poems engraved on some kind of hard material (Fernández 1998–99, 11–18).[5] Two hundred of the latter type can be found in the Iberian Peninsula, including the 20 funerary pieces dealing with the child population (see appendix).[6] In this regard, they all are inscriptions engraved on gravestones or milestones, honoring the deceased children.

Up until not too long ago, it was hard to have access to this material because the existing publications were dispersed despite the many efforts to compile the texts and gather *corpora*. Between 1895 and 1897, Franz Bücheler created the first compilation. These inscriptions were translated into Spanish by Concepción Fernández Martínez in 1998 and 1999. It is difficult for historians to study this material because it is organised according to philological criteria, paying special attention to metrics and overlooking social, geographical or chronological standards. Later on, local studies were carried out and the CIL XVIII, which included *carmina epigraphica* found in the different Roman provinces, was created.[7] Significantly, *corpora* pertaining to the Hispanic provinces have recently been gathered. It is known as XVIII/2. It has been compiled by a group of distinguished scholars in the field of classical philology, such as Concepción Fernández Martínez herself and Joan Gómez Pallarés. The texts making up these *corpora* consist of detailed comments and information, including bibliographic lists and images that are available for consultation in an online database.[8]

This is indeed an attractive object of study for linguists, and hence many studies have focused on its content, textual variety and semantic aspects. The process of reading, transcribing and translating is carried out in great detail, reconstructing fragmented lines, even though some interpretations may be debatable due to the difficulties arising in certain cases. Scholarly work on the *lamentatio*, *consolatio* and *laudatio* is of crucial relevance, as well as studies on the words used to express pain and relatives' reactions to death, regardless of the age of the deceased person (Hernández

2010). There is not much variation in terms of the words and expressions used. It is common to find tributes to the *Manes* or wishes that the earth lies light upon the dead. In addition, one can frequently find information about the life of the deceased person. Pieces honouring dead wives and husbands are worth considering; especially the terms used to praise their masculine and feminine qualities.[9]

There is no question that these studies contribute to expanding and enriching historical scholarship. In this regard, scholarly work on emotions may consider *carmina epigraphica* a valuable object of study, as they are no longer studied by philologists only. These texts clearly show parents' strong affection towards their infants. Similarly, they demonstrate that childhood is a crucial stage in the life of young people. Boys and girls were considered social beings, despite the fact that scholars such as Philippe Ariès thought otherwise.[10] Nowadays, it is accepted that childhood is not only a physical age, but also a social and cultural construction. In this sense, it is argued that children are able to construct their own identities (Minten 2002, 118–120; Juskinson 2005, 92–93).[11]

To be boy or girl in Ancient Rome. Childhood from the *mors immatura*

In Ancient Rome it was widely believed that children were not members of society because they were seen as *liminal beings* (Aasgard 2006, 31). During the early years of life, boys and girls were prepared for their future roles as men and women (Dixon 1992, 98–100). Their dying so young made it impossible to achieve those aspirations. These circumstances were reflected in the epitaphs.[12] It is also true however that boys and girls were considered part of the family and hence they were given specific roles in accordance with their young age. The same occurred to people who reached old age.[13]

According to the information provided by the *carmina epigraphica*, boys and girls share similar biographical characteristics, namely tenderness, obedience and their eagerness to learn (Sigismond 2001, 171). In both cases, emphasis is placed on their love for their parents and their family in general. When parents are mentioned in the texts, reference is made to their deep affection towards their deceased son or daughter. Different stages of childhood were distinguished; the younger the child was, the more difficult it was to consider her or him a *social being*.[14] These attitudes are reflected in the reactions to their deaths, the place chosen for burial, or the funerary ritual, which could be regulated according to laws that went beyond social conventions.

It is noteworthy that children were buried apart from adults – babies in particular were buried underneath houses (Sevilla 2013, 208–209, 213). Burying infants next to their parents or other older family members was in fact exceptional.[15] Leaving aside these norms and conventions, it is clear that families were eager to honor their dead young relatives, even if the latter were just a few months old when they died. The funerary monuments that families dedicated to their dead infants evidence this eagerness. In this regard, they were visible and functionally accessible to the passerby.[16]

As in the case of adults, children's graves were also placed close to the main roads to the city and were part of necropolis similar to those found in Ancient Rome and

Greece. Thereby, it is not uncommon to find a dialogue between the deceased person and the passerby, regardless of the former's age. The dead try to call the passerby's attention in order to stay in the memory of the living (Hualde 1995, 74–79; Fernández 1998, 37–38; Hernández 2001, 229–237).

Rituals performed to say goodbye to boys and girls are very similar. Differences in this type of rituals are in fact determined by age. For instance, most babies who were less than seven months old had no teeth and therefore could not be incinerated. Because of the children's small size, it was thought that the bonfire would be far from large. Similarly, due to their weak bones, it was assumed that they would be rapidly consumed, leaving no human remains at all (Sevilla 2012, 208–209, 213). The time allowed for mourning children that died under 3 years of age was a month for every year they had lived, showing the little importance given to young people (MacWilliam 2001, 7–5 and Sevilla 2012, 208, 228). Funerary ceremonies took place at dawn. These practices are captured by the concept of *funus acerbus*, which means 'bitter.' It can also be translated as *mors immatura*, and hence its bitterness.[17]

It goes without saying that a *mors immatura* is a source of deep pain for parents (Martin-Kilcher 2000; MacWilliam 2001, 78, 193; Sevilla 2010–11; 2012, 200–201; Hernández 2016).[18] An inscription found in Iberian Peninsula greatly accounts for a father's reaction to his daughter's death, whose age remains unknown:

> *Egnacia Florentina* is buried here. May the earth lie light upon thee. What the father thought her daughter should have done to him was prematurely done by the father to his daughter (Martín 2010, C05).

Sorrow was greater when children were involved. Boys left childhood when they were between 15 and 17. At this point they were given the *toga virilis*. Girls, on the one other hand, became adults when they turned 12, the age at which they were considered to be marriageable.[19] These differences are taken into consideration when emphasising children's truncated lives. As far as boys are concerned, stress is laid on the fact that they had not been given the *toga virilis* yet, thus foregrounding their public activity (Dixon 1992, 108; Hernández 2001, 8–11; Laes 2016, 7).[20] Girls, for their part, were buried with their mirrors, dolls, spindles and other elements regarded as being feminine.[21] Dolls are very important, since women left childhood by giving their toys (dolls in particular) away before getting married. It is unknown whether the dolls were offered to the household gods, or left in the temple of goddesses such as *Venus* or *Fortuna Virginalis*.[22] In the Roman Empire, dolls are normally found in funerary contexts, not in domestic spaces (Dasen 2015, 328–334). It is common to find dolls and other toys in children's graves. Interestingly, in Ontur (Albacete) archaeologists found an impressive set of amber and ivory dolls in a girl's grave dating back between 4th and 5th century (Balil 1962).

Funerary monuments usually highlight the fact that the deceased infants were indeed good sons and daughters (Sevilla 2012, 222; Hernández 2001, 186–192). Sometimes they explain the cause of death, which usually involves an illness or an accident, and often express tremendous pain and grief for the loss. Thus, families' wishes that they could take the place of the deceased infant are recurrent. Due to their inability to bear pain, mothers do sometimes follow their daughters in death.[23]

It is also common to find references to the *Manes* and wishes that the earth may lie light upon the dead, evidencing that death was considered a passing phase of life. On the other hand, not always are these monuments explicit about the name of the dead person, the age or social status. The inclusion of nicknames and references to a premature death is enough to learn that a dead child is being honoured.

Paying tribute to a dead infant through poems was popular mainly among the emancipated slave population.[24] The latter engaged in this practice so as to prove that they were up the social ladder. Citizens, free and even slaves also dedicated poems to their dead infants. In this sense, the presence of the mother as the sole signer of the epitaph indicates that she is either a slave or a freedwoman and not a widow. On the other hand, the absence of the mother may be attributed to her being dead or to the tradition of highlighting the figure of the father only.

On reading the *carmina*, the beauty of the text and the suitability of the style, expressions and metrics become evident. Thereby, it can be argued that the sponsors of the monuments hired experts in poetry to write the texts. The influence of the greatest Latin poets (Horace, Ovid, Martial, Juvenal and of course Homer) is felt in many of the poems, as they often quote the aforementioned authors or include some of their most popular themes (Hualde 1995; Fernández 1998, 47–63). Leaving aside aspects such as social status and geographical origin, these pieces demonstrate the way Roman customs were adopted by families and passed to children, although the latter's death blocked assimilation into that way of life. These characteristics, which are clear in the case of Rome and the Italian Peninsula, are also identified in the *carmina epigraphica* found in the Hispanic provinces.

Hispania and the funerary *carmina epigraphica* dedicated to children. From paternal–filial to maternal–filial relationships

The 20 pieces under study here speak volumes about the relationship between parents and their children, the emotions triggered by a *mors immatura*, and the way childhood was conceived in Hispanic provinces and others of the Roman Empire, even though we cannot say for certain that all of these texts do account for the child population.

It is not coincidental that these pieces are found mostly in major cities; that is to say, in Romanised centres inhabited by people who are knowledgeable in Latin language and Greek and Latin literature, especially poetry. In fact, funerary poems are located in Latinised environments, namely *Corduba*, *Emerita*, *Hispalis* or *Castulo*, among other places.[25] The case of *Carthago Noua* is remarkable. A large set of epigraphs from an early stage was located in this community, which was very soon incorporated into the Roman Empire.[26] The first texts located here date back to the 1st century BC. More pieces appeared in the first centuries of our era, especially during the 1st and 2nd centuries. The Christianisation of the imperial society did not put an end to the tradition of *carmina epigraphica*, which continued under the new religious establishment. As a matter of fact, the *corpus* created by Franz Bücheler included Christian texts dating back to the 9th century, many of which were found in the Iberian peninsula.[27]

The pieces contained in the annex present twelve boys and nine girls. A bigger presence of the former was also common in other parts of the empire.[28] Their ages are varied; there is a 7-month-old baby and a 15-year-old teenage boy, who claims that he could not get to wear the *toga virilis*. There are also 1-, 2-, 3-, 8-, 9- and 11-year-old children, who belong to the category of *parvulus*, *puer* and *puella* (Dixon 1992, 104). Most of the epitaphs are not clear about the age infants were when they died. Expressions such as 'dead at a tender age,' 'little daughter,' 'did not get to grow up,' 'boy,' and 'girl' allow us to infer that children are being honoured.[29] The deceased boys and girls mainly represent frustrated hopes, as the protagonist of an inscription from *Baessuci* (today's Vilches, Jaén) claims: 'I was my parents' greatest hope, but my name was lost because I did not get to grow up.' The boy was called *Crescens*, meaning 'the one who is growing up' (Fernández 1998, 29, n. 16; Hernández 2001, 57).[30] Mostly parents are the ones dedicating the monuments to the children. The father is the sole signer in two cases and the mother in four. In six cases there are no references to either the father or the mother, which prevents us from jumping at any conclusions regarding their social status.

The presence of only one of the parents triggers some insights. The sole presence of the father is not strange considering the fact that families in Ancient Rome were patriarchal. What is especially bizarre is that the mother is the only signer of the epitaph. In this regard, the mother is believed to be a slave or a *liberta* that had her daughter or her son when she was a servant. In addition, the daughter or the son may be illegitimate, a fact that would not be accounted for by the funerary monument. Widows are out of the question here, because in that case we would be talking about a legitimate birth, which would be reflected in the monument.

There are a few striking examples of mothers as sole signers of the epitaphs. Two of them present a mother who decided to follow her daughter in death. This event is perfectly described in an inscription from *Carthago Noua* similar to the one opening this chapter:

> The father lost his little daughter and the mother followed her in death. Her name was Salviola.[31]

It is not easy to come to conclusions regarding the social condition of the people featured in Hispanic epitaphs, although it is true that this practice was popular mainly among the slave and the emancipated slave populations (MacWilliam 2001, 93; Sevilla 2012, 223). Even if the *nomen* does not always specify whether or not the text was written in a servile context, what we know is that servants only had one name of non-Latin origin, which underscored their foreignness. In this sense, references to the mother were more common than to the father. A servile status is observed in ten of the selected cases. Their names are not Latin and in three cases the mother is mentioned as the sole signer.[32] Significantly, the inscription dedicated to a boy named *Phillocallus* mentions his mother and sister (see No. 7 in appendix). A reference to *tria nomina* indicates that we are talking about a citizen, which occurs in six cases.[33] The fragmented state of three examples do not enable us to reach any conclusions regarding social status. In this regard, the shortage of population emancipated slave and the great presence of slaves are in fact peculiar. According to the data available, the mothers and their daughters are sometimes buried together; the latter are never buried with their fathers.[34]

Emphasis is usually placed on how premature and cruel the death was. Destiny and fortune are held responsible for these tragedies. There is even one case of murder.[35] Great importance is given to the feelings triggered by these losses. As a matter of fact, there is no shame in expressing pain and grief and there are even direct allusions to tears.[36] The death of boys and girls is regarded as unnatural because it goes against the order of nature. Thus, some parents say that they would graciously take the place of their dead infants. This wish is commonly expressed in the epitaphs that honour children, which can be regarded as a conventional way of expressing pain. This is revealed by the following words, which are uttered by a grieving mother:

> I wish I was dead instead of my daughter. Now you rest in peace. May the earth lie light upon thee.[37]

This wish is in the end realised in the inscription cited on the first page of this chapter, whose protagonist was also a mother. Allusions to pain and love are constant. In order to stop suffering, mothers are encouraged to consider having more children (No. 4 of the appendix), which challenges the idea that mothers did not love their infants.

Mors immatura, childhood and gender. The lamentation of mothers

It is possible to identify several features that keep recurring in the funerary poetry of the Iberian Peninsula, features that are also common to texts found in Rome and the Italian peninsula. I am referring to the dialogues that are established with travellers, the wish that the earth lies light upon the dead or the recommendations that the passerbys make the most of their lives.[38] There are also singular features that are worth considering, especially the detailed descriptions of the societal roles given to boys and girls. Unfortunately, because of their early death, they could not fully follow those gender scripts.

Boys exhibit masculine virtues very early. Stress is laid on the fact that they would perform typically masculine activities when they became adults. This is emphasised in the epitaph to *Crescens* (No. 9), already mentioned, whose death caused severe pain in his parents. He is indeed the protagonist of the text below:

> When you walk past my grave, stop for a moment and read these few words quickly. Here I am, *Crescens*: I was my parents' greatest hope, but my name got lost because I did not get to grow up. All my people's and my country's love has always been with me and my own death attests to that privilege. My courage was not concealed

> by my good speaking abilities and my conception of friendship. My own father engraved these flattering words on my grave as a sign of the impossibility to forget my death. Many will learn this epitaph: you who walk past my grave, be nice to me, may the art of these verses move my *Manes* and, since you have already read them, I say goodbye.[39]

In the case of girls, the situation is very different, as is apparent in a text dedicated to Lesbia by her mother, located in *Iesso* (Guissona, Lérida). Lesbia's beauty is foregrounded:

> *Praepusa* to her eleven-year-old daughter Lesbia, who lies here. What does destiny aim to do when taking away from me the most beautiful thing it has ever created? If we have to submit to the law of the hados, then we will cry in front of the rigid destiny. She was not even twelve. She had never dropped any tear, but now we, her beloved ones, cry over her death. Take care of yourselves, you afflicted parents and stop bothering my *Manes*. We write this epitaph to alleviate our pain and for readers to say: May the earth lie light upon thee![40]

Regardless of gender, all the texts under study show parents' deep affection towards their infants and the pain caused by the death of the latter. However, in the case of boys, emphasis is placed on their physical strength, talent, love for their country and speaking abilities: characteristics that will be also present in their adulthood. Beauty, on the other hand, is the only feature worthy of attention when talking about girls. Regarding parents, whose role is not as prominent as that of their dead infants, one can observe differences between mothers and fathers. In this regard, only two mothers follow their children in death, whereas no father surrenders to death. As far as the level of pain is concerned, differences can also be identified. They are evident in a text dedicated to a 9-year-old girl who is 'cried over by her father and demanded by her mother' (No. 12 in the appendix).

To sum up, the *carmina epigraphica* remain under-studied in historical scholarship. Even though texts dealing with children are scarce in the Iberian Peninsula, they do reveal that gender made a difference in premature deaths. Mothers' and fathers' attitudes towards their dead children were also different. Both conveyed their pain by relying on the gender roles they had been taught, making it clear that their dead infants were on their way to become men and women. Mothers usually surpassed parents when expressing pain. When a woman decided to follow her daughter in death, she showed female *immoderatio*, but, in this case, her attitude aroused respect and admiration. Actually, they reinforced the image of the *bona et pia mater* pervading Roman society.

Acknowledgements

This book chapter is part of the I+D+I Research Project, funded by the Ministry of Economy and Competitiveness of Spain, entitled 'Motherhood and families: continuity, changes, and breakdowns in history'. Ref. HAR2013–42371R.

Notes

1 Epitaph found in *Carthago Noua*, the modern Cartagena (Murcia, Spain). See Appendix No. 1. Due to the difficulties of translating Latin poetry, all passages cited in this text come from Spanish versions, especially from those provided by Carmen Fernández.

2 Epitaphs dedicated to a dead spouse or adult sons and daughters are also very beautifully written. Besides, they stress the affection towards the dead person and the pain caused by his or her death (Hernández 2001, 130–137 and 153–168).

3 Recent works have revisited the figure of the mother and the conception of motherhood. For some examples Cid (2009; 2010) or Hackworth and Salzman-Mitchel (2012). They expand on Dixon's pioneer work, which dates back to 1988.

4 The texts located in Rome and Italy are too many to be considered in this chapter. For this reason, I have selected significant epitaphs found in the Iberian Peninsula. I rely on Concepción Fernández's translations into Spanish (1998–99; 2007) and on the texts compiled by Franz Bücheler (1895–97). Reference is also made to the works of Hernández (2001), Hernández and Gómez (2006) and Martin (2010, 19–23).

5 These data are not updated, for new testimonies have been discovered since then. For more information on the pieces found in Hispania, see Hernández (2001) who carries out a detailed philological study on the words and expressions used in these funerary texts.

6 Corell (1990–91, 165, n.1) claims that there are 220 *carmina epigraphica* in the Iberian Peninsula.

7 For more information on these *corpora* and its evolution, see Fernández (1998, 12–18; 2007, 13–20), Hernández (2001, xvii–xviii) and Martin (2010, 19–23) among others. Sebastián Mariner analysed the case of Hispania in 1952.

8 This database is known as *Carmina Latina Epigraphica Hispaniae. Latin Epigraphic Poetry Database: Iconographic and Textual Researchs*, edited by C. Fernández Martínez, J. Gómez Pallarés and J. del Hoyo Vallejo. [http://cle.us.es/clehispaniae/show-index.jsf? idx=CHAR]. It was finalised in 2013 and includes 173 inscriptions from the Iberian Peninsula. It also includes detailed information about each piece, which is presented using philological standards.

9 Women are referred to as *domiseda, univira* or *lanifica*, as Hernández (2010, 17–19; 2016) points out. This is in fact a frequent practice in the Roman Empire.

10 Minten (2002, 110) foregrounds the conception of children as social beings. Phillipe Ariès (1960) was a pioneer historian who specialised in childhood, although he also analysed modern society. Nowadays, his theses are frequently called into question. Evans and Parkin (2013, 1–6) are some of the scholars in ancient times that criticise Ariès.

11 For a recent view on childhood in ancient times, see, for example, Aasgard (2006) and Evans and Parkin (2013). The particular case of Greece is analysed by Beaumant (2012) and Jouanna (2017), whereas Laes (2016) and Laes and Vuolanto (2017) explore the case of Rome.

12 Children's death in Rome has been explored by scholars such as Neraudeau (1987), King (2000), Minten (2002), Mustakallo *et al.* (2005) and Sevilla (2012).

13 Childhood, maturity and old age are important stages in family life, as Rawson (2003; 2011) argues in his studies on the family, emphasising the role of children in particular.

14 The work of Laes (2016) is crucial to fully grasp these aspects. For a review of the studies on childhood in ancient times, see Minten (2002, 9–10), Aasgard (2006, 25–27) and Laes (2016, 13–18).

15 See George (2013) for an analysis of examples found in Rome.

16 For some insights on children's graves, see King (2000) and Huskinson (2005).

17 For more information on the conception of *funus acerbus*, see Boyancé (1952) and Fernández (2003).

18 Very early Ter Vrugth-Lentz (1960) analysed the *mors immatura.*

19 The minimum marriageable age in Rome is a very controversial issue, although Laes (2016, 1–2) or Evans and Parkin (2013, 6–7) agree on these ages. According to Dixon (1992, 104), the

infans, who does not speak, the *parvulus*, and then the *puer* or *puella*, who is an older boy or girl, were distinguished.

20 See *Festus*' epitaph (Appendix No. 13).

21 Toys are usually found in children's graves (Sevilla 2012, 223–224).

22 Hersch (2010, 65–68) argues that the age at which Roman women got rid of their dolls is unknown.

23 Appendix Inscription No. 6 is a good example of this.

24 Laes (2016, 11) defines the funerary *carmina epigraphica* as 'the voices of ordinary people.'

25 According to Hernández (2001, xvii–xviii) this is a recurring characteristic in all the *carmina epigraphica.*

26 For a view on the epitaphs found in *Carthago Noua*, see Hernández and Gómez (2006).

27 Hernández and Gómez (2006, xvii); Fernández (1998, 30–47).

28 Appendix text No. 17 presents two brothers.

29 These expressions are present in Appendix texts Nos 3, 5, 9, 10, 17 and 12. According to MacWilliam (2001, 14) the Italian funerary epigraphy usually specifies how old the boy or girl was when they died so as to foreground their early age.

30 See Appendix text No. 9

31 Appendix text No. 5. Interpretation and translation by Fernández (1998, n. 1070). Some authors offer different translations. For Hernández and Gómez (2006, n. 5), *Salviola* died in her adult years and after becoming a mother. According to these authors, the inscription says that 'when she was little, the daughter lost her father and, when she became a mother, she followed her father in death.'

32 Appendix texts Nos 1, 5, 9, 11, 12, 13, 14, 17, 19 and 20. For more information about the *nomina* of the Hispanic *carmina epigraphica*, see Limón and Martín (2012).

33 Appendix texts Nos 2, 3, 4, 6, 8 and 15.

34 In two cases the mother and her daughter share the same grave (Appendix Nos 5 and 6). In two other examples there are only references to the siblings (Nos 1 and 17).

35 Cruelty is mentioned in Appendix texts Nos 5 and 6 and destiny is discussed in No. 12. Fortune is mentioned in Nos 4 and 6. There are also allusions to the abandonment of the *Hados* in Nos 1 and 13. Murder is mentioned in text No. 3.

36 This occurs in Appendix Nos 1, 6, 8, 12 and 20 of the annex. Affection is mentioned in Nos 17 and 18 and the loss of the *pignora cara patentes* is lamented in No. 17.

37 Appendix No. 7. This expression is recurrent in inscriptions located in other parts of the Roman Empire, as Hernández points out (2001, 24–27).

38 Direct references to travellers can be seen in Appendix texts Nos 2, 4, 9, 6 and 15 of the annex. The expression *sit tibi terra levis* is commonly found too (texts Appendix Nos 1, 2, 7, 11, 14, 15, 16 and 18).

39 A similar text is present in the epitaph dedicated to *Quintus Lusius Senica*, whose father laments that his son was not strong enough when he died because he had not reached adulthood yet (Appendix text No. 3). The love for the country evokes Cicero. The admiration towards *Lares Patrii is* present in a very fragmented epitaph dedicated to a boy (text No. 15), which reproduces expressions similar to those found in Ovid's *Metamorphosis*, as pointed out by Hernández (2001, 187–188).

40 Appendix text No. 1. Reference should also be made to a poem dedicated to a girl from *Hispalis* who died when she was 1 year 8 months and 12 days old. The text goes as follows: '*Nome* was my name and I was called *Cusucia* upon being born. Both names are present in this inscription. I lived for a short time and while I was alive I always was affectionate towards my father. Now I am buried under this epitaph. I fulfilled all my duties. You, whoever reads these verses, may note the little time I got to live. I beg you to say "may the earth lie light upon

thee'" (Appendix text No. 16). In this case, the girl's affectionate character and compromise to fulfill her duties stand out.

References

Aasgard, R. (2006) Children in Antiquity and early Christianity: Research history and central issues. *Familia* 33, 23–46.

Ariès, Ph. (1960) *L'enfant et la vie familiale sous l'Ancien Régime*. Paris, Plon.

Balil, A. (1962) Muñecas antiguas de España. *Archivo Español de Arqueología* 35(105), 70–85.

Beaumont, L. A. (2012) *Childhood in Ancient Athens: Iconography and Social History*. London/New York, Routledge.

Boyancé, P. (1952) Funus acerbum. *Revue des Etudes Anciennes* 54, 275–289.

Bücheler, F. (1895–97) *Carmina Latina epigraphica. Anthologia Latina* II.1–2 with E. Lommatzsch. II. 3. *Supplementum*, Leipzig, 1926 (reed. Stuttgart, 1982).

Cid López, R. M. (ed.) (2009) *Madres y Maternidades. Construcciones culturales en la civilización clásica*. Oviedo, KRK.

Cid López, R. M. (ed.) (2010) *Maternidades. Representaciones y realidad social. Edades Antigua y Media*. Madrid, Almudayna.

Cohen, A. and Rutter, J. B. (eds) (2007) *Constructions of Childhood in Ancient Greece and Italia (Hesperia* Supplement 41). Princeton, American School of Classical Studies at Athens.

Corell i Vicent, J. (1990–91) Dos epitafios poéticos de *Saguntum*. *Faventia* 12–13, 165–174.

Dasen, V. (2004) *Naissance et petite enfance dans l'Antiquité*. Fribourg/Göttingen, Academic Press/ Vandenhoeck & Ruprecht.

Dasen, V. (2015) *Le sourire d'Omphale. Maternité et petite enfance dans l'Antiquité*. Rennes, Presses Universitaires de France.

Demand, N. (2006) *Birth, Death, and Motherhood in Classical Greece*. Baltimore/London, The Johns Hopkins University Press.

Dixon, S. (1992) *The Roman Family*. Baltimore, The Johns Hopkins University Press.

Dixon, S. (ed.) (2001) *Childhood, Class and Kin in the Roman World*. London, Routledge.

Dixon, S. (1988) *The Roman Mother*. London, Routledge.

Dixon, S. (1992) *The Roman Family*. Baltimore/London, Johns Hopkins University Press.

Evans Grubbs, J.; Tim Parkin, T. and Bell, R. (eds) (2013) *The Oxford Handbook of Childhood and Education in the Classical World*. New York, Oxford University Press.

Fernández Martínez, C. (1998) *Poesía Epigráfica Latina*. I–II. Madrid, Biblioteca Clásica Gredos.

Fernández Martínez, C. (2003) *Acerbus:* la amargura de morir antes de tiempo. *Emerita. Revista de Lingüística y Filología Clásica*. 71(2), 313–317.

Fernández Martínez, C. (2007) Carmina Latina Epigraphica *de la Bética romana. Las primeras piedras de nuestra poesía*. Sevilla, Secretariado de Publicaciones de la Universidad de Sevilla.

Fernández Martínez, C. (2010) De Mulieribus Epigraphicis. *Tradición e innovación*. Sevilla. Secretrariado de Publicaciones de la Universidad de Sevilla.

Fernández Martínez, C. (2016) *Entre la literatura y la vida: elogio fúnebre a la mujer romana*. Sevilla, Secretariado de Publicaciones de la Universidad de Sevilla.

George, M. (2001) Roman funerary monument with a mother and daughter. In Dixon S. (ed.) *Childhood, Class and Kin in the Roman World*. London, Routlegde, 178–189.

Hackworth Petersen, L. and Salzman-Mitchel, P. (eds.) (2012) *Mothering and Motherhood in Ancient Greece and Rome*. Texas, University of Texas Press.

Hernández Pérez, R. (2001) *Poesía Latina Sepulcral de la Hispania Romana: estudio de los tópicos y sus formulaciones*. Valencia, Universitat de Valencia.

Hernández Pérez, R. (2016) *Qui exsitum parentes dederunt*: una formulación en prosa del tópico de la *immatura (praepostera) mors* en una inscripción romana del *ager Tarraconensis* (Renau, Tarragona). *Habis* 47, 187–197.
Hernández Pérez, R. and Gómez Font, X. (2006) Carmina Latina Epigraphica Carthaginis Novae. Valencia, Universitat de Valencia.
Hersch, K. K. (2010) *The Roman Wedding. Ritual and Meaning in Antiquity*. New York, Cambridge University Press.
Hualde Pascual, M. P. (1995) Epitafios infantiles: una tradición literaria grecolatina en la literatura inglesa. *Epos* 13, 73–84.
Huskinson, J. (2005) Dissappearing children? Children in Roman funerary art of the first to the fourth century AD. In H. Mustakallio, J. Hanska, H.-L. Sainio and V. Vuolante (eds) *Hoping for Continuity. Childhood, Education and Death in Antiquity and Middle Ages*. Rome, Institutum Romanum Finlandiae, 91–103.
Jouanna, D. (2017) *L'enfant grec au temps de Pèricles*. Paris, Les Belles Letres.
King, M. (2000) Commemoration of infants on Roman funerary inscriptions. In G. J. Oliver (ed.) *The Epigraphy of Death. Studies in the History and Society of Greece and Rome*. Liverpool, Liverpool University Press, 117–154.
Laes, C. (2016) *Children in the Roman Empire. Outsiders Within* (2nd edition). Cambridge, Cambridge University Press.
Laes, Ch. and Vuolanto, V. (eds) (2017) *Children and Everyday Life in the Roman and Late Antique World*. London/New York, Routledge.
Limón Belén, M. and Martín Adán, L. (2013) Nomina y Cognomina en los CLE de Hispania. In C. Fernández Martínez, M. Limón Belén, J. Gomez Pallarés and J. del Hoyo Calleja (eds) *Ex Officina. Literatura epigráfica en verso*. Sevilla, Secretariado de Publicaciones de la Universidad de Sevilla, 217–234.
MacWilliam, J. (2001) Children among the dead: the influence of urban life on the conmmemoration of children on tomstone inscriptions. In S. Dixon (ed.) *Childhood, Class and Kin in the Roman World*. London, Routledge, 74–98.
Mariner Bigorra, S. (1952) *Inscripciones hispanas en verso*. Barcelona, CSIC.
Martin-Kilcher, S. (2000) *Mors inmatura* in the Roman World. A mirror of society and tradition. In J. Pierce, M. Millet and M. Stuck (eds) *Burial, Society and Context in the Roman World*. Oxford, Oxbow Books, 63–77.
Martín Camacho, J. (2010) *Carmina Latina Epigrahica Baeticae ex schedis: edición y comenario*. Sevilla, Publicaciones de la Universidad de Sevilla.
Minten, E. (2002) *Roman Attitudes towards Children and Childhood. Private Funerary Evidence, c. 50 B.C.–c. A.D 300*. Stockholm, University of Stockholm.
Mustakallio, H., Hanska, J., Sainio, H.-L. and Vuolante, V. (eds) (2005) *Hoping for Continuity. Childhood, Education and Death in Antiquity and Middle Ages*. Rome, Institutum Romanum Finlandiae.
Neraudeau, J. P. (1987) La loi, la coutume et le chagrín. Réflexions sur la mort de enfants. In F. Hinard (ed.) *La mort, les morts et l'au-delà dans le monde romain*. Caen, Université de Caen, 195–208.
Rawson, B. (2003) *Children and Childhood in Roman Italy*. Oxford, Oxford University Press.
Rawson, B. (ed.) (2011) *A Companion to Families in the Greek and Roman Worlds*. Malden/Oxford/Chichester, Wiley-Blackwell.
Sevilla Conde, A. (2010–11) *Mors immatura* en el mundo romanao: los casos documentados en los territorios de la Provincia Tarraconensis. *Anales de Arqueología Cordobesa* 21–22, 197–219.
Sevilla Conde, A. (2012) *Morir ante suum die*. La infancia en Roma a través de la muerte. In D. Justel Vicente (ed.) *Niños en la antigüedad. Estudios sobre la infancia en el Mediterráneo antiguo*. Zaragoza, Prensas Universitarias de la Universidad de Zaragoza, 199–234.
Sigismond, J. (2001) The value of epithets in pagan and Christian epitaphs. In S. Dixon (ed.) *Childhood, Class and Kin in the Roman World*. London, Routledge, 165–177.
Ter Vrugt-Lentz, J. (1960) *Mors Immatura*. Groningen, Wolters.

Appendix

List of Epigraphic *carmina epigraphica* on *mors inmatura* of Children. Selected Testimonials of the Iberian Peninsula

No.	*Bibliographic reference*	*Location*	*Girl/child dead*	*Relatives mentioned*	*Date*	*Age*
1	Hernández 2001 321	*Iesso* (Guissona, Lérida)	*Lesbia*	*Servilia Praepusa* (mother)		11 years 10 months
2	Fernández 1999, no. 2.183	Montán, Castellón	*M. Marius Lasciuos*	–	–	3 years 6 months
3	Fernánde, 1998, no.979; Hernández and Gómez 2006, no. 7	*Carthago Noua* (Cartagena, Murcia)	*Quintus Lusius Senia*[1]	–	1st century AD	(Young age)
4	Fernández 1998, no. 980; Hernández and Gómez 2006, no. 3	*Carthago Noua* (Cartagena, Murcia)	*C. Licinius Thorax* (son of *Caius Licinius*)	Parents	1st century AD	–
5	Fernández 1998, no. 1.070	*Carthago Noua* (Cartagena, Murcia)	*Saluiola (and your mother)*	Parents	1st century BC	(small daughter)
6	Fernández 1998 no. 1.076 = Hernández and Gómez 2006, no. 8	*Carthago Noua* (Cartagena, Murcia)	*Sicinia, (the mother)* *Sicinia Secunda, (the daughter)*[2]	–	–	–
7	Fernández, 1999, no. 1.194; Hernández and Gomez 2006, no. 10.	*Carthago Noua* (Cartagena, Murcia)	*Phillocallus*[3]	Mother	1st–2nd century AD	–
8	Hernández and Gómez 2006, no. 2	*Carthago Noua* (Cartagena, Murcia)	*Publius Pontilenus (son of Lucius)*	Parents	1st cenury BC	–
9	Fernández 1999, no. 1.196	*Baesucci* (Vilches, Jaén)	*Crescens*	Parents		Uncertain
10	Fernández 2007, no. J18	Torredelcampo (Jaén)	*(girl)*	–	1st century AD	–
11	Fernández 1998, no. 193	*Castulo* (Linares, Jaén)	*Antisporo*		2nd century AD	8 years
12	Fernández 1998, no. 445; 2007, no. CO5	*Corduba* (Córdoba)	*Melitine*	*Titilicuta*, (mother) *Carpoforo* (father)	2nd–3rd century AD	9 years 6 months 8 days

No.	*Bibliographic reference*	*Location*	*Girl/child dead*	*Relatives mentioned*	*Date*	*Age*
13	Fernández 2007, CO3	*Corduba*	*Festus*	Mother (?)[4]	2nd–3rd century AD	15 years
14	Fernández 2007, CO18	*Conuentus Cordubensis*	*(girl)*	Mother	1st–2nd century AD	2 years
15	Fernández 2007, CO10	Cortijo de Malpartida, Córdoba	*Son of Marius*	Father	2nd century AD	Uncertain[5]
16	Fernández 1998, No. 1.316	*Hispalis* (Sevilla)	*Nome Cusucia*	Father	–	1 year 8 months 12 days
17	Fernández, 1998, no. 1.158; 2007, no. CA1	*Gades* (Cádiz)	*Sodalis et Festiua (brothers)*	Parents	1st century AD	11 years (girl) 1 year (child)
18	Fernández 1999, no. 1.566	*Gades* (Cádiz)	*Herennia Crocine*	–	–	Uncertain[6]
19	Martín 2010, no. MA1	*Sabora*, (Tolox, Málaga)	*Hermógenes*	–	–	8 years 7 months 13 days
20	Fernández 1999, no. 1.197	*Emerita Augusta*	*Julianus*	Parents	–	7 months

[1] According to Hernández and Gómez, No. 7, *Quintus Lusius Senica* is referred to here; [2] *Sicinia* was the daughter of *Quintus* and *Sicinia Secunda* of *Gaius*; [3] the inscription refers to the freedwoman *Aucta*, the mother and *Adventa*, the sister, who dedicated the monument; [4] Allusions are made to the wet nurse; [5] according to Fernández 2007, 199, both *VIII* and *XVIII ann(orum* could be written on the grave; [6] the youth of the deceased woman is emphasised, without specifying age. We cannot say for certain that it is talking about a girl

Chapter 14

Mater civitatis: forms of patronage, charity and foundations for children

Almudena Domínguez-Arranz

The limits of civic generosity

When the *matres* of a city were chosen, the *honoratae* showed their gratitude by organsiing events to assure a distinguished following and to intervene in the urban landscape by erecting monuments, altars and statues or by making donations of land or money. Epigraphy bears witness to the munificence of these philanthropists towards the *collegia*, whose members received generous gifts, reflecting the social status of these *matres* and the general importance of the mother figure in Roman society.[1] As we shall see, such acts constituted a procedure to obtain social recognition in parallel with the honours garnered by the givers' male counterparts.

Relegated as they were by the nature of Roman gender relations and tradition to the private sphere, leaving public life to men alone, some of these matrons involved themselves in the civic life of the localities with which they had links of some kind, whether by birth or by maternal or paternal origin, constituting the source of the prestige which a given person or family might enjoy in more than one community.[2] The precedent for such behaviour was provided by the Hellenistic monarchies, whose queens sometimes acted and were honoured as public patrons.[3] Like their predecessors, high-status Roman women succeeded in projecting their own social ideals through activities associated with the custom of giving back to the community (Duncan-Jones 1985, 28–33) via initiatives to improve public spaces, the organisation of commemorative games and feasts, endowments and donations, and the creation of foundations. Scholars have shown how some families set up trusts to make contributions to the public finances, allowing their cities to use the rents obtained for the protection of destitute children. One form of women's involvement in the sphere of civic society, to which they were normally denied access, was investment in the urban landscape, contributing more than has hitherto been recognised to the feminisation of the city by sponsoring the construction of public buildings and assuming the liability for taxes payable by their fellow citizens.[4]

Such a matron was one Voconia Avita,[5] who lived in the town of Tagili (modern Tíjola in the province of Almería) in Spain in the Flavian epoch, where she invested in civic improvements, acquiring the site for new bath houses and financing their construction. The inscription recording her munificence adds that she also gifted 10,000 *sestertii* for the perpetual use of the *thermae* in the upkeep of the installations and buildings, and to prevent their deterioration. Voconia was clearly a shrewd lady, *clarissima*, who was well aware of the impact of her actions, and she was careful to organise an *epulum* and circus games for the townspeople to counterbalance the publicity on the opening day of the baths.[6] However, Iunia Rustica, *sacerdos perpetua et prima* of the town of Cartima (modern Cártama near Malaga) went even further, investing very large sums as religion provided her with a different setting in which to practice her philanthropy. The exact amount is not specified in the commemorative inscription, but there are details of both the beneficiaries and the items she paid for, which included porticoes, baths, a cistern and two bronze statues of the gods Cupid and Mars,[7] not to mention the organisation of spectacles. Her interest in tax matters was particularly noteworthy, as she applied a part of her bequest to lighten the burden of the *uectigalia publica* for her fellow citizens by assuming annual indirect tax charges, in all probability the *agri uectigales*.[8] This is one of the very rare documented examples of a matron's accepting the liability for future expenses, which were often onerous for poorer towns and cities receiving donations *ex testamento*. Cartima showed its gratitude by erecting busts of the male members of Iunia Rustica's family, including her son Fabius Iunianus and husband Fabius Fabianus, and of herself, although she defrayed the cost (*remissa impensa*) (Martínez 1990, 219–241). Both literary and legal sources mention that donations of this kind might be made in cash or in kind (land, goods or buildings). The grant of rights to the use and enjoyment of houses and other properties was also common, as was the payment of taxes like the present case (Le Roux 1999, 158–159).

This conduct reveals the wealth of these notables, and it is in fact the only example in the West of a lady, related with the influential family of the *Fabii Fabiani*, personally assuming taxes payable by her fellow citizens. Inscriptions often fail to specify the amount of endowments or the cost of the buildings donated, and we may therefore compare the investment made by Iunia Rustica with the bequests of one *Q. Torius Culeus*, whose philanthropy was on a similar scale, to gain an idea of its importance. *Culeus* was a provincial procurator who financed the construction of the town wall at Castulo (modern Linares in the province of Jaén), gifted land for bath houses and made road repairs, representing a total outlay of some ten million *sestertii* (Curchin 1983, 230), although he did not pay any taxes. It is against these endowments that we may assess the donations made by Iunia Rustica (Donahue 2004, 873–891; Medina 2014, 179 ff). Such traces reveal the role played by local aristocratic ladies in their towns alongside men. We believe giving of this kind was not merely a means to climb the social ladder but must be seen as a personal decision to contribute to the public purse for the benefit of the donors' fellow citizens.

As we have seen in the above examples, the *ludi* and *spectacula* were associated with the inauguration of buildings and the erection of statues, which in the case of female philanthropists were dedicated to male family members and deities in contrast to those put up by male benefactors, who were free to cover a much broader spectrum of possible dedicatees.[9] Meanwhile, architectural projects make up most known female initiatives, and as a general rule the *dedicatio* of a building, whether in Italy or in the provinces, would coincide with a public event at which donations of cash or food might be made, and *epula* or *cenae publicae ob honorem* could be organised.[10] Such celebrations were not in any way obligatory, but were organised by custom and in response to ideological notions of the proper behaviour required of a good citizen (Hemelrijk 2015, 140–141). According to Mrozek's analysis, a *cena* was a more important matter than an *epulum* and was most often, although not always, held upon the grant of some high office. Guests would in principle be drawn from a small circle of people holding the rank of *decurion* or *Augustal* but hardly ever *plebs*, while an *epulum* would be a rather larger event open to the common people.[11] Contemporary accounts confirm that the fare offered at an *epulum* would consist of basic foodstuffs, *panis et uinum*, as well as more costly provender like fish, meat, fruit and cheese, depending on the status and number of guests, and of course the donor's own largesse.

We have seen above the circumstances surrounding the endowments made by Voconia Avita and Iunia Rustica in the Roman *Hispania Baetica*, a province which accounted for the majority of matronly donations linked to feasts organised for the general populace. There is in fact evidence of another 12 banquets held by Hispanic *matres*[12] to express gratitude for the conferral of distinctions, such as the office of priestess,[13] publicise donations made for public works or *opera publica*, and celebrate the dedication of statuary to the imperial family, deities or the donors themselves, or to announce any other kind of public activities beyond those proper to the *domus*. The epigraphic record shows that the women concerned were well aware of the significance of feasts arranged to underscore their position in the community and expected such occasions to create collective memories which would enhance the *honos* earned for themselves and the members of their *gens* (Melchor 2009, 153), so that they would seek to ensure the maximum attendance of magistrates and other notables on the day of the *epulum.*[14] According to Mrozek, giving allowed women to play a high-profile role, and the distribution of food was a priority (Mrozek 1987, 71–75). However, they made up only around 10% of donors, 'Le fait que *l'epulum* appartient aux distributions où la participation des femmes était la plus remarquable n'est pas sans importance pour la qualification d' *epulum* comme un don modeste, car les femmes représentent un groupe de bénéficiaires qui subit généralement une discrimination' (Mrozek 1987, 41).

One unusual case is that of Ummidia Quadratilla, a long-lived lady of Cassino in Italy who died in AD 107. Considered extravagantly rich and somewhat dissolute by her contemporaries, there can be no doubt of her high social standing in the town, where she was elevated to the condition of *femina princeps*, an honour until then only conferred on ladies of the imperial family like Livia and her daughter in law Julia.[15] No-one could have been unaware that Ummidia's prestige came from her family connection with Umidius Durmius Cuadratus, governor of Syria, or that her grandson was a friend of Pliny.[16] In a letter, Pliny paints the 80-year old lady as a ridiculous and disreputable personage without mentioning her philanthropic activities, deploring her pantomime business for arousing the base passions of the populace and casting aspersions on her honour in the vein of contemporary ideas about the kind of women associated with the theatre.[17]

Among the initiatives for which Quadratilla was honoured, we may observe the construction of a temple and an amphitheatre, and the repair of a theatre in *Casinum*, and like the Hispanic ladies mentioned above, she organised an *epulum* to which she invited the *decuriones, populus* and it is said that too *mulieres* (Raepsaet-Charlier 1987, no. 829; Fora 1992, 269–273; Flower 2006, 212; Hemelrijk 2015, 66; Caldelli 2016, 266–267). Presumably, it was this munificence, which immortalised her in the *Fasti Ostienses*, or perhaps it was her marriage, a circumstance that would have made an indelible mark on the memory of the city, or maybe an honour decreed by the *ordo* (Vidman 1982, 48). Around a century later, there lived another wealthy female entrepreneur, Emilia Pudentilla, whose story is known from the *Apologia* written by her second husband, the sophist Apuleius of Madaura. A resident of Oea, this *matrona docta* and *mulier libera*[18] was kept busy not only by her own vast estate but also managed her own trading and lending ventures, at the same time engaging in charitable works and organising banquets. We know, for example, that Apuleius insisted on the couple's holding their wedding outside the city to prevent a horde of plebeians from arriving to demand the distribution of food or cash (*sportula*), as happened at the betrothal of Emilia Pudentilla's eldest son costing her some 50,000 *sestertii*, a significant sum if we consider that it would have been 40–50 times the annual pay of a legionary, although it may appear less so compared with the fortune the writer ascribes to Pudentilla in the text.[19]

We know that some imperial and private ladies would act as benefactors of the populace as a means of further legitimising the state ideology. For example, Livia, the first lady to hold her own immense personal fortune and to use it in a conventionally masculine way, made donations to help the victims of wars[20] and to pay the dowries of girls born to poor families,[21] as well as organising costly public events. Her daughter-in-law Julia also held at least one *epulum* for ladies of the elite on the occasion of the *ovatio* received by Tiberius on his return from Germany,[22] and she may also have offered other banquets together with the Emperor at the Capitolium or on her own initiative in private contexts, as we know Livia did for the *Columbarium Libertorum et Servorum Liviae Augustae*.[23] This custom belonged to the role of first lady, and it was only strengthened by later princesses, whose munificence underpinned respect for their persons and their power relations in each territory. Above all, however, it was the promotion and survival of the dynasty that was at stake, and it was this which heightened their interest in imposing their personal qualities at all times. On this point, we may recall that the emancipation of Roman women from the tutelage to which they were generally subject occurred in parallel with a gradual increase in their personal wealth and gains in their control over their own assets, and it may have been this financial independence which allowed them to invest in their home towns and cities (Van Bremen 1983; Cooley 2013, 29). Thus, the *ius trius liberorum* enshrined among the raft of Augustan laws designed to encourage fertility at a time when the rate of births was at an all time low permitted an increase in female wealth and enabled women legally to inherit and to pass on their own estates.[24]

Child food support, a right or a duty

A similar form of patronage can be observed in the 1st and 2nd centuries AD in the shape of charitable food support programmes, and it cannot be ruled out that the emperors themselves imitated private initiatives in this area, because all evidence suggests that the food foundation set up by Titus Helvius Basila in the Claudian-Neronian period was the first of its kind.[25] It was above all in the 2nd century, however, that the emperors decides to set aside public funds for such purposes (Duncan-Jones 1964), although distributions of free food were far from a novelty by this time, as the *frumentationes*, through which the holders of the *tesserae frumentariae*, would receive either grain or cash had existed since the time of the Republic.[26] Other forms of charitable giving included the *congii* (quotas of wheat, oil, wine and firewood) and the *sportula*, an offering in the form of food or cash provided by the state or private parties in exchange for social advancement, or by an *ordo* or its members in order to win votes in elections, although donations might sometimes be of a more public nature (Mrozek 1987, 33; Blanch-Nougués 2007, 150).[27] However, the *frumentationes* were never intended as charity, although scholars have pointed to their similarity with Trajan's gifts to 5000 plebeian children and with the *alimenta publica* donated to infants and mothers.[28] Our knowledge of both institutions stems from the *Tabula* of *Ligures Baebiani*, the *Tabula alimentaria* of Veleia and epigraphic fragments, providing the subject matter for an intense propaganda disseminated by means of monumental and numismatic iconography[29] (Duncan-Jones 1974; Carlsen 1999; Blanch-Nougués 2007, 126 ff; 2017, 21–37; Cao 2010, 292–294).

In general, it is accepted that the *alimenta* constituted a state programme for loans to landowners in the Italian cities, the returns on which were used to maintain the children of poor families and freedmen until they came of age. The reasons why this system of loans was ever started are still a matter of debate, as is their relationship with the generosity of successive emperors towards the children of mainly Italian cities (Duncan-Jones 1974; Woolf 1990; Patterson 2003). Issues such as the proper nourishment and education of children, their education, inheritance rights and even their social status have been preserved for us in legal codes and are reflected in these food support institutions, which were created both by private parties and by the state, especially under Trajan. It was at this time that women began to make contributions to the municipal treasuries through foundations they themselves set up, so that their study reveals a game of mirrors between the imperial princesses and private matrons in which the latter may have aped the behaviour of the former, although the influence of each on the other was most likely mutual.[30]

It was within this 2nd century policy of beneficence allowing ladies of equestrian or senatorial rank to display their personal wealth and their capacity to manage their own affairs that Matidia the Younger conceived the bequest of a usufruct of property to a foundation for the benefit of children, a donation that was worth as much as one of the two *Veleia* loans and the gifts made by the philanthropist Fabia Agrippina. Surviving texts and prosopographic records have little to say about Matidia and do not even tell us whether she married or had any children of her own.[31] However, they do suggest that she showed scant political ambition and had no influence at court, which seems barely credible in view of her wealth and the size of her estates scattered throughout Italy, Greece and Africa. These she managed personally, allowing her to engage in highly visible patronage and charitable giving.[32]

Hadrian's sister-in-law was a *matrona docta* with connections in the cities of Campania who made a donation to the library of Sessa Aurunca and was involved in the renovation of the theatre and other works to bring fresh water into the city.[33] She was correspondingly honoured with statues which she may herself have paid for, reimbursing the city for the costs incurred as Iunia Rustica did.[34] We know that she left one million *sestertii* to certain *Varianis alumnis masculis feminisque* on her death, which occurred sometime between AD 161 and 170 (Mrozek 1987, 60; Boatwright 1992, 29–30; Hemelrijk 2015, 151).[35] As in the case of other bequests, the function of which was to implement state subsidies, Hadrian's sister-in-law stipulated that each child should receive 50,000 *sestertii* per year. Faustina the Younger was entrusted with carrying out her aunt's wishes after she was appointed executor, and a beneficiary, of her will in AD 162.[36] According to Duncan-Jones, these *Variani* would have enjoyed the benefits of an earlier foundation sponsored by L. Vario Ambibulo, a citizen of Capua and consul in AD 132–133,[37] who figures in Matidia's testament according to Fronton's correspondence with *Marcus Aurelius.* Aside from the texts, almost all of the epigraphs to mention Matidia belong to the period of Antoninus Pius, who wheedled his aunt (*matertera imperatoris Antonini Pii*)[38] into patronising numerous communities with which she had links (Chausson 2008, 236).

The decision to make food bequests was a demonstration of these women's social status and privileged economic circumstances, just as it was for men. Some such benefactresses, like Matidia the Younger, had close ties to the imperial household or provincial governors, and the same may be observed in the case of other endowments (Carlsen 1999, 278–285) such as those made by Fabia *H [adrianil]la* or Agrippina.

The oldest will made by a woman was that of *Fabia H[adrianil]la* (or *H[ispanil]la*), a lady identified as a noble of the Trajan epoch, daughter and wife of consuls, and probably related like Iunia Rustica with the family of the *Fabii*.[39] This Hispanic *clarissima* set up a trust of 50,000 *sestertii* (*in legato*), stipulating that the interest yielded on the principal be used to increase the maintenance distributed to 22 *ingenuae* and 21 *ingenui* by 40 and 30 *sestertii* respectively on Fabia's birthday and that of her deceased husband (Melchor 1999, 30 and 33; Cid 2005, 193–220). By singling out these *dies natalis* for the two payments which her legatees or the town's *curatores* were required to make, Fabia effectively perpetuated the family name while at the same time recalling that this was the custom of the emperors who instituted the *alimenta*. The epigraph tells us that the boys belonged to the *Iuncini, collegia iuuenes* (Medina 2014, 184–185), but there is a gap in the record with regard to the girls, although some believe it may have included the name of the *collegium* referred to as *titianae* in the *Corpus Inscriptionum Latinarum*. This private girls' association seems to have been connected with Sexto Emilio Junco, consul of Tripoli in AD 127 and the possible founder of the *collegium*. This raises the possibility that he, or one of descendants, may have been Fabia's husband and that the girls' college may have taken the name of its benefactress like the *Faustinianae* of Antoninus' state programme[40] (Mirón 2000, 35).

The inscription commemorating *Ag[ripinna]*, daughter or wife of the suffect consul C. Fabius Agrippinus, suggests that she too enjoyed an elevated social position and financial means. She was honoured in this way by the *decuriones* for a donation made to the city[41] (Duncan-Jones 1974, 172; Cao 2010, 210–214; Caldelli 2016, 263–264). This consisted of a trust provided for in her will, which made over the large sum of one million *sestertii* to the city, the interest on which was to be used for three different initiatives – first and foremost to maintain 100 girls in Ostia, second to organise annual games to commemorate Aemilia Agrippina, the matron's mother or grandmother, and third to arrange *cenae* in honour of the *decuriones* three times each year. Both of the latter two public events were intended to underline her munificence and highlight the family name. Agrippina's initiative was without doubt a major bequest, very much larger than that made by *H[adrianil]la* (Duncan-Jones 1974, 228 and 235; Raepsaet-Charlier 1987, 305; Magioncalda 2005, 514–516; Cao 2010, 210), which would yield some 50,000 *sestertii* annually to be distributed, according to other documents, as follows: 16 *sestertii*/month to each girl, making an annual total of 19,200 *sestertii*; some 6600 *sestertii* to cover the cost of the three *cenae* for 110 representatives of the elite, estimated on the basis of other epigraphs stating that the decurions' *sportula* came in at 20 *sestertii* per head; leaving 24,200 *sestertii*, a quite considerable sum, for the organisation of the *ludi*. Hence, the donation not only met the needs of the girls of Ostia but also allowed the matron to win the plaudits of the city elite and the common people at the same time as reflecting the personal gratitude of the *domus* for the favour shown by Antoninus Pius to Fabius' career.

Based on existing research, we may conjecture that both *Ag[ripinna]* and *H[adrianil]la* may have been inspired by the *Puellae Faustinianae* founded by the emperor for his wife (this may actually have been the other way about) (Duncan-Jones 1974, 228; Cao 2010, 572), and it seems likely that the foundation at least influenced their personal decision to benefit girls.[42] To put the matter another way, these private foundations were of a similar kind to other state institutions.

Final remarks

Analysis of the epigraphic record allows us to trace different acts of evergetism by private individuals in Roman cities from support for the erection of buildings through the distribution of cash, the organisation of banquets and feasts, and handouts of one kind or another, as well as the changes that occurred between the early and late empire (Papi 2004, 53–81). Many scholars hold that local elites created a particular system of relationships during the Empire, allowing them to obtain both tangible and intangible benefits. In this way, they were able to project their own personal notions of society by means of interventions in the public space, from building through to the creation of *alimenta propter pueri et puellae*, which we might add reveal a certain discrimination against girls, who benefitted proportionally less than boys and for a shorter time.[43] We even see imperial ladies like Matidia make private donations, although the data is insufficient to establish whether such princesses discharged any further functions in these institutions during their lifetimes. Meanwhile, other wealthy female donors set up trusts to the benefit of their towns and cities to perform commemorative rites in their own honour, celebrate the anniversary of their birth or that of family members, support the priesthood and erect statues (Hemelrijk 2015, 144–147).

Lineage, wealth and some part in the machinery of power were the three main ingredients of power and prestige for such aristocrats. While Roman women were not permitted to take part freely in political life, the law did allow them the option to become rich essentially by inheriting the family estate, and therefore to demand a public role in society and the economy of their times. It was in this way, in fact, that many members of local aristocracies integrated with the Roman empire.

To sum up, these matrons sometimes played an important role in strengthening the local exchequer through their donations despite the ridicule of classical writers, who often held them up as profligate or accused them of interfering in the policies of their husbands employing all manner of rhetorical and literary tropes. The aim of their munificence was not merely to build a reputation as a worthy citizen but was often influenced by a private desire to improve living conditions in their own home towns and cities, which was one of the few ways in which they could gain any visibility in the public sphere. Based on the extant documentation it has been possible to learn the names of some of these women of equestrian or senatorial rank, whose cooperation even went so far (exceptionally) as to defray the cost of general taxes payable by their home municipality. However, certain epigraphs also show that women of more modest means practiced such giving as a way to shed their anonymity (Magioncalda 2005). Whatever their social status, however, these *matres* always acted in the context of the family, seeking to win honours and perpetuate their memory. As Cooley said after making a detailed study of their actions, 'such women were not always imitating imperial models, but were themselves innovators and possibly trend-setters' (Cooley 2013, 43).

Acknowledgements

This chapter is the fruit of research carried out as part of Project I+D+I HAR2013-42371R, 'Demeter. Gender, Motherhood, Gender and Family' and 'OAAEP' Research Groups (the latter financed by the Regional Government of Aragon and FSE).

Notes

1 According to Cenerini (2013, 9–10). See also Hallett (1984) Rowlandson (1998).
2 Raepsaet-Charlier (1987) estimates the numbers of women who were silenced compared to men in percentage terms.
3 Such women were subject to less restrictions than their Roman counterparts according to Bielman (2002, 240).
4 See Martínez (2011) and Cenerini and Rohr (2016) for a discussion of the feminisation of civic relations.
5 Further cases of feminine liberality are described in Melchor (1994–95, 218, 222–225) and Medina (2014, 182–184).
6 IRAL 00048=spectacles-01, 00024=AE 1979, 00352; EDCS-08901014; Melchor (2009, 149–152); Hemelrijk (2015, 512).
7 CIL II 1956; ILS 5512. Cost of the statues in Duncan-Jones (1974, 126–127) and Curchin (1983, 231–232 and 242–243).
8 Cf. Hemerlijk (2015, 148). For an interpretation of this tax, see Duncan-Jones (1990, 187–188). On the *sacerdos*, see Donahue (2004, 87)6.
9 Hemerlijk (2015, 331–332): Male dedicants were not only more numerous, they were also able to include friends, patrons and members of their *domus* and immediate family, not to mention other persons whose relationships with the dedicant are not clearly stated in statue epigraphs.
10 Plin. *Ep.* 10.116. Cf. Stylow and Gimeno (2001, 97–109) who discuss the *cenae publicae* in relation to the interpretation of the *remissio* for feasts offered to fellow townspeople. There is also an inscription in Iporca referring to the *sacerdos* Cornelia Tusca Hemerlijk (2015, 146–147).
11 Mrozek (1987, 37). Guests at either feast would receive cash and other gifts such as *nuces* (X 5849 and 5853).
12 CIL II 1341; 01341=IRPCádiz 00541, EDCS-05501347 (Pomponia Rosciana, *Saepo*); CIL II 964=ERBeturi 00161=CILA-01, 00005=D 05402=SEBarc-09, p. 190, 01=AE 2013, +00107, EDCS-05500974 (Baebia Crinita, *Arucci*); CIL II2/5 631=02, 05514=ILPGranada 00056=CILA-04, 00015, EDCS-08700694 (lady of *Iliberris*); CIL II 3240=(p 949)=EE-09, p 125=CILA-03-01, 00245=D 05764, EDCS-05502659 (Ania Victorina of *Ilugo*); CIL 5488=ILMMálaga 00007, EDCS-05600731 (Valeria Situlina, Cartima); CILA III 101=Spectacles-01, 00029=AE 1958, 00004, EDCS-10200021 (Cornelia Marulina, Castulo); IRPCa 534=AE 1974, 00384=AE 1975, 00496, EDCS-07500255 (Fabia Fabiana, Carteia); CIL II 1278=CILA-02-03, 00951=IUtrera 00030, EDCS-05501282 (Celerina, Salpensa); CIL II 1047=CILA-02-04, 01048, EDCS-05501053 (Cornelia Prisca, Iporca); CIL II 1258=(p. 842)=CILA-01, 00084; EDCS-05501261 (Cornelia Fabula, Iptucci); CIL II 1267=(p. 842)=CIL 09, *00628=CILA-01, 00081, EDCS-05501270 (Suconia Rustica, Ostur); CILA-02-04, 01058=AE 1972, 00270=HEp 1997, 00916=AE 2003, +00841, EDCS-10102156 (Quintia Flacina, Munigua). Cf. Melchor (2009, 149–52; 2011, 267–300).
13 Banquets might also be associated with the conferral of a provincial priesthood or some honorific title, Martínez (1990, 232–234).

14 Plin. *Ep*. 10.116.

15 Ovid styles Livia *Romana princeps* (*Cons. ad Liviam*, 356). In another poem he combines the epithets *femina* and *princeps*, which he knowingly separates by the conjunction *sed* (*Pont*. 3.1.125–128, *Trist*. 1.6.25). In Macrob. *Sat*. 2.5.6, Augustus addresses Livia and Julia as *principes feminas*.

16 Plin. *Ep*. 7.24.

17 CIL VI 28526, X 5183=ILS 5628; PIR, V 606; Sick (1999, 330–348). This is a classic barb aimed at one of a handful of female entrepreneurs, though she was a benefactor of her city and eventually left two-thirds of her fortune to her grandson but only one-third to her granddaughter.

18 We have only the version of the sophist, who refers to her letters (Apul. *Apol*. 84.7–8, 85.1–6, 86.1–2, 87.8, 100.8). The loss of this feminine correspondence is in fact a gender issue, as Apuleius would have been reluctant to publish his wife's private letters in order to preserve her modesty. It was only thanks to Pudentilla that he was able to rise in the social hierarchy, however (Gutsfeld 1992, 250–68; Ceneriri 2007, 16–17).

19 Cf. Hemerlijk (2015, 139), who argues that the example of Pudentilla calls into question the assumption that the frequent feasts and handouts to celebrate family or public events were basically low-cost affairs.

20 Dio. 57.16.2; Val. Max. 4.8.2.

21 Dio. 58.2.

22 Suet. *Aug*. 29.4; Dio., 54.23.1–6, 55.2.4. 55.8. His *damnatio memoriae* conceals Julia's true personality. Cf. Domínguez-Arranz and Gregorio-Navarro (forthcoming).

23 CIL VI 8945.

24 Dio. 49.38.1. The legal aspects involved in women's ownership of property is discussed in Di Bella (2015, 85–94).

25 CIL X 5056.

26 Suet. *Aug*. 40, 42; *Nero*, 11; Carrié 1975. It was at this time too that the *missilia*, consisting of gifts and coins, first appeared in association with games organised by magistrates on their appointment to office. Suet., *Nero*, 11.4; Dio., 66.25; 67.4.6.

27 Marc. I, 59; Juv. I, 117.

28 Plin. *Pan*. 26–28.

29 CIL XI 1147=ILS 6675; CIL IX 1455=ILS 6509, of AD 101. These sources are historiographically controversial. Duncan-Jones (1974); Carlsen (1999); Blanch-Nougués (2007, 126; 2017, 21–37); Cao (2010,292–294).

30 A paradigmatic case was that of Mineia, who may have imitated the behaviour of Livia at Paestum, becoming involved in architectural projects which were commemorated in a series of highly unusual numismatic issues, a public honour towards this *clarissima* without parallel among contemporary imperial ladies (Cooley 2015, 38–42, fig. 3).

31 Chausson (2008, 234) and Wood (2015, 235–236) argue that this cannot be known for certain. She may have married and lost her husband, choosing to remain a widow for fear of reprisals by Hadrian against persons of senatorial rank suspected of plotting parricide. According to Boatwright (1991, 521), she grew up in the *domus* but later went to live at her mother's home if we are to believe the epigraph found on a *fistula acquaria* near the Piazza Vittorio Emmanuele (AE 1954, 72). The only honour she received was a public funeral (Fronto. *Ad Marc. Caes*. 2.16).

32 Boatwright (1991, 524) relates this increased economic freedom and generosity with the distance she maintained from the imperial household. Cf. Reggiani (2007, 23–27).

33 For a discussion of her philanthropy in Campania see Boatwright (1992) and Valeri and Zevi (2004). The text *Matidiae Aug (ustae) Fil (iae)* on a *fistula* found during the excavation of the theatre appears to support her involvement in the renovation of the aqueduct (Cascella 2013, 76).

34 Dedications remain on some of these sculptures: CIL X 4744 to 4747 (Boatwright 1992, 23–24). In addition to those already known, a *Venus Genetrix* in white and *bigio morato* marble may

now be added, which stood in a privileged place dedicated to the family cult (Chausson 2008, 233–259; Wood 2015, 233–259).

35 Fronto. *ad Amicos*, 1.14.1;

36 Fronto. *ad Amicos*, 1.14; *ad Ant. imp.* 2.1. For a discussion of the resulting testamentary disputes, see Boatwright (1992, 29–30).

37 Prosopographia-Imperii-Romani V, 183.

38 According to *Epit. de Caes.* XV 1 and the civic epigraphy of Rome, these were Ephesus, Minturnae, Sessa Aurunca (CIL VI 1007, III 6070a, X 3883 and 4744 to 4747).

39 CIL II 1174, p. 698, 841=CILA 2.1,19; Raepsaet-Charlier (1987, 307–308); Martínez (1990, 222); Mirón (2000, 34–36).

40 CIL II 1174.

41 CIL XIV 4450=350.

42 For the case of *H[adrianil]la*, see Mirón (2003, 226).

43 Surviving documents show that girls received the *alimenta* until the age of 12/13, while boys did so up to 14/15, before recruitment into the army at age 16. Cf. Domínguez and Gregorio (forthcoming).

References

Blanch-Nougués, J. Ma. (2007) *Régimen jurídico de las fundaciones en derecho romano*. Madrid, Dykinson.

Boatwright, M. (1991) The Imperial women of the early second century A.C. *American Journal Philology* 112, 513–540.

Boatwright, M. (1992) Matidia the Younger. *Echoes de Monde Classique* 26, 19–32.

Caldelli, Ma. L. (2016) Evergetismo femminile ad Ostia tra tarda reppublica ed età alto-imperiale. In F. Cenerini and F. Rohr Vio (eds) *Matronae in domo et in re publica agentes. Spazi e occasioni dell'azione femminile nel mondo romano tra tarda repubblica e primo impero*. Trieste, Università di Trieste, 257–275.

Cao, I. (2010) *Alimenta: il racconto delle fonti*. Padova, Poligrafo.

Carlsen, J. (1999) Gli alimenta imperiali e privati in Italia. In D. Vera (ed.) *Demografia, sistemi agrari, regimi alimentari nel mondo antico*. Bari, Edipuglia, 273–288.

Carrié, J. M. (1975) Les distributions alimentaires dans les cités de l'empire romain tardif. *Mélanges de l'École française de Rome* 87, 995–1101.

Cascella, S. (2013) Matidia Minor and Suessa Aurunca. In Th. Opper (ed.) *Hadrian: Art, Politics and Economy*. London, British Museum, 73–88.

Cenerini, F. (2013) The role of women as municipal Matres. In E. Hemerlijk and G. Woolf (eds) *Women in the Roman City in the Latin West*. Leiden/Boston, Brill, 9–22.

Cenerini, F. and Rohr, F. (2016) (eds) *Matronae in domo et in re publica agentes. Spazi e occasioni dell'azione femminile nel mondo romano tra tarda repubblica e primo impero*. Trieste, Università di Trieste.

Chausson, F. (2008) Une dédicace monumentale provenant du théâtre de *Suessa Aurunca*, due à Matidie la jeune, belle-soeur de l'empereur Hadrien. *Journal des savants* 2, 233–259.

Cid, R. M. (2005) La promoción social de las mujeres hispanorromanas: familia y estrategias matrimoniales. In I. Morant (ed.) *Historia de las mujeres en España y América Latina*. Madrid, Cátedra, 193–220.

Cooley, A. E. (2013) Women beyond Rome: Trend-setters or dedicated followers of fashion?. In E. Hemerlijk and G. Woolf (eds) *Women in the Roman City in the Latin West*. Leiden/Boston, Brill, 23–46.

Curchin, L. (1983) Personal wealth in Roman Spain. *Historia* 32(2), 227–244.

Di Bella, F. (2015) *La donna nella storia e nella società romana*. Macerata, Simple.

Domínguez-Arranz A. and Gregorio-Navarro, Ma. C. (forthcoming) La matrona romana y la infancia en los programas alimentarios hasta la dinastía antonina, in Reboreda S. (ed.) *Vues sur l'allaitement dans l'antiquité*. Dialogues d'histoire ancienne 43.

Donahue, J. (2004) Iunia Rustica of Cartima: Female munificence in the Roman West. *Latomus* 63(4), 873–891.
Duncan-Jones, R. (1964) The purpose and organization of the *Alimenta*. *Papers of the British School at Rome* 32, 123–146.
Duncan-Jones, R. (1974) *The Economy of the Roman Empire*. Cambridge, Cambridge University Press.
Duncan-Jones, R. (1985) Who paid for public buildings in Roman cities?. In F. Grew and B. Hobley (eds) *Roman Urban Topography in Britain and the Western Empire*. London, Council for British Archaeology, 28–33.
Duncan-Jones, R. (1990) *Structure and Scale in the Roman Economy*. Cambridge, Cambridge University Press.
Flower, H. (2006) *The Art of Forgetting: Disgrace and Oblivion in Roman Political Culture*. Chapel Hill, North Carolina University Press.
Fora, M. (1992) Ummidia Quadratilla ed il Restauro del Teatro di Cassino. *Zeitschrift für Payrologie und Epigraphik* 94, 269–273.
Gutsfeld, S. (1992) Zur Wirtschaftsmentalität nichtsenatorischer provinzialer Oberschichten: Aemilia Pudentilla und ihre Verwandten. *Klio* 74, 250–268.
Hallett, J. (1984) *Fathers and Daughters in Roman Society*. Princeton, Princeton University Press.
Hemelrijk, E. (2015) *Hidden Lives, Public Personae*. Oxford, Oxford University Press.
Le Roux, P. (1999) Vectigalia et revenus des cités en Hispanie au Haut-Empire. In *Il capitolo delle entrate nelle finanze municipali in occidente ed in oriente*, 155–173. Rome, École française de Rome.
Magioncalda, A. (2005) Donne 'fondatrici.' In A. Buonopane and F. Cenerini (eds) *Donna e vita cittadina nella documentazione epigrafica: atti del II Seminario sulla condizione femminile nella documentazione epigrafica*. Faenza, Fratelli Lega, 503–521.
Martínez, C. (1990) Influencia social de las mujeres en las ciudades de Hispania meridional. In C. Martínez, A. López and A. Pociña (eds) *La mujer en el mundo Mediterráneo antiguo*. Granada, Universidad de Granada, 220–241.
Martínez, C. (2011) *Amantissima civium suorum*: matronazgo cívico en el Occidente romano. *Arenal* 18(2), 277–307.
Medina, S. (2014) *Mujeres y Economía en la Hispania Romana*. Oviedo, Trabe.
Melchor, E. (1994–95) Evergetismo testamentario en la Hispania Romana: legados y fundaciones. *Memorias de Historia Antigua* 15(6), 215–228.
Melchor, E. (1999) *La munificencia cívica en el mundo romano*. Madrid, Arcolibros.
Melchor, E. (2009) Mujeres y evergetismo en la Hispania romana. In J. F. Rodríguez (ed.) *Hispania y la epigrafía romana, cuatro perspectivas*. Faenza, Fratelli Lega, 133–179.
Melchor, E. (2011) Élites supralocales en la Bética: entre la *civitas* y la provincia. In A. Caballos and S. Lefebvre (eds) *Roma Generadora de identidades. La experiencia hispana*. Sevilla, Universidad de Sevilla, 267–300.
Mirón, M. D. (2000) Fabia Hadrianila. In C. Martínez, R. Pastor, Ma. J. de la Pascua and S. Tavera (eds) *Mujeres en la Historia de España*. Barcelona, Planeta, 34–36.
Mrozek, S. (1987) *Les distributions d'argent et de nourriture dans les villes italiennes du Haut-Empire romain*. Bruselles, Latomus.
Papi, E. (2004) A New Golden Age? The northern Prefectura Urbi from the Severans to Diocletian. In S. Swain and M. Edwards (eds) *Approaching Late Antiquity. The Transformation from Early to Late Empire*. Oxford: Oxford University Press, 53–81.
Patterson, J. (2003) The emperor and cities in Italy. In T. Cornell and K. Lomas K. (eds) *Bread and Circuses: Evergetism and municipal patronage in Roman Italy*. London, Rouledge, 89–104.
Raepsaet-Charlier, Th. (1987) *Prosopographie des femmes de l'ordre sénatorial (I^{e}-IIe siècles)*. Louvain, Aed. Peeters.
Reggiani, A. M. (2007) Donne al potere nella famiglia Ulpia. In B. Adembri and R. M. Nicolai (eds) *Vibia Sabina, da Augusta a Diva*. Milano, Electa, 23–27.

Rowlandson, J. (1998) *Women and Society in Greek and Roman Egypt.* Cambridge, Cambridge University Press.

Sick, D. (1999) Ummidia Quadratilla. Cagey business-woman or lazy pantomime-watcher?. *Classical Antiquity* 18(2), 330–348.

Stylow, A. and Gimeno, H. (2001) *Remissis cenis publicis*: las reglas del juego del evergetismo. *Faventia* 23(2), 97–109.

Valeri, C. and Zevi, F. (2004) La statua di Matidia Minore e il teatro di Sessa Arunca. In A. M. Reggiani (ed.) *Adriano. Le memorie al femminile*. Milano, Electa, 128–133.

Van Bremen, R. (1983) Women and wealth. In A. Cameron and A. Kuhrt (eds) *Images of Women in Antiquity*. London, Croom Helm, 223–243.

Wood, S. (2015) Women in action: A statue of Matidia Minor and its contexts. *American Journal of Archaeology* 119(2), 233–259.

Woolf, G. (1990) Food, poverty and patronage: The significance of the epigraphy of the Roman alimentary schemes in early Imperial Italy. *Papers of the British School at Rome* 58, 197–228.

Chapter 15

Mothers and sons in Plutarch's Roman *Parallel Lives. Auctoritas* and maternal influence during the Roman Republic[1]

Borja Méndez Santiago

Introduction

In order to have a better understanding of Plutarch's opinion of women, we need to go further into the *Moralia* than into the *Parallel Lives*. This erroneous approach was one of the most important criticisms made in relation to the work *Plutarque et les femmes* by F. Le Corsú (1981). Spread all over this immense *corpus* of different kinds of treaties, there are several clues which will help us to make a better analysis of those passages which make up the central idea of this text, and which are dealt with below.

At the beginning of the 1990s, some authors defended the revival of the family ideal from the end of the Republic and the beginnings of the Empire, in a process which would coincide in time with the political and legislative reforms made by Augustus in relation to family and marriages (Dixon 1991, 102–103). Therefore, it is no wonder that sons and daughters are, *prima facie*, one of the most important causes of pride for Roman mothers, seeing that they achieved prestige and social standing through their children.[2]

In Plutarch's ideology, daughters and sons are seen as an integral part of each one of the spouses, as they have been created from their union. As has been widely shown, in pre-industrial societies, infancy was never so little valued as Ariès (1960) and Stone (1977) maintained in their works.[3] Childhood and youth are differentiated periods in human life, as is shown in the *Lex Plaetoria* in the Roman case. This law protected the patrimonial interests of youths under 25 against those who might take advantage of their inexperience. Up to that age it was considered that youths may not have fully developed their wisdom (Golden 1990, 6). In practice, in Plutarch's Roman *Lives* his characters' period of youth usually lasts up to the age of 30, the minimum age at which, theoretically, a man could start his political career as a magistrate (Flores 2014, 123–124).

Aside from these considerations, one of the main interests in Plutarch's works has to do with the grief experienced by the family when a child dies an early death.[4] Indeed, as far as we know, he himself had to cope with the death of two of his children, a daughter and a son. In his works, he comes over as a caring father who has brought up his offspring at home with his wife (Soares 2008, 720).[5] In this sense, his *Consolation* can be regarded as a kind of manual for mothers who have recently lost a child. In this work, Plutarch offers them enough support to carry on with rational behaviour even at those hard moments of their lives.[6] On the other hand, it is evident how he criticises those who are invaded by irrational feeling (cf. *Cons. ad Apoll.*, 112E–F, and Seneca, *Ad Marc.* 7.3). In accordance with Plutarch's stoical philosophy, the rational component of human behaviour is what should prevail over others (Hope 2017, 95–96).

In order to guarantee their children's proper education, spouses should ideally keep up a relationship based on companionship (cf. *Brut.* 13), respect and mutual fidelity (Marasco 2008, 663). In several parts of his *Moralia*, Plutarch considers that a man and a woman complement each other, and that women are not inferior to men either in nature or in their learning capacity.[7] Having said this, we should point out that his point of view is not totally egalitarian. According to him, males are ontologically superior to females, who should remain in a subordinate position. In his opinion, women should take a back seat, heeding the wisdom of their husbands, who should take on the role of guide and educator of their wives (*Con. praec.* 145A–C). Therefore, a woman's character should remain as something unknown to everyone, except her husband.

The *auctoritas* within mother–son relationships in Rome. Ties which last a lifetime

In this part, a global perspective on mother–son relationships will be given, taking into consideration everything from the role of mothers in their children's education to their feelings towards them. We will also look at the female *auctoritas* as a means of influence on society in general and especially on their sons. The particular cases of Volumnia[8] and Cornelia will be analysed more thoroughly later on.

As far as education is concerned, a father's and a mother's role are completely different (Dixon 1988, 3–4). Ideally, it was the father who should be in charge of this (*Cat. Ma.* 20.5–6),[9] teaching them their first letters and the basic rules of law. However, if a Roman mother with small children should be a widow, or her husband should be far away for a long period of time, she herself could choose the most suitable instructors for them.[10] Valerius Maximus, in his *Facta et Dicta memorabilia* (V, 8), cites several examples of how fathers, at least at the beginning of the Republic, were not emotionally close to their sons, and it was the mothers who were established as guardian figures primarily prepared to instill traditional values.[11] As we will see, Plutarch's Volumnia fits perfectly into this model. In this way, how they would behave as future citizens may depend on the words they used and the games they played when they were children. Sons and daughters were generally educated by their mothers inside their homes until the age of 7 (Soares 2011, 86), although other providers of care were also common. From that moment onwards, boys and girls began to be separated in terms of education, thus becoming well prepared for the roles they should carry out in society. The objective of this system was to keep some families at the top of the Roman social pyramid (Dixon 1992, 109).

The power of widowed mothers over their children was limited by law. Roman women, for example, could not be the legal guardian of their children.[12] However, the tutor was often limited to looking after the children's estate, keeping it safe until they themselves could manage their own affairs. So, it is understandable that the mothers were in strict control of the tutor, and they were the ones who, in fact, oversaw their children's education.

Undoubtedly, some of the mother figures who appear in Plutarch's *Lives* would still greatly influence their children even when they reach adulthood (Dixon 1988, 134–135; Seneca, *Ad Marc.* 24.1). This could, partly, be due to the peculiar relationship between mothers and sons, which was very different to that of fathers and sons (Golden 1990, 100).[13] Demographic aspects should also be taken into account, as certain statistical studies have shown that only one in four males reached the age of 30 with their father still alive, while for mothers this was nearly 50% (Krause 2011, 630; Parkin 2011, 282). As a result, it was common for women to have a longer-lasting relationship with their sons, which in some cases would last throughout almost all their lives. In the following pages, we will see a mature man, turned down from his candidacy to the consulate (cf. *Cor.* 14–15.3), and how he is publicly scolded by his elderly mother for having become an enemy of Rome. For Plutarch, selfish motives should not be the ones which lead a man into politics (Teodorsson 2008, 341), as it was not regarded as an obligation, but as a way of life (*Bíos*) (cf. Xenophontos, 2015, 343).

For Romans, *pietas* was the basis on which internal family relationships should be sustained (Grubbs 2011, 377). Contrary to what it may seem, Romans went beyond the purely legal meaning of this term (i.e. submission to the *paterfamilias*) to also include mutual affection and duties shared by all the members of the family (Saller 1986, 395, 399; Dixon 1992, 151). Roman sons and daughters should show *obsequium* (obedience) and *reverentia* (respect) towards their parents. They also had the moral, even legal, duty to take care of them in their old age or in sickness.

This perfect state of things could however be violated in certain circumstances. In ideal Roman society, the collective interest should prevail over individuals. Cicero, in *Off.* 1.58, includes a kind of preference order in relation to citizens' duties. The State and the parents would be on the first scale, followed by, in this order: the sons, the household and the relatives.

In Plutarch, very rarely do we see women as active members of their communities. Consequently, when they act outside their traditional roles they are almost always criticised (cf. Stadter 1999, 173). This scholar argues that those actions would only be acceptable if they were carried out in response to male weakness or to violence. The women in his moral treaties (e. g. in his *Mulierum Virtutes*) only abandon their homes in order to defend their land, filled with fervour and determination, in times of general political crises (Cid 2010, 125–126). To try to keep women within the constraints of the home would be to diminish their value inside Roman society, as we would be ignoring certain types of participation which are included in different ancient sources. In this sense, some interesting recent pieces of research have pointed out that, although women did not have *potestas*, as this was exclusively held by a Roman magistrate, they did possess *auctoritas* in the sense that they had the moral obligation to keep society together.[14] In practice, this 'power' could be exercised in certain areas, even in some which were in theory beyond their limits, such as politics.

Next, we will analyse two women in *Parallel Lives* who, in demonstrating their *auctoritas*, and defending the higher interests of the state and their sons, abandoned their homes at critical moments, occupying public spaces and going to places where the greatest decisions were being made. Despite stepping outside the traditional gender roles, they were not socially condemned for their behaviour, but were rather praised for their bravery and patriotism.

Two model mothers? Volumnia and Cornelia in Plutarchean *Lives*

Both *Coriolanus* and the *Gracchi* brothers lost their fathers at an early age. Therefore, to substitute the absent father, both Cornelia and Volumnia, who decided to remain *uniuirae*, had to set themselves up as models to be imitated by their sons.[15] Taking into account these special circumstances, it is not surprising that they would feel entitled to actively intervene in the lives of their adult sons (Dixon 2008, 175–179). This was especially true at those times when their sons were going through moments of physical, political or moral weakness (Xenophontos 2015, 342).

Another common aspect in these two *Lives*, which up to now has not been fully highlighted, is the relationship between the two *matronae* and their daughters-in-law. In the *Lives* of their husbands, they take on a secondary role, appearing as mere companions to their mothers-in-law, who overshadow the other female figures in the story with their brilliance.[16] Now we will focus individually not only on the actions of Cornelia and Volumnia but also on the special relationships that they had with their sons.

The *Life* of Coriolanus is particularly interesting inside the Plutarchean biographies, as in that piece of writing he does not limit himself to merely characterising him, but also tries to go deep into his psyche, so that the reader can catch sight of his true personality.[17] Despite this, Plutarch does not concern himself with delving into Coriolanus' mind, as in general he was not interested in dealing with his protagonists' internal struggles. This kind of worries doesn't bother Plutarch, contrary to what usually happens today in modern biographies (cf. Pelling 2002a, 325–326).

Coriolanus did not receive a good enough education to harness his nature and his behaviour (*Cor.* 1.5).[18] Over time, this lack would become a decisive factor in his character's fall from grace. For Plutarch, a privileged nature alone was not a guarantee of good character, as it had to be moulded by education (cf. Xenophontos, 2016, 61–62).

Plutarch shows us a Coriolanus who is absolutely dependent on his mother. So, right from when he was little, 'he found the chief end of glory in his mother's gladness. That she should hear him praised and see him crowned and embrace him with tears of joy' (4.5).[19] Coriolanus' need for physical contact in this passage reflects his affection towards his mother. Later on, in 33.4, he will again seek physical contact with Volumnia when she comes into the Volscian military camp alongside her daughter-in-law and her grandchildren. Once again, Plutarch's narrative dismantles the image of the old Roman mother as someone who is cold and distant towards her sons and daughters.

The culminating point in Coriolanus' biography is the angry speech in which Volumina criticised her son's action inside the Volscian camp. At that moment he had been a Roman exile and the chief of an Italic coalition which was holding Rome under siege. This 'female embassy', which included, apart from other women, Volumnia, Vergilia and Coriolanus' children, only dared to act once the actions undertaken by the Senate had failed to resolve the crisis. During his mother's speech, Coriolanus would see in her a personification of Rome, according to some researchers.[20] In *Cor.* 33.4 we can see that Volumnia, in her son's absence, is the head of his household. The virtuous Roman women, headed by Valeria, go to Volumnia as they are desperate to find a way of solving the crisis that will preserve the integrity of their land. During the speech itself, Coriolanus was completely overwhelmed by his mother and her powerful rhetoric, and this reduced him to silence.[21]

In contrast to how Coriolanus acted here, Greek and Roman writers tend to praise sons who leave interfering mothers in their places. Otherwise, as happens here, the son's masculinity would be diminished and questioned (Xenophontos, 2015, 341). Here, Coriolanus' reaction to his mother's speech is to accept his defeat, which he does eloquently: 'Thou art victorious, and thy victory means good fortune to my country, but death to me' (*Cor.* 36.4). In fact, shortly afterwards Coriolanus would be killed by the Volscians. The building of the temple of *Fortuna Muliebris* should therefore not be interpreted as a mere triumph of Volumnia's *auctoritas* over her son. Consequently, the temple does not commemorate Coriolanus' submission to his mother but the public benefit achieved by this, which is so unusual for a Roman male.[22]

Lastly, we will analyse the figure of Cornelia, the Gracchi brothers' mother. For many scholars of the Ancient World, Cornelia represents the Roman *matron* par excellence. Nevertheless, the way Plutarch portrays her in her sons' *Lives* is halfway between traditional gender roles and an overthrowing of such roles.

In *TG* 1.6–7 it is written that Cornelia, once widowed, takes charge not only of her son's and daughter's education but also oversees their estates.[23] Her children were brought up in a careful and scrupulous way, giving priority to discretion, magnanimity and kindness. Considering the Hellenistic teaching that Cornelia would have been given in her parents' house, this model is likely to have been used in her children's education.[24] Unlike what we have seen regarding Coriolanus in his *Life*, in this case her son's good nature was accompanied by a good education. Cornelia was highly likely to have been a very cultured woman, as the intellectual conversations held in her villa at *Misenum* have been referred to by many authors.[25] This female wisdom, though regarded with suspicion by many Romans, was socially tolerated as long as the resulting knowledge was used for socially acceptable aims, one of which was the proper education of children.[26]

In *GG.* 4.3–4, Gaius presents Cornelia's intercession as a reason for the withdrawal of a law in which it was written that, if citizens dismissed a magistrate, he could not be eligible for any future public position. Accepting his mother's demands, Gaius tries to come across as somebody who honours his mother. Later on, when he defends her against those who insulted her (*GG.* 4.5–6), Gaius, apart from standing out as a guarantor of his family's reputation,[27] also shows a public demonstration of the strong ties to his mother. Tiberius' instrumental use of his wife and children to manipulate the electorate (cf. *TG.* 13.6) is less compassionate. In this sense, in a critical moment for his faction, he thought that by dressing in mourning and showing his family members as defenseless would be the best way to guarantee the sympathy of the Roman people towards his cause.

Slightly before Gaius' death, Cornelia took an active part in her son's political ambitions. Plutarch wrote that she paid a number of reapers to go to Rome in order to defend Gaius' political measures (*GG.* 13.2).[28] Seneca (*Ad Helv.* 14.2) criticises mothers who, with a woman's passion (*muliebris impotentia*), try to fulfil their own personal ambitions through their children. It could be considered that Cornelia's social triumph or disgrace could only come through her offspring's actions (Hallett 1984, 36), as her father and her husband had died many years before.[29] These reapers could have been seasonal workers taken to Rome by Cornelia as a way of exerting political pressure in favor of her son. This procedure would become common practice in the last century of the Republic.

Unlike many other women, whose behavior was marked predominantly by an element of irrationality, which we have mentioned before, Cornelia accepted the loss of her sons nobly and with spirit. She was, in fact, able to speak to her visitors about them without sorrow or tears, as if they were characters from a long time ago (*GG.* 19.1–3).[30] This ability to accept grief with reasoning, also defended by Plutarch in his *Advice to the Bride and Groom*, differentiates Cornelia and Timoxena from other women, who were overwhelmed with unfathomable grief. In this type of texts, therefore, being able to control emotions is an indicator of social and economic status.

Conclusions

In this text I have tried to highlight above all that, despite the limited role reserved for women by Plutarch in his *Moralia*, the *Lives* show us how some of the most noteworthy among them did step outside those narrow limits without completely breaking away from what society expected of them. This would account for why the bold actions of some women, like Cornelia and Volumnia, have been remembered favourably by many Greek and Roman authors as, ultimately, they were only seeking to guarantee the reinforcement and perpetuation of the patriarchal system.[31]

Despite this, we must remember that this kind of stories are a minority within the *Parallel Lives*. Thus, more than 90% of the women in them correspond to the model of a socially accepted or denigrated woman, so they are only mentioned in passing. The fact that our biographer has returned to the figures of Volumnia and Cornelia in several parts of the *Lives* of their sons, accounts not only for their importance in the narrative but also for the wide range of influence exerted by some women in Roman society. It is a pity that hardly anything is known about these female figures beyond this sort of male-biased reconstructions. But the virtual absence of any type of information related to women belonging to the lower classes is, in my opinion, even more regrettable.

Notes

1 All quotations from classical writers have been taken from the bilingual editions of the Loeb Classical Library.

2 McWilliam (2013, 265) states that 'the procreation of children was the explicit aim of Roman Marriage'; in the same sense, cf. Aulus Gellius, *NA.* 4.3.2 and 1.6.1–8.

3 Eyben (1981) was one of the first scholars to claim that childhood and adolescence should have their own space within the ancient Graeco-Roman world. Golden (1990, 84), from comparative studies, has accurately stated that, in general, children are highly regarded in societies where child mortality is high.

4 The subject of grief surrounding a child's death is talked about, for example, inside the *Lives*, in *Sol.* 6. 2–5.

5 The Roman ideal was not to delegate the care of children to servants. *Tacitus,* in *Dial* 28.6–7, collects examples of mothers well-known for the correct upbringing and education of their sons.

6 For some authors, the *Consolation to His Wife* is a text in which Plutarch tries to indoctrinate his wife about how she should feel in the face of the death of her 2-year-old daughter. Some authors have shown the methodological difficulty of quantifying with literary and epigraphical expression, the extent of the parents' grief when a child dies (cf. Finley, 1981, 159). For a brief, but clever analysis of Plutarch's intentions during the writing of this text, cf. Xenophontos (2016, 56–58).

7 For a similar thought to that of Plutarch, cf. some of the *Discourses* by *Mussonius Rufus.*

8 In Plutarch's work, Volumnia is the name of *Coriolanus'* mother, whereas in the works of *Titus Livius* (II, 40) and *Dionysius of Halicarnassus* (VIII, 40.1–2), she is called Veturia, and Volumnia is the name of *Coriolanus'* wife, who in Plutarch is Vergilia. In my opinion, given that *vetus*, in latin, means 'old', I am more inclined towards Livian and Dionysian version.

9 According to Plutarch, fathers should provide their children with intellectual and moral foundations which will be useful for them in the future (*De aud. Poet.* 15A-B). Therefore, the role of women in their children's education was rather limited.

10 Cornelia, for example, provided her children with the instruction of two Greek teachers, *Blosius* of Cumae and *Diophanes* of Mitylene (*TG.* 8.6). For the use of *exempla* as ways of instilling in young Romans the values and institutions of Rome, see McWilliam, 2013, 269, and Sciarrino, 2013, 236. As regards the importance of education in Plutarch's work, some researchers have

stated that 'es posible que ningún otro griego después de Platón haya concedido a la formación del hombre una importancia tal como Plutarco' (cf. Velázquez 2001, 441).

11 Filial devotion towards their mother is more common in Roman *Lives* than in the Greek ones, where the only cases were Alcibiades and an anecdote included in the *Life* of Solon (cf. 27.7). Plutarch was fully aware that fathers were more lenient towards their daughters, whereas mothers were closer to their sons. In his opinion, this was a result of women needing male support (*Con. Praec.* 143B). For Plutarch, as a woman was weaker than a man, she needed his protection (*Quast. Graec.* 289E). While Hallett (1984, 246) defends this idea, for Dixon (1988, 209, n. 90), this was a very Greek interpretation.

12 Widows, in the *Senatusconsultum Tertullianum*, were obliged to find a tutor for their sons and daughters, and he was named by the magistrate (the praetor or a provincial gobernor), and not by her (cf. Grubbs 2011, 384). If this procedure was not followed, they were in danger of losing their children's hereditary rights.

13 Some authors (cf. Hallett 1984; Dixon 1992, 77), from Freudian theory, have highlighted the fact that the small age gap between mothers who married very young and their sons could bring about a kind of sexual attraction in some cases. They argue that this feeling could give an explanation for the strong feelings of loyalty on the part of women towards their blood relatives in comparison to their husbands. For an example of the (excessive) grief experienced by a son after the death of his mother, cf. *Sert.* 22.9–12.

14 Martínez (2012, 160) stated that women brought to the *ciuitas* 'aquello que era considerado permanente, lo que sustentaba la vida, más allá de las formulaciones coyunturales que los varones eran capaces de crear con la política y las armas'.

15 Some authors, like Hallett (1984, 255–256) have stated that widowed mothers emotionally involved with men other than their sons were looked down on in society.

16 For the suspicion which is constantly cast over mothers-in-law in Latin and Greek literature, see Walcot (1999, 181). For the possibility that newly married young women were educated under the supervision of their mothers-in-law or other female relatives of their husbands soon after their entry into his house, cf. Cid 2001, 38.

17 Christopher Pelling (2002b, 286) has proved the pre-eminence of the irrational element in this biography.

18 Pinheiro (2013, 157) states that Coriolanus did not have the chance to receive a Greek education. This type of tuition, if it was given to Plutarch's biographical characters, would guarantee being dealt with kindly by him. In this sense, the plundering made by Marcellus after the siege of Syracuse (cf. *Marc.* 21.1) was only slightly criticised by Plutarch. After all, all the works of art taken by the Romans were used to make Rome look beautiful for the first time in its history.

19 In Soares' opinion (2008, 724), boys and girls needed their parents' recognition for their success to take on a social and personal meaning. The same author (2011, 93) has pointed out the suffering that could be detected in this little quotation.

20 This line of argument has been followed, among others, by Pérez (2000), Pinheiro (2013, 164) or Buszard (2010, 105–107), who related it to the same episode in Titus Livius' works.

21 For Xenophontos (2016, 65) silence has a different meaning depending on the character. Thus, 'in self- disciplined characters, silence is traditionally a manifestation of self-restraint, whereas in weak characters it points to emotional ambivalence'. For an interesting psychological analysis of this meeting between Coriolanus and his mother, cf. Pelling (2002a, 326–327).

22 Regarding this temple, see Champeaux (1982, 360–373) and Cid (2014).

23 Cornelia is analysed by many authors as a perfect example of the power gained by some women through money (cf. Medina 2014).

24 López (1994, 33) highlights the role of the Scipions in the introduction of Greek culture into Rome. Besides, they were one of the first families to place great importance on their women's education.

25 For Hemelrijk (1999, 97) Cornelia was 'the earliest example of a Roman woman who acted as a patroness of literature and learning'. Van den Bergh (2000, 358) comments on the possibility that some Roman aristocratic women may have continued being educated after marriage in their husbands' houses.

26 In this sense, see Cicero (*Brut.* 104; 211), Quintilian (*Inst.* I, 1, 6) and Tacitus (*Dial.* 28.6), who praised women well-known for giving a correct education to their children.

27 In fact, at this time of his life, after his brother's death, he was already the *paterfamilias.*

28 In this text there are 'dark allusions' to this fact, which may have appeared in Cornelia's famous letters, and which Plutarch undoubtedly knew about. López (1994, 41–42) includes in her work an extensive catalogue both of those who attribute the letters to Cornelia and those who regarded them as a later fiction. More recently, Dixon (2007, 27) has stated, in relation to the letters preserved through the work of Cornelius Nepos, that 'these fragments are at best perverted versions of something she might have written'.

29 Below Cornelia's statue there was originally placed an inscription which shows us how this *matrona* preferred to be remembered as the Gracchi's mother rather than as Scipio's daughter. The text just said: 'Cornelia, mother of the Gracchi' (*CIL* VI, 10043 and *TG.* 8.7). This statue, probably erected at the end of the 2nd century BC, was refurbished during Augustus' government to also include Cornelia's famous father: 'WORK OF TISICRATIS. CORNELIA. D[AUGHTER] OF AFRICANUS OF THE GRACCHI' (*CIL* VI, 31610). For a contextualization of both the statue and the inscription, see Dixon (2007, 29–31; 56–8) and Etcheto (2012, 282–287).

30 Cf. Seneca, *Ad Helv.* 16.6, and *Ad Marc.* 16.3.

31 Some scholars (i.e. Cid 2010 and Hallett 2004, 33) have pointed out the parallelism between the speeches of Veturia-Volumnia and the letters attributed to Cornelia. Hallett has even qualified this kind of behaviour as 'matriotic'.

References

Ariès, P. (1960) *L'enfant et la vie familial sous l'Ancien Régime.* Paris, Plon.

Buszard, B. (2010) The speech of Greek and Roman women in Plutarch's *Lives. Classical Philology*, 105(1), 83–115.

Champeaux, J. (1982) *Fortuna. Le culte de la Fortune à Rome et dans le monde romain. I. Fortuna dans la religión archaïque.* Rome, École Française de Rome.

Cid López, R. M. (2001) La educación de la niña romana: de *puella* a *matrona docta.* In V. Alfaro Bech and R. Francia Somalo (eds) *Bien enseñada: la formación femenina en Roma y el Occidente romanizado.* Málaga, Servicio de publicaciones de la Universidad de Málaga, 19–44.

Cid López, R. M. (2010) Mujeres y actividades políticas en la República. Las matronas rebeldes y sus antecesoras en la Roma antigua. In A. Domínguez Arranz (ed.) *Mujeres en la Antigüedad clásica: género, poder y conflicto.* Madrid, Sílex, 125–152.

Cid López, R. M. (2014) Los santuarios suburbanos y la religiónn de las matronas. El templo de *Fortuna Muliebris* en la Roma republicana. In J. Mangas Manjarrés and M. A. Novillo López (eds) *Santuarios suburbanos y del territorio en las ciudades romanas.* Madrid, Universidad Autónoma de Madrid, 9–29.

Dixon, S. (1988) *The Roman Mother.* London, Routledge.

Dixon, S. (1991) The Sentimental Ideal of the Roman Family. In B. Rawson (ed.) *Marriage, Divorce, and Children in Ancient Rome.* Oxford, Clarendon Press, 99–113.

Dixon, S. (1992) *The Roman Family.* Baltimore/London, Johns Hopkins University Press.

Dixon, S. (2007) *Cornelia. Mother of the Gracchi.* London/New York, Routledge.

Etcheto, H. (2012) *Les Scipions. Famille et pouvoir à Rome à l'époque républicaine.* Bordeaux, Ausonius.

Eyben, E. (1981) Was the Roman 'Youth' and 'Adult' Socially?. *L'Antiquité classique*, 50 (1–2), 328–350.

Finley, M. I. (1981) The elderly in Classical Antiquity. *Greece and Rome* 28, 156–171.

Flores Santamaría, M. (2014) La adolescencia en Roma. In R. Hernández Crespo and A. J. Domínguez Monedero (eds) *Las edades del hombre. Las etapas de la vida entre griegos y romanos*. Madrid, Sociedad Española de Estudios Clásicos, 123–143.

Golden, M. (1990) *Childhood in Classical Athens*. Baltimore/London, Johns Hopkins University Press.

Grubbs, J. E. (2011) Promoting *Pietas* through Roman Law. In B. Rawson, B (ed.) *A Companion to Families in the Greek and Roman Worlds*. Malden/Oxford, Wiley Blackwell, 123–143.

Hallett, J. P. (1984) *Fathers and Daughters in Roman Society: Women and the élite family*. Princeton, Princeton University Press.

Hallett, J. P. (2004) Matriot games? Cornelia, mother of the Gracchi, and the forging of family-oriented political values. In F. McHardy and E. Marshall (eds) *Women's Influence on Classical Civilization*. London, Psychology Press, 26–39.

Hemelrijk, E. A. (1999) Matrona Docta. *Educated Women in the Roman Elite from Cornelia to Julia Domna*. London, Routledge.

Hope, V. M. (2017) A sense of grief. The role of the senses in the perfomance of Roman mourning. In E. Betts (ed.) *Senses of the Empire. Multisensory Approaches to Roman Culture*. London/New York, Routledge, 86–103.

Krause, J.-V. (2011) Children in the Roman Family and beyond. In M. Peachin (ed.) *The Oxford Handbook of Social Relations in the Roman World*. New York/Oxford, Oxford University Press, 623–642.

Le Corsu, F. (1981) *Plutarque et les femmes dans les Vies Parallèles*. Paris, Les Belles-Lettres.

López López, A. (1994) *No sólo hilaron lana. Escritoras romanas en prosa y en verso*. Madrid, Ediciones Clásicas.

Marasco, G. (2008) Donne, cultura e società nelle Vite Parallele di Plutarco. In A. G. Nikolaidis (ed.) *The Unity of Plutarch's work: Moralia themes in the Lives, features of the Lives in the Moralia*. Berlin/New York, Walter de Gruyter, 663–678.

Martínez, C. (2012) Poder integrador de la *mater familias* romana. In P. Díaz Sánchez, G. A. Franco, and M. J. Fuentes Pérez (eds) *Impulsando la historia de las mujeres: la estela de Cristina Segura*, 157–168. Huelva, Universidad de Huelva.

McWilliam, J. (2013) The Socialization of Roman children. In J. Evans Grubbs, T. Parkin and R. Bell (eds) *The Oxford Handbook of Childhood and Education in the Classical World*. Oxford/New York, Oxford University Press, 264–285.

Medina Quintana, S. (2014) *Mujeres y economía en la Hispania romana. Oficios, riqueza y promoción social*. Oviedo, Trabe.

Nuñez Paz, M. I. (2015) *Auctoritas* y mujeres romanas. ¿Ejercicio o sumisión? *Arenal* 22(2), 347–387.

Parkin, T. (2011) The Roman life course and the family. In B. Rawson (ed.) *A Companion to Families in the Greek and Roman World*, 276–290. Malden/Oxford, Wiley Blackwell, 276–290.

Pelling, C. B. R. (2002a) Childhood and personality in Greek biography. In C. B. R. Pelling (ed.) *Plutarch and History, Eighteen Studies*. Swansea, Classical Press of Wales, 301–338.

Pelling, C. B. R. (2002b) Aspects of Plutarch's characterization. In C. B. R. Pelling (ed.) *Plutarch and History, Eighteen Studies*. Swansea, Classical Press of Wales, 283–300

Pérez Jiménez, A. (2000) La Retórica del Silencio: El Discurso de Volumnia en la *Vida* de Coriolano. In L. Van Der Stockt (ed.) *Rhetorical Theory and Praxis in Plutarch. Acta of the IVth International Congress of the International Plutarch Society. Leuven, July 3-6, 1996*. Leuven, Peeters, 341–353.

Pinheiro, J. (2013) Tempo e espaço da Paideia nas *Vidas* de Plutarco. Coimbra, Imprensa da Universidade de Coimbra.

Saller, R. P. (1998) *Pietas*, obligation, and authority in the Roman family. In P. Von Kneissl and V. Losemann (eds) *Alte Geschichte und Wissenschaftsgeschichte: Festchrift für Karl Christ zum 65. Geburtstag*. Darmstadt, Wissenschaftlige Buchgesellschaft, 393–410.

Sciarrino, E. (2011) *Cato the Censor and the Beginnings of Latin Prose: From Poetic Translation to Elite Transcription*. Columbus, Ohio State University.

Soares, C. (2008) Parent-Child Affection and Social Relationships in Plutarch: Common Elements in *Consolation ad uxorem* and *Vitae.* In A. G. Nikolaidis (ed.) *The Unity of Plutarch's work: Moralia themes in the Lives, features of the Lives in the Moralia.* Berlin/New York, Walter de Gruyter, 719–726.

Soares, C. (2011) *Crianças e jovens nas* Vidas *de Plutarco.* Coimbra, Imprensa da Universidade de Coimbra.

Stadter, P. A. (1999) *Philosophos kai Philandros*: Plutarch's view of women in the *Moralia* and *Lives.* In S. B. Pomeroy (ed.) *Advice to the Bride and Groom and A Consolation to His Wife: English translations, commentary, interpretative essays, and bibliography.* Oxford/New York, Oxford University Press, 173–182.

Stone, L. (1977) *The Family, Sex and Marriage in England, 1500-1800.* London, Weidenfeld and Nicolson.

Teodorsson, S.-T. (2008) The education of the rulers in theory (*Mor.*) and practice (*Vitae*). In A. G. Nikolaidis (ed.) *The Unity of Plutarch's work: Moralia themes in the Lives, features of the Lives in the Moralia.* Berlin/New York, Walter de Gruyter, 339–350.

Van Den Bergh, R. (2000) The role of education in the social and legal position of women in Roman society. *Revue internationale des droits de l'antiquité* 47, 351–364.

Velázquez Fernández, A. E. (2001) Presencia y ausencia del educador en las *Vidas* de Plutarco. In A. Pérez Jiménez and F. C. Bordoy (eds) *Estudios sobre Plutarco: misticismo y religiones mistéricas en la obra de Plutarco: actas del VII simposio español sobre Plutarco (Palma de Mallorca, 2-4 de noviembre de 2000).* Madrid, Ediciones Clásicas, 501–514.

Walcot, P. (1999) Plutarch on women. *Symbolae Osloenses* 74, 163–183.

Xenophontos, S. (2015) Plutarch. In M. Bloomer (ed.) *A Companion to Ancient Education.* Malden/Oxford/Chichester, Wiley Blackwell, 335–346.

Xenophontos, S. (2016) *Ethical education in Plutarch. Moralising Agents and Contexts.* Berlin/Boston, Walter de Gruyter.

Chapter 16

Seruae, mothers and the mother–child bond in Roman Italy. The analysis of the epigraphic evidence

Carla Rubiera Cancelas

General considerations on slave families

Overall, a slave had a precarious personal life, also in regard to family, as slave systems were characterised by the lack of respect towards families (Stevenson 1996, viii). They did not exist in the eyes of the law;[1] even more, they were not considered in the eyes of some owners. This precarious situation was strongly connected to the uncertainty of separation. K. R. Bradley speculates about the tension that a slave must always have had in mind: 'the tension between being held in a state of total subjection that denied all sense of personhood on the one hand, and being at the same time a human agent capable of responding to submission in a variety of self-validating ways on the other' (Bradley 1994, 178). This would have affected all kinds of relationship developed within the family. Bradley's assessment is based on the evidence of the slaves from the New World, mainly on slave narratives. These kinds of texts stress two elements: the suffering caused by ill-treatment, and the devastating consequences of families' separation. We can assume that the situation in the Roman world was somehow similar and, as a consequence, family relationships were pretty much likely marked by vulnerability and insecurity. At any moment of life, members of slave families could be separated by the master and, in regard to the very topic of this chapter, mothers could be taken away from their children. Three different scenarios demonstrate the fragility of slave families, as well as of the mother–child bond.

First scenario: sale auctions

Young children could be destined to be sold alone, even without their mothers (Curchin 2000–01, 541; 543). Some sale contracts, most of which were preserved in Egypt, let us visualise isolated children at an early age – e.g., in Oxyrhyncos, an

8-year-old girl was sold alone (AD 77); in Tebtynis, a 7-year-old house-born slave was sold alone (AD 108–116); in Side (Pamphilia), a 10-year-old girl was sold alone for 280 denarii (AD 142), etc. (more examples in Bienzunska 1984, 331–334; Edmonson 2011, 350). A further case from Londonium attests that Fortunata (the Roman name given to her), a 13-year-old girl from Diablintian (Gallia), was sold alone. The text says she was in good health and not a runaway slave, but it does not shed light on whether she travelled with her family (or at least one family member) from Gallia to Britannia (Tomlin 2004, 49–50; Korporowicz 2011, 216–221).

Second scenario: breeding strategies

A second scenario is associated with nursing babies. Basically, owners decided entirely on the upbringing and education of the slave population. This meant that, in some occasions, a slave could feed her offspring, while other times she could be forced to get rid of her baby by abandoning it; by doing this, the woman was available to be rented as a wet nurse of an outside baby.[2] Mothers were taken away from their own children to nurse the offspring of their masters (Joshel 1980). Likewise, female slaves were separated from their children in order to feed babies belonging to other families: wet nursing contracts from Egypt prove this reality.[3] In addition, considering some references regarding the training of slaves, we can also assume that slaves from the *familia urbana* were sometimes sent to the countryside in order to be educated, which could lead to separation (ULPIAN. *Dig.* 33. 7. 12. 42) (Gardner 1987, 208).

Third scenario: owners' death

As H. Mouritsen has recently emphasised: 'Slave families probably found themselves most at risk when the master died, an event that might result in the breaking-up of the entire household' (Mouritsen 2011, 139). When a slaveholder died, his/her slaves might indiscriminately be distributed among the heirs or sold off to different buyers (Edmonson 2011, 350). In Rome, as it happened to properties, slaves and their offspring could be bequeathed to different owners.[4]

Scaevola, in the 2nd century AD, tells us about the provisions of a testator. According to the jurist, the man left all his freedmen their servile consorts, as well as their sons and daughters, with the exception of those who were left to his wife (SCAEV. *Dig.* 32. 41. 2). Another interesting reference, once again from Scevola, explains how a *uilicus* (an administrator) was not in the same legacy of his contubernal and his daughter because they lived in different places: the man lived in the city, while the two women lived in the countryside (SCAEV. *Dig.* 33. 7. 20. 4).

These three scenarios confirm the instability that characterised slave families overall. All these examples allow us to prove the functioning of a system and the result of the application of concrete rules, which affected many aspects of the family life of slaves. If we look at the examples just provided, the mother–child bond was attacked from the very beginning, just after birth and during the period of breastfeeding. Despite this, as the epigraphic evidence attests, slaves were able to create families. Unlike literary and legal sources that speak about them as 'an accident,' the epigraphic records intentionally illustrate this topic. In fact, in order to inquire into the slave family beyond the owner's perspective (offered by many of the preserved sources), it seems necessary to turn to epigraphic records, as they allow us to perceive the other side, even though with a big limitation: we are looking at a very specific picture of a very particular moment. An inscription will never give us the whole biography of a female slave.[5] Overall, it will never tell us about abandoned babies, mothers who were sold or given away, slaves who were separated and, of course, deceased in a context that moves away from the moment when the monument was set up. Despite this, epigraphy serves us as a snapshot of the conformation of the slave family where women appear, among other categories, as mothers.

Female slaves as mothers and the mother-child bond: the evidence from Roman Italy

The existence of a slave system implies the typification and regulation of some forms of slave supply (Scheidel 2011, 287–310). In ancient Rome, various forms were used to increase the slave population, among which we find biological reproduction: 'Slaves come from our enemies or those born of our slaves' (MARCIAN. *Dig.* 1. 5. 5). There are references in literary and legal sources that demonstrate how women were an important part of the slave supply system (Di Nisio 2007, 1493–1517; Rubiera Cancelas 2014, 217–256). This means, their bodies became a source for obtaining house-born slaves, the so-called *uernae* (Scheidel 1997; Harris 1999; Harper 2013, 70). Any child born in these circumstances followed the mother's condition: 'This is the law of nature: somebody of illegitimate birth succeeds to the condition of the mother unless a particular law introduces an alternative outcome'[6] (ULPIAN. *Dig.* 1. 5. 24). Therefore, since marriage between slaves was not legally acknowledged,[7] children of slave men and women were considered illegitimate.

Some literary sources show that masters intervened in the formation of slave couples and encouraged their slaves to have children (Laes 2011, 157–158); '... so they have fellow slaves as wives, from whom they may have children. For from this state of affairs they become more loyal and more attached to the farm' (VAR. *R.* 1. 17. 5). In fact, marital relationships were not necessary for reproduction, only female slaves were (Mouritsen 2011, 134). Thus, where and when needed, slaves were used as wombs for generating new generations of slaves at the service of the owners. We should not also forget that slave boys and girls could be obtained in other ways, for instance through wars and conquests, or even with kidnapping, a method that was illegal but yet recorded in ancient sources (Scheidel 2011, 297).

Slave relations were marked by a dualism inherent to slavery: slaves were objects and subjects. Therefore, women were used by slaveholders as animals of their property for collecting wealth, but at the same time slave women catalogued themselves as mothers in the epigraphic records.[8] The slave context made it difficult for a mother, although not impossible, to maintain a relationship with her offspring, as the epigraphic records belonging to Roman Italy show. The sample we use here was collected during the project carried out at the University of Edinburgh between the years 2014–2016. This sample attempted to cover the whole Italian Peninsula (excluding Rome) in order to have an image as complete as possible. A total of 538 inscriptions, most of them funerary, offer data regarding labour (a minority), personal life and ownership. In these texts, *seruae* are described as mothers in single-parent and in nuclear families. Regarding the first group, which will be discussed below, we have 30 inscriptions in which the slave-mothers appear alone either as dedicators or dedicatees. An example is represented by the following text:

> D(is) M(anibus)/Ianuariae/matri pien/tissimae/Ianu(a)rius Aug(usti)/n(ostri) adiut(or) tabul(ariorum)/f(aciendum) c(uravit). *CIL* 5, 371, Vabriga

In this epitaph Ianuarius, *adiut(or) tabul(ariorum)* of the imperial family, remembers his mother Ianuaria, possibly still a slave, with whom he shares the same name. B. Rawson (2003, 111) as interpreted this as an indicator of how parents would be involved in naming their children, despite not having the right to select the name of their babies because it belonged to the owner. In reality, there is slight information regarding the influence of parents at the moment of naming slave babies. Therefore, we always have to consider 'the owner, the *uilicus* or someone else who was supervising the slaves and the slave parent(s)' (Bruun 2013, 32).

The group of inscriptions that attest slave women as single parents offers a varied panorama of information; some of them, in fact, were set up by sons and daughters commemorating their slave mothers, and these texts reveal details also on the working life of these women. We know of Hygia (InscrIt-4-1, 391, Narnia, AD 71–130) and Egdechome (*CIL* 9, 6316, Teate Marrocinorum, AD 71–130) to whom their *filii*, Fidus and Expectatus respectively, dedicated a funerary monument. These two inscriptions follow the same model: a son, whose age is not given, remembering his mother. In neither of the cases a reference to the father is present, meaning that he is either not in the lives his relatives or, if he is, he cannot be acknowledged in this role in the epitaphs. In both the texts the names of the *seruae* appear followed by those of their owners: Hygia was Autronia Fortunata's slave (*obstetrix*, midwife), and Egdechome was Ateia Acumene's slave. In the funerary monument of the latter, the commissioner added a pair of scissors and a *codex*, objects related to her work activity.[9] Both the examples capture the lives of two slaves associated to personal and work identities, something that is not common, due to the fact that most of the inscriptions in the sample report only details about personal relationships and not work activities.[10]

Mothers also appear as dedicators of their offspring (along with other sons and daughters), who have sometimes passed the stage of *infantia* and *pueritia* (Cenerini 2016, 196); this attests a long relationship in time between the mother and her child, with the latter reaching adulthood. The strength of the mother–child bond and the cohesion of families are here proved despite the circumstances derived from slavery. We have the example of Mercator, an imperial *uerna* of 29 years and 21 days old, who is commemorated by his mother and brothers (*A Epig.* 2006, 265, Albanum, AD 81–130). This rich funerary monument is manifested as a proof of a lasting mother–child relationship, a reality we have known of thanks to the accuracy with which the age of the deceased is reported. In other unfortunate situations, the slaves saw their progeny die at an early age,[11] as in the epitaph of Restituta, a 1-year and 8-month old baby, who is remembered by her mother, whose name has not survived, as a slave of Procula Fidelia (*CIL* 9, 3637, Aveia Vestina). Also in Matilica, a 6-year-old girl named Anaphe is commemorated along with her deceased mother, a 20-year-old woman (*A Epig.* 1981, 313, 50–1 BC).

Some mothers achieved freedom before their offspring, a reality that does not call our attention since there are examples in literary and legal sources that show how slaves are offered freedom in exchange of having a stipulated number of *uernae* (TRYPH. *Dig.* 1. 5. 15). Freedom could be obtained in exchange for work, as the slaves were able to pay for their own freedom. In the examples collected here, despite the improvement of legal status, the slaves continued to maintain a relationship, at least with the children that appear indicated in the epigraphic texts. We have to remember the manumission did not necessarily mean a drastic change in the lives of the *seruae*, who could continue to maintain a relationship with their ex-owners or even continue to work for them (Mouritsen 2011, 225; Edmonson 2011, 343–344). This situation is precisely the one that would have allowed the mothers to keep in touch with their offspring, not affecting their everyday relationship, yet always taking into account that they had no right over it. Vindicia Primigenia, described as a freedwoman, is in charge of the setting up of a funerary monument for her daughter Nympherusa, 18 years old, and her son Nymphius, 22 years old (*A Epig.* 2001, 872, Sipontum, AD 101–200); once more we deal with long-lasting relationships, considering the age of the children. In this case, in light of the information offered by the inscription, this single-parent family would have belonged to the same woman.[12] Other inscriptions attest freed mothers and their slave children, as in the case of Claudia Epiteuxis, whose onomastic reflects that she had a different legal status of that of her daughter Calliste, 20 years old and still a slave at the time of her death (*A Epig.* 2007, 423, Tarentum, AD 70–100). The situation could occur in reverse, of course, with a slave mother and her freed offspring, as we can see in the epitaph of Ursilla, a 40-year-old imperial slave commemorated by her son Ulpius Fortunatus (*A Epig.* 1972, Tarentum, AD 116 98–117).

So far we have mentioned private slaves and those belonging to the imperial family; however, motherhood was experienced also by public slaves, although these are a minority in the epigraphy of Roman Italy, only nine. Occasionally, these slaves are described as *publicae,* other times their names are linked to towns that appear as owners e.g., *Lepora Histoniensium serua* (*CIL* 9, 2889, Histonium), *Thymeleni Corfiniensium serua* (*A Epig* 1983, 323, Corfinium) and Agre, *seruae publica* of Luceria (*CIL* 9, 819). Two of them, Lepora and Agre, are commemorated by their offspring in simple and concise inscriptions; in the second case, the dedicators are not identified with a personal name but by the word *filii*. All the examples discussed so far, being representatives of many others, show the existence of families where no father figure is identified. This leads us to reflect on the identity of the father, and the reasons why he does not appear in the funerary monument: maybe he was already dead at the same of the setting up, or he could not be identified as a father (for instance, when the father was the slave's owner), or he simply did not exist in the life of the slave mother and her offspring.

As disclosed at the beginning of this section, *seruae* were also part of nuclear families. Unlike the previous cases, the following texts present a series of interpretive problems: sometimes it is impossible to know for sure whether a slave was the father or the mother of a third part, that is defined as a son or daughter. These two examples are representative of this situation:

> D(is) M(anibus)/Phileto/Triphosa co[n]/servo et Phile/tus p(atri) b(ene) m(erenti) fe[c(it)]. (*A Epig.* 1983, 216, Venusia, AD 101–150)
>
> [D(is) M(anibus?)]/Statori L(uci) Val(eri)/Potiti ser(vo) Mu/sa cons{s}erva/et Stator filius/[b(ene)] m(erenti) f(ecerunt) v(ixit) a(nnos) XXXV. (*A Epig.* 2012, 399, Heraclea AD 60–120)

In the first inscription, Triphosa sets up a funerary monument to Philetus, whom she defines as a *conseruus*, and so does Philetus to his father. However, the information provided by the epitaph does not allow us to assure that Triphosa is the mother of Philetus. The same happens in the second inscription where Musa, *conserua*, and Stator, *filius*, are commissioners of the funerary monument of Stator senior (father). Again, it is impossible to know with certainty whether Musa was the mother of Stator junior (son) or not. In spite of the complications when interpreting these monuments, I have included them in the group of inscriptions that would focus nuclear families, a total of 55 texts. If we look at the inscriptions of the two Statores, the father and the son carry the same name, unlike what happened in the very first epitaph that we analysed in this section, where the son of Ianuaria was named Ianuarius. Mothers and children sharing name (in masculine or feminine as appropriate) also appear in those epigraphic texts that reveal the existence of nuclear families:

> Lascivo/T(iti) Anini/Numidae/ser(vo) v(ixit) a(nnos) XV/Echio et/Lasciva/f(ilio) piissimo/p(osuerunt). (*A Epig.* 2006, 374, Aveia Vestina)
>
> Restutae Mariorum ancil[l]ae[13]/ann(orum) XXIIII men(sium) VII d(ierum) X/ Restutus fil(ius) [e]t Ep[i]ctetus coniunx/v(ivus) f(ecit) et sibi. (*CIL* 5, 629, Tergeste, AD 101–200)

Although we identified the men, the onomastics could indicate that these are not the biological parents, taking into account that their names, Restitutus and Lascivus, are connected with the mothers' onomastic. In both the examples, the mothers, Lascivia and Restituta, do not specifically indicate their legal status, thus they have to be considered as *incertae*, although there it is very likely that they were still slaves. In relation to naming, we should remember that servile girls and boys belonged to the owner who had, among his rights, the one to name the *uernae* and all other slaves. There is nothing more personal than a name, even if, in the case of slaves, this could have been chosen by an owner, who might have changed the original name following her or his own criteria.[14] There is no obligation to respect the original name of a slave, for instance, after s/he had been sold. Not only masters could give them a new name, but also slave dealers could (McLean 2002, 127). As a result, from that moment, the slave would be recognised according to the new nomenclature as a part of a new identity.[15] Essentially, this practise could be considered as the first step in the 'possession process': renaming as a way to own something or someone. Even if the owners or proprietors were responsible for naming the children of the slaves, they may have done so by basing the children's name on those of the mothers, marking the prevalence of the mother–child bond in a context in which the children follow the legal status of their mothers.

As it happened when we referred to single-parent families, also sons and daughters could achieve freedom before their two parents, as in an inscription from Venusia, AD 130–170, in which we read Philetus and Comice, mother and father (once again a nuclear family) and imperial slaves, were commemorated by their daughter Aelia Philete, an imperial freedwoman (*A Epig.* 2003, 485).[16] Nuclear families also included brothers and sisters who participated as deputies with their parents. So Amoena, slave of Ulpius, is remembered by her mother Ursula, her brother Amoenus and her companion Pyladius (*A Epig.* 2003, 393, Venusia, AD 150–200); Severus a 13-year-5-month-and-5-day-old slave, is remembered by his parents, Utilis and Cypare, as well as his sister Quinta (*A Epig.* 1989, 259, Sulmo, AD 101–200).

Other funerary monuments reflect how the members of the nuclear families belonged to different owners, as in the following inscription, in which we see a slave, her mother, her father and a man defined as *amicus*.[17]

> [P]rimae Accai/[D]eutera Neri/mater Verna/[p]ater Eros amic(us)/pos(uerunt). (*A Epig.* 1989, BC 70–30 AD 258 Sulmo)

It is important to point out that the mother and daughter belonged to different persons; this could mean that they did not live together under the same roof, or that they did not have daily contact, aspects that are not explained, unfortunately, in the epitaph. Otherwise, they may have lived in the same house, but belonging to different people from the same *familia*. The reading of these inscriptions reminds us, to a greater extent, those elements we cited at the beginning of this chapter about the instability and fragility of slave families. However, even in this adverse context, it should be noticed that mother, father and daughter, according to what we have here, maintained their relationship, although unfortunately this epitaph does not include the age of the deceased.

Other sources report the age of the children: Stratonice, an imperial *uerna* commemorated by her father and mother, was victim of a premature death since she died at the age of 1 year, 1 month and 4 days (*CIL* 14, 1642). The same situation can be seen in an inscription from the territory of Interpromium, according to which a father and a mother witnessed the death of their two daughters, of six and one year old respectively (Buonocore *et al.* 1991, 424):

> D(is) M(anibus) [s(acrum)]/Antinoe et Phoebe/duae sunt conservae/sorores servae Vo/lusiorum Marci et Aemiliani/hic sunt positae Phoebe vixit/annis VI m(ensibus) X d(iebus) XV Antinoe/annum d(ies) XX P(h) oebus et Rhodope/filiabus pientissimis et Tertius p(osuerunt). (*A Epig.* 1984, 347, AD 101–200)

In this example, the father and the mother are present, even if they do not explicitly indicate their status. Along with them and the deceased, a third character is listed: Tertius, who may have been their brother (his name could mark the order at birth). In addition to the extensive text, this funerary monument is interesting because of the relief it includes.[18] As F. Cenerini recently published, through the analysis of the epigraphic evidence of the *Regio VIII*, it is not common to find reliefs that commemorate a slave child (Cenerini 2016, 205). This circumstance gives more value to this evidence. The relief has a difficult interpretation regarding the gender and age of the subjects. It is supposed that the image would show two girls, at least considering the text of the epitaph. Here the subjects are hugging. It is unclear if the figure on the right is wearing a *bulla*, which would identify him as a free boy (Cenerini 2016, 196). If, on the other hand, s/he is holding an apple,[19] nothing particular could be said as this fruit is a recurring object in the representation of children. The figure on the left present rounded sinuous forms on the chest that may indicate the character is an adult woman rather that a child. My interpretation suggests that the image, instead of properly representing the two deceased, especially considering that one of them is a baby and therefore would not correspond to any of the relief figures, could be interpreted as a representation of the affection that parents felt for their children (*pietas*).[20] The exchange of apples, as well as the hug, can be interpreted as a sign of affection and love, feelings that in the funerary relief are associated with the figure of an adult woman and a child.

Finally, and with this we close this section, inscriptions also reflect the maternal absence. This is the case of Crescentila, a *uerna* of 2 years and 6 months old, who is remembered by Titus Flavius Epagathus (EDR105347); that of Felicula, *Sempronia Primitiva uernacula*, also 2 years old (*CIL* 11, 5102); and the one of Chloe, 5-years-old and slave of Cneus Pompilius (EE-08-01, 16). In these epitaphs the girls, who are still in the stage of *infantia*, appear isolated without any news of their parents, although they are associated with other people who are not relatives in any degree, or at least they do not manifest any familial bond. On other occasions, we do have a relative, the father, who appears alone, as in the epitaph of Prugia, a 6-year-old slave, and Dercilis, aged 3 and possibly also a slave, only commemorated by their father (Inscrit -10-02, 193, Parentium). A further evidence of maternal absence is found in Brundisium, where Silvana, a 12-year-old slave, is remembered by her grandmother (*A Epig.* 1980, 278). In the absence of a first-degree relative such as the mother, another relative took the place in the dedication of the funerary monument, and most probably also in the girl's everyday life.[21]

Undoubtedly, all these types of inscriptions we have discussed throughout this chapter demonstrate the plural reality in which the slaves took part, either as single mothers or as members of nuclear families. Unfortunately, none of them clarifies the quality of the mother–child bond. The epigraphic evidence shows a very specific moment in time: we have to deal with it by analysing the information we have at our disposal, as well as trying to recover what has been omitted, even if is almost always impossible. Even so, regardless of whether we are interested in motherhood, fatherhood or childhood, in some critical ways, the slavery's mark made slave families very different from other families. 'Unpredictable, fraught and uncertainty,) these have been the words chosen by C. Laes (2011, 157) to define the life of slave children in ancient Roman society. In the same way, these would be the words we need to describe the lives of mothers. There were no guarantees that would ensure the unity of the *seruae* and their offspring; despite this, the mother–child bond survived where the unilateral decisions of those who represented the slave system did not break it.

Conclusions: between the owner's position and the slave's voice

Thanks to the epigraphic records we know that some Roman slaves could enjoy emotional relationships. However, considering the legal references as a starting point, the possibility of creating a family and enjoying a family life was not as big as for free people. On the background of the slave families, there is always the lack of freedom, as well as the unilateral decisions of the owner. And it is at this point that we do not only question ourselves about the data, which are more or less evident, provided by inscriptions, but about the silences. As we have said, there are those sons, daughters and mothers who succumbed to the slavery system. In the margins there are those who were sold, who were abandoned due to the wishes of a third party. Broken relationships have hardly left any evidence behind. Depending on the circumstances and the different scenarios, slaves would have exercised a more or less long motherhood.

When we read about the life of a slave, embodying the role of a mother, even though she appears with a partner (nuclear family), we should remember that the story of the mother–child bond and emotions might have been characterised by instability or fragility, but not by inexistence. The epitaphs surviving from Roman Italy show slaves as mothers, therefore mother–children bonds within slavery. There is no security in the slave union, there is no security in the slave mother–son/daughter relationship. In this way, what is evident is not only the mother–child bond, but also its strength, where it is unprotected, or even where parents and children belonged to different people or had different legal status. Regardless of the existence of a life subject to a stability that responds to the whims of another person. Even so, and this is not clarified by any of the sources that I have been able to analyse so far, not even by the epigraphic evidence, all violence that interrupts the communication between a mother and her offspring generates failures, gaps and traumas on both sides. Despite this, we can hear the voice of the slave mothers and their sons and daughters, beyond Roman prohibitions, which leads us to learn about the incorporated strategies of survival of the slave families.

Acknowledgements

Carla Rubiera Cancelas is junior researcher for the Marie Curie-Clarín Cofund programme (University of Oviedo). This article is part of the I+D project: 'Maternidades, filiaciones y sentimientos en las sociedades griega y romana de la Antigüedad. Familias alternativas y otras relaciones de parentesco fuera de la norma (HAR2017-82521-P)' lead by professor Rosa María Cid López.

Notes

1 As the jurists plainly state that 'the laws do not apply to servile relationships' (*ad leges serviles cognationes non pertinent*, *D* 38.10.10.5, Paul; cf. *D* 38.8.1.2, Ulpian) (Mouritsen 2010, 129).
2 About slaves as *nutrices* (wet nurses) see Bradley (1980; 1986) and Joshel (1980).
3 Some of these contracts are discussed in Masciardi and Montevecchi (1984). An accurate study of this type of sources, which involve enslaved women, is under development.
4 Although some authors have proposed that the slave family could have been divided with little concern for the family units (Bradley 1984, 64–70).
5 'Epitaphs do not offer perfect images of life ... Nevertheless, this information often provides our most direct access to the experience and perspective of an individual; we must rely on the evidence of death as a mirror of life that reflects how men and women saw themselves' (Joshel 1992, 8).
6 For instance the *senatusconsultum Claudianum* 54 AD. See Storchi Marino (1999, 391–426).
7 The Roman slave system did not allow slaves to enjoy *connubium*, but they were free to create *contubernia*. As *contubernium* had no legal validity, the possible offspring was considered illegitimate.
8 About the treatment of enslaved women as animals, see Bradley (2000, 110–125).
9 About meaning of tools on funerary inscriptions see Buonopane (2013, 73–82).
10 N. Tran has recently confirmed speaking about slaves (male and female): 'Aussi, sur leurs inscriptions funeraires, les Italiens choisissaient-ils, dans leur majorite, de ne pas releveler a la posterite leur profession' (2007, 121).
11 About high mortality rate and *uernae* see Hermann-Otto (1994, 230).
12 *SuppIIt* 24, 44.
13 About this word see Mano (2013, 312–313).
14 Renaming slaves was a practice already known in ancient Greece (Robertson 2009, 81–83). Many facts justify this custom in Roman times, including the difficulty in the pronunciation of foreign names, trends and tendencies (Bruun 213, 23).
15 This reflection makes sense speaking about adults becoming slaves.
16 About Aelia Philete: 'La dedicante è la stessa persona di Monumenti 52, dove è ricordata, defunta, dal coniuge Purpurio. I genitori sono morti ancora schiavi, mentre Philete è stata affrancata. La figlia porta, al femminile, il cognome del padre.' *SuppIIt* 20, 2003, 244–245.

17 Latin Oxford Dictionary about *amicus*: '1. A personal friend. 2. A lover. 2. A friend in public life.'
18 http://db.edcs.eu/epigr/bilder.php? bild=PH0003506; PH0003447; PH0003450; PH0003449; PH0003448; PH0003451
19 It may be also a ball. About iconography of childhood in funerary monuments and attributes (apples, pets, birds, scrolls, etc.) see Mander (2012, 36–64).
20 'but slave families, though not recognized such in law, were regarded as bound by *pietas*' (Saller 1994, 112).
21 Other surrogate mothers may have been the wet nurses, that have been discussed, still from the territory of Roman Italy, in a forthcoming publication Rubiera Cancelas. See also note 9.

References

Bradley, K. R. (1994) *Slavery and Society at Rome*. Cambridge, Cambridge University Press.

Bradley, K. R. (1980). Sexual Regulations in Wet-Nursing. Contracts from Roman Egypt, *Klio* 62(2), 321–325.

Bradley, K. R. (1986) Wet-nursing at Rome: a study in social relations. In B. Rawson (ed.) *The Family in Ancient Rome. New Perspectives*. New York, Cornell University Press, 321–324.

Bradley, K. R. (2000) Animalizing the slave: The truth of fiction. *Journal of Roman Studies* 90, 110–125.

Bruun, C. (2013) The owner's choice of names for *Vernae*. In M. George (ed.) *Roman Slavery and Roman Material Culture*. Toronto/Buffalo/London, University of Toronto Press, 19–42.

Buonocore, M. (1991) *Fonti latine e greche per la storia dell'Abruzzo antico*, 1. L'Aquila, Deputazione Abruzzese di storia patria.

Buonopane, A. (2013) Le raffigurazioni di utensili nelle iscrizioni funerarie: da immagini parlanti a simbolo. *Sylloge Epigraphica Barcinonensis (SEBarc)* 11, 73–82.

Cenerini, F. (2016). La rappresentazione epigráfica dell'infanzia servile nella Regio ottava: alcuni esempi. In M. Dondin-Payre and N. Tran (eds) *Esclaves et maîtres dans le monde romain. Expressions épigraphiques de leus relations*, 196–207. Roma, Publications de l'École Française de Rome, 196–207.

Curchin, L. A. (2000–2001) The Roman family: Recent interpretations. *Zephyrus* 53–54, 535–550.

Di Nisio, V. (2007) Osservazioni in tema di *partus ancillae*. In C. Cascione and C. Masi Doria, C. (eds) *Fides humanitas ius: studii in onore di Ligi Labruna*, vo. III, Napoli, Editoriale Scientifica, 1493–1517.

Edmonson, J. (2011) Slavery and the Roman family. In K. Bradley and P. Cartledge (eds) *The Cambridge World History of Slavery. The Ancient Mediterranean World*, vol. 1. Cambridge/New York, Cambridge University Press, 337–361.

Gardner, J. F. (1987) *Women in Roman Law and Society*. London, Indiana University Press.

Harper, K. (2013) *Slavery in the Late Roman World, A.D. 275–425*. Cambridge/New York, Cambridge University Press.

Harris, W. V. (1999) Demography, geography and the sources of Roman slaves. *Journal of Roman Studies* 89, 62–75.

Hermann-Otto, E. (1994) *Untersuchungen zu den <hausgeboren> Sklaven und Sklavinnen im Westen des Römischen Kaiserreiches*. (Forschungen zur antiken Sklaverei; Bd. 24). Stuttgart, Steiner.

Joshel, S. R. (1986) Nurturing the Master's Child: Slavery and the Roman Child-Nurse. *Signs* 12(1), 3–22.

Joshel, S. (1992) *Work, Identity, and Legal Status at Rome. A Study of the Occupational Inscriptions*. Norman, University of Oklahoma Press.

Korporowicz, L. J. (2011) Buying a slave in Roman Britain. The evidence from the Tabulae. *Revue internationale des droits de l'antiquité* 58, 211–224.

Laes, C. (2011) *Children in the Roman Empire. Outsiders Within*. Cambridge/New York, Cambridge University Press.

Latin Oxford Dictionary (1968). Oxford, Clarendon Press.

Mander, J. (2012) *Portraits of Children on Roman Funerary Monuments*. Cambridge, Cambridge University Press.

Mano, S. (2012) La servande dans le monde romain: une figure oubliée. *Pallas: Revue d'études antiques* 90, 311–334.

Masciadri, M. M. and Montevecchi, O. (1984) *I contratti di baliatico*. Milano, CPGrI.

McLean, M. H. (2002) *An Introduction to Greek Epigraphy of the Hellenistic and Roman Periods from Alexander the Great down to the Reign of Constantine (323 B.C–A.D. 337)*. Ann Abor, University of Michigan Press.

Mouritsen, H. (2011) The families of Roman slaves and freedmen. In B. Rawson (ed.) *A Companion to Families in the Greek and Roman Worlds*. Chichester/Malden/Oxford, Wiley-Blackwell, 129–144.

Mouritsen, H. (2011) *The Freedman in the Roman World*. Cambridge/New York, Cambridge University Press.

Rawson, B. (2003) *Children and Childhood in Roman Italy*. Oxford, Oxford University Press.

Robertson, B. (2009) The slave-names of IG I 1032 and the ideology of slavery in Athens. In C. Cooper (ed.) *Epigraphy and the Greek Historian*. Phoenix Supplementary Volume 47. Toronto, University of Toronto Press, 79–118.

Rubiera Cancelas, C. (2014) *La esclavitud femenina en la Roma antigua. Famulae, ancillae et seruae*. Oviedo, Trabe.

Rubiera Cancelas, C. (forthcoming). El uso de esclavas como nodrizas. Más allá de la figura simbólica, *Dialogues d'histoire ancienne*.

Saller, R. P. (1994) *Patriarchy, Property and Death in the Roman Family*. New York, Cambridge University Press.

Scheidel, W. (1997) Quantifying the sources of slaves in the Roman Empire. *Journal of Roman Studies* 87, 159–169.

Scheidel, W. (2011) The Roman slave supply. In K. Bradley and P. Cartledge (eds) *The Cambridge World History of Slavery*. The Ancient Mediterranean World vol. 1, 287–310. Cambridge/New York, Cambridge University Press, 287–310.

Stevenson, B. E. (1996) *Life in Black and White: Family and Community in the Slave South*. New York, Oxford University Press.

Storchi Marino, A. (1999) Restaurazione del more e controllo della mobilità sociale a Roma nel I sec. D.C.: *il senatusconsultum Claudianum de poena feminarum quae servis coniugerentur*. In F. Reduzzi Merola and A. Storchi Marino (eds) *Femmes-esclaves. Modèles d'interprétation anthropologique, économique, juridique. Atti del XXI Colloquio Internazionale GIREA*. Napoli: Jovene Editore, 391–426.

Straus, J. A. (2004) *L'Achat et la vente des esclaves dans l'Egypte romain, Contribution papyrologique à l'étude de l'esclavage dans une province orientale de l'empire romain*. Archiv für Papyrusforschung und verwandte Gebiete, Beiheft 14. Munich/Leipzig.

Supplementa Italica. Nuova Serie 20 (2003) Edizioni Quasar, Roma.

Supplementa Italica Nuova Serie 24 (2009) Edizioni Quasar, Roma.

Tomlin, R. S. O. (2004) The girl in question: A new text from Roman London. *Journal of Roman Society* 34, 49–50.

Tran, N. (2007) La mention épigraphique des métiers artisanaux et commerciaux en Italie centro-méridionale. In J. Andreau and V. Chankowski (eds) *Vocabulaire et expressions de l'économie dans le monde Antique*. Bordeaux, Ausonius, 119–141.

Chapter 17

On the margins of motherhood: images of the *puella docta* and the lover-poet in the Latin love elegy

Rosa Mª Marina Sáez

Introduction

Latin love elegy presents a literary universe on the margins of conventional gender relations, in which women appear in a very different role from that of the *matrona*, the faithful wife and selfless mother of the traditional Roman family.[1] The lifestyle of the *puella docta*, hovering between seduction and luxury, seems in every way at odds with motherhood, and all the more so in the Roman world where social, gender and age roles were strictly delineated. However, we need to remember that the world the poets describe belongs to the sphere of the literary. Both characters, the *puella* and the lover-poet, draw on a literary tradition that does not always match the real world. Leaving aside the historical and social context in which these characters were created, it is the multiplicity of its sources which makes it so difficult to interpret the plot lines and *personae* of elegiac poetry.[2]

The incompatibility between the *puella docta* and motherhood is made explicit in texts like the two elegies in Ovid's *Amores* (II 13 and 14), which concern an abortion provoked by his lover Corinna.[3] It is not my intention to discuss the poet's reflections on this theme at any length here; suffice it to say that they waver between fear for Corinna's life (XIII 4),[4] the possibility that he might be the child's father (XIII 5–6), although he studiously avoids saying that he would have shouldered any responsibility for a living infant,[5] and horror at what he sees as a dreadful crime and at the same time a moment of deadly peril for his beloved (XIV).[6] Very little is said, however, about Corinna's reasons for seeking an abortion, other than the suspicion that she was concerned simply to preserve her figure:[7]

> scilicet ut careat rugarum crimine uenter,
> sternetur pugnae tristis harena tuae? (*Am.* II 14, 8–9)[8]

The poet is not interested in Corinna's actual feelings, and he has nothing to say about her resolve, her fears and cares, or whether she ever thought about having a child. All he cares about is that she acted on the quiet (*Am.* II 13, 3). James remarks on this lack of empathy (James 2003, 173–175), observing that the poems provide a glimpse, hidden among the elegiac literary conventions, into the real lives of Roman courtesans[9], while the poet is quite unable to put himself in his beloved's place.

In the world described by the elegiac poets, a woman's sensuality is defined by the possession of a nubile young body unspoiled by the marks of motherhood. For example, Propertius links the firmness of Cynthia's breasts with the enjoyment of sex for its own sake (*ludere*), while motherhood and its concomitant blemishes would only be an impediment to such pleasures.[10]

> Necdum inclinatae prohibent te ludere mammae:
> viderit haec, si quam iam peperisse pudet. (Prop. II 15, 21–22)[11]

In this light, a woman might fear to lose her looks not so much out of vanity as due to the demands of a lifestyle that is based on physical attractiveness but is full of risks and can only be maintained for a short time (James 2003, 173–175). Without going so far as to identify the *puella* with the *meretrix*, these poems reveal a fear of rejection and abandonment in a world in which the demands of physical appearance only increase (see, for example, Ovid's own *Epistola* from Penelope to Ulysses, in which the classical heroine laments the loss of her looks compared to other beauties who may have beguiled her husband, and the countless invectives against licentious old women to be found in Latin literature). The voices of such women are completely absent from the Latin love elegy, and it is above all that absence which this chapter will now address.

The poet and his duties to sire sons and to fight for his country

Most studies of Latin love elegy focus on the figure of the *puella docta*, whose lifestyle is viewed as a choice open to emancipated women untrammelled by conventional gender roles. In reality, however, it is the poet-lover who chooses the elegiac lifestyle, voluntarily, if temporarily, renouncing his duties as a citizen, which was chiefly to marry and to sire legitimate children. This is irreconcilable with a love life at the side of a woman chosen outside the bounds of social convention (Rambaux 2001, 110–111).[12] In one of his poems Propertius justifies his rejection of a conventional life because he does not wish either to forswear his love for Cynthia or to produce legitimate sons to become soldiers of the *patria*, preferring to opt for his *militia amoris* (Cano 1998, 103):

> Nam citius paterer caput hoc discedere collo
> quam possem nuptae perdere more faces,
> aut ego transirem tua limina clausa maritus,
> respiciens udis prodita luminibus.
> A mea tum qualis caneret tibi tibia somnos,

> tibia, funesta tristior illa tuba!
> unde mihi patriis gnatos praebere triumphis?
> Nullus de nostro sanguine miles erit. (Prop. II 7 7–14)[13]

And he goes on:

> Tu mihi sola places: placeam tibi, Cynthia, solus:
> hic erit et patrio nomine pluris amor. (Prop. II 7, 19–20)[14]

In a later poem, however, Propertius becomes the apologist of a life he had once spurned, and in the homage to Italy he dedicated to Tullus he praises the *patria* as the best of places to seek honours, take a wife and father children.

> haec tibi, Tulle, parens, haec est pulcherrima sedes,
> hic tibi pro digna gente petendus honos,
> hic tibi ad eloquium ciues, hic ampla nepotum
> spes et uenturae coniugis aptus amor. (Prop. III 22, 39–41)[15]

As Fedeli notes (1985, 655), Propertius lists key elements in the life of a *cives romanus*, including his commitment to civic duties via the *cursus honorum* and the practice of rhetoric, and most importantly his obligation to produce legitimate heirs through an honourable marriage to a suitable wife. These matters transcend the private sphere according to Fedeli, being entirely consistent with Augustan policy, and they stand in stark contrast to the attitude towards paternity displayed by Propertius in the previous elegy. Rambaux (2001, 240–242) argues that this thematic shift comes about after the poet has abandoned his *servitium amoris* within his literary universe. Hence, the option to live the life of the *adulescens* is merely a temporary choice, which the poet can change at any time in order to concentrate on more conventional pursuits. The lifestyle of the *puella*, however, is supposed to remain forever unchanging, except for her lovers, until she is no longer a young girl but an old woman or *anus.*

The figure of the *puella* is so markedly a non-mother that she retains at least some of the characteristics of a sophisticated urban woman even when she is assimilated into literary genres like those of the Golden Age or *beatus ille,* in which the description of traditional peasant family life is a central theme, as in Horace (*Epod.* II) or Virgil (*Georgic.* II 523–4),[16] in the manner of Greek pastoral poetry. And, of course, she is childless. A clear example of this is to be found in Tibullus, who several times places Delia in a country setting following the trope of the *beatus ille*:

> fictilia antiquus primum sibi fecit agrestis
> pocula, de facili conposuitque luto.-
> non ego diuitias patrum fructusque requiro,
> quos tulit antiquo condita messis auo:
> parua seges satis est, satis est requiescere lecto
> si licet et solito membra leuare toro.
> quam iuuat inmites uentos audire cubantem
> et dominam tenero continuisse sinu

aut, gelidas hibernus aquas cum fuderit Auster,
securum somnos igne iuvante sequi! (Tib. I I 39–45)[17]

All the tropes surrounding the ideal of the country life appear in this passage, from simplicity through safety to the perils of soldiering, from the rejection of wealth to repose in the bosom of the family. The longing for this way of life, which the poet knows to be unattainable even as he describes it (Lee-Stecum 1998, 46), is represented by the presence of the beloved, his *domina,* and not a *mulier* or *uxor,* and there is of course no mention of any offspring.

Another striking example of absent motherhood, which I discussed in more detail in a paper given at the last Conference of the *Sociedad de Estudios Latinos,* appears in elegy I 5, where the poet relates a complex fantasy of country living in which Delia plays the leading role:

rura colam, frugumque aderit mea Delia custos,
area dum messes sole calente teret,
aut mihi seruabit plenis in lintribus uuas
pressaque ueloci candida musta pede;
consuescet numerare pecus; consuescet amantis
garrulus in dominae ludere uerna sinu.
illa deo sciet agricolae pro uitibus uuam,
pro segete spicas, pro grege ferre dapem.
illa regat cunctos, illi sint omnia curae:
at iuuet in tota me nihil esse domo.
huc ueniet Messalla meus, cui dulcia poma
Delia selectis detrahat arboribus:
Et, tantum uenerata uirum, hunc sedula curet,
huic paret atque epulas ipsa ministra gerat. (Tib. I 5, 21–34).[18]

Despite the obvious links between this text and conventional versions of the *beatus ille* theme, there are marked differences in the gender roles played by the different characteristics. Here, the poet-lover fades into the background (Scioli 2015, 65–66) while Delia takes charge of all matters of husbandry. She is a true *domina*, performing male tasks (Murgatroyd 2001, 167–170), but at the same time she never ceases to be the sophisticated elegiac *puella,* as may be observed in the scene where she is described as playing with the child of a household slave (Lee Stecum 1998, 163–168). The inversion of gender roles is minimised, however, when Tibullus presents Delia as serving Messalla, the poet's patron, in the role of *ministra* proper to a slave girl.

The most interesting feature of these examples is the lack of a traditional family formed by a married couple and their children, contradicting the model demanded by Augustan policy. This absence has attracted the attention of numerous scholars, who have propounded a host of disparate interpretations. Be this as it may, the key feature of these examples as I see it is the proverbial incompatibility between the elegiac couple and conventional matrimony, firstly because the *puella* is not the kind of woman who could become a wife and a mother, and secondly because the poet deliberately turns his back on a conventional lifestyle, at least for the present.[19]

Furthermore, this scenario is not exclusive to Tibullus, appearing not only in elegy III 3 of the *Corpus Tibullianum*[20] but also in Propertius II 16, who paints a picture of the Golden Age in which lovers are faithful and grow old together in their homes, although there is no mention of any offspring:

> Atque utinam Romae nemo esset dives et ipse
> straminea posset dux habitare casa!
> Numquam venales essent ad munus amicae
> atque una fieret cana puella domo (Prop. II 16, 19–22)[21]

In the following example, however, Tibullus does indeed include a wife, children and grandchildren imaging his own old age:

> quin potius laudandus hic est quem prole parata
> occupat in parua pigra senecta casa!
> ipse suas sectatur oues, at filius agnos,
> et calidam fesso comparat uxor aquam.
> sic ego sim, liceatque caput candescere canis
> temporis et prisci facta referre senem (Tib. I 10 39–44)[22]

Tibullus deals with the theme from a different standpoint, that of the *senex*, who has fulfilled his obligations as a Roman, rather than the *adulescens* of the previous poems, who cannot image being surrounded by children. His spouse is denoted by the word *uxor* not *domina.*[23]

This ideal of a happy old age surrounded by grandchildren also appears in Tibullus II 2, a *genethliacon* poem dedicated to Cornutus, and in II 5, 89–94, where the poet describes the agrarian festival of *Palilia*:

> ille leuis stipulae sollemnis potus aceruos
> accendet, flammas transilietque sacras.
> et fetus matrona dabit, natusque parenti
> oscula comprensis auribus eripiet,
> nec taedebit auum paruo aduigilare nepoti
> balbaque cum puero dicere uerba senem (Tib. II 5, 89–94)[24]

In this case, three generations of the pastoral family appear. The central figure is the infant, who captures the full attention of his father and grandfather while his mother, here referred to as *matrona*, stands somewhat apart from this scene of joy, fulfilling the sole function of childbearing in the family.

As these examples show, the elegiac poets paint different pictures of country life depending on the context. Where a poem deals with love for a *puella,* conventional forms are dropped. In other compositions such as dedicatory poems, patriotic verses and praise for the Italian countryside, they return to the established conventions in their descriptions of family life.

The *puella docta* as a maternal figure

Though the *puella* never appears as the mother of his children, she is sometimes described as a maternal figure in her relationship with the poet himself. The most obvious examples are to be found in Propertius, although Tibullus I 5 has also been interpreted in this way. The case discussed here comes from Propertius' elegy I 11 in a passage which Fedeli (1980, 226) represents as full of pathos and almost hymn-like in its tone. In it, the poet treats Cynthia above his own mother, calling her alone his home and family:

an mihi nunc maior carae custodia matris?
aut sine te uitae cura sit ulla meae?
tu mihi sola domus, tu, Cynthia, sola parentes.
omnia tu nostrae tempora laetitiae (Prop. I 11, 21–24)[25]

The first two lines are particularly problematic in terms both of textual criticism and identification of the referent for the term *matris.* In this case, I prefer to follow the reading and interpretation proposed by Fedeli (1980, 280), currently the majority view, according to which *matris* is the poet's own mother. This links the passage to certain texts of Roman comedy like Plaut. *Truc.* 662, where the dramatist places his love of a woman above his feelings for his own mother (Camps 1966, 72; Fedeli 1980, 282; Coutelle 2005, 269).

The third line, meanwhile, picks up on some words of Andromache spoken to Hector in the *Iliad* (Il. VI 429–430), which are also echoed in Ter. *Phorm.* 496 and Catull. 72 3–4, a passage which Fedeli (1980, 282) sees as Propertius' principal model:

Dilexi tum te non tantum ut vulgus amicam,
sed pater ut gnatos diligit et generos.[26]

What has most attracted the attention of researchers is not the expression *per se*, however, but the fact that the poet addresses it to his beloved where it is usually directed by a woman to a man, which implies a reversal of gender roles (Wike 1989, 25–47; Greene 1995, 303–318; Baker 2000, 123, Coutelle 2005, 271). This is a highly unusual detail, which Newman explains by arguing that Roman men sometimes lacked the language to express sexual love and commitment, and they therefore needed to borrow the women's words for such matters (Newman 1997, 315–316). Meanwhile, Greene (1998, 64) observes a profound confusion in the poem's construction of gender relations. The poet imagines himself as *custos* of his mother,[27] tying in with his depiction of Cynthia as a woman who needs to be controlled. More importantly, however, he compares Cynthia to a mother in contrast with earlier images in the poem where she is described as wanton; now she is desexualised by the use of the term *parentes* and represented as chaste and fertile, the opposite of the *puella*, while the poet appears as a dependent child.[28]

The matter is put much more clearly in another passage, where Propertius tells his beloved that he will take the place of the brothers and sons she lacks:

Cum tibi nec frater nec sit tibi filius ullus,
frater ego et tibi sim filius unus ego. (Prop. II 18 d. 33–34)[29]

Once again the text is modelled on *Iliad* VI 429–30 and Catul. 72, 3–4 (Fedeli 2005, 550–551), and once again it is open to different interpretations, as expounded by Grimal (1963, 173), Rambaux (2001, 137) and Fedeli (2005, 551), among others. While avoiding the controversy over possible incestuous impulses, which form the basis for the psychoanalytic critique of this text, the latter argues that a brother or child could stand in for an absent father in the traditional Roman family, exercising control over the womenfolk in the role of *paterfamilias*. On this view, what the poet desires is to gain some kind of authority over an emancipated woman, which was of course impossible in reality.

To conclude, the literary universe created by the elegiac poets is rooted in male fantasies and the desire for a lifestyle that is free of any kind of responsibility. The *docta puella* is the ideal partner in this universe, not because she too chooses to turn her back convention, but because she is defined as non-conventional, a woman who is beyond marriage or motherhood even if she can be imagined as a mother figure by her lover. Unlike the character of the poet-lover, who is constructed from features proper to the *adulescens* found in the comedy of Plautus and Terentius but can at any time drop the mask to reinvent himself as a responsible citizen, the *puella* can never become a *matrona* under any circumstances. It is because of this that the poets can rework traditional literary tropes and defend a lifestyle like the *beatus ille* that conforms to the ideals of Augustan policy, only replacing the familiar depictions with scenes that are more in accord with characters beguiled by a love without commitments. All of this contrasts with other more traditional approaches to the theme, in which the character of the poet adapts to his new circumstances while the *puella* is simply replaced by the figure of the *uxor*.

Notes

1 This disjunction impressed Cano (1998, 103), who saw such women as combining features of both the *matrona* and the courtesan. The elegiac poets were not interested in the family ideal, but in the continuation of a roughly stable relationship compounded of both passion and *fides*. According to Keith (2008, 87), the love of expensive jewellery and dresses displayed by Propertius' Cynthia, her lifestyle and her Greek name distinguish her either as a high-class courtesan or as an independently wealthy member of the Roman elite who chooses to live like one. On the matter of Cynthia's identity, see the exhaustive study in Newman (1997, 278–337), who takes the possible allusion to a *docto ... avo* in III 20a 8 as showing that Cynthia is a woman of some social standing, refuting the view of her as a mere *meretrix* or *libertina* of lowly origins.

2 The relationship between reality and fiction in this literature has been the subject of a fascinating debate (Wike 1987, 1989; Greene 1998, 37–66) on the textual figure of the *puella*.

3 See Laigneau (1999, 248–272) for a discussion of abortion and contraception in Rome. This was a novel topic for love poetry according to Booth (1991, 70), although the reasons for his beloved's illness and the poet´s own interest in it are common themes. Cf. Tib. I 5, 8–6, Prop. II 9, 25–28, Ov. *Ep.* 19(20) 129–142, 20(21), 183–206.

4 See Aristotle, *Politics* 1335b on the risks inherent in the practice of abortion.

5 Booth (1991, 157) highlights the absurdity of the poet's patriarchal reaction to the supposed loss of an illegitimate child.

6 Such admonishments have nothing to do with any kind of legislation to protect the *nasciturus*, who would not in any event have been considered human in the classical age, but are concerned rather with the right of the father to decide whether to abort or to bring up the child. See Cantarella (1991, 252–254).

7 As explained in (Booth 1991, 162), this is one of the arguments made by moralists to explain why some women shun childbirth (Sen. *Dial.* XII 16.3; Gel. XII 1.8). The mention of stretch marks caused by pregnancy and the need to hide them is also found in Ov. *Ars* III 785. For the extolment of a flat stomach, see Ov. *Am.* I 5, 21. For further evidence of these matters, see McKeown (1998, 247).

8 'Can it be that to spare your bosom the reproach of lines, you would scatter the tragic sands of deadly combat?' (Trans. Showerman 1914, 423). The Latin text cited is from McKeown's edition (1987).

9 The social status of these women is debatable. For example, Propertius sometimes describes Cynthia as an upper class lady (I 6), but her behaviour often appears to be that of a courtesan. In any case, we should not forget that this is an eminently poetical fiction, in which elements from a range of traditions appear.

10 Fedeli 2005, 453. Cf. Ov. *Am.* II 4, 45–46, who claims to be attracted not only by young but also by mature women, who have other allures besides beauty alone.

11 'It's not as though sagging breasts bar you from fun and games: leave that worry to her who knows the shame of having given birth' (trans. Gold 1990, 165).

12 Fedeli (2005, 233) notes that the purpose of marriage was to pass on a man's name and estate, but that the poet was by convention *pauper* and thus had nothing to pass on. In support of this argument, he cites Catullus (61, 66–69), who tells us that illegitimate sons could not be expected to defend the *patria*.

13 'For sooner should I let my head be severed from my neck than I could quench the torch of love to humour a bride's whim, or as a married man pass by your barred threshold, looking back with tearful eyes at the house I had betrayed. Ah, Then what dire slumbers would my wedding-flute warble for you, that flute more dismal than the trumpet of death! How should I furnish sons for our country's triumphs? No soldier shall ever be born of my blood' (trans. Gold 1990, 141). The Latin text cited is from Fedeli's edition (2005).

14 'You are my only joy: be I your only joy, Cynthia: this love means more to me than the name of father' (trans. Gold 1990, 140).

15 'This, Tullus, is the land that gave you birth, this your fairest home; here you should seek the high office to match your noble birth. Here are citizens for your eloquence to sway, here rich hope of offspring, here awaits you perfect love from your bride to be' (trans. Gold 1990, 343). The Latin text cited is from Fedeli's edition (1985).

16 For a discussion of different models of the rural Roman family, see Dyson (2003, 2011).

17 'Earthen were the drinking-cups which the ancient yokel made himself, modelling them from pliant clay.
I ask not for the riches of my sires or the gains which garnered harvests brought to my ancestors of yore. A small field's produce is enough – enough if I may sleep upon my bed and the mattress ease my limbs as heretofore. What delight to hear the winds rage as I lie and hold my love safe in my gentle clasp; or when the stormy South Wind sheds the chilling showers, to follow the road of untroubled sleep, the rain my lullaby!' (trans. Postgate 1921, 195). The Latin text cited is from Postgate's edition (1915).

18 '"In the country," I said, "I will live. My Delia shall be there to keep watch upon the grain, while the threshing-floor winnows the harvest in the blazing sun; or she shall watch the grapes in the brimming trough when the quick feet tread the gleaming must. She shall learn to count

the flock; she shall teach the prattling serf-child to play on a loving mistress' lap. To the god that tends the country she will know what gifts to offer – for vines a cluster, spiked ears for cornfield, drink offering for flock. All folk shall she direct, and all things be her care. I shall love to be but a cipher in the house. Hither shall come my own Mesalla. From chosen trees shall Delia pull him down sweet fruit. In homage to his greatness she shall give him zealous tendance, and prepare and carry him the repast, herself his waiting maid' (trans. Postgate 1921, 219).

19 This has been interpreted in various ways. Johnson (1989, 103) wonders why there should be this absence, while Norwick (1990, 116) speculates that Delia may represent some kind of maternal figure for the poet.

20 In this elegy, which has been attributed to Lygdamus, the poet-lover aspires to a simple, happy life with Neaera, whom he even calls his *cara coniuge* (v. 32), but he expresses no yearning for children.

21 'Oh, would that no man were rich at Rome and even our leader could live in a hut of straw! Never then would our girl-friends sell themselves for a gift, and a maiden would grow grey in a single house' (trans. Gold 1990, 170–171).

22 'Nay, the hero is he whom, when his children are begotten, old age's torpor overtakes in his humble cottage. He follows his sheep, his son the lambs, while the good wife heats the water for his weary limbs. So let me live till the white hairs glisten on my head and I tell in old man's fashion of the days gone by' (trans. Postgate 1921, 247).

23 Murgatroyd (1980, 290) observes that the family is a pillar of rural life, which here appears in contrast to the existence of the inhabitants of the netherworld described in vv. 35–38.

24 'Full of drink, he will fire the light straw heaps in the appointed way, and leap across the sacred flames. Then shall his dame bear offspring, and the child take hold of his father's ears to snatch the kiss; nor shall the grandsire find it irksome to watch by his Little grandson's side, nor, for all his years, to lisp in prattle with the child' (trans. Postgate 1921, 277).

25 'Ah, I could not show a more watchful care for my dear mother or have any thought for life without you. You alone are my home, Cynthia, you alone my parents, you are my every moment of happiness' (trans. Gold 1990, 79). We may note that Gold follows the textual variant *ah* for *an* as in Fedeli's edition (1980), from which the Latin text cited is taken. However, this does not materially change the interpretation of the poem.

26 'I love you then, not only as the common sort love a mistress, but as a father loves his sons and sons-in-law' (trans. Cornish 1921, 153). The Latin text is from the edition by Bardon (1973). According to Greene (1989, 64), Propertius goes further than the mere comparison drawn by his predecessor. See also Baker (2000, 122) and Coutelle (2005, 271). The sentiment also appears in Ovid (*Ep.* 3, 52). Fedeli (1980, 279) also observes that the poem recalls Catullus (68, 35–36), despite the difference in meaning.

27 Fedeli (1980, 280–281) and Coutelle (2005, 269) place these lines in the context of Propertius own life, as the poet lost his own father as a child according to elegy IV (1, 127–128), which may have meant that his mother came under his tutelage and care.

28 Green (1995, 315–316) highlights this ambivalent portrayal of Cynthia as both mistress and mother, dissolute and virtuous in a work with psychoanalytic overtones. Coutelle (2005, 271) also points up the paradox. According to Rambaux (2001, 50), the poet presents himself as reliant upon a mature, self-assured Cynthia, behaving upon her departure like a child who cannot bear the momentary absence of his parents.

29 'since you have no brother and no son, let me and no other be for you a brother and a son' (trans. Gold 1990, 179).

References

Baker, R. J. (2000) *Propertius I. With an Introduction, Translation and Commentary*. Oxford, Aris & Philips.

Bardon, H. (1973) *Catullus. Carmina.* Stuttgart, Teubner.

Booth, J. (1991) *Ovid. Amores II, ed. with Translation and Commentary.* Warminster, Aris & Philips.
Camps, W. A. (1966) *Propertius. Elegies Book I* (2nd edition). Cambridge, Cambridge University Press.
Cano Alonso, P. L. (1988) Sobre los personajes de Propercio. *Faventia* 20(2), 101–108.
Cantarella, E. (1991) *La calamidad ambigua. Condición e imagen de la mujer en la antigüedad griega y romana.* Madrid, Ediciones Clásicas.
Cornish, F. W., Postgate, J. P. and Mackail, J. W. (1921) (trans) *Catullus, Tibullus, Pervigilium Veneris* (reprint of 1913 edition). (Loeb Classical Library 6). London, William Heinaman/New York, G. P. Putnam's sons.
Coutelle, E. (2005) *Poétique et métapoesie chez Properce. De l'Ars amandi à l' Ars scribendi.* Leuven/Paris/Dudley MA, Peeters.
Dyson, S. L. (2003) *The Roman Countryside.* London, Duckworth.
Dyson, S. L. (2011) The family and the Roman countryside. In B. Rawson (ed.) *A Companion to the Families in the Greek and Roman Worlds.* Malden/Oxford/Chichester, Willey-Blackwell, 431–444.
Fantham, E. (2006) The image of woman in Propertius' poetry. In H.-C. Günther (ed.) *Brill's Companion to Propertius.* Leiden/Boston, Brill, 183–197.
Fedeli, P. (1980) *Properzio: Il primo libro delle Elegie.* Firenze, Leo S. Olschi editore.
Fedeli, P. (1985) *Properzio: Il libro terzo delle Elegie.* Bari, Adriatica.
Fedeli, P. (2005) *Properzio. Elegie libro II, Introduzione, testo e commento.* Cambridge, Francis Cairns.
Gaisser, J. (1971) Structure and tone in Tibullus 2.6. *American Journal of Philology* 92(2), 202–216.
Goold, G. P. (1990) (trans.) *Propertius. Elegies.* (Loeb Classical Library). Cambridge MA/London, Harvard University Press.
Greene, E. (1995) Elegiac woman: Fantasy, materia and male desire in Propertius I 3 and I 11. *American Journal of Philology* 116 (2), 303–318.
Greene, E. (1998) *The Erotics of Domination. Male Desire and the Mistress in Latin Love Poetry.* Baltimore/London, John Hopkins University Press.
Grimal, P. (1963) *L' amour à Rome.* París, Hachette.
James, S. L. (2003) *Learned Girls and Persuasión. Gender and Reading in Roman Love Elegy.* Berkeley/Los Angeles/London, University of California Press.
James, S. L. (2012) Elegy and New Comedy. In B. K. Gold (ed.) *A Companion to Roman Love Elegy.* Malden/Oxford/Chichester, Willey-Blackwell.
Keith, A. (2008) *Propertius. Poet of Love and Leisure.* London, Duckworth.
Labate, M. (1977) Tradizione elegiaca e società galante negli 'Amores. *Studi Classici e Orientali* 27, 283–339.
Laigneau, S. (1999) *La femme et l' amour chez Catulle et les élégiaques augustéennes.* Bruxelles, Latomus.
Lee-Stecum, P. (1998) *Powerplay in Tibullus.* Reading Elegies 1. Cambridge, Cambridge University Press.
McKeown, J. C. (1987) *Ovid: Amores. Text, Prolegomena and Commentary in Four Volumes, vol I. Text and Prolegomena.* Leeds, Francis Cairns.
McKeown, J. C. (1998). *Ovid: Amores. Text, Prolegomena and Commentary in Four Volumes, vol III. A Commentary on Book 2.* Leeds, Francis Cairns.
Murgatroyd, P. (2001) *Tibullus I. A Commentary on the First Book of the Elegies of Albius Tibullus* (reprint of 1980 edition). London, Bristol Classical Press.
Myers, K. S. (1986) The poet and the procuress: the *lena* in Latin Love elegy. *Journal of Roman Studies* 86, 1–21.
Newman, J. K. (1997) *Augustan Propertius. The Recapitulation of a Genre.* Hildesheim/Zürich/New York, Olms.
Posgate, I. P. (1915) *Tibulli aliorumque carminum libri tres.* Oxford, Clarendon.
Rambaux, C. J. (2001) *Properce ou les difficultés de l´ emancipation féminine.* Bruxelles, Latomus.
Scharrock, A. (2000) Constructing characters in Propertius. *Arethusa* 33, 263–284.
Showerman, G. (1914) *Ovid. Heroides and Amores.* (Loeb Classical Library). London, William Heineman/New York, MacMillan.
Wike, M. (1987) Written women: Propertius' *Scripta puella. Journal of Roman Studies* 77, 47–61.
Wike, M. (1989) Mistress and metaphor in Augustan elegy. *Helios* 16, 25–47.

Chapter 18

Childhood and maintenance. Legal norms related to education and guardianship of minors, from Antoninus Pius to Justinian

María Isabel Núñez Paz

Initial considerations. Food, *patria potestas* and *expositio infantes*

In this chapter, we will deal with the obligation that parents had in ancient Rome to provide food for their children. Only in a late period, from the emperors Antoninus Pius and Marcus Aurelius onwards, did conditions under which certain relatives had to give assistance to each other if necessary start to be regulated. At that time, as will be seen in the next section, an extraordinary procedural way appears, the *cognitio extra ordinem*, through which it is possible to claim this right judicially. Until Justinian there are consecutive reforms in the legal regime of the *obligatio alimentorum*. This study will deal only with the obligation that the father and mother had to provide food for their under-age children, precisely when they were in conditions of greater vulnerability.

In the Spanish Civil Code, the obligation of providing sustenance is included in the article 142:

> 'Se entiende por alimentos todo lo que es indispensable para el sustento, habitación, vestido y asistencia médica. Los alimentos comprenden también la educación e instrucción del alimentista, mientras sea menor de edad y aún después cuando no haya terminado su formación por causa que no le sea imputable. Entre los alimentos se incluirán los gastos de embarazo y parto en cuanto no estén cubiertos de otro modo.'[1]

In this article, which is reproduced with some variations in all European legislation, appear some of the fundamental characteristics of the maintenance obligation, which were already present in Roman law.[2] Precisely such characteristics were configured throughout the evolution of the Roman law. Among these is their very personal nature; therefore, in the first place we can refer to the maintenance obligation as a legal duty *intuitu personae*; secondly, obligations between relatives or other persons linked together by other types of relationships (such as affinity and adoption) are part of the *pietas* duty that links the closest to each other. Third, the duty of maintenance is not only limited to maintenance or clothing, but also includes custody, care and education. Fourth, it is necessary to adjust the needs of those who need maintenance (maintenance debtor) to the economic capacity of the one who is by law obliged to supply it (maintenance creditor). In this sense, the amount of the benefit must have certain proportionality with the availability of financial means of the person obliged to provide maintenance, so that he can also meet his own needs and those of other members of his family. Fifth and last, among the maintenance obligations are included the disbursements made due to pregnancy and birth, linking in this sense with the emblematic Roman figure of the *curator ventris*, the male caregiver or guardian of the female womb. Later I will return to this question when referring to the importance that, by influence of the praetor and the jurisprudence, is progressively acquiring *cognaticio* kinship (by female line) in Roman law.

The ultimate basis for obliging parents to provide their offspring with maintenance is found in a *ius naturale* that ordered humans and animals alike to take care of their own offspring and feed them:

> *Ius naturale est quod natura omnia animalia docuit. Nam ius istud non humani generis proprium, sed ómnium animalium, quae in terra, quae in mari nascuntur, avium quoque commune est, hinc descendit maris atque feminae coniunctio, quam nos matrimonio appellamus, hic liberorum procreatio hinc educatio.* D.1,1, 3 (Ulp. *Inst.* lib 1)

Now, what is considered to be natural law in the imperial era (to which corresponds the text that we have just transcribed) is not considered natural at all in monarchical or republican times. We think it is essential to make a prior reference to the consideration that homeless newborns had in the early Roman days. For this, we must consider the peculiar content of parental authority that father had over those subjected to him by the link of the *agnatio*.

The first Roman laws (from the monarchical period) not only did not force the father to maintain or feed the offspring, but also contemplated with absolute naturalness the fact that newborns were abandoned. According to the *ius vitae et necis* (right of life and death) that the *paterfamilias* had over the members of his family, he freely decided, without being subject to control of any kind, whether to accept the son or daughter as a new member of the family community or to reject them by 'exposing' them, that is, leaving them to their fate. It is well known that frequent use was given in Rome to the so-called *Columna Lactaria* ('milk column') in the *Holitorium forum*, where unwanted children were deposited waiting for someone to take them in and where traders and nurses formalised many breastfeeding contracts (Cid López 2016, 129–138: ns 37–41). The exercise of the *ius exponendi* meant, in many cases, not only the civil death but also the physical death of the newborns. Since they were deposited on the ground at the feet of the pater in a ritual ceremony, he could either lift them, take them in his arms (*tollere* or *suscipere liberos*) or leave them where they had been deposited, giving, with this gesture, the implicit order to abandon them. If the father decided not to accept newborn children, they were exposed in the forum and their legal capacity remained in the hands of chance, according to the legal status of the person who took it in. That is to say, the child could become a slave or have better luck and acquire the status *libertatis* or *civitatis*, if the one who welcomed them was in a position to transmit status.

The *ius vitae et necis* of the *paterfamilias* had different content depending on whether they were daughters or sons. In the case of girls, the acceptance ceremony was more complex. If the father decided to accept her into the family, he had to make the explicit gesture of clearly ordering her to be fed (*alere iubere*). Otherwise, she was considered an *exposita* or to have been abandoned.

According to Dionysius of Halicarnassus, the first limitation to the *expositio infantes* was established when a *lex regia* imposed a patrimonial sanction on those who abandoned a male child or a firstborn daughter (the *expositio* or abandonment of the younger daughters was not sanctioned). Probably for demographic reasons it became necessary to curb the massive abandonment of newborns, establishing a penalty for those who abandoned their firstborn children. Out of this limitation, the offspring could be abandoned with impunity. It was one of the *pater*'s prerogatives: one more of the rights that constituted his parental authority and that gave him absolute freedom to provoke abortions in the women subjected to him, to abandon the newborns to their fate or to apply the death penalty to members of his family. In a volume dedicated to motherhood, it does not seem superfluous to highlight the absolute contempt for the will of the mother, whether this woman was *liberta*, *ingenua* or even a Roman citizen already in the republican era. A pregnant Roman woman (*filia familias* or *uxor*) could deeply desire to be a mother, but if the *pater* decided that it was not convenient to accept a new member, he could force her to abort without any legal repercussion until the imperial age. Something similar happened with the newborns that were born with serious deformities (*monstrua, prodigia, portenta*), including hermaphrodites. This happened with a certain *Frosinon*, whose uncertain sex was considered a proof of divine wrath (*foedum ac turpem prodigium*). The father who abandoned one of those monstrous children to his fate was not, in accordance with Romulus legislation, exposed to the penalties provided for the abandonment of newborns.[3]

> *cito (necatus) tamquam ex XII Tabulis insignis ad deformitatem puer* (Tab IV 1: Cicero, *De Legibus* 3, 8,19)

The only requirement needed of the father to proceed with the abandonment of the creature was the summoning of five neighbours to testify that the newborn was deformed (monstrous). The practice of abandoning was maintained with few variations until the Justinian era.[4]

To understand Roman parent–child relationships, we must start from the existence of a legitimate marriage. This happens in all periods of Roman law. Although the fundamental changes and the replacement of the *adgnatio* by *cognatio* (that is to say, of the bonds of submission to the *pater* through the biological links or through the maternal line) will not occur until the imperial age, when female kinship begins to be relevant and the obligation to feed the children becomes procedurally enforceable. The concept of an original family is based on patrimonial reasons. The motives of economic convenience that led to a marriage *cum manu*, an *adoptio* or an *adrogatio* could discourage the accceptance of a new mouth to feed in the family, even if it was a biological son of the *pater*. It could be more productive in economic terms to abandon it or to give it away for a price (*venum duit*) to a third party. It should not be surprising, therefore, that the same Law that neglected the abandoned offspring, however, prescribed the need to feed the debtors. This is how it is read in the law of the Twelve Tables, where in the regulation of the *manus iniectio* it is prescribed that the debtor, who does not comply with the sentence, can be taken prisoner by the creditor and this in turn should provide them with food:

> *Post deinde manus iniectio esto, in ius ducito. Ni iudicatum facit aut quis endo eo in iure vindicit, secum deducito, vincito aut Nervo aut compedibus XV pondo, ne minore, aut si volet maiore vincito. Si volet suo vivito. Ni suo vivit, qui eum vinctum habebit, libras farris endo dies dato, si volet plus dato* (L. Twelve Tables III, 1 6: Aulus Gellius, 20, 1, 45–47)

The law of the Twelve Tables also meticulously determined both the weight that the debtor's chains should have and the exact amount of cereal (emmer wheat) with which the creditor had to sustain him in case the prisoner did not want or could not be fed on his own.[5]

Another previous consideration that seems necessary before proceeding to the examination of the legal sources of the obligation of maintenance is that, when we refer to Roman law, we usually cover a wide temporal arc that includes since the beginning of the Monarchy in the 8th century BC, until the death of Justinian in the 6th century AD. It is therefore logical that the changes that take place in many aspects of the legislation (such as the right to be recognised as *filius legitimus* and the right to food) are of great magnitude. At the time of Constantinus, the obligation to provide food to minors not only had civil effects, but criminal sanctions were established both for the presumption of *expositio infantes* and for other types of failure to provide maintenance.

> *Imp. Constantinus a. ad Ablavium pf. p. Quicumque puerum vel puellam proiectam de domo, patris vel domini voluntate scientiaque, collegerit ac suis alimentis ad robur provexerit, eundem retineat sub eodem statu, quem apud se collectum voluerit agitare, hoc est sive filium sive servum eum esse maluerit: omni repetitionis inquietudine penitus summovenda eorum, qui servos aut liberos scientes propria voluntate domo recens natos abiecerint. Dat. xv. kal. mai. Constantinopoli, Basso et Ablavio coss* (CTh.5.9.1 [=Brev.5.7.1])

Later the emperors Honorius and Theodosius go a step further to establish that the *pater* who abandons or proceeds to the *expositio* of a child will never be able to recover them

> *nullum dominis vel patronis repetendi aditum relinquimus si expositus quedammodo ad mortem voluntas misericordiae smica collegerit, nec enim dicere suum poterit, quem pereuntemcontempsit; si modo testis episcopalis subscriptio fuerit subsecuta, de qua nulla penitus ad securutatem possit ese cunctatio ... Impp. Honorius et Theodosius aa. Melitio pf. p. Nullum dominis vel patronis repetendi aditum relinquimus, si expositos quodammodo ad mortem voluntas misericordiae amica collegerit (nec enim dicere suum poterit, quem pereuntem contempsitit); si modo testes episcopalis subscriptio fuerit subsecuta, de qua nulla penitus ad securitatem possit esse cunctatio. Dat. xiv. kal. april. Ravenna, Honorius ix. et Theodosius v. aa. coss.* (CTh.5.9.2 [=Brev.5.7.2])

One of the most significant texts is attributed to Paulus in the Digest: 'It is not only those who deliberately suffocate the newborn provoke its death, but also whoever denies food or even who exposes it to the houses of mercy of a mercy that he does not have':

> *Necare videtur non tantum is qui partum praefocat, sed et is qui abiit (et qui alimonia denegat et is quis publicis locis misericordiae causa exponit, quam ipse non habet.* (D. 25, 3, 4, 1 (Paul. Sent. I, 24))

The *pietas* and the *charitas*, already present in texts by Cicero and Seneca, are gradually incorporated into the *humanitas* as protection of the weakest or most vulnerable, until it becomes a true principle that inspires the Law (Pugliese 1984, 31–76; Palma 1992, 19–47, 179–196; Garofalo 2005, 4). The first institutions dedicated to the care of orphaned children appear from Nerva and Trajan onwards. Later in the Christian era, the *humanitas* is progressively impregnated with Christian connotations such as mercy.[6] The emperors Valentinian Valens and Gratian already clearly estimate that the *expositio infantes* constitutes a serious crime and, as such, deserves to be punished with the maximum penalty. The death penalty is prescribed for the parent who abandons the newborn to his or her fate, with no difference in sex between daughters and sons.

> *Si quis necandi infantis piaculum adgressuss adgressare sit sciat se capitali supplicio esse punniendu.* (C. 9,16, 8: a. 374)

Definitively Justinian in the Novel 153 of the year 541 considers that whoever commits this crime has absolutely no *humanitas* and deserves the death penalty: *erit capitali istud malum.*

While it is true that Christianity contributed to definitively configure the content of parental authority as a tuition or guardian institution, removed from its original configuration as a mechanism of power over the subject, it is also observed that, until the end, traces of the old force of the *patria potestas* survive. The abandonment of the offspring is considered an act of mercy in cases of families in extreme poverty *propter nimiam paupertatem egestatemque*. The idea is consolidated in the times of the very Christian Emperor Justinian when it is considered an act of mercy the abandonment of sons and daughters or their surrender to a third party for a price (*venditio ne in hoc tantummodo casu valente*) when the family is so poor that they can not feed them.[7]

Kinship by maternal line. *Cognatio* (consanguinity) and *extra ordinem* procedural exigibility of food

The members of a family can only demand mutual assistance (food) from each other when the kinship by maternal line begins to be relevant to the Law. The first praetor and the *Tertullianus* senate consulted by Hadrian and *Orfitianus* (AD 178) represent an important step forward for mothers and their children to have inheritance rights among themselves.[8] But with regards to food, the change did not take place until the legislation of the Antonine emperors. The legal texts are explicit: If *paternal pietas* (family affection) is not enough for parents to provide food to their children, go to the coercive force of law. The consuls, in a summary procedure and by extraordinary means (*cognitio extra ordinem*), respond to the request for maintenance. It is also prescribed the duty of children to provide relief to their father and mother.

Gradually the obligation extends to other members of the blood or cognative family: *Item divus Pius significat, quasi avus quoque maternus alere compellatur* (Lanfranchi 1953, 45; Zoz 1970, 323 ff.; De Francesco 2001, 60; Alburquerque 2006, 13–15; 2007, 9–30; Sandirocco 2013, 1–24, see ns 3–4)

> *Si patrem tuum officio debito promerueris, paternam pietatem tibi non denegabit. Quod si sponte non fecerit, aditus competens iudex alimenta pro modo facultatium praestari tibi iubebit.* C. 5. 25. 4 (Imp. Severus and Antoninus a. 197)
>
> *Parentum necessitatibus liberos succurrere iustum est.* C. 5,25,1 (Imp. Antoninus Pius, *sine die et consule*)

As we saw above, the principle of *humanitas* was changing the Law. The figure of the mother becames stronger at the same time that the *patria potestas* was weakened as an absolute power. The road had been very long and the obligation of relatives to provide food to each other was ethical long before it was legal. The etymology of the term foods (*alimentum*) is very significant in this sense. It is important to remember that *alo* ('to feed') has the same root that *allevo* ('to raise'), and in the initiatory rite of admission into the family *communi iure*, the creature was deposited on the ground and the father made the gesture of taking him/her in his arms, recognised them as his own and accepted them into his family, from which his obligation to feed them was inferred. The term *alumnandus* designated the boy or girl that was given to be nursed or fed. On the other hand, Cicero already referred to a moral *lex alimentaria* and later Seneca mentions the content of the paternal and maternal *auctoritas*; this includes the moral duties of the children of obedience towards their parents and the restitution of the benefits provided by the parent, father or mother.[9]

There comes a time when *alere* becomes an enforceable legal right. There is the possibility to sue the courts for the maintenance obligation thanks to the *interpretatio* that the jurists make of the imperial constitutions.

> *Denique idem Pius ita rescripsit: 'aditi a te competentes iudices ali te a patre tuo iubebunt pro modo facultatium eius, si modo, cum opificem te esse dicas, in ea valetudine es, ut operis sufficere non possis'* D. 25,3,5, 5–7 (Ulpianus, book II *de officio consulis*):

> *Si vel parens neget filium idcircoque alere se non debere contendat, vel filius neget parentem, summatim iudices oportet super ea re cognoscere. Si constiterit filium vel parentemesse, tunc ali iubebunt: ceterum si non constiterit, nec decernent alimenta.* (D. 25. 3. 5. 8, Ulp. 2 (*de off. Cons.*))

The two texts of the Digest transcribed here refer to the *senatus consultum, de liberis agnoscendis*. The jurists treat in a unitary way the recognition of the descendants as their own and the obligation to maintain them and provide them with everything necessary for their subsistence.[10]

Prior to determining what and how much to pay for food, they had to make sure that the children really belong to the person from whom food was being claimed. Even though the mother is clear, the father is not so much. It is therefore a question of a preliminary ruling, of a *praeiudicium* to which a large part of the Senate is dedicated: *Quod si patrem negabit, quaestionem istam in primis idem iudex examenbit*. The legal problem posed by the recognition of children as their own always worried the Romans. Those who were born out of a legitimate marriage lacked inheritance and food rights with respect to their father. However, in this new era it was no longer the father arbitrarily who decided whether to accept a child as his own, but in the case of having celebrated an *iustum matrimonium*, it was presumed that the child was the husband's: *pater est quem nuptias demostrant*.[11]

The father 'maintenance debtor': *pater est quem nuptias demostrant.* The father is he who is married to the mother

From a proven fact such as marriage, another fact can be deduced as being very probable: the legitimacy of the offspring conceived or born inside it. In this sense, the son or daughter is legitimated to file an action of filiation against the father, as well as to judicially demand the provision of food from him.

The issue of legitimate fatherhood and female fidelity was the subject of intense legal discussions in Rome along its history. While male adultery went unpunished, that of the wife was always punished with very serious penalties. Widows were forbidden to remarry until a reasonable time had elapsed to prevent the possibility that a pregnancy from another man could provoke the *turbatio sanguinis*; the so-called *tempus lugendi* (an approximate year of compulsory mourning) was intended to dispel doubts about the legitimacy of any offspring. Arduous discussions between doctors and moralists ended up establishing a period ranging from 7 months from the beginning of the marriage, to 10 months after its termination, death or divorce. If birth occurred during this time, paternity was attributed to the husband or ex-husband, although evidence of the contrary was admitted, both by the father and by the mother. According to the jurist *Iulianus*, paternity cannot be attributed if it is shown that the father ahs been absent for years or suffers from physical illness or limitation that makes him unable to procreate.[12]

The *senatus consultum de liberis de agnoscendis* deserved a complete rubric in the edict from *praetor urbanus* and a complete title in the *Digest* of Justinian.[13] Its breadth shows that issues of paternity were recurrent before the administration of justice; it was necessary to determine whether the children of the married, widowed or divorced mother were also the children of her husband or ex-husband. From the moment the boy or girl was 3 years old, they had the right to action against the father for any food that was due to them. The attribution of paternity and the correlative obligation of maintenance was resolved equally in the case of male and female children: *filiam suam pater exhibeat, si constiterit apud iudicium iuste eam procreatam.*[14]

In title 25.3 of the *Digest*, to which we have been referring, the previous legislation on the matter is incorporated; specifically, it mentions a *senatus consultum plancianum* (probably from Vespasian times) about the legitimacy of the children; this was complemented with another one by Hadrian. In the first one, doubts about paternity arise at the end of the marriage; in the second, doubts about the paternity of the son who is in gestation appear already during the marriage (*constante matrimonio*) (Zoz 1970, 323–355; Tafaro 1990, 1278–1302):

> *Quia Plancianum senatus consultum ad eos partus pertinet quipost divortium eduntur, aliud senatus consultum temporibus divi Hadriani factum est, ut, etiamsi constante matrimonio partus sit editus, de agnoscendo eo agatur.* (D. 25,3, 3, 3, 1 (Ulp. 34 ad ed.))

In the complex casuistry presented by Ulpianus, mothers appear claiming that their partners or former partners recognise their children and provide them with maintenance; there are also men who claim not to be the biological parents and oppose the *ius alimentorum*. If the father who denies paternity does not meet all the requirements of the law (make the necessary inquiries, require the pregnant woman to say if she was pregnant or not, ask for expert evidence, and finally formally notify her that there was no pregnancy), then he can be forced to recognise his paternity through the extraordinary procedure (*cognitio extra ordinem*). Moreover, in this case if the woman denounces him as the father of her children, the fact of marriage works as proof and it is he – the presumed father – who has to prove the opposite, that is, that the child is not his. The burden of proof was therefore reversed, since if the husband or ex-husband could not prove it, it was formally recognised by a judicial decision as a father and as a maintenance debtor.

Other men, on the other hand, are very interested in having offspring and recognising their children as their own. Especially interesting is the case of Rutilius, a man who, after divorcing Domitia, suspects that she tries to hide from him that she is pregnant and the issue reaches the court. The problem arises due to the unusual fact that the woman continues to deny her status of *praegnans*, a situation for which there was no legal response, nor any interpretation of the *senatus consultum plancianum,* nor any norm in force until then. For this reason, the praetor Valerius Priscianus consults the emperors to solve the question. These, Marcus Aurelius and Lucius Verus (161–169 D.C.) pronounce a rescript on the matter, subjecting Domitia to vigilance; she is given a 'guardian of the womb' (*custos ventris*) and complex obstetric inspections are prescribed for her.[15]

In another case, there is a mother, Ticiana, who goes to the *Divi Fratres* Marcus Aurelius and Lucius Verus, to claim food from Claudius, the father of her daughter. The answer of these is restrictive. If the woman is able to prove to the judge that the son is Claudius's, then he has to feed him.[16]

A progressive extension of the concept is observed, in the sense that food is not only understood as food, clothing or medical assistance but 'everything that is necessary for the descendants'; that is, attention is shown for the psychophysical health of the offspring, with instruction and education occupying a preferential place.[17]

In the interpretation of the *senatus consultum* is also frequently that cases are solved in order of the appeal to the *humanitas*: minors must be fed, without prejudging whether or not they are somebody's children child; therefore, the duty to provide maintenance appears unconnected to the *patria potestas*:

> *Sed utrum eos tantum liberos qui sunt in potestate cogatur quis exhibere, an vero etiam emancipatos vel ex alia causa sui iuris constitutos, videndum est. Et magis puto, etiamsi non sunt liberi in potestate, alendos a parentibus et vice mutua alere parentes debere.* (D. 25. 3. 5. 1 (Ulp. 2 *de off. cons.*))

We could conclude that, in the long title of the *Digest* that we are commenting on, three aspects are decisive: first, the link between the recognition of children and the legal obligation to provide them with food; secondly, the concept of food is progressively broadened, which not only includes basic needs such as food, hygiene or housing, but education and spiritual care of the offspring; thirdly, the ultimate reason for the *ius alimentorum* is not linked to the *patria potestas*, but to the *humanitas*, the *naturalis ratio*, the *pietas* or the charitas implied in the maternal consanguinity.

A constitution by Diocletian from AD 294 confirms the previous provisions, in the sense that the father can never stop recognising his own children or refuse to provide for them.

> *Nec filium negare cuiquam esse liberum Senatus Consulta de partu agnoscendo ac denuntiata poena, item praeiudicium edicto perpetuo propositum et remedium alimentorum apud praesidem maiori trimo petenti monstratum iure manifesto declarant* (C. 8.46. (47) 9; AD 294–305).

The mother 'maintenance debtor': *mater semper certa est, etiam si vulgo conceperit*[18]

We have seen how, in the sphere of the family, the legal obligation of maintenance starts from the fertilisation of the wife united to her husband in *iustum matrimonium*. Based on the principle that has been called 'pure semen', the original legal bond is established between the male and his progeny (descendants in *iustae nuptiae*). If, as mentioned above, at first the mother was not considered a relative of her children, now, however, the relevance given to female or consanguineal kinship means that the unborn children of legitimate marriage (whether they are *spurii*, that is, born of a stable relationship – concubinage – or *vulgar concepti* – born of a sporadic relationship) also have the right to be always fed by the mother.[19] Likewise, we have referred earlier to the progressive extension of the concept of food ... *non solum alimenta praestari debent*. When the concept of food begins to include the psychophysical well-being of the child, the mother can be considered an educator, with preference over the father. This is clearly shown in the title II of book 27 of the *Digest*: *Ubi pupillus educari vel morari debeat et de alimentis ei ei praestandis.*

The discretion of the judge is absolute and he should only attend to what is most convenient for the child by ensuring that the son or daughter is 'always fed and educated free from malicious suspicions.' Therefore, it is sometimes prescribed that the child receives food from one of the parents, but lives with another or even with a third person if neither of the parents behaves in an appropriate way.[20]

From the end of the 3rd century AD it is clearly stated that the father is not always the best *alimentarius*. With good judgment, Fasolinus considers that for the first time in Diocletian's time the so-called 'best interest of the child' is configured. Attending to what is most convenient for the child, the distribution of the children is decided by sex (girls are guarded by the mother and boys by the father), good manners (*pudicitia*) and even the better economic conditions of the father or mother. The mother is preferred over the father whenever she is 'a woman of recognised authority.' The traditional republican model of the exemplary mother, transmitter of moral values and rules of behavior towards the gods, the ancestors and the society is maintained in this sense.[21]

> *Si disceptetur, ubi morari vel ubi educari pupillum oporteat, causa cognita id praesidem statuerit oportebit, in causa e cognitione evitandi sunt quae pudicitiae impubere possunt indisiari.* (D.27.2,5 (Ulp. 3 *de officio proconsulis*))

In the age of Justinian the content of the so-called 'best interest of the child' changes. This is configured according to the trend of the new morality, contrary to divorce and the mother's second marriage; the pragmatic criterion of the greatest patrimony also appears. That is, instead of taking into account which one of the parents can better educate the child, they opt for the 'richest.'[22]

In any case, the *ratio legis* of the Christian emperors remains that the mother is always and in any case the maintenance debtor of her offspring, both marital and extramarital ones. The children *vulgo concepti*, of an unmarried mother, must be fed by her. The statement that appears in the Sentences of Paulus (4, 9, 5): *Septimo mense natus matri prodest* ('the mother has benefits when the child is born after the 7th month') does not mean any benefit anymore. The only thing it shows is the operation of the presumption of paternity and that the mother can file a claim *extra ordinem* for the maintenance of her children against the father. Now, if the father does not comply, the obligation corresponds to the mother ('always certain'). The titles of the *Codex Theodosianus* are explicit in this sense: *De naturalibus filiis et matribus eorum*, as well as of its successor the *Codex Justinianeus*: *De naturalis liberis et matribus eorum ex quibus casibus iusti efficiuntur*.[23]

In the Post-classic and Justinian texts timid statements appear in the sense that the father not only owes maintenance to those born inside a legitimate marriage; from what seems to be inferred *sensu contrario* that they also the extramarital children are entitle to it. The fundamental change that occurs from Emperor Constantinus onwards is the tendency for parents united in a stable relationship or concubinage to regulate their situation by contracting a Christian marriage. In the legislation of the Christian emperors, the new marriage, not anymore based on continuous but initial consent, is linked to a progressive tendency towards the restriction of divorce, which breaks abruptly with the consolidated idea of free and by mutual consent divorce. The concubinage begins to have a pejorative consideration and the tendency is that those who live in sin are united in marriage. Only in this way, children born out of wedlock also receive maintenance *per subsequens matrimonium* of their parents. It should be noted in this regard that in Rome the spouses were never able to claim maintenance from each other through a court action; this would only be possible later, in common law.[24]

> *Ac primum quidem quisquisex complexibus (nequem enim nuptias vocabimus nefariis vel incestis vel damnatis procreator est, ist neque naturalis vocabiturneque a patribus aletor neque cum praesenti lege quicquam communi habebit.* (Novela 89, 15. (AD 539))[25]

Justinian's opinion is determinant in the sense that those born from a relationship of concubinage can receive maintenance from the father, as long as he marries the mother; but those born of 'loathsome incestuous or condemned' unions have no right to be maintained; that is, children born from unstable relationships. Discrimination against extramarital children is still evident in Justinian's time and goes *in crescendo* in the Civil Law.

Acknowledgements

This publication belongs to the I+D+I Research Project, funded by the Ministry of Economy and Competitiveness, entitled 'Motherhood and families: continuity, changes, and breakdowns in history. Between ancient and contemporary societies' (HAR 2013–42371-R).

Notes

1 'Food is understood as all that is essential for sustenance, housing, clothing and medical assistance. Food also includes the education and instruction of the maintenance creditor, as long as he/she is a minor and even later when he/she has not completed his/her training without being responsible. Expenses for pregnancy and childbirth will be included in the food as long as they are not covered otherwise' (Author´s translation).

2 The right to food is found throughout European law; in this sense, see also article 9.7 of the Spanish Civil Code; with regards to European regulation Council Regulation (EC) No 4/2009 of

18 December 2008, on jurisdiction, applicable law, recognition and enforcement of decisions and cooperation in matters relating to maintenance obligations; in American regulations, see the Inter-American Convention on Food Obligations of 15 July 1989 of Montevideo (Uruguay), which regulates the law applicable to food obligations, competence and international procedural cooperation.

3 Dion. Hal. *Ant Rom.* 2, 15, 2; Plut. *Rom* 22,3; Plinius the Young: Plin *epist.* 3,12 2; Núñez (2015, 982–993).

4 D. 1, 5, 14 (Paulus) D.50 16, 135 (Ulpianus) *Cod Iust* 6, 29,3 (AD 530). Rather than an exercise of paternal brutality, it is necessary to think about rites to which the *prodigia* were subdued (Wacke 1990, 678–711; Cantarella 1996, 271–272, 288).

5 Gayo, *Inst* 4, 21–25; Sandirocco (2013, 5).

6 Although the strength of parental authority is always observed by Gaius: *Inst* 1, 55 ... *quos is proprium civium romanorum est; fere enim nulli alii sunt homines qui talem in filios suos habent postestatem, qualem nos habemus,* it is the judge who determines the conditions in which parents and children or other relatives should be fed, highlighting that, although the children are not already under parental authority, they must also be fed by the parents D. 25, 3, 5, 1 (Ulp. *de off. const.* II).

7 C.th 5, 9,1; C. 4, 43, 2 (a. 329); Biondi (1954, 193–195, 290–297; Churruca 1999, 9–22). The constitutions of Constantinus on the non-provision of food to sons and daughters are used as a legislative model by Liuvigild (L. V 4,4,1 Cth. 5 10 1 (LRW 4 10 1). In Christian and Visigothic legislation the sale of children is considered a lesser evil in front of the expositio and this one less evil in the face of infanticide and abortion (d'Ors 1969, 133–151); on nutritional crime and its historical projection (Morán 2002, 451–452).

8 It was relevant the blood kinship in the *plebeian* families, unlike what happened in the primitive *patricia* family *proprio iure* or *communi iure* regulated by the *ius Quiritarium*, based on the *mores maiorum*; D 38, 17 (Ulp. 13 *ad Sab.*).

9 Cic., *De rep.* 7,8; *De off* 1, 18,59; *Ad Att.* 1,5–77; Snn. *Controversiae* 1,1, *casus VII*; regarding the nutritional meaning of *victus* D. 4, 43, 2 (Wycisk 1972, 217; Sandirocco 2013, n. 24).

10 The full title is: *De agnoscendis et alendis liberis vel parentibus vel patronis vel libertis*: Together with the reciprocal obligation of food between ascendants and descendants, the reciprocal obligation between freedmen and employers is also discussed, probably dating back to the beginnings of the the Principate of Augustus, where the *Lex Aelia Sentia* (AD 4) expressly states the employer's duty to feed the freedman (Zoz 1970, 324–325; 330 ff.; Gell. *Noct. Att.* 5, 13, 2.; about its consideration as *officium*, Cremades 1988, 101).

11 *Qui mater quidem certa patrem autem incerto nati sunt, spuri appellantur* (Ulp. Reg.4, 2); D.2,4,5 (Paul. *ad ed.*4); D 22, 3 2 (*Paul ad ed.* 69); Gai *Inst.* 1, 56; 1.64), with special relevance in inheritance law since those born after ten months had no right to the legitimate inheritance D. 38,16,3,11 (Ulp.10 Sab.); the presumption that has passed to modern codifications, for example, in Spanish law presumed to be children of the husband those born after the celebration of marriage and before the 300 days following its dissolution or the legal or de facto separation of the spouses; vine. Articles 116 and 117 of the Spanish Civil Code.

12 Gell., *Noct. Att.*3, 16 (12–13); Gayo, 1, 56; Paulo, *Sent.* 4, 9, 5; infra nota 17 (D 25, 3, 14 (Ulp. *ad ed.* 34); *Partus maturior videatu ... Qui centessimuo octogessimo secundo die natus est Hippocrates scripset et divus Pius pontificibus scripsit iusto tempore videri natum;* D.1, 5, 12 (Paul 19 *Resp.*); according to the opinion of the emperor Hadrian, until ten or eleven months the son is considered the husband's); D.1, 6,6 (Ulp.9 *ad Sab.*)

13 Lenel 1927–2000, 117: *De liberis et de uentre*; *De agnoscendis liberis*; D. 25, 3.

14 D. 25. 3. 3. 1. pr., Ulp. 34 *ad ed.*

15 On Domitia, the *curator ventris* and the allocation of food by the praetor to the pregnant mother (pregnant, divorced or widowed) were destined directly to the *nasciturus* (Núñez 201, 432–435).

16 C. 5. 25. 3, *Divi fratres: Si competenti iudici eum, quem te ex Claudio enixam esse dicis, filium eius ese probaveris, alimenta ei pro modo facultatum praestari iubebit. Idem, an apud eum educari debeat, aestimabit,* A. Pius (a 162).
17 Vid. infra note 23.
18 *Digestum* 2,4,5 (Paul. 4 *ad ed.*)
19 D. 50, 16, 195,1; D.50, 16,195,6 (Ulp. 46 *ad ed*); D. 25, 3, 5–7; the progressive recognition of the mother figure makes a huge difference with the treatment that in Greece was given to non-marital children *nothoi* compared to the legitimate ones or *gnesioi* (Gardner 1987, 114–208; Patterson 1990, 40 ff.; Pomata 1996, 43–64).
20 C 5,49 1 (a 223), D. 43, 30,1,3 (Ulp 71 ad ed.); 3, 5 (h.t.); Fasolino (2013, 244, 236–249) highlights the analogy with guardianship as a way to fill gaps in legislation in this regard (Masarotto 1977, 354–365; Sandirocco 2013, ns 22–23).
21 D. 37, 10, 6,5; C. 5, 24, 1 (a. 294); in any case, the demands on the woman-mother are always greater, as is the case when she is allowed to exercise the guardianship (Centola 2013, 187; Núñez 2015, 364).
22 C. 6, 61, 8 (AD 531). Nov 117,7; Nov 12,4.
23 C. *th.* 4, 6, 0; C.5, 27,0; Reg. Ulp.4,2; D. 1,5, 19 (Celsus, 91 *dig.*).
24 It is also possible the legitimisation *per oblationem curia y per rescritum principis*; D 27, 2, 1, 1 (Ulp 34 *ed.*); C. 5, 27; *Inst.* Iust 10,3; Nov. 74,3; Nov.89,7; Nov 117,10; regarding the new Christian marriage and the concubinage (Núñez 1988, 40–59; 65 ff.).
25 It is difficult to know if they are genuine texts, or if the compilers introduced changes in the previous texts (Albertario 1933, 249 ff.; Biondi 1954, 189–200, 290–297; Sacoccio, 2014, 1–40).

References

Albertario, E. (1933) Sul diritto agli alimenti. In *Studi di diritto Romano.1. Persone e familia.* Milano, Giuffrè.

Alburquerque Sacristán, J. M. (2006) Notas, conjeturas e indicios previos a la regulación de Antonino Pio y Marco Aurelio acerca de la prestación de alimentos en Derecho romano, *Anuario da Facultade de Dereito da Universidade da Coruña* 10, 9–32.

Alburquerque Sacristán, J. M. (2007) Aspectos de la prestación de alimentosen el derecho romano: especial referencia a la reciprocidad entre padre e hijo, ascendientes y descendientes. *Revista jurídica Universidad Autónoma de Madrid* 15, 9–30.

Biondi, B. (1954) *Il Diritto romano cristiano.* Milano, Giuffre.

Bradley, K. (1991) Remarriage and the structure of the upper class in the Roman family. In B. Rawson (ed.) *Marriage, Divorce and Children in Ancient Rome.* Oxford, Clarendon Press, 79–98.

Cantarella, E. (1991) *I supplizi capitali in Grecia e a Roma. Origini e funzioni della pena di norte nell.antichità classica.* Milano, Feltrinelli.

Cao, I. (2010) *Alimenta. Il racconto delle fonti.* Padova, Il Poligrafo.

Centola, A. (2013) Alcune osservazioni sull'origine del diritto agli alimenti, *Teoria e Storia del diritto privato* VI, 1–39.

Cid López, R. M. (2016) Madres sustitutas y oficios femeninos. Nodrizas y niñeras en la Roma antigua. In M. Picazo and A. Delgado (eds) *Los trabajos de las mujeres en el mundo antiguo. Cuidado y mantenimiento de la vida.* Tarragona, Institut català de Arqueologia clásica, 129–138.

Cremades Ugarte, J. (1988) El *officium* en el derecho privado romano. León, Servicio de Publicaciones de la Universidad de León.

Critini, N. (2010) La fortuna della tabula alimentaria di *Veleia. Ager Velias*, 1–10.

d'Ors, A. (1960–2014) *El código de Eurico, Edición, Palingenesia e Índice.* Estudios Visigóticos II. Roma/ Madrid, Boletín oficial del Estado (Leyes históricas de España).

De Francesco, A. (2001) Il diritto agli alimenti fra genitori e figli. Un'ipotesi ricostruttiva, *Labeo* 47, 29–63.
De Francesco, A. (2002) Giudizi alimentari e accertamento sulla filiazione. In *Diritto e giustizia nel Processo. Prospettive storiche, costituzionale e comparativistiche*. Napoli, Editoriale Scientifica, 93–141.
Fasolino, F. (2003) L'affidamento dei figli a Roma. In A. Palma (ed.) *Studi in onore di Francesco Guizzi*. Torino, Giappichelli Editore, 236–249.
Foxhall, L. (2013) *Studying Gender in Classical Antiquity*. Cambridge, Cambridge University Press.
Gardner, J. F. (1987) *Women in Roman Law and Society*. London, Routledge.
Garofalo, L. (2005) L'*humanitas* nel pensiero della giurisprudenza classica. In L' "*Humanitas" nel mondo antico: filantropia, cultura, "pietas". Convegno Nazionale di Studi, Treviso, 22 novembre 2003*. Treviso, Fondazione Cassamarca, 27–43.
Lanfranchi, F. (1954) *Ricerche sulle azioni di stato nella filiazione*. Modena, Publicazioni della Facoltà di Giurisprudenza della Università di Modena.
Lenel, O. (1889) *Palingenesia Iuris Civilis*. Aalen, Scientia Verlag
Lenel, O. (1927) (Reimp. Aulen 1985). *Das Edictum Perpetuum. Ein Versuch zu seiner Wiederherstellung*, Leipzigp, Bernhard Tauchnitz.
Massarotto, M. (1977) In merito ai decreti di Antonino Pio sull affidamento della prole alla madre. *Rivista dell'Istituto di diritto romano* 80, 354–365
Morán Martín, R. (2002) *Historia del Derecho Privado, Penal y Procesal*. Madrid, Coley
Núñez Paz, M. I. (1998) *Consentimiento matrimonial y divorcio en Roma*. Salamanca, Universidad de Salamanca.
Núñez Paz, M. I. (2015a) Review of V. Rodríguez Ortiz. 2014. El aborto hasta fines de la Edad Media castellana, Su consideración social y jurídica. Madrid, Aranzazu *Glosssae* 12, 982–993
Núñez Paz, M. I. (2015b) *Auctoritas* y mujeres romanas. ¿Ejercicio o sumisión?, *Arenal. Revista de Historia de las mujeres* 22 (2), 347–387.
Núñez Paz, M. I. (2017) Mujeres romanas, filiación y divorcio. Del deber de procrear al *favor liberorum*. In L. Suárez Llanos (ed.) *El derecho y la justicia*. Madrid, Tirant le Blanch, 419–442.
Patterson, C. B. (1990) Those Athenian bastards, *Classical Antiquity* 9, 40–73.
Pomata, G. (1996) Blod ties and semen ties, consanguinity and agnation. In M. J. Maynes, A. Waltner, B. Soland and U. Strasser (eds) *Gender Kinship and Power. A Comparative and Interdisciplinary History*. London/New York, Routledge, 43–64.
Pugliese, G. (1984) Assistenza all'infanzia nel principato e 'piae causae' del diritto romano cristiano. *Sodalitas Guarino* 7, 31–76.
Saccoccio, A. (2014) Dall'obbligo alla prestazione degli alimenti all' *obligatio ex lege* nella teoría delle fonti romane. *Roma e America. Diritto romano commune* 35, 35–40.
Sandirocco, L. (2013) Non solum alimenta praestari debent, *Rivista di diritto romano* XIII, 1–23
Tafaro, S. (2009) Diritti di fanciulli. In *Scritti in onore di G Melillo* III. Napoli, Sartura editrice, 1278–1302.
Wycisk, F. (1972) 'Alimenta' et 'victus' dans le droit roman classique, *Revue historique de droit francais ed étranger* 50 (2), 205–228
Zoz, M. G. (1970) In tema di obbligazioni alimentari, *Bullettino dell'Istituto di Diritto Romano ·Vittorio Scialoja* 12, 323–355
Zoz, M. G. (1999) Rapporti di patronato: la interpretazione giurisprudenziale in tema dee alimenti. In *Studi in onore di A. Metro* VI. Milano, Giuffrè, 539–554.

Chapter 19

The relationship of Iulia Mamaea and Alexander Severus, a young imperator. A review through literary sources

Pedro David Conesa Navarro

Introduction

Iulia Avitae Mamaea[1] was remembered for being the mother of Alexander Severus, last emperor of the Severan Dynasty. In turn, her fame comes given to belong to one of the most important dynasty of Roman empresses: those known as 'Syrian empresses' (Turton 1974, 2). If we play attention to written sources, they were able to exert a strong influence over the emperors. In a certain way, it was posible because, with the exception of Septimius Severus, in the Severan Dynasty there was no powerful male member who could stop the power of these empresses, as well as the political skills and ambitions that they had, which allowed them to participate in political matters of great importance (Cleve 1988, 196–197). Prejudices were formed during antiquity when there were women who were not only limited to the domestic sphere. From the origins of the history of Rome to the present, women have been subjected to the watchful eye of men. Women like Livia, Messalina or the famous Amazons, who had transgressed their domestic sphere, were criticised by classical authors. This is a view that has been maintained in Western culture, therefore we should not be surprised that the empresses such as those of the Severan Dynasty were described as unscrupulous people, capable of establishing alliances to ensure that their position within the court did not diminish (Martínez López 1991, 411–426; Cid López 2010, 687–693; Conesa Navarro 2015, 87–101; 2016, 206). According to María José Hidalgo de la Vega:

> 'Realmente la historia de estas princesas sirias, Julia Domna, su hermana Julia Maesa y las dos hijas de esta última, Soemias y Julia Mamaea, fue una historia en la que se conjugaban el poder, la filosofía, la religión siria, el drama e incluso la tragedia'[2] (Hidalgo de la Vega 2012, 131).

Without a doubt, Iulia Domna would be the most important representative of all of them, as well as the most important source of inspiration for her succesors. All the classic sources, without exception, describe Iulia Mamaea as one of the main instigators of bringing her son to power. She had no objection to participating in plots and aliances when the Elagabalus's rule came to an end (Kosmetatou 2002, 398). The records that have survived about her life are more abundant than those containing information about her sister Iulia Soaemias. Acording to Benario, this situation allowed that the historiography cared about his historial importance since the beginning of the 20th century, with studies that focused on the data provided by epigraphy and literary sources.[3] Iulia Mamaea's personality made it posible for her to be considered as beng closest to the political cleverness and intelligence of Iulia Domna (Wild 1917, 20).

From the moment in which Domna became empress, after her husband Lucius Septimius Severus was proclaimed imperator by the troops, great figures coming from the East and Africa were introduced into the court (Okoń 2012, 42–43; 2015, 159–160). In fact, the Empress was blamed for introducing foreign customs in detriment of Roman traditions. In addition to the various personalities of eastern origin who came to the court of Severus, including part of the Domna family, there was also an opening to the oriental world with the introduction of jurists who were part of the circle of the emperors (Millar 1992, 27; Conesa Navarro 2012, 401). On the religious level, authors such as von Domaszewski (1895, 72; 1908, 223–229) thought that Iulia Domna was one of the great culprits of Orientalisation that occurred during the 3d century AD. These foreign cults were introduced at first in the provincial areas, acquiring a larger dimension under the Elagabalus's rule (Cid López 1993, 252; Carbó García 2010, 592). In fact, it is difficult to assure the true transcendence of the Eastern cults under the reign of Septimius Severus, as Roman customs continued to be maintained, in addition to the fact that the traditional pantheon of gods remained the predominant one. Iulia Domna's sister, Iulia Maesa, was in Rome with her daughters during the government of Septimius Severus. We have registered that Iulia Soaemias was one of the 110 matrons who participated with the Vestal Virgins in the proccesion that was led by Iulia Domna in honor of *Iuno Regina* and Diana during the Saecular Games of the AD 204[4] (Faure 2013, 373; Icks 2013, 56; Lusnia 2014, 109; Rantala 2017a, 115–117; 2017b, 95–96). At the same time, it is very interesting to note that these princesses came from a very important priestly dynasty of Emesa. Both Iulia Domna and Iulia Maesa were daughters of the priest Iulius Basianus.[5] Therefore, we know that Soaemias and Mamaea received careful training to which, we could add, they were in Rome within the most important intelectual circles of the moment.

In this paper we try to analyse the figure of the Empress Iulia Mamaea and the relationship maintained with her son Alexander Severus. We will also have a look at the maternal role developed by the Alexander Severus's mother, as well as her influence on historical development. We will also consider the following questions: What role did Iulia Mamaea play into the court? What were the motivations for classical authors to describe her like that? Was she really as powerful as literary references want to convey to us? All these questions will be answered from the main references that the classical authors gave us.

Beginning of Iulia Mamaea's political influence

Alexander Severus was emperator in AD 222 when he was 13 years old. Once more a teenager came to power after a violent confrontation that had ended with the assassination of the previous leader.[6] From the beginning, Iulia Maesa along with her daughter Iulia Mamaea, who was immediately granted the title of *Augusta* (Kettenhofen 1979, 44; Comucci Biscardi 1987, 31–32), and Ulpianus, praetorian prefect, were responsible for conducting the reins of the Empire.[7] After the death of the first, 2 years after the appointment of his grandson,[8] Iulia Mamaea remained the only support of Alexander Severus. As opposed to Elagabalus, whose government was marked from the beginning by femininity, tyranny and transgression, in addition to an infinity of vices, the arrival of the new imperator was seen as a return to lost traditions and customs.[9] In reality, one of the best-known measures that he introduced was the religious "counter-reformation", possibly helped by his grandmother and mother. This consisted in returning to Rome the traditional gods and turning away from Eastern religious currents (Cid López 1993, 264). Breaking with traditions was seen as an uncommon act of a good emperor. It is clear that these stereotypes of the 'good' and 'bad' emperor were artificial, depending on the classic authors who portrayed them. But what is meant by a good emperor? The good emperors respected the established norm already from the republican period, in which the Senate played a fundamental role. Virtues such as *clementia* or *ciuilitas*, which meant rejecting tyrannical principles, were fundamental for a good emperor. To these, we could add others such as *pietas*, in the sense of absolute respect for the traditions of the State, the *mos maiorum* and the gods. Finally, as a representative of the Roman people, the emperor had to embody self-control towards his wishes, putting particular issues before the good of the Roman people (Van Haeperen 2008, 147).

In addition, the Severan Dynasty was a difficult period and the reason why the figure of the *princeps* was object of careful consideration by the literary sources. It was expected that the emperor would be able to reconcile the Empire to the glorious channels of the Augustan period (Gascó 1988, 119). Thus, the descriptions of the different princeps and *Augustae* provided by classical authors must be taken with caution, since not only did they write from the patriarchal position, but also from a privileged social position that determined their views on the matter. For example, Cassius Dio was a senator and under his ideology he understands, narrates and judges his reality as Fernando Gacó has expressed (Gascó 1988, 115). Another important problem is that concerning the *Vita Alexandri* that Lampridius wrote and that is found in the *Historia Augusta*. The study of the Late Empire is essential, according to Meckler this compedium of biographies is the most complete text for understanding the reality of the 2nd and 3rd centuries AD (Meckler 1996, 364). However, there are many problems: not only those deriving from the date of the work, or even the authorship, but also those deriving from the authenticity of the facts that it contains. According to Barnes, the biography of Septimius Severus by Lampridius constitutes a turning point in the *Historia Augusta*. From this moment onwards, fantastic and anachronistic facts are introduced in detriment of historical ones (Barnes 1976, 48). Therefore, when we analyse a source we always have to take it with caution, in this case even more, because Alexander's biography is full of negative references to the emperor that are not objective.

The hopes that Romans had in the new *Augustus* vanished almost at the beginning of his reign. He tried to get away from the Eastern fashions that his cousin and predecessor had developed, although it was not enough. The influence of his mother on him meant that the literary sources were critical of Alexander Severus (Madsen 2016, 157). Herodian presents him as a puppet in the hands of his progenitor without a firm authority.[10] Eutropius, on the other hand, describes him as an extremely pious being with Iulia Mamaea.[11] In part, this benevolent attitude may have been due to the peaceful and affable character he always maintained.[12] That did not stop Mamaea from occasionally offending with her attitude: Herodian says that Mamaea was characterised by greed. In fact, he says that sometimes she pretended to be raising money to distribute it among the soldiers, when really what he was doing was enlarging his patrimony. Much of the reticence towards the government of the last Severus was due to the attitude adopted by Mamaea, as it often confiscated by force the properties of individuals without his consent.[13]

However, Alexander always remained faithful to his mother, despite not being satisfied with all the decisions taken. The *Historia Augusta* is sometimes referred to as *Alexander Mamaeae*:[14] even some buildings were built in the name of the Empress, as was the case of some pavilions located in the palatial residence called Mamaea's Salas – traditionally they was known as *ad Mammam*. In addition, we need to add a palace in Bayas and a pond, that was called *Mameo.*[15] Apart from his failure to curb the pretences and desires of Iulia Mamaea, Alexander Severus's attitude was not reprehensible. He ruled sensibly, for he showed clemency to his subjects, in addition to administering justice well and maintaining good relations with the Senate. In fact, part of his *consilum principis* was composed of 16 senators with experience in judicial matters.[16] This was possibly an attempt to re-establish the power that the Senate had already lost from the end of the 2nd century AD to the detriment of the *ordo equester*.[17] Likewise, it can be interpreted as a return to the time of Septimius Severus. We know that in the court of the first emperor of the dynasty there were important figures related to the law, to such an extent that it was thought that possibly the *Constitutio Antoniniana* promulgated in the year AD 212 by the Emperor Caracalla, was the result of decisions taken by the *consilum principis* of his father or Septimius Severus himself, because he had extensive legal knowledge (Mignot 2008, 325; González Fernández and Fernández Ardanaz 2010, 162 n. 14; Conesa Navarro 2012, 401).

Before Alexander Severus became emperor, Iulia Maesa, seeing that Elagabalus was losing supporters and becoming increasingly hated, tried to remedy the situation. Therefore, she ensured that, in the presence of her and Julia Soemia, Elagabalus adopted his cousin as his son and successor in front of the Senate.[18] Herodian clearly states that Maesa's intention went beyond preserving Elogabalus in power. The clever Augusta's intention was to secure her superior position in the imperial court.[19] This information could be in tune with that transmitted by Cassius Dio, because the senator of Bhytinia comments that, when Iulia Maesa saw that her older grandson losing support, she declared that she wanted him to be dethroned.[20] This provoked a conflict between Iulia Mamaea and her other daughter, Iulia Soaemias, and with the prefect Ulpian (Syme 1970, 320–321). The adoption was hardly credible for the people and, in fact, said Herodianus, the senators mocked it.[21–22] There are disagreements about the date in which the title of Caesar was conferred. In different passages of the *Historia Augusta* this event occurred after Macrinus's death, in AD 218. However, if we confront Cassius Dio and Herodian, as Jardé (1925, 11) has done, that date is not correct, so the adoption had to take place before June of the AD 221 because, in these sources, Elagabalus's proclamation as Emperor and Alexander Severus as Caesar did not take place at the same time (Moreno Ferrero 1983, 100).

To the new son of Elagabalus, in addition to granting him the title of *Caesar*, he shared with his cousin the consulate.[23] He was included in the school of the *sodales Antonini*[24] and received the title of *princeps iuuentutis* (Okoń 2013, 82). He formally obtained the name of Marcus Aurelius Alexander, to which would be added later that of Severus.[25] With this manoeuver he managed to become related to the founder of the dynasty, reigning with the name of Marcus Aurelius Severus Alexander (Varner 2004, 196; González Fernández and Conesa Navarro 2017, 137–152). The change of *nomen* was a strategy orchestrated by Iulia Maesa and her daughter to convince the Senate that a new era was beginning, a return to the government style of Septimius Severus (Hidalgo de la Vega 2012, 157; 2013, 515). In fact, Lampridius says that Elogabalus was the last to receive the name of Antoninus due to the customs and the way of life.[26] On the other hand, in the *Historia Augusta* it is mentioned that the Senate offered to call him Alexander Antoninus and that it was he who refused despite the relationship he had with Caracalla. The same thing happened with the title *Magno*, which was also offered to Alexander and rejected by him.[27]

Mamaea was concerned to offer the Emperor a traditional education, based on literature and military arts. The fear of repeating the situation with Elogabalus conditioned him to show special interest in the study of Greek and Latin authors, in addition to taking part in various properly virile exercises. Among other things, all Alexander's teachers who were not to the liking of Mamaea and the emperor were banished or executed. The concern that Mamaea showed in educating her children following the Greek and Latin precepts can be observed not only with Alexander, but also with her other daugther, Teoclia. A passage of the *Historia Augusta* states that, at a certain time, Alexander Severus wrote a letter to his mother to inform her that he would give his sister in marriage to Maximin the Younger, son of his General, Maximin the Elder. Nevertheless, he chose not to do it because the candidate presented certain barbaric traits that would have provoked his sister's rejection.[28]

Elogabalus thought that his sucesor would follow his example. However, his hatred against Iulia Mamaea made him regret the adoption.[29] Narrator Lampridius was so irritated that he proposed in a session of the Senate that the title of *Caesar* be removed from Alexander. Following the silence of the senators, since they felt affection and respect towards the heir, the Emperor made the decision to try to eliminate Alexander Severus.[30] However, it was Elogabalus who found death, as both he and his mother were assassinated at the hands of the praetorians.[31] The fall of the Emperor brought with it that of Iulia Soaemias, as well as the later *damnatio memoriae* to which they were subjected.[32] Herodian mentions that all Elagabalus' supporters perished as well as those suspected of participating in his tyrannical government. After killing, mutilating and dragging them throughout the city, they were finally thrown into the sewers that flowed into the Tiber River.[33]

After the death of Iulia Maesa, in the year 223 AD,[34] Mamaea was alone with her son. Herodian says that he made an effort to continue with his mother's legacy and she educated and directed Alexander Severus with great firmness. Therefore, he intensified the surveillance of all his actions, in addition to controlling the people with whom he interacted with. To prevent him from having a licentious life, he occupied himself with judicial tasks and activities worthy of his condition.[35] She dealt with all matters that were related to him, including a wife, Sallustia Orbiana, whose name is not reflected in any literary source Syme (1971, 157). Despite being an arranged marriage, Alexander Severus came to love her. However, the harmony did not last long, for Mamaea, afraid to be eclipsed by the young *Augusta*, felt jealous and expelled Alexander's wife from the palace. In contrast, the attitude shown by the emperor was faultless. So much so that Orbiana's father, Lucius Seius Sallustius, a member of one of the aristocratic families of the city and related to the *Barbii* of Aquileia, showed affection towards his son-in-law. Given the aggressive attitude of Iulia Mamaea, Lucius Seius had to hide and took refuge in the camp to escape the insults that led him to his daughter, Alexander Severus's mother. Finally, the opposition of the emperor would not help, since Seius was condemned and the young *Augusta* sent to Libya to exile.[36] As a result of this fact, Herodian critized the attitude undertaken by the emperor for not coming before the wishes of his mother.[37] We could say, as Held has pointed out, that once Orbiana was eliminated from the public sphere, Mamea's only threat had dissipated (Heil 2001, 233). However, there was still the hardest aspect that she could not break and that was the army and Fidelity to Alexander Severus and herself.

Death of Alexander Severus and Iulia Mamaea. The end of the Severan Dynasty

At the beginning of AD 235 Alexander Severus and his mother were killed in the *uicus Britannicus* (Varner 2004, 196; Körner 2011, 88). Although there are authors who set an exact date, there are different interpretations, but what seems to be confirmed is that it occurred in February–March (Schumacher 2004, 2). As happened previously with Elogabalus and Iulia Soaemias, those who executed the final blow were the troops. The position of these women in the front line of government meant that they were participants along with the emperors in both their achievements and their failures. Herodian says that the death of both occurred as follows: the news that came to the Emperor was not good. Apparently, the Germans had crossed the area of the Rhine and the Danube and were devastating everything in their path. The Illyrian territories, bordering Italy, were in danger and claimed the presence of the Emperor with all his army. The soldiers who had helped the Emperor to fight against the Persians blamed Alexander for not doing anything about the situation that was taking place in the northern part of the Empire.

So he finally chose to embark on the journey to the conflict zones with a large garrison. Before engaging in combat, he sent embassies to the Germans, in addition to promising them large sums of money in order not to enter into conflict. This attitude was seen by the army as an act of cowardice and to be improper of an emperor. In the meanwhile, one of his generals, Maximinus, showed strength and courage, winning the support of the *ordo equester.* Alexander's charisma, in contrast, began to fade and the troops named Maximinus as the new Emperor. It only remained to find a way to get rid of Mamaea's son. When he heard what had happened, Alexander was afraid and urged the soldiers to protect him. However, his efforts did not get any response. He barely managed to reach his tent and, where he hugged his mother and, blamed her for his fate since he was the true culprit of his misfortune. Finally, Maximinus sent a tribune and some centurions to kill the Emperor, Mamaea and all his supporters.[38]

When Lampridius speaks in the *Historia Augusta* of the death of Alexander Severus, he also mentions that it happened in a tent when the imperator was waging war against the Germans. However, he does not allude to the situation of Empress Iulia Mamaea.[39] Only indirectly is she mentioned and the reference is merely that she perished. He speaks of a party that was decreed by the Senate in honour of Alexander Severus and his mother. The date of celebration was the Emperor's birthday.[40]

The version offered by Zosimus differs from the one explained above. Alexander, who was in the area of the Rhine, learned of the uprising that had led Maximinus to be named emperor, so he decided to return to Rome. Until his last days he pursued a policy of being peaceful and ready for dialogue, so the Greek author says that the Emperor came to promise the rebel soldiers, and the usurper himself, that if they ceased in their attempt to overthrow him they would be forgiven. However, he was killed just like Mamaea and the praetorian prefects who had gone to help the previous Severus.[41]

It is surprising that one of the causes of the death of Alexander Severus and Iulia Mamaea was the Empress herself. It is in *Historia Augusta* where we can see that different causes are argued for. Some authors thought that the trigger for the army to get angry and take the decision to eliminate them was Mamaea's attitude towards her son. She had persuaded him to abandon the war against the Germanic tribes and return to the East. However, Lampridius says that, in the end, that idea was just an excuse to justify and hide a real crime against an extraordinary emperor; a crime aggravated by the fact that the murdered Alexander was executed by a friend of his, Maximinus.[42] On the other hand, Iulius Capitolinus, in the life of the two Maximini, speaks about the causes and death of the Emperor. He tells us that there are different versions. The two traditional ones are also mentioned; either that Mamaea was the cause, because she encourage her son to abandon the confrontation against the Germans and go to the East or that it could have been the treachery of Maximinus or other barbarian tribes. One of the consequences could also have been the attitude of Alexander himself, as his character was not strong.[43] Like Lampridius, Capitoline does not speak of the Mamaea's death, suggesting therefore that Herodian was the only source for it.

Julia Mamaea appears to have had the same honorary titles of her predecessors, especially of Iulia Domna (Kosmetatou 2002). It seems that the power assigned to her by classical authors may be over-rated. However, there are issues in the epigraphic testimonies that deserve to be clarified. The exaltation of motherhood through the granting of different honours is not a novelty, since all the empresses from Livia onwards received similar decorations. The novelty in the Severan Dynasty we can see in the first place in the inclusion of the women of the imperial house in the *miliarii*. With the exception of the example of Matidia Minor in *Suessa Aurunca*, there is no evidence that the names of previous empresses appeared on milestones. It was from the Severan Dynasty that all members of the *domus* appeared in these singular inscriptions. Therefore, it was undoubtedly an effective and quick way to demonstrate the union and prosperity of the ruling house in the most remote parts of the Empire (Bertalozzi 2015, 427–428; González Fernández 2017, 314–316). But, undoubtedly, one thing to keep in mind would be that, in the inscriptions relating to Alexander Severus, at no time was his father mentioned and it was Iulia Mamaea who gave legitimacy to her son. We could think that it was an authentic proof to affirm that this Empress had a considerable weight in the Empire, however, it is also true that it was the only point of union with Septimius Severus, since Caracalla had no offspring. In short, whether she had power or not, what does seem is that she was used as an instrument of legitimation, materialised especially with its her appointment as *Mater Universi Generis Humani*,[44] encompassing not only the most prominent social layers of Roman society, but also to every being that inhabited the known world.

The imperator and the mother. From the Julio-Claudian to Severa dynasty

Leaving aside the *Historia Augusta*, the fundamental sources of information were undoubtedly the Cassius Dio and Herodian. We observe that, in this case, unlike Elagabalus, a distinction is made between the figures of Alexander Severus and his mother. The Emperor embodies the virtues of the stereotype of the 'good emperor.'

He was pious with his mother to the extreme, lenient with his subjects, showing respect and attention to the Senate, in addition to restoring Roman traditions not only religiously but also socially and politically. However, Iulia Mamaea is described as an authentic manipulator, capable of directing her son as well as acting without his approval. If we compare Mamaea with the descriptions made of Livia or Agripina the Younger, they have in common that the latter, as indicated by Rosa Cid, are identified as influential women in the politics of Ancient Rome, whose biographies are directly related to the predominance of women in the exercise of public tasks and to the supposed that they caused in the society their time (Cid López 2014, 179). Comparing different periods always entails a certain danger because the social and political realities are totally different, but specifically in the case of the Iulio-Claudian Dynasty, where the last two empresses were inserted, and the Severan Dynasty which included Mamaea, certain parallels in the descriptions of classical authors can be seen. Greco-Roman writers, male and conditioned to a patriarchal society, portrayed these women as ambitious beings and, at times, without scruples for the simple fact of participating or pretending to participate in imperial political decisions. Roman literature was the product of a phallocentric culture that reproduced a gendered binary in which the behavior of both sexes were prescribed (Palacios 2014, 94). These prejudices have been reproduced with the passage of time, as we see, for example, in the poisoning of Livia – protagonist of the television series *I Claudius* (Cid López 2014, 179) – or in the case of Agripina, who comes to qualify as a *femina* who acted as *dux* (Santorio L'Hoir 1994, 6), the allusion of general woman, *dux femina*, that corresponds with the qualification propounded by Virgil in the *Aeneid* of princess Dido of Carthage.[45] The imperial women emerged as secondary figures, subordinated to the strong control of the male and so rebuilding their identities is impossible. Authors such as Tacitus, Suetonius or Cassius Dio were most prolific when it came to portraying women of the imperial *domus* (Hidalgo de la Vega 2013, 78). These authors, despite not being contemporaries in time, attribute to the imperial princesses a series of stereotypes that have endured over time and it is difficult to obtain particular and objective fact.

Tacitus began book 13 of his *Annales* with the murder of M. Iunius Silanus, proconsul of Asia and Octavia's fiancé, whose order of execution came from the empress herself, who ordered P. Celer and the freedman Helius to poison him in a banquet.[46] It was the *prima nouo principatur mors*,[47] that is to say, the first death that took place under Nero's rule following Agrippina's wishes. Immediately after, Tacitas talks about the suicide of the freedman Narcisus, abut which the classic author comments that it was provoked by the Empress herself.[48] The death of emperor Claudius, before Nero became emperor, was also her fault and was accomplished through poisoning.[49] Tacitus, throughout his work whenever he talks about Nero's mother, presents her under negative stereotypes, not only as a murderer and as a commander, but also for carrying out transgressive sexual practices to order to reach power (Ginsburg 2006, 131). As with Livia, the women of the Iulio-Claudian Dynasty acquire a certain dimension in Tacitus's work for two reasons. Fundamentally the author was a defender of traditional society, so he rejected all female participation in government affairs. To do this, he contrasts women with men to demonstrate that women can not transgress the silent plane of the domestic sphere in any way. On the other hand, he rejected the regime implemented by Augustus and to discredit it uses the princesses of the imperial *domus* and their attitude as a weapon (Cid López 2014, 185–186).

Focusing on the relationship maintained between Agrippina and her son Nero, there are differences with respect to Iulia Mamaea and Alexander Severus. Unlike what happened with the Emperor Severus, the Emperor Iulio-Claudius was in open conflict with his mother that that would lead him to be killed by order of his son in the year AD 59[50] (Hidalgo de la Vega 2007, 406; 2012, 45; Conesa Navarro and González Fernández 2016, 607–608). The reality of the Iulio-Claudian Dynasty has nothing to do with what happened in the Severan period. Not even the support of those who supposedly served these women to get their children proclaimed emperors. On the one hand, at the time of Agrippina, power was held by the Senate and during the governments of Claudius and Nero freedmen exercised an important influence, while under the Severan Dynasty it was the army that had important decision-making power at the time of the proclamation of the new emperor. However, despite the possible differences, these examples illustrate that the role attributed by classical sources to these women in the court is similar: these were women who, through plots and intrigues, got their children to be emperors and, with it, played an important role in the imperial house.

Conclusions

Despite the attempts made by Iulia Mamaea to prevent repetiion of the situation with Elogabalus, she could not stop the wrath of the army that would eventually end her life and that of the Emperor and mean the end of the Severan Dynasty. At first it seemed that the situation was going to be different, since Alexander was received as the saviour of Rome after a tyrannical and oriental government. However, the classical sources, despite praising the Emperor's behaviour, were critical when talking about the relationship he had with Mamaea. Alexander's rule was the last chance to maintain the dynastic unit inaugurated by Septimius Severus (Saavedra-Guerrero 2006, 726) but that unity was not achieved because of the attitude of the *Augusta* regarded by most of her contemporaries as being guilty of the assassination of the emperor. Undoubtedly, Alexander's young age allowed his mother to guide his steps. To this we would have to add the political capacity that Mamea had in belonging to one of the most important lineages of Roman Syria, which had motivated her to participate in political and social circles of the time. All the achievements and failures that Alexander Severus had were undoubtedly due to the work of his mother who, along with his grandmother, set the guidelines for the new Emperor's performance. Therefore, as this text reflects precisely on maternal and child relationships we believe that here a great example of how some women exerted their influence over men and could act and be participants in historical evolution in Rome, although in principle female power was vetoed

Finally, we cannot ignore the questions we asked ourselves at the beginning. What role would Julia Mamaea play within the imperial court? What were the motivations for the different classical authors to describe Mamaea in such a way and finally, was she as powerful as the literary sources indicate? If we follow traditional discourse, we observe that all the classical texts portray her as a manipulative woman with authentically reproachful behaviour. However, as we have observed through comparison with other empresses, stereotypes that were already marked in women since the Iulio-Claudian Dynasty continued to be reproduced in Mamaea. However, despite the fact that the literary references were written by men, we can not entirely reject the information transmitted. It is true that it is very diffiuclt to make an objective reading and we will never know with complete certainty the role that she played in the court.

It is clear that the insults given to Mamea by the illustrious male historians respond to the fact that she was not completely in the background, but we cannot know for sure if she had such important control over her son in the empire. Similarly, it is clear that these same historians developed a contrast between masculinity, in this case embodied by an emperor who shows moderation towards his subjects and clemency, above the influence of a woman who could respond to the canons of the *femme fatale*. Julia Mamaea did not represent what was expected of an empress, as representative of all the women of Rome. The *Augusta* should have always been in the domestic sphere and accompanied by her son. However, we see a powerful woman who even treasured a great fortune. Therefore, the disqualifications respond to a desire of the classical authors to demonstrate a patriarchal vision of reality and even to justify in some way the possible mistakes that Alexander Severus made during his reign. It is impossible to know exactly if she was a woman as powerful as the literary sources have transmitted, but we can say that she was powerful in the sense that, through her, a whole propaganda policy with the desire to return to the period was developed by Septimius Severus, considering that Iulia Mamaea was the direct descendant of the empress Iulia Domna.

Acknowledgements

This chapter was elaborated thanks to a Predoctoral Contract FPI of the Fundación Séneca. Agencia Territorial de Ciencia y Tecnología de la Región de Murcia (19829/FPI/15).

Notes

1 *PIR*^{2} I 649; Kienast (2004, 180–181).

2 In truth the story of these Syrian princesses, Julia Domna, her sister Julia Maesa and the two daughters of the latter, Soaemias and Julia Mamaea, was a story in which power, philosophy, the Syrian religion, drama and even tragedy were involved.

3 'Julia Mamaea does not present problems similar to those which face us concerning her sister. She has long since been the subject of a careful study and, in even more than a half century, little new evidence has come to hand' (Benario 1959, 13).
4 Hdn., 5, 3, 2–4.
5 *PIR*^{2} I 202.
6 About Elagabalus's death cf. DC. 79 (80), 20, 2; Hdn., 5, 8, 8–9; Lamp. *Elag.* 16, 4–5; 17, 1–4; 18, 2–3.
7 Zonar. 12, 15; Calderini (1949, 116); Hidalgo de la Vega (2012, 157; 2013, 515).
8 The date when Iulia Maesas died was 3 August AD 224. Cf. Kienast (2004, 181).
9 Lamp. *Alex Sev.*, 41, 2; Okoń (2013, 108); Baugman (2017, 107).
10 Hdn. 6, 8, 3; Baugman (2017, 113).
11 Eutr. 8, 23.
12 Hdn. 6, 1, 6–7.
13 Hdn 8, 1, 8. On the news of the Mamaea's wealth at the expense of private individuals, also describes Zonaras 12, 15. It is possible that he consulted the work of Herodian. There is evidence through a fistula found in the vicinity of the church of San Giovanni in Laterano, in Rome, that Mamea had a property in the city. Cf. CIL XV 7336; Granino Cecere (2010, 118–119).
14 Lamp. *Alex Sev.* 5, 2; Vopiscus, *Div. Aurelianus*, 42, 4; Id. *Carus et Numerarianus*, 3, 4.
15 Lamp. *Alex Sev.* 26, 9–10; Barnes (1970, 32).
16 Hdn. 6, 1, 4; Syme (1971, 147); Blázquez (1990, 34); González Fernández and Sancho Gómez (2006, 68); Kosmetatou (2002, 399). The *Historia Augusta* shows different personalities that they was part of the *consilum.* Cf. Lamp. *Alex Sev.* 68, 1–2.
17 Comucci Biscardi (1987, 32). Sobre la cuestión del sector ecuestre en el siglo III d.C., cf. Conesa Navarro (2012, 375–406).
18 D.C. 80, 17, 2.
19 Hdn. 5, 7, 1.
20 D. C. 80, 19, 1[1].
21 Hdn. 5, 7, 4.
22 Hdn. 5, 7, 2–3.
23 Hdn. 5, 7, 4.
24 *Acta sodales Antoniniani* (*CIL* VI, 2001).
25 25 For her part, Danuta Okoń points out that Severus' cognomen was used before the proclamation of the Emperor, thus being a novelty. Cf. Okoń (2013, 107).
26 Lamp. *Elag.* 18, 1–2.
27 Lamp. *Alex. Sev.* 5, 3–5; 12, 2–4. On the speeches delivered during that session of the Senate, cf. Lamp. *Alex. Sev.* 6, 1–5; 7, 1–6; 8, 1–5; 9, 1–7; 10, 1–8; 11, 1–4; 12, 1. Okoń (2013, 107).
28 Capitol. *Maximin*, 29,3, 1–5.
29 Hdn. 5, 7, 5–6. In the *Historia Augusta*, in addition to mentioning that he received a traditional education Alejandro Severo, he offers in detail a list of professors that he had. cf. Lamp. *Alex. Sev.* 3, 1–5 (Calderini 1949, 442; Comucci Biscardi 1987, 32; De Arrizabalaga y Prado 2010, 33).
30 Lamp. *Elag.* 13, 1–4. About the description of the death of the empress given by the *Historia Augusta*, cf. Lamp. *Elag.* 13, 5–8.
31 Eut. 8, 22; (González Fernández and Sancho Gómez 2006, 67).
32 About this question. Cf. Varner (2004, 188–195).
33 Hdn. 5, 8, 8–9.
34 The apotheosis of the Empress was recognized in a series of denarii and sesterces and with the legend of *Diva Maesa Aug (usta)*, while on the reverse came the word *Consacratio*. Cf. *RIC* IV^2, p. 66; p. 101 n°. 377–378; p. 127 n° 712–714; *BMC* VI, pp. 135–136 n° 217–218. There is a case in which the legend of the reverse refers to the *Fecunditas*. In the mint of Antioch. Cf. *RIC* IV^2, p. 101

nº 380. According to the *BMC*, p. 136, this last coin would correspond rather to an irregular copy of Mesa, with the obverse also ill-informed.
35 Hdn. 6, 1, 5–6.
36 Hdn. 6, 1, 9–10; Zonaras, 12, 15 Fink (1939, 326–327).
37 Hdn. 6, 1, 10 y 6, 2, 1.
38 About the complete story that we have described, cf. Hdn. 6, 7, 1–10; 6, 8, 1–8; 9, 1–8; Schumacher (2004, 2–3).
39 Lamp. *Sev. Alex*, 61, 1–7.
40 Lamp. *Sev. Alex.*, 63, 3–4.
41 Zos. 13, 2–3; Mennen (2011, 160).
42 Lamp. *Alex. Sev*. 63, 5–6.
43 Capitol. *Maximin*, 7, 4–6.
44 This title was found on an inscription of *Hispania* in *Tarraconensis*. Cf. *CIL* II, 3413.
45 Virg. *Eneid*. 1, 364.
46 Tac. *Ann*. 13, 1, 1–2.
47 Tac. *Ann*. 13, 1, 1.
48 Tac. *Ann*. 13, 1, 3.
49 Tac. *Ann*. 12, 66–67.
50 Tac. *Ann*. 14, 8, 5.

References

Barnes, T. D. 1970. The lost Kaisergeschichte and the Latin historical tradition. In *Bonner Historia-Augusta-Colloquium. 1968/1969*. Bonn, Rudolf Habelt, 13–43.

Barnes, T. D. (1976) *The Sources of the Historia Augusta*. Bruxelles, Latomus.

Baugman, K. E. (2017) Mamaea's little man: Alexander Severus, his mother, and the Germanic War. In D. Cooper and C. Phelan (eds) *Motherhood in Antiquity*. Cham, Spinger Link, 107–121.

Benario, H. W. (1959) The titulature of Julia Soemias and Julia Mameae: Two notes. *Transactions and Proceedings of the American Philological Association* 90, 9–14.

Bertolazzi, R. (2015) The depiction of Livia and Julia Domna by Cassius Dio: some observations. *Acta Antiqua Academiae Scientiarum Hungaricae* 55, 413–432.

Bertolazzi, R. (2018) On the alleged treachery of Julia Domna and Septimius Severus' failed siege of Hatra. In C. Dunn and E. Carney (eds) *Royal Womenand Dynastic Lolalty*, Cham, Palgrave McMillan, 67–86.

Blázquez, J. M. 1990. Alejandro Magno, modelo de Alejandro Severo. In J. M. Croisille (ed.) *Neronia IV. Alejandro Magno, modelo de los emperadores romanos. Actes du IVe Colloque international de la SIEN*. Bruxelles, Latomus, 25–36.

Calderini, A. (1949) *I Severi. La crisi dell'Impero nel III secolo*. Bologna, Licinio Capelli Editore.

Carbó García, J. R. (2010) La problématique del Sol Invictus. Le cas de la Decie Romaine. *Numen* 57(5), 583–618.

Cid López, R. Mª. (1993) Las emperatrices sirias y la religión solar. Una nueva valoración. In J. Alvar, C. Blánquez and C. G. Wagner (eds) *Formas de difusión de las religiones antiguas. Segundo encuentro-coloquio de Arys. Jarandilla de la Vega, diciembre 1990*. Madrid, Ediciones Clásicas, 245–268.

Cid López, R. Mª. (2010) Mujeres 'poderosas' del Imperio romano en la historiografía moderna. Algunas notas críticas a las visiones de la Ilustración y su influencia. In C. Fornis, J. Gallego, P. M. López Barja de Quiroga and M. Valdés Guía (eds) *Dialéctica histórica y compromiso social: homenaje a Domingo Plácido*. Madrid, Libros Pórtico, 687–693.

Cid López, R. Mª. (2014) Imágenes del poder femenino en la Roma antigua. Entre Livia y Agripina. *Asparkía. Investigació feminista* 25, 179–201.

Cleve, F. S. (1988) Some male relatives of the Severan women. *Historia. Zeitschrift für Alte Geschichte* 37(2), 196–197.
Comucci Biscardi, B. (1987) *Donne di rango e donne di popolo nell'età dei Severi*. Firenze, Olschki.
Conesa Navarro, P. D. (2012) (2014 ed). La prefectura del pretorio: Auge y 'declive' de un cargo militar romano *Antigüedad y Cristianismo. Monografías históricas sobre la Antigüedad Tardía* 29, 375–406.
Conesa Navarro, P. D. (2015) De salvajes a domesticadas: Aproximación a un ensayo sobre la justificación de la condición femenina en el mundo romano. *Revue des Etudes Anciennes* 117(1), 87–108.
Conesa Navarro, P. D. (2016) Estudios sobre mujeres en la Antigua Roma. Estado de la cuestión, problemas y progreso científico en un campo histórico consolidado. *Minius. Historia, arte e xeografía* 24, 205–226.
Conesa Navarro, P. D. and González Fernández, R. (2016) *Mors honesta*. Suicidas y muertes inducidas de mujeres en la antigua Roma. In R. Rodríguez López and M. J. Bravo Bosch (eds) *Mujeres en tiempos de Augusto. Realidad social e imposición legal*. Valencia, Tirant Humanidades, 587–609.
De Arrizabalaga y Prado, L. (2010) *The Emperor Elagabalus: Fact of Fiction?*. Cambridge, Cambridge University Press.
Faure, P. (2013) *L'aigle et le cep. Les centurions légionnaires dans l'Empire des Sévères*. Bordeaux, Ausonius Éditions.
Fink, R. O. (1939) Lucius Seius Caesar, Socer Augusti. *American Journal of Philology* 60(3), 326–332.
Gascó, F. (1988) Buenos y malos emperadores en Casio Dión. In J. M[a] Candau Morón, F. Gascó and A. Ramínez de Verger (eds) *La imagen de la realeza en la Antigüedad*. Madrid, Editorial Coloquio, 115–140.
Ginsburg, J. (2006) *Representing Agrippina. Constructions of Female Power in the Early Roman Empire*. Oxford, Oxford University Press.
González Fernández, R. and Conesa Navarro, P. D. (2017) La dinastía Severa y el *nomen Aurellius*. Septimio Severo y la *gens Aurelia*, *Athenaeum. Studi di letteratura e Storia dell'antichità* 105(1), 137–152.
González Fernández, R. and Fernández Ardanaz, S. (2010) Algunas cuestiones en torno a la promulgación de la *Constitutio Antoniniana*. *Gerión. Revista de Historia Antigua* 28(1), 157–191.
González Fernández, R. and Sancho Gómez, M. P. (2006) Pautas para el estudio de la relación emperadores-senado (197–251). *Antigüedad y Cristianismo. Monografías históricas sobre la Antigüedad Tardía* 23, 57–77.
Granino Cecere, M. G. (2010) Propietà di Augustae to Rome in Latium vetus. In A. Kolb (ed.) *Augustae. Machtbewusste Frauen am römischen Kaiserhof?*. Berlin/Boston, De Gruyter, 111–127.
Heil, M. (2001) Severus Alexander und Orbiana. Eine Kaiserehe. *Zeitschrift für Papyrologie und Epigraphik* 135, 233.
Hidalgo de la Vega, M[a]. J. (2007) La imagen de 'la mala' emperatriz en el Alto Imperio: Mesalina, meretrix Augusta. *Gerión. Revista de Historia Antigua* 25(1), 395–409.
Hidalgo de la Vega, M[a]. J. (2012) *Las emperatrices romanas. Sueños de púrpura y poder oculto*. Salamanca, Universidad de Salamanca.
Hidalgo de la Vega, M[a]. J. (2013) Mujeres poderosas: las emperatrices sirias, sucesión dinástica, imagen pública. In R. M[a] Cid López and E. B. García Fernández (eds) *Debita verba. Estudios en homenaje al profesor Julio Mangas Manjarrés*. Oviedo, Universidad de Oviedo, 499–518.
Icks, M. (2013) *The Crimes of Elagabalus. The Life and Legacy of Rome's Decadent Boy Emperor*, London/New York, IB Tauris.
Jardé, A. (1925) Études critiques sur la vie et le règne de Sévère Alexander. Paris, de Boccard.
Kettenhofen, E. (1979) *Die syrischen Augustae in der historischen Überlieferung. Ein Beitrag zum Problem der Orientalisierung*. Bonn, Rudolf Habelt.
Kienast, D. (2004) *Römische Kaisertabelle. Grundzüge einer römischen Kaiserchronologie* (3rd edition). Darmstadt, Wissenschaftliche Buchgesellschaft.

Körner, Ch. (2011) Transformationsprozesse im Römischen Reich des 3. Jahrhunderts n. Chr. *Millennium-Jahrbuch* 8, 87–123.

Kosmetatou, E. (2002) The public image of Julia Mamaea. An epigraphic and numismatic inquiry, *Latomus. Revue d'*études latines 61(2), 398–414.

Lusnia S. S. (2014) *Creating Severan Rome. The Architecture and Self- Image of L. Septimius Severus (A.D. 193–211).* Bruxelles, Latomus.

Madsen, J. M. (2016) Criticising the benefactors: The Severans and the return of dynastic rule. In C. H. Lange and J. M. Madsen (eds) *Cassius Dio. Greek Intellectual and Roman Politician.* Leiden/Boston, Brill, 136–158.

Martínez López, C. (1991) De Livia a *feminae*: romper el silencio de las mujeres en el mundo antiguo. In C. Bernis, V. Demonte, E. Garrido González, T. C. Calbert and I. de la Torre (eds) *Los estudios sobre la mujer: de la investigación a la docencia. Actas de las VIII Jornadas de Investigación Interdisciplinaria.* Madrid, Instituto Universitario de Estudios de la Mujer, 411–426.

Meckler, M. (1996) The beginning of the Historia Augusta. *Historia: Zeitschrift für Alte Geschichte* 45(3), 364–375.

Mennen, I. (2011) *Power and Status in the Roman Empire, AD 193–284.* Leiden/Boston, Brill.

Mignot, D. A. (2008) République et citoyenneté a l'aube du second siècle. Une certaine idée de la république chez Pline le Jeune. *Gerión. Revista de Historia Antigua* 26(1), 313–326.

Millar, F. (1992) *The Emperor in the Roman World (31 BC–AD 337).* London, Duckworth.

Moreno Ferrero, I. (1983) La adopción de Alejandro Severo y su nombramiento como Cesar. *Studia Historica. Historia Antigua* 1, 99–103.

Okoń, D. (2012) *Septimius Severus et Senatores. Septimius Severus'Personal Policy Towards Senators in the Light of Prosopographic Research (193–211 A.D.).* Szczecin, Uniwersytet Szczeciński.

Okoń, D. (2013) *Imperatores Severi et Senatores. The History of the Imperial Personnel Policy*, Szczecin, Uniwersytet Szczeciński.

Okoń, D. (2015) Consuls and consulars of the Severan period – a new approach. In P. Briks (ed.) *Elites in the Ancient World. Szczecińskie Studia nad Starożytnością* II. Szczecin, Uniwersytet Szczeciński, 153–165.

Palacios, J. (2014) Miradas romanas sobre lo femenino: discurso, estereotipos y representación. *Asparkía. Investigació feminista* 25, 92–110.

Rantala, J. (2017a) Promoting family, creating identity. Septimius Severus and the imperial family in the rituals of the ludi saeculares. In W. Vanacker and A. Zuiderhoek (eds) *Imperial Identities in the Roman World.* London/New York, Routledge, 110–124.

Rantala, J. (2017b) *The Ludi Saeculares of Septimius Severus. The Ideologies of a New Roman Empire.* London/New York, Routledge.

Saavedra-Guerrero, Mª. D. (2006) *Augustae, uxores, mulieres et matres.* Mujeres y ficción en la dinastía de los Severos. *Mélangues de l'Ecole française de Roma* 118(2), 719–728.

Santorio L'Hoir, F. (1994) Tacitus and women's usurpation of power. *Classical World* 88(1), 5–25.

Schumacher, L. (2004) Die *Sicilia* in Mainz-Bretzenheim. Zur Lokalisierung der Ermordung des Kaisers Severus Alexander. *Mainzer Zeitschrit* 99, 1–10.

Syme, R. (1970) Three Jurists. In *Bonner Historia-Augusta-Colloquium 1968/1969*, 309–323. Bonn, Rudolf Hablet Verlag.

Syme, R. (1971) *Emperors and Biography. Studies in the Historia Augusta.* Oxford: Clarendon Press.

Turton, G. (1974) *The Syrian Princesses. The Women Who Ruled Rome, AD 193–235.* London. Book Club Associates.

van Haeperen, F. (2008) L'impiété, une caractéristique des «mauvais» empereurs. *Mythos. Rivista di Storia delle Religioni* 2, 147–158.

Varner, E. R. (2004) *Mutilation and Transformation. Damnatio Memoriae and Roman Imperial Portraiture.* Leiden/Boston, Brill.

von Domaszewski, A. (1895) *Die Religion des römischen Heeres.* Trier, F. Lintz
von Domanszewski, A. (1908) Die politische Bedeutung der Religion von Emesa. *ARW (Abhandlungen zur ròmischen Religion)* 11, 223–229.
Wild, P. S. (1917) Two Julias. *Classical Journal* 13(1), 14–24.

Chapter 20

Representations of women, motherhood and childhood in Spanish primary school textbooks

Silvia Medina Quintana

Introduction

More than four decades of studies on the history of women allows a greater knowledge of the past, in which we trace the mechanisms developed by the patriarchy to justify alleged female inferiority, as well as the gender relations that are at the basis of our social organisation. Therefore, although there are still many issues to be studied, we now have enough information to reject the traditional, androcentric and classist history that gave women the role of mere spectators. However, this theoretical knowledge does not seem to have been transmitted beyond the specialised spheres. The contribution of the history of women has to be present in the educational field, but textbooks, both from primary and secondary school, and university manuals, are far from inclusive; the same as the educational messages of most archaeological museums with just a few exceptions.

In order to foster a view of the present among children that steers them away from stereotypes and to bring them closer to a richer past, educators should include classroom resources that address the presence and participation of women throughout history. For this reason, from the didactics of the social sciences it is necessary to promote research around this issue, with the aim of improving the quality of teaching in disciplines such as history. It is evident that, as a tool to understand the world in which we live, the social sciences can offer a more integrating perspective in the classroom.

This study is part of a broader line of research on teaching–learning about the role of women in history, such as their presence in school textbooks (Medina Quintana and García-Morís 2015) or the gender perspective in educational paths and itineraries (Medina Quintana 2014). In turn, it links with other analyses that we are carrying out on the use of iconographic sources in primary school and in the initial training of teachers (García-Morís *et al.* 2016).

This chapter does not seek to make a comprehensive or systematic analysis on the representation of motherhood and childhood in textbooks, but rather offers a qualitative and interpretive approach to the subject, through examples from several publishing houses of different years and different subjects. First, an approach to the Francoist education will be made to see what image of motherhood was offered in the textbooks of the time; then, we will review some current textbooks made under the last Spanish educational law (2014).

Textbooks as an educational tool

Although today, partly due to the new ICT (Information and Communications Technologies), there are many didactic resources available to teachers, most of them continue to use the textbook as a fundamental support for the teaching-learning process (Gómez *et al.* 2014). In this way, the book is the point of reference for this process, both for students and teachers. This explains why, today, we continue to ask ourselves what role women are given in school textbooks (Blanco 2000) and, in the case at hand, how motherhood and childhood are reflected.

As established by Jurjo Torres decades ago, the educational curriculum in Spain is at the service of certain interests, and, therefore, so are the school textbooks that follow it. Thus, textbooks, more or less intentionally, leave out necessary information and perspectives and can distort the reality by omission, deletion, addition or deformation of the information given (Torres 1989).

Although some publishers express a greater concern than others, it is evident that, in general, the images that represent women are not in agreement with the actual historical reality. Faced with this dynamic, it is necessary to include in the textbooks representations where the relationship between genders is not always unequal and where the real importance that women had in the past is appreciated. This is desirable both in the case of famous characters who, despite having been rescued by the history of women, remain invisible within the school environment and also those anonymous characters without whose presence history cannot be understood, showing the relevance of activities such as maintenance and care, including motherhood.

Given that education is a basic tool in achieving equality, an effort should be made to adapt school books (not only in their theoretical contents but also in the images and use of language) and curriculum, in general, to the new perspectives that are being reached through research. This is about offering real models, far removed from a restricted and partial history, where boys and girls can feel reflected and that illustrate the diversity that existed in past societies (Sant and Pagès 2011).

Consequently, in a world where the visual prevails and in which the media and the outreach of social media networks mean that, on many occasions, the power of the images is trivialised, it is advisable to promote a critical eye among our students on everything that surrounds them, in their environment. Not without reason one of the competencies that the primary school curriculum establishes directly relates to the ability of analysis and interpretation of texts, in its broad sense, both written and imagined. It is necessary that we encourage work that enhances a critical vision among primary school children and that is why this issue must be addressed in the Bachelor Degree of Primary Education, in order to train future teachers' ability to be critical when working with textbooks and when choosing materials and teaching resources (Gámez Ceruelo *et al.* 2013).

The image of motherhood and childhood in the Francoist manuals (1939–1975)

Brief historical context

From the beginning of the 20th century, a progressive discourse had been developed in Spain that demanded a new role for women, and in which the renewing educational movements, such as the Free Institution of Education, played an important role. Not surprisingly, it is worth noting the educational momentum of the Second Republic and the importance that teachers had for the country in opening up in all areas, including the education of women (García Galán 2015).

After the civil war, the unique accepted model for women in the whole country was the traditional one. Motherhood was linked to certain values, such as love, surrender and self-sacrifice, which characterise 'good mothers.' It is understood that certain characteristics spring naturally from the fact of being a woman, essentially associating motherhood and femininity. Those traits are sweetness and delicacy, but also discretion and diligence; a model of domesticity of which there is evidence, in our culture, as early as the 4th century BC, with *The Oeconomicus* by Xenophon (Iriarte Goñi 2000) and that, in contemporary times, is incarnated by the model of the Angel in the House. At the same time, Francoism exalted the figure of the country embodied in a mother, as in many other examples where the female body and motherhood are used as a metaphor to refer to the nation (González Arias 1999).

The educational model of this period sought to indoctrinate the values of the regime, among which gender roles played an important part and transmitted a feminine image that was linked to the home and whose primary functions were marriage and motherhood (Di Febo 2003; Domingo 2007). However, the male role was understood as the family father (precisely, the Roman *pater familias*) that provided economic support in the home (Nuño 2010). In this sense, school textbooks of this time reinforced the image of women as selfless mothers in the service of their husbands and their offspring, and urged the girls to follow this model, marking these gender roles from a very early age.

As has been studied, the period of Francoism was not uniform; however differences can be established between decades. Without going into detail, in the 1960s the regime tried to open up, in a more apparent than real way; thus, we have focused on manuals that did not belong to the beginning of Franco's regime, but to its final stages; however, the discourse on women and motherhood was identical to that of the earliest times.

Motherhood and childhood in Franco's manuals

According to an Order of October 1939, textbooks were to be sent to the Ministry, where they were analysed and approved, or not, for publication and use in schools (Sánchez-Redondo Morcillo 2004). In this sense, school textbooks had to comply with the rules and values of the regime. These books reinforced the aforementioned maternal values of self-denial and sacrifice, turning them into an essential reference for women. The feminine and the maternal are linked to such an extent that this image included the teachers themselves, due to their role as caregivers and educators, a role that was always well accepted for women and that allowed them to access certain professions, such as teaching or nursing, but always in a lower range than men. Some examples of fragments refer to that image of the teachers as mothers.[1]

> Beloved teacher, my teacher. Her eyes caressed us and her mouth gave us smiles. She was so good! She gives advice like a **mother** and calls her (female) students **'my children'**.
>
> It is possible that in your heart you have almost as much space for some good friends, including your teachers, as you have for your **family**.

Although it is important to recognise that, sometimes, the male teacher was also valued as a father, not only due to the respect and figure of authority but also for the affection that he was able to demonstrate, most allusions to those signs of affection refer to women.

As it could not be otherwise, these manuals are examples of women of the past who serve as a reference for the roles of boys and girls: for the girls, a model to imitate, and for the boys, to know what is expected of a woman. Among the female characters that appear in these texts is Isabel I of Castile, which they present as a female example with the following words: 'honourable as a woman, diligent and loving as wife and mother.'[2] Although they allude to her capacities as queen and exemplary ruler, in no case does her political role match that of her husband, Fernando de Aragón.

Another recurring female character in the Francoist manuals is Teresa de Jesús, and we find that even in the biography of the saint her 'maternal sweetness' is mentioned, again essentially linking feminine nature with the qualities of a good mother. The regime tried to inculcate this model as a reference for girls, which is why they are considered as potential mothers, reminding them that their future inevitably passes through the exercise of a virtuous motherhood:

> You, girl, are probably going to be a mother some day. When you already are, the love treasures from your heart will pour on your child ... You will live more for them than yourself. You will suffer more for their sorrows than your own. They

> will, in turn, correspond your love by loving you more than anything else in the world (Sáinz-Amor, in Sánchez-Redondo 2004).
>
> You love him so much, especially because he awakens your maternal sense. He evokes the child that every woman feels sleeping in her heart ... because for a little girl, any family child wonderfully embodies the hope of being a future mum.

In order to instil that motherly role in girls, the educational texts insist on their role as caretakers of their little brothers in a preparation of what it was considered a sacred feminine task.[3]

In short, with respect to childhood, during the Franco regime the educational model of indoctrination was applied, in which the minds of children were recipients to be filled with the knowledge of their teachers; above all, they sought to take advantage of the stage of childhood as that age in which to model the behaviours and inculcate the roles that the regime defended. In this way, motherhood was presented before children as the destiny of any woman, something they should aspire to above anything else.

Changes and recurrences in current textbooks (2014)

Gender and educational laws since 1975

After the Francoist dictatorship, a series of reforms was developed during the decade of the 1980s to adapt the General Law of Education, promulgated in the 1970s, to the new reality of the country. In some cases, these changes continued in a similar line and, in others, they meant a rupture with the previous model, although the way in which women were treated in the curriculum and in the textbooks was not significantly different.

In contrast to previous reforms, with the LOGSE (Organic Law of General Management of the Educational System) of the 1990s, the principle of equality appears in the school curriculum for the first time. However, textbooks continued to offer a sexist image of women, both in content, illustrations and language (Ruiz Oliveras and Vallejo Martín-Albo 1999). The following educational reform, the Organic Law of Education (LOE) of 2006, placed special emphasis on equality within the curriculum and, specifically in the area of social sciences, the role of women in the past was given special value.

We will now focus on textbooks adapted to the latest educational reform, the LOMCE (Organic Law for the Improvement of Educational Quality), promulgated in 2014, to analyse the image of women, motherhood and childhood in the most recent textbooks.

Motherhood and childhood in the textbooks of the LOMCE

Previous studies had already pointed out the need to analyse the image of women in this material, that is, textbooks, given their prominent use in the classroom (Medina and García-Morís 2015). In an analysis made by two Spanish publishers (Santillana and SM) of the social sciences books of Year 5 of primary school, adapted to the LOMCE, there was a significant difference between men and women, especially in the history units (with 74% of male characters versus 26% of female), while in the geography units there was a greater balance (58% of males and 42% of females). Of course, beyond the figures, it is interesting to see what kind of actions and values are attributed to each gender and how both are represented and, in the case at hand, what meaning is given to motherhood and childhood.

Textbooks are a product made for children and it is significant that a balance is sought in the way minors are represented. In this sense, there is a more egalitarian representation between boys and girls than among adults: 47% of girls and 53% of boys against adult characters, with a (dis) proportion of 29% female and 71% male.

On this occasion, we have broadened the scope of analysis and reviewed textbooks related to other disciplines, apart from the social sciences, to see what image is offered of motherhood and childhood; thus, manuals of natural sciences and religion have also been consulted alongside with those of social sciences. Women appear as mothers but are rarely presented as pregnant. In the Santillana edition, in unit 6 (*The passage of time)* of Year 1 of primary school, a woman is shown pregnant with her second child, since she is accompanied by her older daughter. It is the only example found in the social sciences books (publishers Santillana, SM and Edebé).

On the contrary, in the natural sciences books the subject of gestation appears linked to human reproduction. It offers, therefore, a biological vision of the issue, with images focused on the formation of the foetus and the development process of the pregnancy.

In the manuals of religion, motherhood is undoubtedly personified in the Virgin Mary, who appears in a maternal attitude with the baby Jesus. However, beyond this representation, something interesting is the image offered of the current family model. Heterosexual couples appear inside the home, performing domestic tasks in a balance of roles, since both the father and the mother are doing the work (cooking, ironing, washing the dishes ...). This shows a transformation compared to previous decades, where women were presented as 'queens' of the home. In some cases the grandfather or the grandmother are also included, and there are always children's characters.

As in other matters, religious books show a change in the idea of family, a fact that is reflected in the representation (both in drawing and in photography) of families of other ethnic groups or with different skin colours. But, as expected, there are no homosexual couples or single-parent families. The social sciences units of Year 1 of primary school also deal with the concept of family and images are used that illustrate a co-responsibility in the domestic work, with the presence of the father and the children doing some tasks in the kitchen, under the epigraph 'The coexistence in family' or the message 'We must collaborate in the housework,' addressed to the students. Likewise, the existence of adoption and of single-parent families is mentioned, thus expanding the notion of family and showing it as a rich and varied reality, so that textbooks, in this case, fulfil their task of reflecting reality.

As for the units of prehistory and ancient history, which appear in the book of Year 4 of primary school (based on what was established by the curriculum), two publishers have been reviewed: Santillana and Edebé. Before beginning with the historical subjects, one talks about the historic-cultural heritage and the necessity to know it and preserve it; this section includes some images of archaeological excavations, in relation to the method of research and writing of history. It is interesting to see that women are practicing archaeology and, as was pointed out for geography units, an attempt is made to present them performing roles similar to men. The difference comes from the history units, where that attempt to present a gender balance is not appreciated.

In the subjects of prehistory and ancient history few images of women are used, compared to men. In the representation of the tasks developed during prehistory, a distinction of roles is shown, since the male sector is awarded activities such as metallurgy and stone carving, as well as prehistoric art, which continues to be understood as mainly male work. Women appear in other activities such as the grinding of cereals and the working of animal skins for shelter. This is a mistake, since models from later times are being applied to an era when there is no evidence of such division. Recent research offers another image of the Palaeolithic groups, with more importance given to collection and collaboration among people. In any case, there is information that we do not have, such as the award of parietal art production exclusively to male hands, which is systematically reproduced in textbooks and in museums. Even in an image in which a woman appears next to a rock painting, she seems to be in a 'secondary' position, as an assistant, while the man next to her is acting.

Some representations of motherhood appear in this prehistory unit, both in the Palaeolithic and Neolithic stages, as a woman holding a baby in her arms; again, there are no figures of pregnant women. Children are also appreciated, such as a child near the oven in which ceramic pieces are being introduced for cooking; this is a significant change from other times when the important role of children in the communities of the past was not taken into account.

Looking at the units that refer to the Roman age, few women appear and, in addition, some of them are seen from their backs, which takes importance away from them. They are not doing anything concrete but they seem to be walking or, in some case, buying in the market. In other editorials, although not in the ones studied here, there is a section called 'the Roman woman,' which refers to clothing or distinctive ornaments, just as it happens in many museums.

Faced with the scarcity of women, male characters are depicted as soldiers or senators, and specific examples are cited, such as Viriato, Augusto, Adriano or Seneca, but no female name linked to Roman Hispania is mentioned. Without entering into this information, and as was the case in the prehistory sections, a biased feminine image continues to be given, which does not reflect the research provided by the history of women. This portrait links them to the domestic world, leaving for men the public sphere of economics and politics, as well as the army, so that an image of passivity or lack of action is transmitted, depriving women of any leading role.

With regard to children, it is worth noting that there are representations of girls and boys integrated in the city, and there is, specifically, a section on children's games from the time, under the epithet 'What did Roman children play?' At this point, we can point out that language, in most textbooks, is not inclusive, but the generic masculine is used to refer to the entire population.[4] The use of children's games is a good element to facilitate historical empathy and to encourage the students' interest in the past by approaching the habits of people their own age; thus, it is essential to include references to the childhood of the different historical times in school textbooks.

Conclusions

From the Francoist model, which intrinsically linked women to a maternal duty, there have been differences in the way both motherhood and childhood have been represented in school textbooks. Nowadays, one can appreciate the attempt to reflect a more balanced society in the geography units, as well as in manuals of other disciplines, such as the natural sciences, when they refer to the present. However, this does not happen in the history units (in this case, as far as prehistory and ancient history are concerned). Thus, the images present in the history units of primary school textbooks continue to convey a traditional image of women, despite the fact that this role has been refuted after years of research.

In any case, although the image of women as mothers is used, given that they appear with some boy or girl, there are hardly any representations of pregnancies. As said before, pregnancy only appears when dealing with the issue of reproduction and is therefore given a biological perspective. It should be remembered at this point that with the LOGSE they implemented the subject 'knowledge of the environment,' which, from an integrated perspective, brought together content from the natural and the social sciences. With some exceptions, this approach had a positive impact for the understanding of reality as something global in which aspects of both matters are interrelated. With regards to the representation and understanding of motherhood, this link was positive.

The image of the female population in the prehistory units of the books analysed seeks to offer the diversity of tasks performed by these groups, although there is a clear division by gender. However, in the case of the Ancient Age they appear almost as decorative characters, which are included to complete the mosaic of Roman society, and sometimes alluding to aesthetic aspects, but without addressing economic or political activities; there is no real criticism of that society as a patriarchal structure, which would at least allow to establish a debate about the past, as could happen with the issue of slavery.

For its part, it seems that the representation of children has achieved a greater role in school textbooks in the last decades. It is true that children already appeared in textbooks, but, for example, in the history units they are now represented not only as minors playing but as actors and actresses with historical importance, something that, in most occasions, is denied to women.

Once again, we stress the need to use educational resources at school that include women, especially in historical contexts; otherwise, women will be perpetually portrayed as inactive and confined to the domestic sphere, which is the result of carrying on stereotypes that are far from reality, especially in the case of the popular classes. School textbooks are a fundamental piece in the teaching-learning process of our time, so they must be analysed to know what values and ideas are being transmitted and to demand, if necessary, their update. In the case of the History of women, this is a common claim since, as has been pointed out, the latest contributions of research in this discipline do not seem to transcend the specialised field. Hence, it is necessary to encourage in the future teachers, who are currently in training, a critical vision and the necessary skills to detect these deficiencies and to find alternative materials that complement textbooks.

Acknowledgements

This work is set in the Research Project 'Patrimonio Arqueológico, Nuevas Tecnologías, Turismo, Educación y Rentabilización Social: un nexo necesario para la ciudad histórica,' funded by the Spanish Ministry of Economy, Industry and Competitiveness (Dirección General de Investigación Científica y Técnica y Subdirección General de Proyectos de Investigación) (Ref.: HAR2015–68059-C2-1-R; Subprograma Retos de la Sociedad).

Notes

1 The fragments are collected from Bolinaga and Sáinz-Amor in Sánchez-Redondo (2004), and have been translated by Violeta Ruano Posada.
2 Maillo, in Sánchez-Redondo (2004) (trans. Violeta Ruano Posada).
3 Sáinz-Amor in Sánchez-Redondo (2004) (trans. Violeta Ruano Posada).
4 From organisations like the Royal Academy of the Spanish Language (RAE), it is argued that the masculine gender should include the feminine as well; however, feminist theory rejects the false 'generic masculine' and since the seventies has advocated the need to use an inclusive language, assuming the idea that what is not named does not exist (Bengoechea 2015).

References

Bengoechea Bartolomé, M. (2015) *Lengua y género*. Madrid, Síntesis.

Blanco, N. (2000) Mujeres y hombres para el siglo XXI: El sexismo en los libros de texto. In M. A. Santos Guerra (ed.) *El harén pedagógico. Perspectiva de género en la organización escolar*. Barcelona, Graó, 119–147.

Ciencias Sociales 1º de Primaria (2014) Santillana, Madrid.

Ciencias Sociales 4º de Primaria. (2015) Santillana, Madrid.

Ciencias Sociales 4º de Primaria. (2015) Edebé, Madrid.

Ciencias Sociales 5º de Primaria. (2015) Santillana, Madrid.

Ciencias Sociales 5º de Primaria, Savia. (2014) SM, Madrid.
Di Febo, G. (2003) Nuevo Estado, nacionalcatolicismo y género. In G. Nielfa (ed.) *Mujeres y hombres en la España franquista: sociedad, economía, política, cultura.* Madrid, Universidad Complutense de Madrid, 19–44.
Domingo, C. (2007) *Coser y cantar. Las mujeres bajo la dictadura franquista.* Barcelona, Lumen.
Gámez Ceruelo, V., Molina Neira, J., Cardona Gómez, G. and Rojo Ariza, M. C. (2013) Cómo se enfrenta a las imágenes el alumnado de grado de educación primaria. In J. J. Díaz Matarranz, A. Santisteban Fernández and A. Cascajero Garcés (eds) *Medios de comunicación y pensamiento crítico. Nuevas formas de interacción social.* Alcalá de Henares, Universidad de Alcalá, 445–454.
García Galán, S. (2015) *Mujeres entre la casa y la calle. Educación, feminismos y participación política en Asturias, 1900 1931.* Oviedo, Trabe.
García-Morís, R., Medina Quintana, S., López Fernández, J. A. and Martínez Medina, R. (2016) Literacidad visual y alteridad. La construcción "del otro" en las narraciones del alumnado del grado en educación primaria. In A. Arroyo (ed.) *Deconstruir la alteridad desde la Didáctica de las Ciencias Sociales: Educar para una ciudadanía global.* Las Palmas de Gran Canaria, Universidad de las Palmas de Gran Canaria, 151–164.
Gómez, C., Cózar. R. and Miralles. P. (2014) La enseñanza de la historia y el análisis de libros de texto. Construcción de identidades y desarrollo de competencias. *Revista de la Facultad de Educación de Albacete,* 29(1), 11–25.
González Arias, L. M. (1999) Nacionalismo y feminismo: la conceptualización del cuerpo femenino en la literatura irlandesa contemporánea. In M. P. Cuder Domínguez (coord.) *Exilio femenino.* Huelva, Universidad de Huelva, 35–44.
Iriarte Goñi, A. (2000) Fronteras intramuros en el 'Económico' de Jenofonte. In P. M. López Barja and S. Reboreda (coord.) *Fronteras e identidad en el mundo griego antiguo.* Vigo, Universidad de Vigo, 267–279.
Medina Quintana, S. (2014) Un recorrido didáctico a través de las esculturas femeninas de Oviedo. In E. Tonda Monllor and R. Martínez Medina (eds.) *Nuevas perspectivas conceptuales y metodológicas para la educación geográfica,* 289–300. Murcia, Universidad de Córdoba and Grupo de Didáctica de la Geografía.
Medina Quintana, S. and García-Morís, R. (2015) Las imágenes de mujeres en los libros de texto de Educación Primaria. In O. Fernández Álvarez (coord.) *Mujeres en riesgo de exclusión social. Una perspectiva transnacional.* Madrid, McGraw Hill-España, 311–321.
Nuño, L. (2010) *El mito del varón sustentador. Orígenes y consecuencias de la división sexual del trabajo.* Barcelona, Icaria.
Ruiz Oliveras, L. and Vallejo Martín-Albo, C. (1999) ¿Qué queda del sexismo en los libros de texto?. *Revista Complutense de Educación* 10(2), 125–145.
Sánchez-Redondo Morcillo, C. (2004) *Leer en la escuela durante el franquismo.* Cuenca, Universidad de Castilla-La Mancha.
Sant Obiols, E. and Pagès i Blanch, J. (2011) ¿Por qué las mujeres son invisibles en la enseñanza de la Historia?. *Historia y Memoria* 3, 129–146.
Torres Santomé, J. (1989) Libros de texto y control del currículum. *Cuadernos de pedagogía* 168, 50–55.

Chapter 21

Women and children omitted in the teaching of history: causes and consequences

Antonia Garcia Luque

Introduction

On 9 December 2013 Spain's Official State Gazette published the legislation on the Organic Law for Improving Educational Quality – referred to as LOMCE in Spanish – which was designed to amend without repealing the previous Organic Law on Education (referred to as LOE in Spanish) adopted on 3 May 2006 by the previous government. Since the adoption of Spain's first constitution in 1812 there have been many laws implemented on education, although successive changes from one to another have taken place more rapidly, largely coinciding with a transformation in the state political system state or with a change of government and, therefore, the colour of the ideology in power (Table 21.1). Moreover, there is a plethora of regulations or provisions that have been issued both nationally and regionally to modify specific aspects of the generic legislation.

Formal education in Spain has never been neutral and has historically reflected the ideological parameters of the political class or social leader of the time, which has imposed its thinking through the use of greater or lesser mechanisms of enforcement. This can be seen in the narrative used in legal texts, the teaching/learning models, the structuring of the materials, and other curricular elements – objectives, selected content, competencies to be developed, evaluation criteria and so on.

In this sense, with regard to gender, the legislation on education is also a mirror of the partisan ideology dominant at a given time. There are obvious improvements and setbacks in relation to gender equality in the various laws depending on the different kinds of positioning: progressive or conservative.

In a recent paper, I carried out a critical reflection on the regression that has taken place with regard to gender in the latest law (LOMCE). To this end, I analysed this legislation from a gender perspective, focusing on the presence or absence of gender

Table 21.1: Descriptive table of educational laws approved in Spain since 1975 (source: author)

Governing parties in Spain in democracy	*Years of government*	*Approved educational law*
Unión de Centro Democrático	1977–1982	LOECE/1980
Partido Socialista Obrero Español	1982–1996	LODE/1985; LOGSE/1990; LOPEG/1995
Partido Popular	1996–2004	LOCE/2003
Partido Socialista Obrero Español	2004–2011	LOE/2006
Partido Popular	2011– actual	LOMCE/2013

identities and affective-sexual diversity in both the curriculum and in the ideology on which it is based. I also carried out a diagnosis of the educational measures and actions that it includes aimed at the prevention and eradication of gender violence (García Luque 2016).

Analysis of gender in the current education legislation

The LOMCE's lines of highly competitive educational progress, chiefly in agreement with European education, cloak an involution of women's human rights by removing or omitting from the social and historical content any related to gender diversity – affective-sexual diversity, sex-gender system, feminist theory, etc. Prior to the adoption of the LOMCE, the publication of the draft Law sparked controversy and many feminist voices denounced the offence committed in this new legislation regarding gender issues relative to several key issues:

- Use of sexist language in drafting the text, in breach of Organic Law 3/2007 of 22 March for effective equality between women and men whose SECTION II on public policies for equality, CHAPTER I, art. 14.10 obligates *The implementation of non-sexist language in the administrative field and its encouragement in all social, cultural and artistic relations.*

  In this regard, our attention is drawn by the fact that sexist language is not used when reference is made to the student body, which is referred to in the masculine and feminine forms (in Spanish) as *alumnos/alumnas* – in Spanish, *male students/ female students* respectively, but rather when speaking of teachers and directors in the masculine form. We are surprised, first because teaching is a feminised profession, and secondly because, by mentioning directors only in the masculine form, this law effects an absolutely intentional whitewashing, in my opinion, aimed at maintaining a patriarchal ideology that underpins the famous *glass ceiling*.
- Public funding for sex-segregated education under the argument of freedom of education, opening the door to education that is differentiated for boys and girls based on a system of ideas – mainly religious – of certain schools that defend the scientific reasons that back sex-based differences and reflective coeducation. In their paper analysing co-education in the LOMCE in the past two reports of the

CEDAW (2013; 2014) Fernández-González and González Clemares[1] question whether public funding of single-sex schools are or are not in breach of the treaty, as under Article 10 of the CEDAW, States Parties sign on to the obligation to take measures to eliminate discrimination against women in education, and states one of these as encouraging coeducation (Fernández-González and González Clemares 2015). Let us recall that the segregated school supported with public funds is contrary to the inclusive paradigm advocated by the LOE.

- Elimination of the subject of Education for Citizenship and Human Rights – hereinafter ECHR – Ethics and History of Philosophy. We are not going to analyse what the effect was of the first modification of the content of ECHR contained in Royal Decree 1190/2012 of 3 August, the immediate antecedent of the elimination of the subject itself which was adopted 16 months later with the LOMCE (García Luque and Peinado 2012). Nor will we delve into what the effect has been of the inclusion of two new subjects, Social and Civic Values and Ethical Values, whose objectives, content and ideological foundations have little or nothing to do with ECHR (Fernández-González and González Clemares 2015; Peinado and García Luque 2015). In this regard, note should be taken not only of the clear decline in gender matters brought about by the elimination of specific gender topics from its objectives and content, but also by the new perspective they have taken, far distant from the reflection and critical spirit so necessary for the deconstruction of the patriarchal system and to achieve true gender equality. The situation is exacerbated even more if we take into account that they have become an optional alternative – to be chosen by the parents or legal guardians – to the subject of religion given academic value in the context of a secular and non-denominational State whose values are sustained on an indisputable patriarchal ideology, with beliefs about sexuality, reproduction, gender identities and the social role of women that are clearly contrary to feminist discourse, which demands the real and effective equality of women and men.

  Regarding the subject of philosophy, it remains as a compulsory core subject for all modalities in the first year of *bachillerato* – equivalent to UK A levels – but history of philosophy ceases to be one in the second year, becoming an elective for students choosing the humanities and social sciences study programme. Thus, much of the student body will never know the evolution of schools of thought from the classical period to our days, which will prevent them from reflecting on the changes that have occurred with the passage of time, as well as becoming familiar with feminism as a contemporary school of thought and its historical background.
- The omission of gender identities and affective-sexual diversity. Our reality in matters of social gender is not binary and is composed of different gender identities that are constructed, dynamic and changeable, so it is illogical and paradoxical that formal education works with cultural referents that conform to the hetero-normative systems of sex, gender and sexuality in order to thereby maintain and perpetuate a social order established and standardised based on

patriarchal assumptions. The various institutional areas also advocate for the binary – man/woman – construct of social control which marginalised the abnormal, i.e. leaving out non-normative identities outside of this reality built on artificial dichotomies.

The LOMCE follows standardised social patterns, so that ideological principles underlying the actions of this law reflect heterosexist logic. No reference is made to the gender diversity existing in our current social context or to the plurality of sexualities. Although the LOMCE is not open to these gender topics, there are autonomous regions that, within the framework of their autonomy in educational matters, are strongly committed to gender equality (García Luque 2016). All the comprehensive laws on sexual diversity and gender identities that are being passed in the various autonomous regions include a specific chapter of measures in the field of education.

On the other hand, affective-sexual diversity and different gender identities have been part of the curriculum reflected in the LOE, although it became hidden in actual practice, and absent from the curriculum in the LOMCE, thus leaving out the fact that sexual identities are historical and social products, fluid and changeable, and that the need to fix them corresponds to the need for social control, so that the binary *man/woman formula itself excludes other possibilities and ultimately denies the constructive nature of sex and sexuality* (Planella and Pié 2012, 271).

That which falls outside what is established and standardised is directly excluded and omitted from the LOMCE; the exclusion represents the dark side of standardisation, the definition of that which is pathological. [...] The techniques of exclusion are constant in pedagogy: individuals, identities, practices, as well as forms of constructing knowledge are excluded (Planella and Pié 2012, 275).

Women in what is taught in primary school history: absent or present?

In the following lines we will analyse women as an object of study in primary school history classes by investigating both the official, as well as the hidden, curriculum.

Female invisibility in the curricula

It should be noted that history as a separate subject does not exist in primary school, but rather the historical content is currently included in the subject of social sciences. One of the major structural changes produced by the LOMCE's reorganisation of subjects was the replacement of the inclusive and globalising subject of knowledge of the natural, social and cultural environment with two separate subjects: natural science and social science, which has produced a regression to a dichotomous nature/social positivist model. This change directly affected both the objectives of each subject as well as the selection of content, so that, in relation to gender, there was a significant shift in that specific content from the subject of knowledge of the

Table 21.2: Spanish educational legislation by levels of curricular concretion (source: author)

National area	Organic Law 8/2013, of December 9, for the improvement of educational quality. LOMCE Royal Decree 126/2014, of February 28, establishing the basic curriculum of Primary Education.
Autonomous area, first level of concretion Example: Andalusia	Decree 97/2015, of March 3, establishing the management and the curriculum of the Primary Education in the Autonomous Community of Andalusia.
Autonomous area, second level of concretion	Order of March 17, 2015, which develops the curriculum corresponding to Primary Education in Andalusia.

environment which was the *identification of the role of men and women in history* in the Stage II, and *Evaluation of the role of men and women as subjects of the story* in Stage III (appendix II of R. D. 1513/2006), disappeared. Thus, the previous legislation generated an optimal space for the inclusion of women as social actors in the teaching practices of historical knowledge.

We can go back to 1981, when UNESCO adopted in Belgium the text of the *Planification de l'*éducation pour la réduction des inégalités: Un séminaire de l'*IIPE*, which demonstrated the need to generate new initiatives to combat sexist prejudices using education; or the text of the 1990 Organic Law on the General Organisation of the Education System – referred to in Spanish as LOGSE – itself, whose second article stated that all educational activity must reflect the effective equality of rights between the sexes.

Prior to analysing the current situation of the historical content, it is necessary to briefly explain how the curriculum of subjects in the Spanish education system is legislated and formulated. There are three levels curriculum specification, ranging from national to regional, since in Spain the various autonomous regions have competencies in education (Table 21.2). Thus, following the adoption of the LEO, which regulates the structuring of the educational system, the specification of the curriculum of subjects at the different stages of education is regulated through Royal Decrees, and curriculum specification at the regional level can be done through orders and instructions, as in the case, for example, of Andalusia.

In the current curriculum legislation, the selected content has been grouped into blocks that allow for the identification of the main aspects that make up the area of social sciences (Table 21.3). The historical content fall within Block 4 which, at the national level, is not divided by academic years, while at the regional level they are sequenced by stages (Table 21.4).

In view of the content, we can affirm that – at least at the regulatory curricular level – no reference is made to women as social actors of history nor is the teaching of the history of women included. There is commitment to choosing positivist-type content, as there is continued predomination of the teaching of political history, in which women have had a limited presence based on the patriarchal social model, so

Table 21.3: Curricular contents of the subject of social sciences (source: author)

Order of March 17, 2015, which develops the curriculum corresponding to Primary Education in Andalusia
Block 1. Common contents
Work techniques with which to approach the area. Technological progress and development models. The use of information and communication technologies.
Block 2. The world we live in
The Universe, the representation of the Earth and the orientation in space. Of the geography of the surroundings, to the one of Andalusia and Spain. Natural spaces and their conservation. Water and responsible consumption. Climate and climate change. Landscape and human intervention in the middle. The Andalusian landscapes. From the analysis of the near reality, discover the richness of geographic and cultural diversity to learn to value and care for it.
Block 3. Living in society
Characteristics of different social groups, respecting and valuing their differences, who their members are, how they are distributed in physical space, how the work is distributed among its members, how consumer goods are produced and distributed, economic life of the citizen. The entrepreneurial capacity of the members of society and the study of the company, which will understand the dynamising role of business activity in society. The social, political and territorial organization and the knowledge of the European institutions. Population, production sectors, as well as elementary financial education. Responsible use of resources.
Block 4. The traces of time
Understanding concepts such as historical time and its measurement, the ability to temporarily order some historical facts and other relevant facts using the basic notions of succession, duration and simultaneity. Great historical stages of Humanity, five ages of History, associated with the events that mark its beginnings and its endings. Historical conditions, events and figures of the different periods. The historical, social and cultural construction of Andalusia.

that when women have appeared, they do so as *minor characters* (Sant and Pagés 2011, 133), in the best of cases.

As the legislation states, the proposal of content is not due to any kind of hierarchical order for being addressed, and so it should not be understood as a proposal for didactic organisation. However, the vast majority of textbook publishers follow this organisation with absolute rigidity. History content is always included in the last units, which typically are taught more rapidly, hurried by the lack of time. Potential planning errors and the student's own fatigue after a long academic year hinder the assimilation of the content of the last topics in the books. Let us recall that textbooks remain the most used teaching material in the classroom and have enormous teaching power and:

- they are not neutral, but rather reflect the intentionalities of the contextual political power and each publisher's own particular ideology. They do not limit themselves to merely conveying some innocent knowledge, but rather transfer the social, cultural, values-related models which they seek to maintain

Table 21.4: Curricular contents of history. Subject of social sciences (source: author)

BLOCK 4. THE TRACES OF TIME	
Royal Decree 126/2014, of February 28, establishing the basic curriculum of Primary Education.	Order of March 17, 2015, which develops the curriculum corresponding to Primary Education in Andalusia.
Historical time and its measure. Historical sources and their classification. The Ages of History: Duration and dating of significant historical facts that limit them. The timelines. The Iberian Peninsula in Prehistory. The Iberian Peninsula in the Old Age. The Peninsular Kingdoms in the Middle Ages. The Hispanic Monarchy in the Modern Age. Spain in the Contemporary Age (I): the nineteenth century. Spain in the Contemporary Age (II): the 20th and 21st centuries. Our historical and cultural heritage.	FIRST CYCLE (1st and 2nd grade. Students age: 6–8 years old) 4.1. Changes in time. 4.2. The calendar. 4.3. Notions of duration, succession and simultaneity. 4.4. Remains of the past: care and conservation. 4.5. Characters of History. Andalusian characters SECOND CYCLE (3rd and 4th grade. Students age: 8–10 years) 4.1. Historical time and its measure. 4.2. The ages of history. Duration and date of the significant historical facts that limit them. The timelines. 4.3. The prehistory. Stone Age (Paleolithic and Neolithic) Age of Metals. Dating and characteristics of life, significant inventions. Cultural, artistic and architectural manifestations of Prehistory. The man of Orce and his past as a fact relevant to science and Andalusia. 4.4. The Ancient Age. Characteristics. Forms of life, economic activities and productions of the human beings of the Old Age. Romanisation. The Roman cultural legacy. THIRD CYCLE (5th and 6th grade. Students age: 10–12 years old 4.1. The Middle Ages. Kingdoms peninsular. The Germanic invasions and the Visigothic kingdom. Al-Ándalus: political evolution, economy, social organisation, traditions, religion, culture, science and art. Your cultural heritage. The Christian kingdoms: their origin and process of formation, the Reconquest and the repopulation, the social organisation, the Way of Santiago, art and culture. 4.2. The coexistence of the three cultures: Muslim, Jewish and Christian. The Modern Age: The Hispanic Monarchy. The Reign of the Catholic Monarchs: the dynastic union, the conquest of Granada, the expulsion of the Jews, the discovery of America. The rise of the Hispanic monarchy in the 16th century during the reigns of Charles I and Philip II; the organisation of the Empire; internal and external problems. The decadence of the empire in the 17th century. Renaissance and Baroque: the great figures of the Golden Age. The War of Succession and the Treaty of Utrecht. Illustration. The Illustrated Despotism of Carlos III. Goya and his time. Andalusian characters.

Table 21.4 (contd)

	4.3. Spain in the Contemporary Age: the 19th century. The War of Independence and the work of the Cortes de Cádiz (1808–1813). Political evolution: from the reign of Fernando VII to the regency of Maria Cristina (1814–1902). The economic and social transformations of the 19th century. Art and culture of 19th-century Spain. Spain in the Contemporary Age: the 20th and 21st centuries. The reign of Alfonso XIII and the dictatorship of Primo de Rivera (1902–1931). The Second Republic and the Civil War (1931–1939). The dictatorship of Franco (1939–1975). The transition to democracy and Constitution of 1978. Our recent history. The political organisation of Spain today.
	4.4. Spain in the European Union. Art and culture of Andalusia and Spain of the 20th and 21st centuries.

- their content is hardly challenged by teaching professionals, who convey it without conducting an exercise of critical reflection, due to both their lack of training and their employment situation.

Sexism in curricular materials: the case of textbooks

Taking into account the previous lines, it is not surprising that the analysis if the role of women in textbooks has been the focus of a large number of research projects since the late '80s (Moreno 1986; Garreta and Careaga 1987; Subirats 1993; Prendes 1997; see also Medina, this volume), primarily focused on the study of the illustrations in the different stages of education, mainly in higher (secondary) education and on the analysis of gender stereotypes (Blanco 2000a; 2000b; Lomas 2002; Valls 2007; Terrón and Cobano 2008; Saiz 2011; López-Navajas 2014; Bel 2016). We lack studies of sexism in curricular materials for the first stages of education, which are crucial to the comprehensive education of the student, from both the cognitive as well as behavioural – values-related – perspective.

The need to eliminate gender biases and stereotypes in educational programmes and curricular materials to ensure the empowerment of women and the elimination of gender inequalities was already declared at the IV World Conference on Women in Beijing organised by the United Nations in 1995. This concern remains in force as shown by the latest *Global Education Monitoring Report* (GEM) prepared by UNESCO,[2] which devotes a section to this issue, noting the *urgent* need for governments to review and amend school textbooks, since they are responsible for disseminating values of equality in every society. According to the report, the presence of gender bias in textbooks is a subtle and covert mechanism that prevents the progress towards equality in education and the empowerment of women for economic development. It shows a positive result in that the content of gender equality has increased in textbooks across the world, as some authors have found in their recent research

(Terrón and Cobano 2008; López-Navajas 2014; Bel 2016). It also warns that there are countries like Algeria, France, Pakistan, Uganda, Zimbabwe and Spain where the invisibility of women in educational materials and teaching is a concern because these continue to use stories, images or examples that either do not include women, or show them in a traditional, submissive and dependent role, serving men.

Another example of the need to include formulas and strategies for equality between men and women in educational materials is the numerous statutory regulations in the legislative framework that call for this, both in education laws as well as specific gender equality laws.

Despite gradual progress in the last decade in this regard, it remains insufficient. As noted in recent studies by López-Navajas (2014) and Bel (2016), although the presence of women in illustrations has increased, men and groups of men continue to have greater representation, and the number of female historical characters with proper names continues to be alarmingly underrepresented – three out of ten. Women are increasingly represented in public spaces, which remain priorities in teaching history, compared to the imperceptible increase of men in private spaces, and their dominance over women in public spaces continues to be overwhelming.

The teaching of the history of political and economic power – public domain – in which the activities of producing and maintaining life remain marginalised, as do – indirectly – the women who conduct them. According to Terrón and Cobano (2008), this is due in large part to the general consideration that activities carried out in public environments require greater knowledge. In our view, the activities of producing and maintaining life require some important and complex knowledge, both of the production stages as well as of the necessary technologies and how they function which have to be transmitted in teaching-learning processes generation after generation – endoculture. The problem is not that these activities require less knowledge, but rather that they are undervalued and marginalised in the construction of the androcentric patriarchal historical knowledge focused on upper-class Western white men and this has generated that belief in people's collective imaginary. The 5.5% of representations of images of women in an affection attitude or carrying out a specific caring action towards other people from among the 1062 images analysed in the study of 222 books from Anaya, 401 from Everest and 439 from SM is, thus, derisory.

The permanence of the androcentric bias in teaching materials transfers a model of society to students that is far from the reality they experience and, at the same time, conveys some content in which the absence of women in past and recent history prevents girls from identifying with this content, and thus they lack gender models that boys do have as the result of the positivist-type political history prevailing in the classroom (García Luque 2016).

In conclusion, studies show us that there are underrepresented gender and age groups, with women, children and the elderly being affected the most (Terrón and Cobano 2008), which generates a biased transmission of the past which produces cognitive conflicts in students with regard to the present.

Causes of the omission of women in the teaching of history at school

Throughout this text, we have indicated some possible causes for the absence of women in the teaching of history at school already discussed in previous papers (García Luque 2015), which we will now summarise:

1. Political interference in textbooks: let us remember that textbooks are not neutral, but rather reflect the intentionalities of the prevailing political power that legislates the official curriculum.
2. Predominance of political history in textbooks: the historical positivism focused its efforts on the development of political events, and on the characters considered of great importance in these events, i.e. historical subjects were reduced to the *major characters*. The issue is to reflect on who were considered *major characters*, why, and by whom. The students' conception of history is not that of a social process, but rather a war-based process associated with specific events and exceptional characters, a partial and androcentric history. For students, history is perceived as a literary construction, and they are ignorant of the analytical, methodological and epistemological mechanisms of the process of historical synthesis (Miralles and Belmonte 2004).
3. Lack of transfer of the progress and developments in historical research in the teaching of history. Historical science is constantly evolving and should have some kind of influence on teaching, so as to not perpetuate outdated discourses that convey to students social obsolete social models in which women had no presence and, therefore, are not recognised or identified.

   There is an absolute disconnection between historical research and the teaching of history (Fernández 2001; Miralles and Belmonte 2004). Obviously, the teaching of history cannot be dependent on historiography, even more so at the beginning levels – pre-school and primary–, but a pedagogical effort should be made to include new historiographical approaches. As noted by Miralles and Belmonte (2004), the origin of the teaching is not in the historiographical changes, but if we want to innovate and improve the teaching of history, these have much to contribute.

   The enormous advances in the historiography of gender have not been reflected in the teaching of history at school: not in the selection of curricular content, not in the teaching practice, nor in the teaching resources or materials. It is not enough to investigate history from the perspective of gender, but rather gender should influence teaching at all levels.
4. Permanence of the belief that the history of women is a women's thing. It is necessary to reflect on how the idea that the history of women is a women's thing, confusing the subject with the purpose of study, something that does not happen in any other line of inquiry. It is a fact that, even today, gender studies are done in their vast majority by women; in fact, studies that have analysed the readiness of future teachers to include women in teaching about the past demonstrate the

increased readiness of women compared to men (Maldonado 2004). This leads us to the following cause.

5. Absence of gender training at the start of the training programme for teachers, to whom historiographical developments do not reach in order to broaden their critical and reflective vision.

As stated by Maldonado (2004), scientific and didactic update in the disciplines studied by future teachers is the key to initiating a change beginning in the basic levels of the educational activity. Therefore, the path is to go towards a critical and reflective training to train male and female teachers to look at gender, either through the specific grades of early childhood and primary education, or through Masters of Secondary Education.

Some improvement strategies for including women in the teaching of history

1. *Change the choice of the type of history that is taught in school.* While the selection of curricular content depends on the dominant power and remains positivist, the teaching methodology is open and flexible, allowing us to include new perspectives when conveying the selected content. As noted by García Luque and De la Cruz (2017), we must commit to the teaching of a history that:
   - Enhance the value of the culture of that which is of routine nature in historical processes, including maintenance activities to the teaching of historical knowledge – pregnancy and childbirth, parenting, food processing, textile activity, care and hygiene of persons and places, etc. This way, caring can be conveyed didactically as an ethical manner of existence, which recovers the silenced voices of women and elevates them to a human and political category. We start from the premise that, order to survive, we human beings need to care for each other, since we are [sic] self-sufficient; consequently, men and women should be educated with an aim to a moral autonomy rooted in solidarity and concern for the well-being of the other, of themselves and of the environment (López-Francés 2012). Giving historical and social value to maintenance activities empowers women in the spaces and tasks historically attributed to them that have been undervalued – and even omitted – from historical discourses, while giving them the importance and value that they have had facilitates learning co-responsibility among children and youths.
   - Incorporate women's production in the teaching/learning of the Social Sciences in an integrated manner and not as isolated chapters in history at the periphery of educational materials: their scientific, material, reproductive, creative, production, etc.

     There should be a focus not only on the characters, but also on people.

2. *Initial and ongoing training of teachers for their awareness and commitment to gender equality.* Future teachers must be trained in the relativity of knowledge and given theoretical and practical tools for detecting gender, class, ethnicity, age, etc. biases, so that they become aware of their consequences in the construction of historical knowledge and, thus, in their teaching. It is not enough to train; we must engage teachers with gender equality so that they carry out effective coeducational practices in their classrooms.

   This initial training is aimed at future teachers being able to:

   - Reflect on the need to change the type of history that has been and is being taught.
   - Include the gender perspective in the teaching of history.
   - Analyse textbooks and other curricular materials from a gender perspective with critical, thoughtful and committed thinking, in order to choose materials without gender bias in the classroom, in both written as well as visual discourse.
   - Use inclusive language in their teaching practice, as well as detecting and penalising the use of sexist language in any aspect of education.
   - Denounce sexist teaching practices and situations of gender discrimination in academia.
3. *Training of actors involved in the production of curricular materials (websites, educational publishers, male and female illustrators, etc.) to make them aware of and committed to gender equality.* They must be trained in the new feminist historiographical approaches, as well as being made aware of the importance of including gender in their productions in order to avoid the biases that they are often subconsciously responsible for. To this end, we must equip them with strategies and resources.

   According to Terrón and Cobano (2004, 399), there is an issue to consider when studying these, and it is the *lack of definition and ambiguity represented by many of the figures*, considering that, in order to address how the issue of gender is treated, asexual figures are chosen for illustration. In our opinion, this is not the right strategy to break androcentric biases and have a more neutral, partial and comprehensive representation. This may reflect the difficulty of illustrators in including gender as a category in their work due to a lack of training. They choose asexual representation to somehow avoid the imbalances of male and female representations that have been demonstrated and denounced in all research conducted and for which they feel responsible.
4. *Didactically transfer theoretical academic advances to real praxis.* There are R&D projects on educational innovation related to including gender in schools whose results are not transferred to the classroom and which are, therefore, reduced to the context of academic debate, but without actual implementation. The transfer of the results of research to the classroom is necessary in order to change the educational paradigm. To this end, it is necessary to generate effective transfer strategies to the actors involved

in formal education – active teachers; publishers; training centres for continuing education of teachers, educational managers; school management teams, etc.

Conclusions

School is a political instrument for projecting equalities or inequalities, and in educational practice we must reflect on what content and what teaching strategies we want in order to aim for another kind of school, regardless of the regression produced in matters of gender in the current legislation on education. The progressive and insufficient increase of the presence of women in teaching materials –primarily textbooks– does not imply equality, since it is not just a matter of numbers. We must reflect on how we want to include women in the teaching of history, in what contexts and in what actions. We must include their agencies and activities and give them the social and historical value that they have had. It is not just about including women who were *important* just because they occupied male spaces and positions. It is significant to highlight female cultural models that came to visible power, but it is also necessary to teach women in their day-to-day activities and spaces as models. As noted by Sánchez and Miralles (2014, 285) *the study of the woman must transcend the gender perspective and recognise and include the plurality of women that are present in history.*

It is not enough to change the curricula or textbooks to include women; we must train teachers to engage them in the struggle for gender equality so that they train and engage their students based on a critical and reflective view against gender prejudices and stereotypes. This will create a spider web in favour of equality in formal education that will transcend society.

Notes

1 Convention on the Elimination of All Forms of Discrimination against Women (UN)
2 See the Report on Gender at the following link: http://es.unesco.org/gem-report/

References

Bel Martínez, J. C. (2016) El papel de las mujeres en la historia según las imágenes de los libros de texto. Comparación de manuales editados durante la LOE y la LOMCE. *AULA Revista de pedagogía de la Universidad de Salamanca* 22, 219–233.

Blanco, N. (2000a) *El sexismo en los materiales educativos de la ESO*. Sevilla, Instituto Andaluz de la Mujer.

Blanco, N. (2000b) Mujeres y hombres para el s. XXI: El sexismo en los libros de texto. In M. Á. Santos Guerra (coord.) *El harén pedagógico: perspectiva de género en la organización escolar*. Barcelona, Grao, 119–147.

Fernandez, A. (2001) *Las mujeres y la enseñanza de las Ciencias Sociales*. Madrid, Síntesis.

Fernández-González, N. and González Clemares, N. (2015) La LOMCE a la luz de la CEDAW un análisis de la coeducación en la última reforma educativa. *Journal of Supranational Policies of Education* 3, 242–263.

García Luque, A. (2013) *Igualdad de género en las aulas de la Educación Primaria: apuntes teóricos y guía orientativa de recursos*. Colección Cuadernos de trabajo. Jaén, Servicio de publicaciones de la Universidad de Jaén.

García Luque, A. (2015) Mujeres visibles e invisibles en la enseñanza de la Historia en la Educación Primaria: cambios y pervivencias al amparo de la LOMCE. In A. Mª. Hernández, Carretero, J. L. García Ruiz, J. L. de la Montaña (coords.) *Una enseñanza de las ciencias sociales para el futuro: Recursos para trabajar la invisibilidad de personas, lugares y temáticas*. Cáceres, Universidad de Extremadura-Asociación Universitaria de Profesores de Didáctica de las Ciencias Sociales, 163–173.

García Luque, A. (2016). La LOMCE bajo una mirada de género/s: ¿Avances o retrocesos en el s. XXI?. *Revista Educación, Política y Sociedad* 1(2), 100–124.

García Luque, A. and Peinado, M. (2012) Género y ciudadanía en la educación obligatoria: de la intencionalidad a la realidad. In M. Martín Clavijo (ed.) *Más Igualdad. Redes para la Igualdad*. Almería, Editorial Arcibel, 291-301.

García Luque, A. and Peinado, M. (2015) LOMCE: ¿es posible construir una ciudadanía sin la perspectiva de género? *IBER. Didáctica de las Ciencias Sociales* 79, 65–72.

García Luque, A. and De la Cruz Redondo, A. (2017) La educación como herramienta de cambio de las desigualdades de género: directrices educativas para combatir la violencia de género. *UNES: Universidad, Escuela y Sociedad* 2, 30–50.

Garreta, N. y Careaga, P. (1987) *Modelos masculino y femenino en los textos de la EGB*. Madrid, Publicaciones del Instituto de la Mujer 14, Estudios.

Lomas, C. (2002) El sexismo en los libros de texto. In A. González and C. Lomas (coords.) *Mujer y educación: educar para la igualdad, educar desde la diferencia*. Barcelona, Grao, 193–209.

López-Francés, I. (2012) Educación para la igualdad y prevención de la violencia de género. In I. Vázquez Bermúdez (coord.) *Investigación y género, inseparables en el presente y en el futuro: IV Congreso Universitario Nacional Investigación y Género*. Sevilla, Unidad para la Igualdad, Universidad de Sevilla, 989–999.

Maldonado, L. (2004) El alumnado de Magisterio ante la Historia de las Mujeres: percepción y actitudes. In M. I. Vera Muñoz and D. Pérez i Pérez (coords.) *Formación de la ciudadanía: las TICs y los nuevos problemas. Simposio Internacional de Didáctica de las Ciencias Sociales* 15, 1–7.

Miralles, P. and Belmonte, P. (2004) Historiografía, historia de las mujeres y enseñanza de la historia. In Mª. I. Vera and D. Pérez (eds) *Formación de la ciudadanía: las TIC y los nuevos problemas*. Alicante: Asociación Universitaria de Profesorado de Didáctica de las Ciencias Sociales, 619–629.

Moreno, A. (1986) *El arquetipo viril protagonista de la Historia*. Barcelona, LaSal. Edicions de les dones.

Planella, J. and Pié, A. (2012) Pedagoqueer: resistencias y subversiones educativas. *Educación XXI* 15(1), 265–283.

Rodríguez Izquierdo, R. (1998) La imagen y el papel de la mujer en los libros de texto escolares en España. *Escuela Abierta* I, 257–265.

Ruiz Oliveras, L. and Vallejo Martín-Albo, C. (1999) ¿Qué queda de sexismo en los libros de texto? *Revista Complutense de Educación* 10(2), 125–145.

Sánchez, R. and Miralles, P. (2014) Pensar a las mujeres en la historia y enseñar su historia en las aulas: estado de la cuestión y retos de futuro. *Revista Tempo e Argumento, Florianópolis* 6(11), 278–298.

Sant, E. and Pagés, J. (2011) ¿Por qué las mujeres son invisibles en la enseñanza de la Historia? *Revista Historia y Memoria* 3, 129–146.

Subirats, M. (1993) (coord.) *El sexismo en los libros de texto: análisis y propuesta de un sistema de indicadores*. Madrid, Instituto de la Mujer.

Terrón, Mª. T. and Cobano-Delgado, V. (2008) El papel de la mujer en las ilustraciones de los libros de texto de Educación Primaria. *Foro de Educación* 10, 385–400.